Webster's New World 33,000 WORD BOOK

Compiled by
SHIRLEY M. MILLER
and based upon

Webster's New World Dictionary

of the American Language
Second College Edition

Editor in Chief
DAVID B. GURALNIK

WILLIAM COLLINS
PUBLISHERS, INC.

INTRODUCTION

YOU NEED NO SPECIAL INSTRUCTIONS to use this book. But to get the most from it in the shortest time, you should first read the following guide to the use of the book. It explains the content and special features.

HOW TO USE THIS BOOK

Each of the words listed alphabetically in this book will be referred to here as an *entry* or an *entry word*.

1. Content

Webster's New World Word Book is easy to use. It is a quick, accurate, up-to-date guide to the correct spelling and syllabification of more than 33,000 words, based on the widely used *Webster's New World Dictionary of the American Language, Second College Edition.* A special feature is the *Word Finder Table,* which will help you locate a word even though all you know about the word is how to pronounce it.

Many of the entries will settle questions as to whether a certain term is written as one word or with a hyphen or as two words. Answers to specific questions such as the following can be found easily: Do I want the word *anecdote* or *antidote?* When is *hanged* preferred as the past tense and past participle of *hang?* Is the word I want spelled *moot* or *mute?* When is *ringed* used correctly as a verb?

An almost infinite number of words can be formed through the addition of certain prefixes or suffixes to base words. Many of these derived words have been entered. Those that present any question of spelling have been included. For example:

a·gree′a·ble	di·ag′o·nal	di·dac′tic	gar′lic
a·gree′a·bly	di·ag′o·nal·ly	di·dac′ti·cal·ly	gar′lick·y

Obsolete, rare, and archaic forms have been omitted. Many technical terms, especially those in general use, and many colloquial words in common use have been included.

At the back of the book is a section covering punctuation usage.

In all, this book has been designed to be as complete and timesaving an aid to spelling and syllabification as possible.

2. Word Division

All the entry words have been divided into syllables. Each syllable break is indicated by a centered dot, an accent mark, or, in certain cases, a hyphen. Wherever a hyphen *is* used in an entry word, that hyphen is part of the spelling of the word.

A word can be divided from one line to the next between any of its syllables except in the following cases:

a. Never separate from the rest of the word a first or last syllable of only one letter or, if you can avoid it, two letters.

b. Never divide a hyphenated word at any point other than the hyphen.

3. Accent Marks

Accent marks are included to help you find words more quickly. In some cases the accent mark will distinguish one word from another word spelled almost the same way.

lo′cal / lo·cale′   kar′at / ka·ra′te

Two kinds of accent marks are used. The accent mark in heavy type shows that the syllable preceding it receives the main stress, or accent. The lighter one, wherever used, indicates that the preceding syllable receives less stress than the main one but somewhat more than an unmarked syllable.

ag′gra·vate′ / dem′on·stra′tion / su′per·vise′

4. Parts of Speech

Part-of-speech labels (*n.* = noun, *v.* = verb, *adj.* = adjective, *adv.* = adverb) are included here only in special cases. Sometimes this label will give you information about current usage. In all cases the main purpose is to help you be sure you have the word you are looking for. Two of these special cases are explained here.

a. Sometimes a word is accented and syllabified in one way as one part of speech and differently as another. These changes in accent and syllabification are indicated, and the word is appropriately labeled; for example: re·cord′ *v.* / rec′ord *n.*

b. Sometimes two words are related in meaning and close in spelling and pronunciation. A part-of-speech label is all that is needed to identify each word:

<table>
<tr><td>ad·vice′ n.</td><td>proph′e·cy n.</td></tr>
<tr><td>ad·vise′ v.</td><td>·cies</td></tr>
<tr><td>·vised′ ·vis′ing</td><td>proph′e·sy′ v.</td></tr>
<tr><td></td><td>·sied′ ·sy′ing</td></tr>
</table>

5. Inflected Forms

Inflected forms include the plurals of nouns, the parts of the verb, and the comparative and superlative forms of the adjective and adverb. All irregularly formed inflected forms have been entered as part of the entry for the base word. To save space, these forms have been shortened in most cases to show only those syllables that are different from the base word. For example:

<table>
<tr><td>please</td><td>li′a·bil′i·ty</td><td>pic′nic</td></tr>
<tr><td>pleased pleas′ing</td><td>·ties</td><td>·nicked ·nick·ing</td></tr>
<tr><td>fly</td><td>eas′y</td><td>date</td></tr>
<tr><td>flies</td><td>·i·er ·i·est</td><td>dat′ed dat′ing</td></tr>
<tr><td>flew flown fly′ing</td><td></td><td></td></tr>
</table>

For verbs, when two forms are given, the first is the past tense and past participle and the second is the present participle. When three forms are given, the first is the past tense, the second is the past participle, and the third is the present participle. Noun, adjective, and adverb forms are easy to identify.

Again to save space, inflected forms of some compound words and derived words have been omitted. These forms can easily be found with the entry for the base word. For example:

<table>
<tr><td>po·lice′man</td><td>pre·pack′age</td><td>un′der·score′</td></tr>
</table>

Occasionally certain inflected forms are used for certain meanings. These are identified. For example:

staff	ring
staffs *or* staves	rang rung ring′ing
(*stick; music*)	(*sound . . .*)
staffs	ring
(*people*)	ringed ring′ing
	(*circle . . .*)

This system of entering inflected forms as part of the entry for the base word accomplishes at least three things: (1) It helps you distinguish between words that might be confused if entered separately, as in:

hop	hope
hopped hop′ping	hoped hop′ing

(2) It saves the time and trouble of searching for a word you might think is spelled one way but is, in fact, spelled differently, as in:

swim
swam swum swim′ming

(3) It establishes, without further identification under a separate entry, the specific inflected form that you are looking for (see *fly* above).

One last point: when an entry contains verb forms, this does not necessarily mean that the word is used only as a verb. On the contrary, many of the entries represent the spelling for more than one part of speech. If, for example, a word used as an adjective is already entered as a verb form, and the spelling and syllabification are exactly the same, this word is not entered again separately. You may accept the verb form as the correct spelling for the adjective (see *please* above). If, too, a noun has the same spelling as a verb, no special notation is given (see *picnic* above). Where confusion might exist, some kind of identification is given.

6. Use of Identifying Definitions

It is no doubt clear that this book is not meant to replace the dictionary. It is also clear that in attempting to learn the correct spelling for a specific word, you may run into the difficulty of confusing another word with it. Many instances of such confusion are present in the English language. To help you find the exact word you are seeking, this book contains many cross-references. Each cross-reference supplies you with a very short *identifying definition* and refers you to another word that may be the one you want.

Confusion may result for any of several reasons. Two of the most common are: (1) similar (but not exactly the same) pronunciation:

mou′ton′
(*fur;* SEE mutton)

mut′ton
(*food;* SEE mouton)

(2) exactly the same pronunciation but, usually, a different spelling (such words are called *homonyms*):

la′ma
(*monk;* SEE llama)

leak
(*escape;* SEE leek)

lla′ma
(*animal;* SEE lama)

leek
(*vegetable;* SEE leak)

Often the words involved are very close alphabetically. In such cases only the identifying terms are given, as in:

less'en
  (*make less*)
less'er
  (*smaller*)
les'son
  (*instruction*)
les'sor
  (*one who leases*)

An important thing to note here is that these *identifying definitions* are meant only as an aid to your locating or identifying the word you want. They are not meant to replace or by any means cover the entire dictionary definition.

7. More Than One Accepted Spelling

Many words in the English language have more than one accepted spelling in use today. Because of space limitations, only the variant spellings of the more common words have been included. To help you identify them as variants of the same word, this book, in most cases, enters them together, as part of the same entry. Usually, the first spelling given is the one more frequently used. Sometimes, if they are far apart alphabetically or if necessary for some other reason, they are entered as separate entries. Whichever variant spelling you decide on, it is advisable to be consistent and use that same spelling throughout any one piece of writing.

8. Prefixes

Many derived words have been entered in this book. Since all such words cannot possibly be included, the information given below about a certain group of prefixes will be helpful.

The prefix . . .	*is usually added to the base word . . .*
self	with a hyphen.
out	without a hyphen.
over	without a hyphen.
anti pre pro semi un	without a hyphen *except* when the prefix is followed by a capital letter.
non	without a hyphen *except* when the prefix is followed by a capital letter or a word that has a hyphen in it.
re	without a hyphen *except* to distinguish between a word in which the prefix means *again* or *anew* and a word having a special meaning (*re-lay* and *relay*).

WORD FINDER TABLE

HAVE YOU EVER tried to look up a word in order to find its spelling when you don't have any idea how to find it—simply because you can't spell it? This *Word Finder Table,* which gives the most common spellings for sounds, will help you end this vicious circle.

Think of the word in terms of its pronounced syllables. *Be sure you are pronouncing the word correctly.*

If the sound is like the . . .	try also the spelling . . .	as in the words . . .
a in fat	ai, au	pl*ai*d, dr*au*ght
a in lane	ai, ao, au, ay, ea, ei, eigh, et, ey	r*ai*n, g*ao*l, g*au*ge, r*ay*, br*ea*k, r*ei*n, w*eigh*, sach*et*, th*ey*
a in care	ai, ay, e, ea, ei	*ai*r, pr*ay*er, th*e*re, w*ea*r, th*ei*r
a in father	au, e, ea	g*au*nt, s*e*rgeant, h*ea*rth
a in ago	e, i, o, u, *and combinations, as* ou	*a*gent, san*i*ty, c*o*mply, foc*u*s, vici*ou*s
b in big	bb	ru*bb*er
ch in chin	tch, ti, tu	ca*tch*, ques*ti*on, na*tu*re
d in do	dd, ed	pu*dd*le, call*ed*
e in get	a, ae, ai, ay, ea, ei, eo, ie, u	*a*ny, *ae*sthete, s*ai*d, s*ay*s, br*ea*d, h*ei*fer, l*eo*pard, fr*ie*nd, b*u*ry
e in equal	ae, ay, ea, ee, ei, eo, ey, i, ie, oe	alumn*ae*, qu*ay*, l*ea*n, fr*ee*, dec*ei*t, p*eo*ple, k*ey*, mach*i*ne, ch*ie*f, ph*oe*be
e in here	ea, ee, ei, ie	*ea*r, ch*ee*r, w*ei*rd, b*ie*r
er in over	ar, ir, or, our, re, ur, ure, yr	li*ar*, elix*ir*, auth*or*, glam*our*, ac*re*, aug*ur*, meas*ure*, zeph*yr*
f in fine	ff, gh, lf, ph	cli*ff*, lau*gh*, ca*lf*, *ph*rase
g in go	gg, gh, gu, gue	e*gg*, *gh*oul, *gu*ard, prolo*gue*

xi

If the sound is like the . . .	try also the spelling . . .	as in the words . . .
h in hat	wh	*wh*o
i in it	a, e, ee, ia, ie, o, u, ui, y	us*a*ge, *E*nglish, b*ee*n, carr*ia*ge, s*ie*ve, w*o*men, b*u*sy, b*ui*lt, h*y*mn
i in kite	ai, ay, ei, ey, ie, igh, uy, y, ye	*ai*sle, *ay*e, sl*ei*ght, *ey*e, t*ie*, n*igh*, b*uy*, fl*y*, r*ye*
j in jam	d, dg, di, dj, g, gg	gra*d*uate, ju*dg*e, sol*di*er, a*dj*ective, ma*g*ic, exa*gg*erate
k in keep	c, cc, ch, ck, cqu, cu, lk, q, qu, que	*c*an, a*cc*ount, *ch*orus, ta*ck*, la*cqu*er, bis*cu*it, wa*lk*, *q*uick, li*qu*or, baro*que*
l in let	ll, sl	ca*ll*, i*sl*e
m in me	chm, gm, lm, mb, mm, mn	dra*chm*, paradi*gm*, ca*lm*, li*mb*, dru*mm*er, hy*mn*
n in no	gn, kn, mn, nn, pn	*gn*u, *kn*eel, *mn*emonic, di*nn*er, *pn*eumatic
ng in ring	n, ngue	pi*n*k, to*ngue*
o in go	au, eau, eo, ew, oa, oe, oh, oo, ou, ough, ow	m*au*ve, b*eau*, y*eo*man, s*ew*, b*oa*t, t*oe*, *oh*, br*oo*ch, s*ou*l, d*ough*, r*ow*
o in long	a, ah, au, aw, oa, ou	*a*ll, *U*t*ah*, fr*au*d, th*aw*, br*oa*d, *ou*ght
oo in tool	eu, ew, o, oe, ou, ough, u, ue, ui	man*eu*ver, dr*ew*, m*o*ve, sh*oe*, gr*ou*p, thr*ough*, r*u*le, bl*ue*, fr*ui*t
oo in look	o, ou, u	w*o*lf, w*ou*ld, p*u*ll
oi in oil	oy	t*oy*
ou in out	ough, ow	b*ough*, cr*ow*d
p in put	pp	cli*pp*er
r in red	rh, rr, wr	*rh*yme, be*rr*y, *wr*ong
s in sew	c, ce, ps, sc, sch, ss	*c*ent, ri*ce*, *ps*ychology, *sc*ene, *sch*ism, mi*ss*

If the sound is like the . . .	try also the spelling . . .	as in the words . . .
sh in ship	ce, ch, ci, s, sch, sci, se, si, ss, ssi, ti	ocean, machine, facial, sure, schwa, conscience, nauseous, tension, issue, fission, nation
t in top	ed, ght, pt, th, tt	walked, bought, ptomaine, thyme, better
u in cuff	o, oe, oo, ou	son, does, flood, double
u in use	eau, eu, eue, ew, ieu, iew, ue, ui, you, yu	beauty, feud, queue, few, adieu, view, cue, suit, youth, yule
ur in fur	ear, er, eur, ir, or, our, yr	learn, germ, hauteur, bird, word, scourge, myrtle
v in vat	f, lv, ph	of, salve, Stephen
w in will	o, u, wh	choir, quaint, wheat
y in you	i, j	onion, hallelujah
z in zero	s, sc, ss, x, zz	busy, discern, scissors, xylophone, buzzer
z in azure	ge, s, si, zi	garage, leisure, fusion, glazier

Sometimes, certain letter combinations (rather than single sounds) cause problems when you are trying to find a word. Here are some common ones:

If you've tried . . .	then try . . .	If you've tried . . .	then try . . .	If you've tried . . .	then try . . .
pre	per, pro, pri, pra, pru	cks, gz	x	fiz	phys
		us	ous	ture	teur
per	pre, pir, pur, par, por	tion	sion, cion, cean, cian	tious	seous
				air	are
is	us, ace, ice	le	tle, el, al	ance	ence
ere	eir, ear, ier	kw	qu	ant	ent
wi	whi	cer	cre	able	ible
we	whe	ei	ie	sin	syn, cin, cyn
zi	xy	si	psy, ci		

A

aard'vark'
aard'wolf'
·wolves'
ab'a·cus
·cus·es or ·ci'
ab'a·lo'ne
a·ban'don
a·base'
·based' ·bas'ing
a·bash'
a·bat'a·ble
a·bate'
·bat'ed ·bat'ing
ab'a·tis
ab'at·toir'
ab'ax'i·al
ab'ba·cy
·cies
ab'bé
ab'bess
ab'bey
ab'bot
ab·bre'vi·ate'
·at'ed ·at'ing
ab·bre'vi·a'tion
ab·bre'vi·a'tor
ab'di·cate'
·cat'ed ·cat'ing
ab'di·ca'tion

ab'di·ca'tor
ab'do·men
ab·dom'i·nal
ab·duct'
ab·duc'tion
ab·duc'tor
ab·er'rant
ab'er·ra'tion
a·bet'
·bet'ted ·bet'ting
a·bey'ance
ab·hor'
·horred' ·hor'ring
ab·hor'rence
ab·hor'rent
a·bide'
·bode' or ·bid'ed
·bid'ing
a·bil'i·ty
·ties
ab'ject
ab·jec'tion
ab'ju·ra'tion
ab·jure'
·jured' ·jur'ing
ab'la·tive
a·blaze'
a'ble
·bler ·blest
a'ble-bod'ied
ab·lu'tion
ab'ne·gate'
·gat'ed ·gat'ing
ab'ne·ga'tion

ab·nor'mal
ab'nor·mal'i·ty
·ties
ab·nor'mi·ty
·ties
a·board'
a·bode'
a·bol'ish
ab'o·li'tion
A'-bomb
a·bom'i·na·ble
a·bom'i·nate'
·nat'ed ·nat'ing
a·bom'i·na'tion
a·bom'i·na'tor
ab'o·rig'i·nal
ab'o·rig'i·ne
·nes
a·bort'
a·bor'ti·cide
a·bor'ti·fa'cient
a·bor'tion
a·bor'tive
a·bound'
a·bout'-face'
·faced' ·fac'ing
a·bove'board'
ab'ra·ca·dab'ra
ab·rade'
·rad'ed ·rad'ing
ab·ra'sion
ab·ra'sive
ab're·act'
ab're·ac'tion

a·breast'
a·bridge'
　·bridged'
　·bridg'ing
a·bridg'ment
　or ·bridge'ment
a·broad'
ab'ro·gate'
　·gat·ed ·gat'ing
ab'ro·ga'tion
ab'ro·ga'tor
a·brupt'
ab'scess
ab'scessed
ab·scis'sa
　·sas or ·sae
ab·scond'
ab'sence
ab'sent adj.
ab·sent' v.
ab'sen·tee'ism
ab'sent-mind'ed
ab'sinthe or ·sinth
ab'so·lute'
ab'so·lu'tion
ab'so·lut'ism
ab·solve'
　·solved' ·solv'ing
ab·solv'ent
ab·sorb'
　·sorbed' ·sorb'ing
ab·sorb'a·ble
ab·sorb'en·cy
ab·sorb'ent

ab·sorp'tion
ab·stain'
ab·ste'mi·ous
ab·sten'tion
ab'sti·nence
ab'sti·nent
ab·stract'
ab·strac'tion
ab·struse'
ab·surd'
ab·surd'i·ty
　·ties
a·bun'dance
a·bun'dant
a·buse'
　·bused' ·bus'ing
a·bus'er
a·bu'sive
a·but'
　·but'ted ·but'ting
a·but'ment
a·but'ter
a·bys'mal
a·bys'mal·ly
a·byss'
a·ca'cia
ac'a·de'mi·a
ac'a·dem'ic
ac'a·dem'i·cal
ac'a·dem'i·cal·ly
a·cad'e·mi'cian
ac'a·dem'i·cism
a·cad'e·my
　·mies

ac'a·jou'
a·can'thus
　·thus·es or ·thi
a' cap·pel'la
A'ca·pul'co
ac·cede'
　·ced'ed ·ced'ing
　(agree; SEE
　exceed)
ac·cel'er·an'do
ac·cel'er·ant
ac·cel'er·ate'
　·at'ed ·at'ing
ac·cel'er·a'tion
ac·cel'er·a'tor
ac·cel'er·om'e·ter
ac'cent
ac·cen'tu·al
ac·cen'tu·al·ly
ac·cen'tu·ate'
　·at'ed ·at'ing
ac·cen'tu·a'tion
ac·cept'
　(receive; SEE
　except)
ac·cept'a·bil'i·ty
ac·cept'a·ble
ac·cept'a·bly
ac·cept'ance
ac'cep·ta'tion
ac·cept'ed
　(approved; SEE
　excepted)
ac·cep'tor

2

ac′cess
(approach; SEE excess)
ac·ces′si·bil′i·ty
ac·ces′si·ble
ac·ces′sion
ac·ces′so·ry
or ·sa·ry
·ries
ac′ci·dent
ac′ci·den′tal
ac′ci·den′tal·ly
ac·claim′
ac′cla·ma′tion
ac′cli·mate′
·mat′ed ·mat′ing
ac·cli′ma·tize′
·tized′ ·tiz′ing
ac·cliv′i·ty
ac·cli′vous
ac′co·lade′
ac·com′mo·date′
·dat′ed ·dat′ing
ac·com′mo·da′·
tion
ac·com′pa·ni·
ment
ac·com′pa·nist
ac·com′pa·ny
·nied ·ny·ing
ac·com′plice
ac·com′plish
ac·com′plished
ac·cord′

ac·cord′ance
ac·cord′ant·ly
ac·cord′ing
ac·cor′di·on
ac·cost′
ac·count′
ac·count′a·bil′·
i·ty
ac·count′a·ble
ac·count′a·bly
ac·count′ant
ac·count′ing
ac·cou′ter
ac·cou′ter·ments
ac·cred′it
ac·cred′it·a′tion
ac·cre′tion
ac·cru′al
ac·crue′
·crued′ ·cru′ing
ac·cul′tu·rate′
·rat′ed ·rat′ing
ac·cul′tu·ra′tion
ac·cu′mu·la·ble
ac·cu′mu·late′
·lat′ed ·lat′ing
ac·cu′mu·la′tion
ac·cu′mu·la′tive
ac·cu′mu·la′tor
ac′cu·ra·cy
ac′cu·rate
ac′cu·rate·ly
ac·curs′ed or
ac·curst′

ac·cus′al
ac′cu·sa′tion
ac·cu′sa·tive
ac·cu′sa·to′ry
ac·cuse′
·cused′ ·cus′ing
ac·cus′tom
ac·cus′tomed
a·cer′bi·ty
·ties
ac′e·tate′
ac′e·tone′
a·cet′y·lene′
ache
ached ach′ing
a·chiev′a·ble
a·chieve′
·chieved′
·chiev′ing
a·chieve′ment
ach′ro·mat′ic
a·chro′ma·tism
a·chro′ma·tize′
·tized′ ·tiz′ing
A′chro·my′cin
ach′y
ach′i·er ach′i·est
ac′id-fast′
ac′id-form′ing
a·cid′ic
a·cid′i·fi′er
a·cid′i·fy′
·fied′ ·fy′ing
a·cid′i·ty

ac'i·do'sis
a·cid'u·late'
 ·lat'ed ·lat'ing
a·cid'u·lous
ac·knowl'edge
 ·edged ·edg·ing
ac·knowl'edge·
 a·ble
ac·knowl'edg·
 ment *or*
 ·edge·ment
ac'me
ac'ne
ac'o·lyte'
ac'o·nite'
a'corn
a·cous'tic *or*
 ·ti·cal
a·cous'ti·cal·ly
ac·quaint'
ac·quaint'ance
ac'qui·esce'
 ·esced' ·esc'ing
ac'qui·es'cence
ac'qui·es'cent
ac·quir'a·ble
ac·quire'
 ·quired' ·quir'ing
ac·quire'ment
ac'qui·si'tion
ac·quis'i·tive
ac·quit'
 ·quit'ted
 ·quit'ting

ac·quit'tal
a'cre
a'cre·age
ac'rid
a·crid'i·ty
ac'ri·mo'ni·ous
ac'ri·mo'ny
ac'ro·bat'
ac'ro·bat'ic
ac'ro·bat'i·cal·ly
ac'ro·nym
ac'ro·pho'bi·a
a·crop'o·lis
a·cross'
a·cros'tic
a·cryl'ic
act'a·ble
act'a·bil'i·ty
act'ing
ac·tin'i·um
ac'ti·nom'e·ter
ac'ti·no·my'cin
ac'tion
ac'ti·vate'
 ·vat'ed ·vat'ing
ac'ti·va'tion
ac'ti·va'tor
ac'tive
ac'tiv·ism
ac'tiv·ist
ac·tiv'i·ty
 ·ties
ac'tiv·ize'
 ·ized' ·iz'ing

ac'tor
ac'tress
ac'tu·al
ac'tu·al'i·ty
 ·ties
ac'tu·al·ize'
 ·ized' ·iz'ing
ac'tu·al·ly
ac'tu·ar'i·al
ac'tu·ar'y
 ·ies
ac'tu·ate'
 ·at'ed ·at'ing
ac'tu·a'tion
ac'tu·a'tor
a·cu'i·ty
 ·ties
a·cu'men
ac'u·punc'ture
a·cute'
a·cute'ly
ad'age
a·da'gio
 ·gios
ad'a·mant
a·dapt'
 (*fit;* SEE adept,
 adopt)
a·dapt'a·bil'i·ty
a·dapt'a·ble
ad'ap·ta'tion *or*
 a·dap'tion
a·dapt'er *or*
 a·dap'tor

4

a·dap′tive
add′a·ble *or* ·i·ble
ad·den′dum
 ·da
ad′der
 (*snake*)
add′er
 (*one who adds*)
ad′dict
ad·dic′tion
ad·dic′tive
ad·di′tion
 (*an adding;* SEE
 edition)
ad·di′tion·al
ad·di′tion·al·ly
ad′di·tive
ad′dle
 ·dled ·dling
ad′dle-brained′
ad·dress′
ad′dress·ee′
ad·duce′
 ·duced′ ·duc′ing
ad·duc′i·ble
ad·duc′tion
ad′e·noi′dal
ad′e·noids′
ad·ept′
 (*skilled;* SEE
 adapt, adopt)
ad′e·qua·cy
ad′e·quate
ad′e·quate·ly

ad·here′
 ·hered′ ·her′ing
ad·her′ence
ad·her′ent
ad·he′sion
ad·he′sive
ad′ hoc′
ad′ hom′i·nem′
a·dieu′
ad in′fi·ni′tum
ad in′ter·im
ad′i·pose′
ad·ja′cen·cy
ad·ja′cent
ad′jec·tive
ad·join′
 (*be next to*)
ad·journ′
 (*suspend*)
ad·judge′
 ·judged′
 ·judg′ing
ad·ju′di·cate′
 ·cat′ed ·cat′ing
ad·ju′di·ca′tion
ad·ju′di·ca′tor
ad′junct
ad′ju·ra′tion
ad·jure′
 ·jured′ ·jur′ing
ad·just′
ad·just′a·ble
ad·just′er *or*
 ·jus′tor

ad·just′ment
ad′ju·tant
ad′-lib′
 -libbed′ -lib′bing
ad′man′
 ·men′
ad·min′is·ter
ad·min′is·tra·ble
ad·min′is·trate′
 ·trat′ed ·trat′ing
ad·min′is·tra′tion
ad·min′is·tra′tive
ad·min′is·tra′tor
ad′mi·ra·ble
ad′mi·ra·bly
ad′mi·ral
ad′mi·ral·ty
 ·ties
ad′mi·ra′tion
ad·mire′
 ·mired′ ·mir′ing
ad·mir′er
ad·mis′si·bil′i·ty
ad·mis′si·ble
ad·mis′si·bly
ad·mis′sion
ad·mit′
 ·mit′ted ·mit′ting
ad·mit′tance
ad·mit′ted·ly
ad·mix′
ad·mix′ture
ad·mon′ish
ad′mo·ni′tion

5

ad·mon'i·to·ry
ad' nau'se·am
a·do'
a·do'be
ad'o·les'cence
ad'o·les'cent
a·dopt'
(choose; SEE
adapt, adept)
a·dop'tion
a·dop'tive
a·dor'a·ble
ad'o·ra'tion
a·dore'
·dored' ·dor'ing
a·dorn'
a·dorn'ment
ad·re'nal
ad·ren'al·in
a·drift'
a·droit'
ad·sorb'
ad·sor'bent
ad·sorp'tion
ad'u·late'
·lat'ed ·lat'ing
ad'u·la'tion
a·dul'ter·ant
a·dul'ter·ate'
·at'ed ·at'ing
a·dul'ter·a'tion
a·dul'ter·er
a·dul'ter·ess n.
a·dul'ter·ous adj.

a·dul'ter·y
a·dult'hood
ad·um'brate
·brat·ed ·brat·ing
ad' va·lo'rem
ad·vance'
·vanced'
·vanc'ing
ad·vance'ment
ad·van'tage
ad'van·ta'geous
ad'ven·ti'tious
ad·ven'ture
·tured ·tur·ing
ad·ven'tur·er
ad·ven'ture·some
ad·ven'tur·ous
ad'verb
ad·ver'bi·al
ad'ver·sar'y
·ies
ad·verse'
(opposed; SEE
averse)
ad·verse'ly
ad·ver'si·ty
·ties
ad·vert'
ad·vert'ent
ad'ver·tise' or
·tize'
·tised' or ·tized'
·tis'ing or
·tiz'ing

ad'ver·tise'ment
or ·tize'ment
ad·vice' n.
ad·vis'a·bil'i·ty
ad·vis'a·ble
ad·vis'a·bly
ad·vise' v.
·vised' ·vis'ing
ad·vis'ed·ly
ad·vise'ment
ad·vis'er or
·vi'sor
ad·vi'so·ry
ad'vo·ca·cy
ad'vo·cate'
·cat'ed ·cat'ing
Ae·ge'an
ae'gis
ae'on
aer'ate'
·at'ed ·at'ing
aer·a'tion
aer'a·tor
aer'i·al
aer'i·al·ist
aer'ie or ·y
aer'o·bal·lis'tics
aer'o·bat'ics
aer'obe
aer'o·dy·nam'i·
cal·ly
aer'o·dy·nam'ics
aer'o·me·chan'·
ics

6

aer'o·med'i·cine
aer'o·nau'ti·cal
aer'o·nau'tics
aer'o·neu·ro'sis
aer'o·sol'
aer'o·space
aer'o·stat'ics
Ae'sop
aes'thete'
aes·thet'ic
aes·thet'i·cal·ly
aes·thet'i·cism
af'fa·bil'i·ty
af'fa·ble
af'fa·bly
af·fair'
af·fect'
 (*to influence;* SEE
 effect)
af'fec·ta'tion
af·fect'ed
af·fec'tion
af·fec'tion·ate
af·fec'tive
 (*of feelings;* SEE
 effective)
af·fi'ance
 ·anced ·anc·ing
af'fi·da'vit
af·fil'i·ate'
 ·at·ed ·at·ing
af·fil'i·a'tion
af·fin'i·ty
af·firm'

af'fir·ma'tion
af·firm'a·tive
af·firm'a·tive·ly
af·fix'
 ·fixed' *or* ·fixt'
 ·fix'ing
af·flict'
af·flic'tion
af'flu·ence
af'flu·ent
 (*rich;* SEE
 effluent)
af·ford'
af·fray'
af·front'
af'ghan
a·fi'cio·na·do
a·field'
a·fire'
a·flame'
a·float'
a·fore'men'tioned
a·fore'said'
a·fore'thought'
a·fore'time'
a·foul'
a·fraid'
A'-frame'
a·fresh'
Af'ri·can
af'ter
af'ter·birth'
af'ter·burn'er
af'ter·damp'

af'ter·ef·fect'
af'ter·glow'
af'ter·im'age
af'ter·life'
af'ter·math'
af'ter·noon'
af'ter·shock'
af'ter·taste'
af'ter·thought'
af'ter·ward
a·gain'
a·gainst'
a·gape'
ag'ate
ag'ate·ware'
age
 aged, ag'ing *or*
 age'ing
age'less
age'long'
a'gen·cy
 ·cies
a·gen'da
a'gent
age'-old'
ag·glom'er·ate'
 ·at·ed ·at·ing
ag·glom'er·a'tion
ag·glu'ti·nant
ag·glu'ti·nate'
 ·nat·ed ·nat·ing
ag·glu'ti·na'tion
ag·gran'dize'
 ·dized' ·diz'ing

7

ag·gran′dize·
  ment
ag′gra·vate′
  ·vat′ed ·vat′ing
ag′gra·va′tion
ag′gre·gate′
  ·gat′ed ·gat′ing
ag′gre·ga′tion
ag·gres′sion
ag·gres′sive
ag·gres′sor
ag·grieve′
  ·grieved′
  ·griev′ing
a·ghast′
ag′ile
ag′ile·ly
a·gil′i·ty
ag′i·tate′
  ·tat′ed ·tat′ing
ag′i·ta′tion
ag′i·ta′tor
ag′it·prop′
a·gleam′
ag′let
a·glow′
ag·nos′tic
ag·nos′ti·cal·ly
ag·nos′ti·cism
a·gog′
ag′o·nize′
  ·nized′ ·niz′ing
ag′o·ny
  ·nies

ag′o·ra·pho′bi·a
a·grar′i·an
a·gree′
  ·greed′ ·gree′ing
a·gree′a·bil′i·ty
a·gree′a·ble
a·gree′a·bly
ag′ri·busi′ness
ag′ri·cul′tur·al
ag′ri·cul′ture
ag′ri·cul′tur·ist
  or ·tur·al·ist
a·gron′o·my
a·ground′
a′gue
a′gu·ish
a·head′
aid
  (help)
aide
  (assistant)
aide′-de-camp′ or
  aid′-de-camp′
  aides′- or aids′-
ail
  (be ill; SEE ale)
ai′le·ron′
ail′ing
ail′ment
aim′less
air
  (gases; SEE heir)
air base
air′borne′

air brake
air′bra′sive
air′brush′
air coach
air′-con·di′tion
air′-con·di′tioned
air conditioner
air conditioning
air′-cool′
air′-cooled′
air′craft′
air′drome′
air′drop′
  ·dropped′
  ·drop′ping
air′-dry′
  -dried′ -dry′ing
air express
air′field′
air′foil′
air force
air′frame′
air gun
air hole
air′i·ly
air′i·ness
air′ing
air lane
air′lift′
air′line′
air′lin′er
air lock
air′mail′

8

air′man
·men
air′-mind′ed
air′mo′bile
air′plane′
air′port′
air pressure
air′proof′
air pump
air raid
air′scape′
air′ship′
air′sick′
air′space′
air′speed′
air′-sprayed′
air′stream′
air′strip′
air′tight′
air′waves′
air′wor′thy
air′y
air′i·er air′i·est
aisle
(passage; SEE isle)
a·kim′bo
Al′a·bam′a
al′a·bas′ter
a′ la carte′
a·lac′ri·ty
à′ la king′
a′ la mode′
or à′ la mode′
a·larm′ing

a·larm′ist
A·las′ka
al′ba·core′
al′ba·tross′
al·be′it
al′bi·nism
al·bi′no
·nos
al′bum
al·bu′men
(egg white)
al·bu′min
(class of proteins)
Al′bu·quer′que
al′che·mist
al′che·my
al′co·hol′
al′co·hol′ic
al′co·hol′i·cal·ly
al′co·hol·ism
al′cove
al′der·man
·men
ale
(a drink; SEE ail)
a′le·a·to′ry
ale′house′
a·lert′ly
A·leu′tian
ale′wife′
·wives′
al·fal′fa
al·fres′co
al′gae

al′gae·cide′
al′ge·bra
al′ge·bra′ic
al′ge·bra′i·cal·ly
a′li·as
al′i·bi′
·bis′
·bied′ ·bi′ing
al′ien
al′ien·ate′
·at′ed ·at′ing
al·ien·a′tion
a·light′
·light′ed or ·lit′
·light′ing
a·lign′ or a·line′
·ligned′ or ·lined′
·lign′ing or
·lin′ing
a·lign′ment
or a·line′ment
a·like′
al′i·men′ta·ry
(nourishing; SEE
elementary)
al′i·mo′ny
al′i·quant
al′i·quot
a·live′
al′ka·li′
·lies′ or ·lis′
al′ka·line
al′ka·lize′
·lized′ ·liz′ing

9

al'ka·loid'
al'kyd
all'-A·mer'i·can
all'-a·round'
al·lay'
·layed' ·lay'ing
all'-clear'
al'le·ga'tion
al·lege'
·leged' ·leg'ing
al·leg'ed·ly
Al'le·ghe'ny
al·le'giance
al'le·gor'i·cal
al'le·go·rize'
·rized' ·riz'ing
al'le·go'ry
·ries
al'le·gret'to
al·le'gro
al'le·lu'ia
al'ler·gen
al'ler·gen'ic
al·ler'gic
al'ler·gist
al'ler·gy
·gies
al·le'vi·ate'
·at'ed ·at'ing
al·le'vi·a'tion
al'ley
·leys
(*narrow lane;*
SEE ally)

al'ley·way'
al·li'ance
al·lied'
al'li·ga'tor
all'-im·por'tant
all'-in·clu'sive
al·lit'er·ate'
·at'ed ·at'ing
al·lit'er·a'tion
al'lo·cate'
·cat'ed ·cat'ing
al'lo·ca'tion
al·lot'
·lot'ted ·lot'ting
al·lot'ment
al·lot'tee'
all'-out'
all'o'ver
al·low'
al·low'a·ble
al·low'ance
al·lowed'
(*permitted;* SEE
aloud)
al'loy
all'-pur'pose
all right
all'spice'
all'-star'
all'-time'
al·lude'
·lud'ed ·lud'ing
(*refer to;* SEE
elude)

al·lure'
·lured' ·lur'ing
al·lu'sion
(*mention;* SEE
elusion, illusion)
al·lu'sive
(*mentioning;* SEE
elusive, illusive)
al·lu'vi·al
al·lu'vi·um
·vi·ums *or* ·vi·a
al·ly' *v.* al'ly *n.*
·lied' ·ly'ing
·lies
(*join; partner;*
SEE alley)
al'ma ma'ter
al'ma·nac'
al·might'y
al'mond
al'mon·er
al'most
alms
a·loft'
a·lo'ha
a·long'shore'
a·long'side'
a·loof'
a·loud'
(*loudly;* SEE
allowed)
al·pac'a
al'pen·stock'
al'pha·bet'

al'pha·bet'i·cal
al'pha·bet'i·cal·ly
al'pha·bet·ize'
 ·ized' ·iz'ing
al·read'y
al'so·ran'
al'tar
 (*table for worship*)
al'ter
 (*to change*)
al'ter·a'tion
al'ter·cate'
 ·cat'ed ·cat'ing
al'ter·ca'tion
al'ter·nate'
 ·nat'ed ·nat'ing
al'ter·na'tion
al·ter'na·tive
al·ter'na·tor
al·though'
al·tim'e·ter
al'ti·tude'
al'to
 ·tos
al'to·geth'er
al'tru·ism
al'tru·is'tic
a·lu'mi·num
a·lum'na *n.fem.*
 ·nae
a·lum'nus
 n.masc.
 ·ni

al'ways
a·mal'ga·mate'
 ·mat'ed ·mat'ing
a·mal'ga·ma'tion
a·man'u·en'sis
 ·ses
am'a·ryl'lis
am'a·teur'
am'a·to'ry
a·maze'
 ·mazed'
 ·maz'ing
a·maze'ment
Am'a·zon'
am·bas'sa·dor
am·bas'sa·do'ri·al
am'ber
am'ber·gris'
am'bi·ance
am'bi·dex·ter'i·ty
am'bi·dex'trous
am'bi·ent
am'bi·gu'i·ty
am·big'u·ous
am·bi'tion
am·bi'tious
am·biv'a·lence
am'ble
 ·bled ·bling
am·bro'sia
am'bu·lance
am'bu·late'
 ·lat'ed ·lat'ing
am'bu·la·to'ry

am'bus·cade'
 ·cad'ed ·cad'ing
am'bush
a·me'ba
 ·bas *or* ·bae
a·mel'io·rate'
 ·rat'ed ·rat'ing
a·mel'io·ra'tion
a·mel'io·ra'tive
a·me'na·bil'i·ty
a·me'na·ble
a·mend'
 (*revise;* SEE emend)
a·mend'ment
a·men'i·ty
 ·ties
A·mer'i·can
A·mer'i·ca'na
A·mer'i·can·ism
A·mer'i·can·i·za'tion
A·mer'i·can·ize'
 ·ized' ·iz'ing
Am'er·ind'
am'e·thyst
a'mi·a·bil'i·ty
a'mi·a·ble
a'mi·a·bly
am'i·ca·bil'i·ty
am'i·ca·ble
am'i·ca·bly
a·mid'
a·mid'ships

11

a·midst'
a·mi'no
Am'ish
a·miss'
am'i·ty
·ties
am'me·ter
am·mo'nia
am·mu·ni'tion
am·ne'sia
am·ne'si·ac' *or*
am·ne'sic
am·nes'ty
·ties, ·tied ·ty·ing
a·moe'ba
·bas *or* ·bae
a·mok'
a·mong'
a·mongst'
a·mon·til·la'do
a·mor'al
a·mor·al'i·ty
am'o·rous
a·mor'phous
am·or·ti·za'tion
am'or·tize'
·tized' ·tiz'ing
a·mount'
a·mour'
am'per·age
am'pere
am'per·sand'
am·phet'a·mine'
am·phib'i·an

am·phib'i·ous
am'phi·the'a·ter
am·pho·ra
·rae *or* ·ras
am'ple
am'pli·fi·ca'tion
am'pli·fi'er
am'pli·fy'
·fied' ·fy'ing
am'pli·tude'
am'ply
am'pul
am·pul'la
·las *or* ·lae
am'pu·tate'
·tat'ed ·tat'ing
am'pu·ta'tion
am'pu·tee'
a·muck'
am'u·let
a·muse'
·mused'
·mus'ing
a·muse'ment
a·nach'ro·nism
a·nach'ro·nis'tic
an'a·con'da
a·nae'mi·a
a·nae'mic
an'aes·the'sia
an'aes·thet'ic
an·aes'the·tize'
·tized' ·tiz'ing
an'a·gram'

a'nal
an'al·ge'si·a
an'al·ge'sic
an'a·log' computer
a·nal'o·gize'
·gized' ·giz'ing
a·nal'o·gous
a·nal'o·gy
·gies
a·nal'y·sis
·ses'
an'a·lyst
(*one who
analyzes;* SEE
annalist)
an'a·lyt'i·cal
or an'a·lyt'ic
an'a·lyt'i·cal·ly
an'a·lyze'
·lyzed' ·lyz'ing
an'a·pest'
an·ar'chic
or an·ar'chi·cal
an'ar·chism
an'ar·chist
an'ar·chis'tic
an'ar·chy
·chies
an'as·tig·mat'ic
a·nas'tro·phe
a·nath'e·ma
·mas
a·nath'e·ma·tize'
·tized' ·tiz'ing

an'a·tom'i·cal
  or an'a·tom'ic
an'a·tom'i·cal·ly
a·nat'o·mist
a·nat'o·mize'
  ·mized' ·miz'ing
a·nat'o·my
  ·mies
an'ces·tor
an·ces'tral
an'ces'tress
an'ces'try
  ·tries
an'chor
an'chor·age
an'cho·rite'
an'cho'vy
  ·vies
an'cient
an'cil·lar'y
an·dan'te
and'i'ron
and/or
an'dro·gen
an'ec·dot'al
an'ec·dote'
  (*story;* SEE
  antidote)
a·ne'mi·a
a·ne'mic
a·nem'o·graph'
an'e·mom'e·ter
a·nem'o·ne'
an'er·oid'

an·es·the'sia
an·es·the'si·
  ol'o·gy
an·es·thet'ic
an·es'the·tist
an·es'the·tize'
  ·tized' ·tiz'ing
an'gel
  (*spirit;* SEE angle)
an·gel'fish'
an·gel'ic
  or an·gel'i·cal
an·gel'i·cal·ly
An'ge·lus
an'ger
an·gi'na
an'gle
  ·gled ·gling
  (*corner; scheme;*
  SEE angel)
an'gler
an'gle·worm'
An'gli·can
An'gli·cism
An'gli·cize'
  ·cized' ·ciz'ing
an'gling
An'glo-A·mer'i·
  can
An'glo·ma'ni·a
An'glo·phile'
An'glo·Sax'on
An·go'ra
an'gos·tu'ra

an'gri·ly
an'gry
  ·gri·er ·gri·est
an'guish
an'gu·lar
an'gu·lar'i·ty
  ·ties
an'gu·la'tion
an·hy'drous
an'ile
a·nil'i·ty
an'i·mad·ver'·
  sion
an'i·mal
an'i·mal'cule
an'i·mal·ism
an'i·mal·is'tic
an'i·mal·ize'
  ·ized' ·iz'ing
an'i·mate'
  ·mat'ed ·mat'ing
an'i·ma'tor
  or ·mat'er
an'i·ma'tion
an'i·mism
an'i·mos'i·ty
  ·ties
an'i·mus
an'i'on
an'ise
an'i·seed'
an'i·sette'
ankh
an'kle

13

an'kle·bone'
an'klet
an'nal·ist
(*a writer of
annals;* SEE
analyst)
an'nals
An·nap'o·lis
an·neal'
an'ne·lid
an·nex' *v.*
an'nex *n.*
an'nex·a'tion
an·ni'hi·late'
·lat'ed ·lat'ing
an·ni'hi·la'tion
an·ni'hi·la'tor
an·ni·ver'sa·ry
·ries
an'no·tate'
·tat'ed ·tat'ing
an'no·ta'tion
an·nounce'
·nounced'
·nounc'ing
an·nounce'ment.
an·nounc'er
an·noy'
an·noy'ance
an'nu·al
an'nu·al·ly
an·nu'i·tant
an·nu'i·ty
·ties

an·nul'
·nulled'
·nul'ling
an'nu·lar
an·nul'ment
an'nu·lus
·li' *or* ·lus·es
an·nun'ci·ate'
·at'ed ·at'ing
(*announce;* SEE
enunciate)
an·nun'ci·a'tor
an·ode'
an'o·dize'
·dized' ·diz'ing
an'o·dyne'
a·noint'
a·nom'a·lous
a·nom'a·ly
·lies
an'o·mie
an'o·nym'i·ty
a·non'y·mous
a·noph'e·les'
an·oth'er
an'swer
ant·ac'id
an·tag'o·nism
an·tag'o·nis'tic
an·tag'o·nize'
·nized' ·niz'ing
ant·al'ka·li'
·lies' *or* ·lis'
ant·arc'tic

Ant·arc'ti·ca
an'te
·ted *or* ·teed
·te·ing
an'te- *prefix*
(*before;* SEE
anti-)
ant'eat'er
an'te·bel'lum
an'te·cede'
·ced'ed ·ced'ing
an'te·ced'ence
an'te·ced'ent
an'te·cham'ber
an'te·date'
an'te·di·lu'vi·an
an'te·lope'
an'te me·ri'di·em
an·ten'na
·nae *or* ·nas
an'te·pe'nult
an·te'ri·or
an'te·room'
an'them
an'ther
an·thol'o·gist
an·thol'o·gy
·gies
an'thra·cite'
an'thrax
·thra·ces'
an'thro·poid'
an'thro·pol'o·gist
an'thro·pol'o·gy

an'thro·po·mor'·
  phic
an'ti- *prefix*
  (*against;* SEE
  ante-)
an'ti·air'craft
an'ti·bac·te'ri·al
an'ti·bi·ot'ic
an'ti·bod'y
  ·ies
an'tic
  ·ticked ·tick·ing
an·tic'i·pant
an·tic'i·pate'
  ·pat·ed ·pat·ing
an·tic'i·pa'tion
an·tic'i·pa·to'ry
an'ti·cli·mac'tic
an'ti·cli'max
an'ti·de·pres'sant
an'ti·dote'
  (*remedy;* SEE
  anecdote)
an'ti·freeze'
an'ti·gen
an'ti·he'ro
an'ti·his'ta·mine'
an'ti·knock'
an'ti·la'bor
An·til'les
an'ti·ma·cas'sar
an'ti·mat'ter
an'ti·mo'ny
an'ti·nov'el

an'ti·par'ti·cle
an'ti·pas'to
an'ti·pa·thet'ic
an·tip'a·thy
  ·thies
an'ti·per'son·nel'
an'ti·phon
an·tiph'o·nal
an·tip'o·dal
an'ti·pode'
an·tip'o·des'
an'ti·quar'i·an
an'ti·quar'y
  ·ies
an'ti·quate'
  ·quat·ed
  ·quat·ing
an·tique'
  ·tiqued'
  ·tiqu'ing
an·tiq'ui·ty
  ·ties
an'ti·Sem'ite
an'ti-Se·mit'ic
an'ti-Sem'i·tism
an'ti·sep'sis
an'ti·sep'tic
an'ti·so'cial
an·tith'e·sis
  ·ses'
an'ti·thet'i·cal
an'ti·thet'i·
  cal·ly
an'ti·tox'in

an'ti·trust'
ant'ler
an'to·nym'
an'trum
  ·trums *or* ·tra
a'nus
  ·nus·es *or* ·ni
an'vil
anx·i'e·ty
  ·ties
anx'ious
an'y·bod'y
an'y·how'
an'y·one'
an'y·thing'
an'y·way'
an'y·where'
A'-OK' *or*
  A'-O·kay'
a·or'ta
  ·tas *or* ·tae
a·pace'
a·part'heid
a·part'ment
ap'a·thet'ic
ap'a·thet'i·
  cal·ly
ap'a·thy
  ·thies
a·pe·ri·tif'
ap'er·ture
a'pex
  a'pex·es *or*
  ap'i·ces

a·pha′si·a
aph′o·rism
aph′ro·dis′i·ac′
a′pi·ar′y
·ies
a·piece′
a·plomb′
a·poc′a·lypse′
a·poc′a·lyp′tic
a·poc′ry·phal
ap′o·gee′
a·pol′o·get′ic
a·pol′o·get′i·
cal·ly
ap′o·lo′gi·a
a·pol′o·gize′
·gized′ ·giz′ing
ap′o·logue′
a·pol′o·gy
·gies
ap′o·plec′tic
ap′o·plex′y
a·pos′ta·sy
a·pos′tate
a′ pos·te′ri·o′ri
a·pos′tle
ap′os·tol′ic
a·pos′tro·phe
ap′os·troph′ic
a·pos′tro·phize′
·phized′
·phiz′ing
a·poth′e·car′y
·ies

ap′o·thegm′
(*short saying*)
ap′o·them′
(*math. term*)
a·poth′e·o′sis
·ses
Ap′pa·la′chi·an
ap·pall′ or ·pal′
·palled′ ·pal′ling
ap′pa·loo′sa
ap′pa·ra′tus
·tus or ·tus·es
ap·par′el
·eled or ·elled
·el·ing or ·el·ling
ap·par′ent
ap′pa·ri′tion
ap·peal′
ap·pear′ance
ap·peas′a·ble
ap·pease′
·peased′
·peas′ing
ap·pease′ment
ap·peas′er
ap·pel′lant
ap·pel′late
ap′pel·la′tion
ap·pend′
ap·pend′age
ap·pend′ant or
·ent
ap′pen·dec′to·my
·mies

ap·pen′di·ci′tis
ap·pen′dix
·dix·es or
·di·ces′
ap′per·cep′tion
ap′per·tain′
ap′pe·tite′
ap′pe·tiz′er
ap′pe·tiz′ing
ap·plaud′
ap·plause′
ap′ple·jack′
ap′ple·sauce′
ap·pli′ance
ap′pli·ca·bil′i·ty
ap′pli·ca·ble
ap′pli·cant
ap′pli·ca′tion
ap′pli·ca′tor
ap·plied′
ap′pli·qué′
·quéd′ ·qué′ing
ap·ply′
·plied′ ·ply′ing
ap·pog′gia·tu′ra
ap·point′
ap·point′ee′
ap·point′ive
ap·point′ment
ap·por′tion
ap′po·site
ap′po·si′tion
ap·prais′a·ble
ap·prais′al

16

ap·praise'
  ·praised'
  ·prais'ing
  (*estimate;* SEE
  apprise)
ap·prais'er
ap·pre'ci·a·ble
ap·pre'ci·ate'
  ·at'ed ·at'ing
ap·pre'ci·a'tion
ap·pre'ci·a·tive
ap'pre·hend'
ap'pre·hen'sion
ap'pre·hen'sive
ap·pren'tice
  ·ticed ·tic·ing
ap·prise' *or*
  ·prize'
  ·prised' *or*
  ·prized'
  ·pris'ing *or*
  ·priz'ing
  (*inform;* SEE
  appraise)
ap·proach'
ap·proach'·
  a·ble
ap'pro·ba'tion
ap·pro'pri·ate'
  ·at'ed ·at'ing
ap·pro'pri·ate·ly
ap·pro'pri·a'tion
ap·prov'a·ble
ap·prov'al

ap·prove'
  ·proved'
  ·prov'ing
ap·prox'i·mate'
  ·mat'ed ·mat'ing
ap·prox'i·mate·ly
ap·prox'i·ma'·
  tion
ap·pur'te·nance
a'pri·cot'
A'pril
a' pri·o'ri
ap'ro·pos'
ap'ti·tude'
apt'ly
aq'ua·cade'
aq'ua·lung'
aq'ua·ma·rine'
aq'ua·naut'
aq'ua·plane'
a·quar'i·um
  ·i·ums *or* ·i·a
a·quat'ic
aq'ua·tint'
aq'ue·duct'
a'que·ous
aq'ui·line'
ar'a·besque'
A·ra'bi·an
Ar'a·bic
ar'a·ble
a·rach'nid
ar'bi·ter
ar'bi·tra·ble

ar·bit'ra·ment
ar'bi·trar'i·ly
ar'bi·trar'i·ness
ar'bi·trar'y
ar'bi·trate'
  ·trat'ed ·trat'ing
ar'bi·tra'tion
ar'bi·tra'tor
ar'bor
ar·bo're·al
ar·bo·re'tum
  ·tums *or* ·ta
ar'bor·vi'tae
arc
  arced *or* arcked
  arc'ing *or* arck'ing
  (*curve;* SEE ark)
ar·cade'
ar'chae·o·log'i·cal
ar'chae·ol'o·gy
ar·cha'ic
arch·an'gel
arch'bish'op
arch'dea'con
arch'di'o·cese
arch'duch'y
  ·ies
arch'duke'
arched
arch'en'e·my
  ·mies
ar'che·o·log'i·cal
ar'che·ol'o·gy
arch'er·y

ar'che·type'
arch'fiend'
ar'chi·pel'a·go'
 ·goes' or ·gos'
ar'chi·tect'
ar'chi·tec·ton'ics
ar'chi·tec'tur·al
ar'chi·tec'tur·
 al·ly
ar'chi·tec'ture
ar'chi·trave'
ar'chives
arch'priest'
arch'way'
arc'tic
ar'dent
ar'dor
ar'du·ous
ar'e·a·way'
a·re'na
aren't
Ar'gen·ti'na
ar'gon
ar'got
ar'gu·a·ble
ar'gu·a·bly
ar'gue
 ·gued ·gu·ing
ar'gu·ment
ar'gu·men·
 ta'tion
ar'gu·men·ta·
 tive
a'ri·a

a·rid'i·ty
ar'id·ness
a·rise'
 ·rose' ·ris'en
 ·ris'ing
ar'is·toc'ra·cy
 ·cies
a·ris'to·crat'
a·ris'to·crat'ic
a·ris'to·crat'i·
 cal·ly
Ar'is·to·te'li·an
Ar'is·tot'le
a·rith'me·tic' n.
ar'ith·met'ic adj.
ar'ith·met'i·cal
ar'ith·met'i·
 cal·ly
ar'ith·me·ti'cian
Ar'i·zo'na
ark
 (enclosure;
 SEE arc)
Ar'kan·sas'
ar·ma'da
ar'ma·dil'lo
 ·los
ar'ma·ment
ar'ma·ture
arm'chair'
armed
arm'ful
 ·fuls
arm'hole'

ar'mi·stice
arm'let
ar'mor
ar'mored
ar'mor-plat'ed
ar'mor·y
 ·ies
arm'pit'
arm'rest'
ar'my
 ·mies
ar'ni·ca
a·ro'ma
ar'o·mat'ic
ar'o·mat'i·cal·ly
a·round'
a·rous'al
a·rouse'
 ·roused'
 ·rous'ing
ar·peg'gio
 ·gios
ar·raign'
ar·range'
 ·ranged'
 ·rang'ing
ar·range'ment
ar·rang'er
ar'rant
ar·ray'
ar·ray'al
ar·rear'age
ar·rears'
ar·rest'

ar·riv'al
ar·rive'
·rived' ·riv'ing
ar'ro·gance
ar'ro·gant
ar'ro·gate'
·gat·ed ·gat·ing
ar'ro·ga'tion
ar'row·head'
ar'row·root'
ar·roy'o
·os
ar'se·nal
ar'se·nic
ar'son
ar'son·ist
ar'te·fact'
ar·te'ri·al
ar·te'ri·o·scle·
ro'sis
ar·te'ri·o·scle·
rot'ic
ar'ter·y
·ies
ar·te'sian
art'ful
art'ful·ly
ar·thrit'ic
ar·thri'tis
Ar·thu'ri·an
ar'ti·choke'
ar'ti·cle
ar·tic'u·late'
·lat·ed ·lat·ing

ar·tic'u·late·ly
ar·tic'u·la'tion
ar'ti·fact'
ar'ti·fice
ar·tif'i·cer
ar'ti·fi'cial
ar'ti·fi'cial·ly
ar'ti·fi'ci·al'i·ty
·ties
ar·til'ler·y
art'i·ness
ar'ti·san
art'ist
ar·tiste'
ar·tis'tic
ar·tis'ti·cal·ly
art'ist·ry
art'less
art'mo·bile'
art'sy-craft'sy
art'y
·i·er ·i·est
Ar'y·an
as·bes'tos
as·cend'
as·cend'a·ble
as·cend'an·cy
as·cend'ant
as·cen'sion
as·cent'
(*a rising;* SEE
assent)
as·cer·tain'
as·cet'ic

as·cet'i·cal·ly
as·cet'i·cism
a·scor'bic
as'cot
as·crib'a·ble
as·cribe'
·cribed'
·crib'ing
as·crip'tion
a·sep'tic
a·sep'ti·cal·ly
a·sex'u·al
a·shamed'
ash'can'
ash'en
ash'es
a·shore'
ash'y
·i·er ·i·est
A'sia
A'si·at'ic
as'i·nine'
as'i·nin'i·ty
·ties
a·skance'
a·skew'
a·sleep'
a·so'cial
as·par'a·gus
as'pect
as'pen
as·per'i·ty
as·perse'
·persed' ·pers'ing

19

as·per'sion
as'phalt
as·phyx'i·a
as·phyx'i·ant
as·phyx'i·ate'
·at'ed ·at'ing
as·phyx'i·a'tion
as·phyx'i·a'tor
as'pic
as'pir·ant
as'pi·rate'
·rat'ed ·rat'ing
as'pi·ra'tion
as'pi·ra'tor
as·pire'
·pired' ·pir'ing
as'pi·rin
as·sail'
as·sail'ant
as·sas'sin
as·sas'si·nate'
·nat'ed ·nat'ing
as·sas'si·na'tion
as·sault'
as·say'
(*analyze;* SEE
essay)
as·sem'blage
as·sem'ble
·bled ·bling
as·sem'bly
·blies
as·sem'bly·man
·men

as·sent'
(*consent;* SEE ascent)
as·sert'
as·ser'tion
as·ser'tive
as·sess'
as·ses'sor
as'set
as·sev'er·ate'
·at'ed ·at'ing
as·sev'er·a'tion
as·si·du'i·ty
as·sid'u·ous
as·sign'
as·sign'a·ble
as'sig·na'tion
as·sign·ee'
as·sign'ment
as·sim'i·la·ble
as·sim'i·late'
·lat'ed ·lat'ing
as·sim'i·la'tion
as·sim'i·la'tive
as·sim'i·la'tor
as·sist'
as·sist'ance
as·sist'ant
as·size'
as·so'ci·ate'
·at'ed ·at'ing
as·so'ci·a'tion
as·so'ci·a'tive
as'so·nance
as'so·nant

as·sort'
as·sort'ed
as·sort'ment
as·suage'
·suaged'
·suag'ing
as·sua'sive
as·sum'a·ble
as·sume'
·sumed'
·sum'ing
as·sump'tion
as·sur'ance
as·sure'
·sured' ·sur'ing
as·sur'ed·ly
As·syr'i·a
as'ter·isk'
as'ter·oid'
asth'ma
asth·mat'ic
asth·mat'i·cal·ly
as·tig·mat'ic
as·tig·mat'i·cal·ly
a·stig'ma·tism
as·ton'ish
as·tound'
a·strad'dle
as'tra·khan
or ·chan
as'tral
a·stride'
as·trin'gen·cy
as·trin'gent

as'tro·dome'
as'tro·labe'
as·trol'o·ger
as'tro·log'i·cal
as·trol'o·gy
as'tro·naut'
as'tro·nau'ti·cal
as'tro·nau'tics
as·tron'o·mer
as'tro·nom'i·cal
  or ·nom'ic
as'tro·nom'i·cal·ly
as·tron'o·my
as'tro·phys'i·cal
as'tro·phys'i·cist
as'tro·phys'ics
as·tute'
a·sun'der
a·sy'lum
a·sym·met'ri·cal
  or ·met'ric
a·sym'me·try
as'ymp·tote'
at'a·vism
at'a·vis'tic
at'el·ier'
a'the·ism
a'the·ist
a'the·is'tic
ath'lete'
ath·let'ic
ath·let'i·cal·ly
at-home'
a·thwart'

a·tin'gle
At·lan'tic
at'las
at'mos·phere'
at'mos·pher'ic
at'mos·pher'i·
  cal·ly
at'oll
at'om
a·tom'ic
a·tom'ics
at'om·ize'
  ·ized' ·iz'ing
at'om·iz'er
a·ton'al
a'to·nal'i·ty
a·tone'
  ·toned' ·ton'ing
a·tone'ment
a'tri·um
  ·tri·a or ·tri·ums
a·tro'cious
a·troc'i·ty
  ·ties
at'ro·phy
  ·phied ·phy·ing
at·tach'
at'ta·ché'
at·tach'ment
at·tack'
at·tain'
at·tain'a·ble
at·tain'der
at·tain'ment

at·taint'
at'tar
at·tempt'
at·tend'
at·tend'ance
at·tend'ant
at·ten'tion
at·ten'tive
at·ten'u·ate'
  ·at'ed ·at'ing
at·ten'u·a'tion
at·ten'u·a'tor
at·test'
at'tes·ta'tion
at'tic
at·tire'
  ·tired' ·tir'ing
at'ti·tude'
at'ti·tu'di·nal
at·tor'ney
  ·neys
at·tract'
at·trac'tion
at·trac'tive
at·trib'ut·a·ble
at'tri·bute' n.
at·trib'ute v.
  ·ut·ed ·ut·ing
at'tri·bu'tion
at·trib'u·tive
at·tri'tion
at·tune'
  ·tuned' ·tun'ing
a·typ'i·cal

a·typ'i·cal·ly
au'burn
auc'tion
auc'tion·eer'
au·da'cious
au·dac'i·ty
·ties
au'di·bil'i·ty
au'di·ble
au'di·bly
au'di·ence
au'di·o
au'di·ol'o·gy
au'di·o·vis'u·al
au'di·phone'
au'dit
au·di'tion
au'di·tor
au'di·to'ri·um
au'di·to'ry
au'ger
(*tool;* SEE augur)
aught
(*anything;* SEE ought)
aug·ment'
aug'men·ta'tion
aug·ment'a·tive
au gra'tin
au'gur
(*soothsayer;*
SEE auger)
Au'gust
au jus'

au na·tu·rel'
au'ra
·ras *or* ·rae
au'ral
(*of the ear;* SEE oral)
au're·ole'
Au're·o·my'cin
au' re·voir'
au'ri·cle
(*earlike part;* SEE oracle)
au·ric'u·lar
au·ro'ra bo're·a'lis
aus'cul·ta'tion
aus'pi·ces'
aus·pi'cious
aus·tere'
aus·tere'ly
aus·ter'i·ty
·ties
Aus·tral'ia
au·then'tic
au·then'ti·cal·ly
au·then'ti·cate'
·cat'ed ·cat'ing
au·then'ti·ca'tion
au'then·tic'i·ty
au'thor
au·thor'i·tar'i·an
au·thor'i·ta'tive
au·thor'i·ty
·ties

au'thor·i·za'tion
au'thor·ize'
·ized' ·iz'ing
au'to
·tos
·toed ·to·ing
au'to·bi'o·graph'ic *or*
graph'i·cal
au'to·bi·og'ra·phy
·phies
au·toc'ra·cy
·cies
au'to·crat'
au'to·crat'ic
au'to·crat'i·cal·ly
au'to·graph'
au'to·mate'
·mat'ed ·mat'ing
au'to·mat'ic
au'to·mat'i·cal·ly
au'to·ma'tion
au·tom'a·tism
au·tom'a·ton'
·tons' *or* ·ta
au'to·mo·bile'
au'to·mo'tive
au'to·nom'ic
au·ton'o·mous
au·ton'o·my
·mies

au'top'sy
·sies
au'to·sug·ges'·
tion
au'tumn
au·tum'nal
aux·il'ia·ry
·ries
a·vail'a·bil'i·ty
a·vail'a·ble
a·vail'a·bly
av'a·lanche'
·lanched'
·lanch'ing
a·vant'-garde'
a·vant'-gard'ism
a·vant'-gard'ist
av'a·rice
av'a·ri'cious
a·venge'
·venged'
·veng'ing
a·veng'er
av'e·nue'
a·ver'
·verred'
·ver'ring
av'er·age
·aged ·ag·ing
a·verse'
(*unwilling;* SEE
adverse)
a·ver'sion
a·vert'

a'vi·ar'y
·ies
a'vi·a'tion
a'vi·a'tor
a'vi·a'trix
av'id·ly
av'o·ca'do
·dos
av'o·ca'tion
a·void'a·ble
a·void'a·bly
a·void'ance
av'oir·du·pois'
a·vow'al
a·vowed'
a·vun'cu·lar
a·wait'
a·wake'
·woke' *or*
·waked',
·waked',
·wak'ing
a·wak'en
a·wak'en·ing
a·ward'
a·ware'
a·weigh'
awe'some
awe'-struck'
aw'ful
aw'ful·ly
aw'ful·ness
a·while'
awk'ward

awn'ing
a·wry'
ax *or* axe
ax'es
axed ax'ing
ax'i·om
ax'i·o·mat'ic
ax'i·o·mat'i·
cal·ly
ax'is
ax'es
ax'le
Ax'min·ster
a·zal'ea
az'i·muth
Az'tec
az'ure

B

bab'bitt
bab'ble
·bled ·bling
ba·boon'
ba·bush'ka
ba'by
·bies
·bied ·by·ing
ba'by-sit'
-sat' -sit'ting
baby sitter
bac'ca·lau're·ate

23

bac'ca·rat'
bac'cha·nal
bac'cha·na'li·an
bac'chant
·chants or
bac·chan'tes
bac·chan'te
bach'e·lor
ba·cil'lus
·li
back'ache'
back'bite'
·bit', ·bit'ten or
·bit', ·bit'ing
back'bend'
back'board'
back'bone'
back'break'ing
back'court'
back'date'
·dat'ed ·dat'ing
back'door'
back'drop'
back'field'
back'fire'
·fired' ·fir'ing
back'gam'mon
back'ground'
back'hand'
back'lash'
back'list'
back'log'
·logged'
·log'ging

back'rest'
back'side'
back'slide'
·slid', ·slid' or
·slid'den, ·slid'ing
back'space'
·spaced'
·spac'ing
back'spin'
back'stage'
back'stairs'
back'stop'
back'stretch'
back'stroke'
·stroked'
·strok'ing
back'track'
back'up' or
back'-up'
back'ward
back'wash'
back'wa'ter
back'woods'man
·men
ba'con
bac·te'ri·a
(sing. bac·te'ri·um)
bac·te'ri·cide'
bac·te'ri·o·log'i·
cal·ly
bac·te'ri·ol'o·gist
bac·te'ri·ol'o·gy
bad
worse worst

badge
badged badg'ing
badg'er
bad'i·nage'
·naged' ·nag'ing
bad'lands'
bad'min·ton
bad'-tem'pered
baf'fle
·fled ·fling
bag
bagged bag'ging
bag'a·telle'
ba'gel
bag'ful'
·fuls'
bag'gage
bag'gy
·gi·er ·gi·est
bag'pipe'
ba·guette' or
·guet'
Ba·hai'
Ba·ha'mas
bail
(money; SEE
bale)
bai'liff
bai'li·wick
bails'man
·men
bait'ed
(lured; SEE
bated)

24

bake
  baked bak'ing
bak'er
bak'er·y
  ·ies
bal'a·lai'ka
bal'ance
  ·anced ·anc·ing
bal'ance·a·ble
bal·brig'gan
bal'co·ny
  ·nies
bal'der·dash'
bald'faced'
bald'head'ed
bald'ness
bale
  baled bal'ing
  (bundle; SEE
  bail)
bale'ful
balk'y
  ·i·er ·i·est
ball
  (round object;
  SEE bawl)
bal'lad
bal'lad·eer'
bal'last
ball bearing
bal'le·ri'na
bal'let
bal·lis'tic
bal·loon'ist

bal'lot
ball'park'
ball'play'er
ball'room'
balm'y
  ·i·er ·i·est
ba·lo'ney
bal'sa
bal'sam
Bal'tic
Bal'ti·more'
bal'us·ter
bal'us·trade'
bam·bi'no
  ·nos or ·ni
bam·boo'
bam·boo'zle
  ·zled ·zling
ban
  banned ban'ning
ba'nal
ba·nal'i·ty
  ·ties
ba·nan'a
band'age
  ·aged ·ag·ing
band'-aid' or
  band'aid'
ban·dan'na
band'box'
ban·deau'
  ·deaux'
ban'de·role'
ban'dit

band'mas'ter
ban'do·leer'
  or ·lier'
band saw
bands'man
  ·men
band'stand'
band'wag'on
ban'dy
  ·died ·dy·ing
ban'dy·leg'ged
bane'ful
ban'gle
bang'-up'
ban'ish
ban'is·ter
  or ban'nis·ter
ban'jo
  ·jos or ·joes
ban'jo·ist
bank'book'
bank note
bank'roll'
bank'rupt
bank'rupt·cy
  ·cies
ban'ner
banns or bans
  (marriage notice)
ban'quet
ban'tam
ban'tam·weight'
ban'ter
ban'zai'

25

bap'tism
bap·tis'mal
bap'tis·ter·y
 or ·tis·try
 ·ies or ·tries
bap'tize
 ·tized ·tiz·ing
bar
 barred bar'ring
bar·bar'i·an
bar·bar'ic
bar'ba·rism
bar·bar'i·ty
 ·ties
bar'ba·rous
bar'be·cue'
 ·cued' ·cu'ing
barbed wire
bar'bel
 (*hairlike growth*)
bar'bell'
 (*bar with weights*)
bar'ber
bar'ber·shop'
bar'bi·tal'
bar·bi'tu·rate
bar'bule
bare
 bared bar'ing
 (*uncover*; SEE
 bear)
bare'back'
bare'faced'
bare'fac'ed·ly

bare'foot'
bare'foot'ed
bare'hand'ed
bare'head'ed
bare'leg'ged
bare'ly
bar'gain
barge
 barged barg'ing
bar'i·tone'
bar'keep'er
bark'en·tine'
bark'er
bar'ley·corn'
bar'maid'
bar'man
 ·men
bar mitz'vah or
 bar miz'vah
bar'na·cle
bar'na·cled
barn'storm'
barn'yard'
bar'o·graph'
ba·rom'e·ter
bar'o·met'ric
bar'on
 (*nobleman*; SEE
 barren)
bar'on·ess
bar'on·et
ba·ro'ni·al
ba·roque'
ba·rouche'

bar'racks
bar'ra·cu'da
bar·rage'
 ·raged' ·rag'ing
barred
bar'rel
 ·reled or ·relled
 ·rel·ing or
 ·rel·ling
bar'ren
 (*empty*; SEE
 baron)
bar·rette'
 (*hair clasp*;
 SEE beret)
bar'ri·cade'
 ·cad'ed ·cad'ing
bar'ri·er
bar'ring
bar'ris·ter
bar'room'
bar'row
bar'tend'er
bar'ter
Bart'lett pear
bas'al
bas'al·ly
ba·salt'
bas'cule
base
 bas'es
 based bas'ing
 (*foundation*; *vile*;
 SEE bass)

26

base'ball'
base'board'
base'born'
base'burn'er
base hit
base'less
base line
base'ly
base'man
·men
base'ment
base'ness
bas'es
(pl. of base)
ba'ses
(pl. of basis)
bash'ful
bash'ful·ly
bash'ful·ness
bas'ic
bas'i·cal·ly
bas'il
ba·sil'i·ca
ba'sin
ba'sis
·ses
bas'ket
bas'ket·ball'
bas'ket·work'
bas'-re·lief'
bass
(singer; SEE base)
bass
(fish)

bass clef
bass drum
bas'set
bass horn
bas'si·net'
bas·soon'
bass viol
bass'wood'
bas'tard
baste
bast'ed bast'ing
bas·tille'
bas'tion
bat
bat'ted bat'ting
batch
bate
bat'ed bat'ing
ba·teau'
·teaux'
bat'ed
(held in; SEE baited)
bathe
bathed bath'ing
bath'er
bath'house'
bath'i·nette'
ba'thos
bath'robe'
bath'room'
bath'tub'
bath'y·sphere'
ba·tik'

ba·tiste'
bat mitz'vah or
bat miz'vah
ba'ton'
bat·tal'ion
bat'ten
bat'ter
bat'ter·y
·ies
bat'ting
bat'tle
·tled ·tling
bat'tle-ax' or -axe'
bat'tle·dore'
bat'tle·field'
bat'tle-ground'
bat'tle·ment
battle royal
battles royal
bat'tle-scarred'
bat'tle·ship'
bau'ble
baux'ite
bawd'y
·i·er ·i·est
bawl
(shout; SEE ball)
bay'o·net'
·net'ed or ·net'ted
·net'ing or ·net'ting
bay'ou
ba·zaar'
(market; SEE
bizarre)

27

ba·zoo'ka
be
  was *or* were,
  been be'ing
beach
  (*shore;* SEE
  beech)
beach'comb'er
beach'head'
bea'con
bead'ing
bead'work
bead'y
  ·i·er ·i·est
bea'gle
beak'er
bean'bag'
bean'stalk'
bear
  (*animal;* SEE
  bare)
bear
  bore, borne *or*
  born,
  bear'ing
  (*carry;* SEE bare)
bear'a·ble
bear'a·bly
beard'ed
bear'ish
bear'skin'
beast'li·ness
beast'ly
  ·li·er ·li·est

beat
  beat beat'en
  beat'ing
be'a·tif'ic
be·at'i·fi·ca'tion
be·at'i·fy'
  ·fied' ·fy'ing
be·at'i·tude'
beat'nik
beau
  beaus *or* beaux
  (*sweetheart;* SEE
  bow)
beau'te·ous
beau·ti'cian
beau'ti·fi·ca'tion
beau'ti·fi'er
beau'ti·ful
beau'ti·ful·ly
beau'ti·fy'
  ·fied' ·fy'ing
beau'ty
  ·ties
bea'ver
bea'ver·board'
be·calm'
be·cause'
beck'on
be·come'
  ·came' ·come'
  ·com'ing
bed
  bed'ded
  bed'ding

bed'bug'
bed'cham'ber
bed'clothes'
bed'cov'er
be·dev'il
  ·iled *or* ·illed
  ·il·ing *or* ·il·ling
bed'fast'
bed'fel'low
bed'lam
Bed'ou·in
bed'pan'
bed'post'
be·drag'gle
  ·gled ·gling
bed'rid'den
bed'rock'
bed'roll'
bed'room'
bed'side'
bed'sore'
bed'spread'
bed'spring'
bed'stead'
bed'time'
beech
  (*tree;* SEE beach)
beech'nut'
beef
  beeves *or* beefs
beef'eat'er
beef'steak'
beef'y
  ·i·er ·i·est

28

bee′hive′
bee′keep′er
bee′line′
beer
  (*drink;* SEE bier)
beer′i·ness
beer′y
  ·i·er ·i·est
bees′wax′
Bee·tho·ven
bee′tle
bee′tle-browed′
be·fall′
  ·fell′ ·fall′en
  ·fall′ing
be·fit′
  ·fit′ted ·fit′ting
be·fog′
  ·fogged′
  ·fog′ging
be·fore′hand′
be·friend′
be·fud′dle
  ·dled ·dling
beg
  begged beg′ging
be·get′
  ·got′, ·got′ten or
  ·got′, ·get′ting
beg′gar
be·gin′
  ·gan′ ·gun′
  ·gin′ning
  (*start;* SEE beguine)

be·gin′ner
be·gird′
  ·girt′ or ·gird′ed,
  ·girt′, ·gird′ing
be·gone′
be·gon′ia
be·grime′
  ·grimed′
  ·grim′ing
be·grudge′
  ·grudged′
  ·grudg′ing
be·guile′
  ·guiled′ ·guil′ing
be·guine′
  (*dance;* SEE begin)
be·half′
be·have′
  ·haved′ ·hav′ing
be·hav′ior
be·head′
be·he′moth
be·hest′
be·hind′hand′
be·hold′
  ·held′ ·hold′ing
be·hold′en
be·hoove′
  ·hooved′
  ·hoov′ing
beige
be·jew′el
  ·eled or ·elled
  ·el·ing or ·el·ling

be·la′bor
be·lat′ed
be·lay′
  ·layed′ ·lay′ing
belch
be·lea′guer
bel′fry
  ·fries
be·lie′
  ·lied′ ·ly′ing
be·lief′
be·liev′a·bil′i·ty
be·liev′a·ble
be·liev′a·bly
be·lieve′
  ·lieved′ ·liev′ing
be·liev′er
be·lit′tle
  ·tled ·tling
be·lit′tler
bel′la·don′na
bell′boy′
  (*errand boy*)
bell buoy
  (*signal bell*)
belle
  (*pretty girl*)
belles-let′tres
bell′-bot′tom
bel′li·cose′
bel′li·cos′i·ty
bel·lig′er·ence
bel·lig′er·en·cy
bel·lig′er·ent

29

bell'-like'
bell'man
·men
bel'low
bell'weth'er
bel'ly
·lies
·lied ·ly·ing
bel'ly·band'
be·long'
be·lov'ed
be·low'
belt'ing
be·mire'
·mired' ·mir'ing
be·moan'
bend
bent bend'ing
be·neath'
ben'e·dict'
Ben'e·dic'tine
ben'e·dic'tion
ben'e·fac'tion
ben'e·fac'tor
ben'e·fac'tress
ben'e·fice
be·nef'i·cence
be·nef'i·cent
ben'e·fi'cial
ben'e·fi'ci·ar'y
·ar'ies
ben'e·fit
·fit·ed ·fit·ing
be·nev'o·lence

be·nev'o·lent
ben'ga·line'
be·night'ed
be·nign'
be·nig'nan·cy
be·nig'nant
be·nig'ni·ty
ben'i·son
be·numb'
ben'zene
(*in chemistry*)
ben'zine
(*cleaning fluid*)
be·queath'
·queathed'
·queath'ing
be·queath'al
be·quest'
be·rate'
·rat'ed ·rat'ing
be·reave'
·reaved' or ·reft'
·reav'ing
be·reave'ment
be·ret'
(*flat cap;* SEE
barrette)
ber'i·ber'i
Berke'ley
Ber·mu'da
ber'ry
·ries
·ried ·ry·ing
(*fruit;* SEE bury)

ber·serk'
berth
(*bed;* SEE birth)
ber'yl
be·ryl'li·um
be·seech'
·sought' or
·seeched'
·seech'ing
be·set'
·set' ·set'ting
be·side'
be·sides'
be·siege'
·sieged' ·sieg'ing
be·smirch'
be·sot'
·sot'ted ·sot'ting
Bes'se·mer
bes'tial
bes'ti·al'i·ty
·ties
be·stow'
best seller
bet
bet or bet'ted
bet'ting
be'ta·tron'
be·tray'al
be·troth'
be·troth'al
be·trothed'
bet'ter
(*compar. of* good)

bet′tor *or* ·ter
(*one who bets*)
be·tween′
be·twixt′
bev′a·tron′
bev′el
·eled *or* ·elled
·el·ing *or* ·el·ling
bev′er·age
bev′y
·ies
be·wail′
be·ware′
·wared′ ·war′ing
be·wil′dered
be·witch′
be·yond′
bez′el
bi·an′nu·al
bi·an′nu·al·ly
bi′as
·ased *or* ·assed
·as·ing *or* ·as·sing
Bi′ble
Bib′li·cal
Bib′li·cal·ly
bib·li·og′ra·phy
·phies
bib′li·o·phile′
bib′u·lous
bi·cam′er·al
bi·car′bon·ate
bi·cen·te′nar·y
·ies

bi·cen·ten′ni·al
bi′ceps
·ceps *or* ·ceps·es
bick′er
bi·cus′pid
bi′cy·cle
·cled ·cling
bi′cy·clist
bid
bade *or* bid,
bid′den *or* bid,
bid′ding
bid′da·ble
bi·det′
bi·en′ni·al
bi·en′ni·al·ly
bier
(*coffin stand;* SEE
beer)
bi′fo·cals
bi′fur·cate′
·cat′ed ·cat′ing
big
big′ger big′gest
big′a·mist
big′a·mous
big′a·my
·mies
big′gish
big′heart′ed
big′horn′
big·no′ni·a
big′ot
big′ot·ed

big′ot·ry
·ries
bi′jou
·joux
bi·ki′ni
bi·la′bi·al
bi·lat′er·al
bilge
bi·lin′gual
bil′ious
bill′board′
bil′let
bil′let-doux′
bil′lets-doux′
bill′fold′
bill′head′
bil′liards
bill′ing
bil′lings·gate′
bil′lion
bil′lion·aire′
bill of fare
bill of lad′ing
bill of sale
bil′low
bil′low·i·ness
bil′low·y
·i·er ·i·est
bil′ly
·lies
bi·man′u·al
bi·man′u·al·ly
bi·me·tal′lic
bi·met′al·lism

31

bi·month'ly
bin
  binned bin'ning
bi'na·ry
bind
  bound bind'ing
bind'er
bind'er·y
  ·ies
binge
bin'go
bin'na·cle
bin·oc'u·lars
bi·no'mi·al
bi·no'mi·al·ly
bi'o·as'tro·
  nau'tics
bi'o·chem'ist
bi'o·chem'is·try
bi'o·cide'
bi'o·e·col'o·gy
bi·og'ra·pher
bi'o·graph'i·cal
bi'o·graph'i·cal·ly
bi·og'ra·phy
  ·phies
bi'o·log'i·cal
bi'o·log'i·cal·ly
bi·ol'o·gy
bi·on'ics
bi'o·phys'ics
bi'op'sy
  ·sies
bi'o·sat'el·lite'

bi·par'ti·san
bi·par'tite
bi'pro·pel'lant
bi·quar'ter·ly
bi·ra'cial
bird'bath'
bird'call'
bird'ie
bird'lime'
bird'man'
  ·men'
bird'seed'
bird's'-eye'
bi·ret'ta
birth
  (*being born*; SEE
  berth)
birth'day'
birth'mark'
birth'place'
birth'rate'
birth'right'
birth'stone'
bis'cuit
bi·sect'
bi·sec'tion
bi·sec'tor
bi·sex'u·al
bi·sex'u·al·ly
bish'op
bish'op·ric
bis'muth
bi'son
bisque

bis'tro
bitch
bite
  bit, bit'ten *or*
  bit, bit'ing
bit'ter
bit'tern
bit'ter·sweet'
bi·tu'men
bi·tu'mi·nous
bi·va'lent
bi'valve'
biv'ou·ac'
  ·acked' ·ack'ing
bi·week'ly
  ·lies
bi·year'ly
bi·zarre'
  (*odd*; SEE bazaar)
bi·zarre'ly
black'-a-moor'
black'-and-blue'
black'ball'
black'ber'ry
  ·ries
black'bird'
black'board'
black'en
black'face'
black'guard
black'head'
black'heart'ed
black'jack'
black'list'

black′mail′
black′out′
black′smith′
black′top′
 ·topped′
 ·top′ping
blad′der
blam′a·ble or
 blame′a·ble
blame
 blamed blam′ing
blame′wor′thy
blanc·mange′
blan′dish
blan′ket
blare
 blared blar′ing
blar′ney
bla·sé′
blas·pheme′
 ·phemed′
 ·phem′ing
blas′phe·mous
blas′phe·my
 ·mies
blast′off′ or
 blast′-off′
bla′tan·cy
 ·cies
bla′tant
blaze
 blazed blaz′ing
blaz′er
bla′zon

bleach′ers
bleak′ly
blear′i·ness
blear′y
 ·i·er ·i·est
blear′y-eyed′
bleed
 bled bleed′ing
blem′ish
blend
 blend′ed or blent
 blend′ing
blend′er
bless
 blessed or blest
 bless′ing
bless′ed·ness
blight
blind′fold′
blintz
bliss′ful
bliss′ful·ly
blis′ter
blithe
blithe′some
blitz′krieg′
bliz′zard
bloat′ed
bloc
 (group)
block
 (solid piece)
block·ade′
 ·ad′ed ·ad′ing

block′bust′ing
block′head′
block′house′
blond or blonde
blood bank
blood count
blood′cur′dling
blood′hound′
blood′i·ness
blood′i·ly
blood′less
blood′let′ting
blood′mo·bile′
blood pressure
blood′shed′
blood′shot′
blood′stained′
blood′stream′
blood test
blood′thirst′y
blood vessel
blood′y
 ·i·er ·i·est
 ·ied ·y·ing
Bloody Mary
blos′som
blot
 blot′ted blot′ting
blotch′y
 ·i·er ·i·est
blot′ter
blouse
 bloused
 blous′ing

blous'on
blow
　blew blown
　blow'ing
blow'gun'
blow'hole'
blow'out'
blow'pipe'
blow'torch'
blow'up'
blow'y
　·i·er ·i·est
blowz'y
　·i·er ·i·est
blub'ber
blu'cher
bludg'eon
blue
　blued, blu'ing or
　blue'ing
blue'ber'ry
　·ries
blue'bird'
blue'-blood'ed
blue book
blue'-chip'
blue'-col'lar
blue'fish'
blue'grass'
blue jay
blue law
blue'-pen'cil
　·ciled or ·cilled
　·cil·ing or ·cil·ling

blue'print'
blue'stock'ing
bluff'er
blu'ing or
　blue'ing
blu'ish or
　blue'ish
blun'der
blun'der·buss'
blunt'ly
blur
　blurred blur'ring
blur'ri·ness
blur'ry
　·ri·er ·ri·est
blus'ter
blus'ter·y
bo'a
boar
　(*hog;* SEE bore)
board'er
board foot
　board feet
board'ing·house'
boarding school
board'walk'
boast'ful
boast'ful·ly
boat'house'
boat'ing
boat'load'
boat'man
　·men
boat'swain

bob'bin
bob'ble
　·bled ·bling
bob'o·link'
bob'sled'
　·sled'ded
　·sled'ding
bob'white'
bode
　bod'ed bod'ing
bod'ice
bod'ied
bod'i·ly
bod'kin
bod'y
　·ies
bod'y·guard'
bo'gey
　·geys
　·geyed ·gey·ing
　(*golf term*)
bog'gy
　·gi·er ·gi·est
　(*like a bog*)
bo'gus
bo'gy
　·gies
　(*spirit*)
boil'ing
bois'ter·ous
bold'face'
bold'faced'
bo·le'ro
　·ros

boll
  (*pod;* SEE bowl)
boll weevil
boll′worm′
bo·lo′gna
bol′ster
bom·bard′
bom·bar·dier′
bom′bast
bom·bas′tic
bom·bas′ti·cal·ly
bomb′proof′
bomb′shell′
bomb′sight′
bo′na fi′de
bo·nan′za
bon′bon′
bond′age
bonds′man
  ·men
bone′-dry′
bon′fire′
bon′go
  ·gos
bon′i·ness
bon′ mot′
  bons′ mots′
bon′net
bon′ny
  ·ni·er ·ni·est
bon·sai′
bo′nus
bon′ vi·vant′
  bons′ vi·vants′

bon′ voy·age′
bon′y
  ·i·er ·i·est
boo′by
  ·bies
boo′hoo′
  ·hoos′
  ·hooed′ ·hoo′ing
book′bind′er
book′case′
book club
book′end′
book′ish
book′keep′er
book′keep′ing
book′let
book′mak′er
book′mark′
book′mo·bile′
book′plate′
book′rack′
book′sell′er
book′shelf′
  ·shelves′
book′stack′
book′stall′
book′stand′
book′store′
book′worm′
boom′er·ang′
boom′let
boon′docks′
boon′dog′gle
  ·gled ·gling

boor′ish
boost′er
boot′black′
boot′ee
  (*baby's shoe;* SEE
  booty)
boot′leg′
  ·legged′
  ·leg′ging
boot′leg′ger
boot′strap′
boo′ty
  ·ties
  (*spoils;* SEE
  bootee)
bo′rax
bor′der
bor′der·line′
bore
  (*dull person;*
  SEE boar)
bore
  bored bor′ing
bore′dom
born
  (*brought into*
  life)
borne
  (*participle of*
  bear)
bor′ough
  (*town;* SEE burro,
  burrow)
bor′row

borsch *or* borsht
bos'om
boss'i·ness
boss'y
 ·i·er ·i·est
bo·tan'i·cal
bot'a·nist
bot'a·ny
botch
both'er·some
bot'tle
 ·tled ·tling
bot'tle·neck'
bot'tle·nose'
bot'tom
bot'u·lism
bou·clé' *or*
 bou·cle'
bou'doir
bouf·fant'
bough
 (*tree branch;*
 SEE bow)
bought
bouil'la·baisse'
bouil'lon
 (*broth;* SEE
 bullion)
boul'der
boul'e·vard'
bounce
 bounced
 bounc'ing
 bounc'er

bound'a·ry
 ·ries
bound'en
bound'less
boun'te·ous
boun'ti·ful
boun'ti·ful·ly
boun'ty
 ·ties
bou·quet'
bour'bon
bour·geois'
bour'geoi·sie'
bourse
bou·tique'
bou'ton·niere'
bo'vine
bow
 (*curve;* SEE beau)
bow
 (*of a ship;* SEE
 bough)
bowd'ler·ize'
 ·ized ·iz'ing
bow'el
bow'er
Bow'er·y
bow'ie knife
bow'knot'
bowl
 (*dish;* SEE boll)
bow'leg'ged
bow'line
bowl'ing

bow'sprit'
bow'string'
bow tie
box'car'
box'er
box office
box'wood'
boy
 (*child;* SEE buoy)
boy'cott
boy'friend'
boy'hood'
boy'ish
boy'sen·ber'ry
 ·ries
brace
 braced brac'ing
brace'let
brack'et
brack'ish
brad'awl'
brag
 bragged
 brag'ging
brag·ga·do'ci·o'
brag'gart
Brah'ma
Brah'man·ism
braid
Braille
brain'child'
brain'i·ness
brain'pow'er
brain'storm'

brain'wash'
brain wave
brain'y
 ·i·er ·i·est
braise
 braised brais'ing
 (*cook;* SEE braze)
brake
 braked brak'ing
 (*stop;* SEE break)
brake'man
 ·men
bram'ble
branch'ing
bran'dish
brand'-new'
bran'dy
 ·dies
 ·died ·dy·ing
bras'sard
brass'ie *n.*
bras·siere'
brass'i·ness
brass'ware'
brass'-wind' *adj.*
brass winds
brass'y *adj.*
 ·i·er ·i·est
braun'schwei'ger
bra·va'do
brave
 braved brav'ing
brave'ly
brav'er·y

bra'vo
 ·vos
brawl
brawn'y
 ·i·er ·i·est
braze
 brazed braz'ing
 (*solder;* SEE
 braise)
bra'zen
bra'zen·ness
bra'zen·faced'
bra'zier
Bra·zil'
bra·zil'wood'
breach
 (*a gap;* SEE
 breech)
bread'bas'ket
bread'board'
bread'box'
breadth
 (*width;* SEE
 breath)
breadth'ways'
bread'win'ner
break
 broke bro'ken
 break'ing
 (*smash;* SEE
 brake)
break'a·ble
break'age
break'down'

break'fast
break'front'
break'neck'
break'out'
break'through'
break'up'
break'wa'ter
breast'bone'
breast'-feed'
 -fed' -feed'ing
breast stroke
breast'work'
breath
 (*air;* SEE breadth)
breath'a·lyz'er
breathe
 breathed
 breath'ing
breath'er
breath'less
breath'tak'ing
breech
 (*rear;* SEE
 breach)
breech'cloth'
breech'es
breech'-load'ing
breed
 bred breed'ing
breez'i·ly
breez'i·ness
breeze'way'
breez'y
 ·i·er ·i·est

breth'ren
bre'vi·ar'y
·ies
brev'i·ty
brew'er·y
·ies
brib'a·ble
bribe
bribed brib'ing
brib'er·y
·ies
bric'-a-brac'
brick'bat'
brick'lay'ing
brick'work'
brick'yard'
brid'al
(wedding; SEE
bridle)
bride'groom'
brides'maid'
bridge
bridged
bridg'ing
bridge'a·ble
bridge'head'
bridge'work'
bri'dle
(harness; SEE
bridal)
brief'case'
bri'er or bri'ar
bri·gade'
brig'a·dier'

brig'and
brig'an·tine'
bright'en
bril'liance
bril'liant
bril'lian·tine'
brim
brimmed
brim'ming
brim'ful'
brim'stone'
brin'dled
brine
brined brin'ing
bring
brought
bring'ing
brin'i·ness
brink'man·ship'
brin'y
·i·er ·i·est
bri·oche'
bri·quette'
or ·quet'
bris'ket
brisk'ly
bris'tle
·tled ·tling
bris'tli·ness
bris'tly
·tli·er ·tli·est
Bris'tol board
Brit'ain
(place)

Brit'i·cism
Brit'on
(person)
brit'tle
brit'tle·ly or
brit'tly
broach
(open; SEE
brooch)
broad'ax' or ·axe'
broad'cast'
·cast' or ·cast'ed
·cast'ing
broad'cloth'
broad'leaf'
broad'-leaved'
broad'loom'
broad'-mind'ed
broad'side'
broad'sword'
bro·cade'
·cad'ed ·cad'ing
broc'co·li
bro·chette'
bro·chure'
bro'gan
brogue
broil'er
bro'ken-down'
bro'ken·heart'ed
bro'ker
bro'ker·age
bro'mide
bro·mid'ic

bro′mine
bro′mo selt′zer
bron′chi·al
bron·chi′tis
bron′chus
·chi
bron′co
·cos
bron′to·sau′rus
bronze
bronzed
bronz′ing
brooch
(*pin*; SEE broach)
brood′i·ness
broom′stick′
broth′el
broth′er-in-law′
broth′ers-in-law′
brougham
brought
brou′ha·ha′
brow′beat′
·beat′ ·beat′en
·beat′ing
brown′ie
brown′out′
brown′stone′
browse
browsed
brows′ing
bruise
bruised bruis′ing
bruis′er

bru·net′ *or*
bru·nette′
brush′wood′
brush′work′
brusque
brusque′ly
brusque′ness
Brus′sels sprouts
bru′tal
bru·tal′i·ty
·ties
bru′tal·ize′
·ized′ ·iz′ing
brut′ish
bub′ble
·bled ·bling
bub′bler
bub′ble-top′
bub′bly
bu·bon′ic
buc′ca·neer′
buck′board′
buck′et·ful′
·fuls′
bucket seat
buck′le
·led ·ling
buck′-pass′er
buck′ram
buck′saw′
buck′shot′
buck′skin′
buck′tooth′
·teeth′

buck′toothed′
buck′wheat′
bu·col′ic
bud
bud′ded bud′ding
Bud′dha
Bud′dhism
budge
budged budg′ing
budg′et
budg′et·ar′y
buf′fa·lo′
·loes′ *or* ·los′
buff′er
buf′fet
buf·foon′er·y
bug′bear′
bug′gy
·gies
·gi·er ·gi·est
bu′gle
·gled ·gling
build
built build′ing
build′up′ *or*
build′-up′
built′-in′
built′-up′
bul′bar
bul′bous
bulge
bulged bulg′ing
bulg′i·ness
bulk′i·ness

39

bulk'y
·i·er ·i·est
bull'dog'
bull'doze'
·dozed' ·doz'ing
bull'doz'er
bul'let
bul'le·tin
bul'let·proof'
bull'fight'er
bull'frog'
bull'head'ed
bull'horn'
bul'lion
(gold; SEE
bouillon)
bull'ish
bull'ock
bull'pen'
bull's'-eye'
bull'whip'
bul'ly
·lies
·lied ·ly·ing
bul'rush'
bul'wark
bum'ble·bee'
bum'bling
bump'er
bump'kin
bump'tious
bump'y
·i·er ·i·est
bun'combe

bun'dle
·dled ·dling
bun'ga·low'
bung'hole'
bun'gle
·gled ·gling
bun'ion
bunk'er
bun'ting
Bun'sen burner
buoy
(marker; SEE boy)
buoy'an·cy
buoy'ant
bur'ble
·bled ·bling
bur'den·some
bu'reau
·reaus or ·reaux
bu·reau'cra·cy
·cies
bu'reau·crat'
bu'reau·crat'ic
bu'reau·crat'i·
cal·ly
bu·rette' or ·ret'
bur'geon
bur'glar
bur'gla·rize'
·rized' ·riz'ing
bur'gla·ry
·ries
Bur'gun·dy
bur'i·al

bur'lap
bur·lesque'
·lesqued'
·lesqu'ing
bur'ley
(tobacco)
bur'li·ness
bur'ly
·li·er ·li·est
(muscular)
burn
burned or burnt
burn'ing
burn'a·ble
bur'nish
bur·noose'
burn'out'
bur'ro
·ros
(donkey; SEE
burrow, borough)
bur'row
(hole; SEE burro,
borough)
bur'sa
·sae or ·sas
bur'sar
bur·si'tis
burst
burst burst'ing
bur'y
·ied ·y·ing
(cover; SEE
berry)

bus
  bus'es *or* bus'ses
  bused *or* bussed
  bus'ing *or* bus'sing
  (*motor coach;* SEE
  buss)
bus'boy'
bus'by
  ·bies
bush'el·bas'ket
bush'ing
bush'man
  ·men
bush'rang'er
bush'whack'er
bush'y
  ·i·er ·i·est
bus'i·ly
busi'ness
busi'ness·like'
busi'ness·man'
  ·men'
busi'ness·wom'an
  ·wom'en
bus'kin
bus'man
  ·men
buss
  (*kiss;* SEE bus)
bus'tle
  ·tled ·tling
bus'y
  ·i·er ·i·est
  ·ied ·y·ing

bus'y·bod'y
  ·ies
bus'y·ness
butch'er·y
but'ler
butte
but'ter·fat'
but'ter·fin'gers
but'ter·fly'
  ·flies'
but'ter·milk'
but'ter·nut'
but'ter·scotch'
but'ter·y
but'tocks
but'ton·down'
but'ton·hole'
  ·holed' ·hol'ing
but'tress
bux'om
buy
  bought buy'ing
buz'zard
buz'zer
by'gone'
by'law'
by'line'
by'pass'
by'path'
by'play'
by'prod'uct *or*
  by'-prod'uct
by'road'
by'stand'er

by'way'
by'word'

C

ca·bal'
  ·balled' ·bal'ling
cab'a·lism
ca·bal·le'ro
  ·ros
ca·ba'na
cab'a·ret'
cab'bage
cab'driv'er
cab'in
cab'i·net
cab'i·net·mak'er
cab'i·net·work'
ca'ble
  ·bled ·bling
ca'ble·gram'
ca·boose'
cab'ri·o·let'
cab'stand'
ca·ca'o
cac·cia·to're
cache
  cached cach'ing
ca·chet'
cach'in·nate'
  ·nat'ed ·nat'ing
cach'in·na'tion

cack'le
 ·led ·ling
ca·cog'ra·phy
ca·coph'o·nous
ca·coph'o·ny
cac'tus
 ·tus·es or ·ti
ca·dav'er
ca·dav'er·ous
cad'die or ·dy
 ·dies
 ·died ·dy·ing
 (in golf)
cad'dish
cad'dy
 ·dies
 (tea box)
ca'dence
ca·den'za
ca·det'
cad'mi·um
ca'dre
ca·du'ce·us
 ·ce·i
Cae·sar'e·an
cae·su'ra
 ·ras or ·rae
ca·fé' or ca·fe'
caf·e·te'ri·a
caf'fe·ine or ·in
cage
 caged cag'ing
ca'gey or ca'gy
 ·gi·er ·gi·est

ca'gi·ly
ca'gi·ness
cais'son
cai'tiff
ca·jole'
 ·joled' ·jol'ing
ca·jole'ment
ca·jol'er·y
cake
 caked cak'ing
cal'a·bash'
ca·lam'i·tous
ca·lam'i·ty
 ·ties
cal·car'e·ous
cal'ci·fi·ca'tion
cal'ci·fy'
 ·fied' ·fy'ing
cal'ci·mine'
 ·mined' ·min'ing
cal'ci·um
cal'cu·la·ble
cal'cu·late'
 ·lat'ed ·lat'ing
cal'cu·la'tion
cal'cu·la'tor
cal'cu·lus
 ·li or ·lus·es
cal'dron
cal'en·dar
 (table of dates)
cal'en·der
 (roller; SEE
 colander)

cal'ends
ca·les'cent
calf
 calves
calf'skin'
cal'i·ber or ·bre
cal'i·brate'
 ·brat'ed ·brat'ing
cal'i·bra'tion
cal'i·co'
 ·coes' or ·cos'
Cal'i·for'ni·a
cal'i·pers
ca'liph
cal'is·then'ics
calk
call'board'
cal·lig'ra·phy
cal'lous adj.
cal'low
call'-up'
cal'lus n.
 ·lus·es
calm'ly
ca·lor'ic
cal'o·rie or ·ry
 ·ries
cal'o·rim'e·ter
cal'u·met'
ca·lum'ni·ate'
 ·at'ed ·at'ing
ca·lum'ni·ous
ca·lum·ny
 ·nies

Cal'va·ry
(*Biblical place;*
SEE cavalry)
calve
calved calv'ing
Cal'vin·ism
ca·lyp'so
ca'lyx
ca'lyx·es *or*
ca'ly·ces'
ca'ma·ra·de·rie
cam'ber
cam'bric
Cam'bridge
cam'el
ca·mel'li·a
Cam'em·bert'
cam'e·o'
·os'
cam'er·a
cam'er·a·man'
·men'
cam'er·a-shy'
cam'i·sole'
cam'o·mile'
cam'ou·flage'
·flaged' ·flag'ing
cam·paign'
cam'pa·ni'le
·les *or* ·li
camp'er
camp'fire'
camp'ground'
cam'phor

cam'phor·ate'
·at'ed ·at'ing
camp'o·ree'
camp'site'
camp'stool'
cam'pus
cam'shaft'
can
canned can'ning
Ca'naan
Can'a·da
Ca·na'di·an
ca·naille'
ca·nal'
ca·nal'boat'
ca·nal'ize
·ized ·iz·ing
ca'na·pé
(*food;* SEE
canopy)
ca·nard'
ca·nar'y
·ies
ca·nas'ta
can'can'
can'cel
·celed *or* ·celled
·cel·ing *or*
·cel·ling
can'cel·la'tion
can'cer
can'cer·ous
can·de·la'bra
·bras

can·de·la'brum
·bra *or* ·brums
can·des'cence
can·des'cent
can'did
(*frank;* SEE
candied)
can'di·da·cy
·cies
can'di·date'
can'died
(*sugared;* SEE
candid)
can'dle·light'
candle power
can'dle·stick'
can'dle·wick'
can'dor
can'dy
·dies
·died ·dy·ing
can'dy-striped'
cane
caned can'ing
ca'nine
can'is·ter
can'ker
can'na·bis
can'ner·y
·ies
can'ni·bal
can'ni·bal·ize'
·ized' ·iz'ing
can'ni·ly

can'ni·ness
can'non
  (*gun;* SEE canon,
  canyon)
can'non·ade'
  ·ad'ed ·ad'ing
can'not
can'ny
  ·ni·er ·ni·est
ca·noe'
  ·noed' ·noe'ing
can'on
  (*law;* SEE cannon,
  canyon)
ca·non'i·cal
can'on·ize'
  ·ized' ·iz'ing
can'o·py
  ·pies
  (*hood;* SEE
  canapé)
can·ta'bi·le'
can'ta·loupe'
  or ·loup'
can·tan'ker·ous
can·ta'ta
can·teen'
can'ter
  (*gallop;* SEE
  cantor)
can'ti·cle
can'ti·le'ver
can'to
  ·tos

can'ton
can·ton'ment
can'tor
  (*singer;* SEE
  canter)
can'vas
  (*cloth*)
can'vass
  (*to solicit*)
can'yon *or* ca'ñon
  (*valley;* SEE
  cannon, canon)
caou·tchouc'
cap
  capped cap'ping
ca'pa·bil'i·ty
  ·ties
ca'pa·ble
ca'pa·bly
ca·pa'cious
ca·pac'i·tance
ca·pac'i·tor
ca·pac'i·ty
  ·ties
ca'per
cap'ful'
  ·fuls'
cap'il·lar'y
  ·ies
cap'i·tal
  (*city; chief;* SEE
  capitol)
cap'i·tal·ism
cap'i·tal·is'tic

cap'i·tal·is'ti·
  cal·ly
cap'i·tal·i·za'tion
cap'i·tal·ize'
  ·ized' ·iz'ing
cap'i·tal·ly
cap'i·ta'tion
cap'i·tol
  (*building;* SEE
  capital)
ca·pit'u·late'
  ·lat'ed ·lat'ing
ca·pit'u·la'tion
ca'pon
ca·price'
ca·pri'cious
cap'ri·ole'
  ·oled' ·ol'ing
cap'size
  ·sized ·siz·ing
cap'stan
cap'stone'
cap'su·lar
cap'sule
  ·suled ·sul·ing
cap'sul·ize'
  ·ized' ·iz'ing
cap'tain
cap'tain·cy
  ·cies
cap'tion
cap'tious
cap'ti·vate'
  ·vat'ed ·vat'ing

cap'tive
cap·tiv'i·ty
·ties
cap'tor
cap'ture
·tured ·tur·ing
car'a·cul
ca·rafe'
car'a·mel
car'a·mel·ize'
·ized' ·iz'ing
car'a·pace'
car'at
(weight; SEE
caret, carrot)
car'a·van'
car'a·van'sa·ry
·ries
car'a·way'
car'bide
car'bine
car'bo·hy'drate
car·bol'ic
car'bon
car'bo·na'ceous
car'bon·ate'
·at'ed ·at'ing
car'bon·a'tion
car'bon-date'
-dat'ed -dat'ing
car'bon·if'er·ous
car'bon·ize'
·ized' ·iz'ing
car'bo·run'dum

car'bun·cle
car'bu·re'tion
car'bu·re'tor
car'cass
car·cin'o·gen
car·ci·no'ma
car'da·mom
card'board'
card'-car'ry·ing
car'di·ac'
car'di·gan
car'di·nal
car'di·o·gram'
car'di·o·graph'
card'sharp'
care
cared car'ing
ca·reen'
ca·reer'
care'free'
care'ful
care'ful·ly
care'less
ca·ress'
ca·res'sive·ly
car'et
(insert mark; SEE
carat, carrot)
care'tak'er
care'worn'
car'fare'
car'go
·goes or ·gos
car'hop'

Car'ib·be'an
car'i·bou'
car'i·ca·ture
·tured ·tur·ing
car'i·ca·tur·ist
car'ies
(decay; SEE
carries)
car'il·lon'
car'load'
car'man
·men
car'mine
car'nage
car'nal
car'nal·ly
car·na'tion
car·nel'ian
car'ni·val
car'ni·vore'
car·niv'o·rous
car'ol
·oled or ·olled
·ol·ing or ·ol·ling
car'ol·er or ·ol·ler
Car'o·li'nas
Car'o·lin'i·an
car'om
car'o·tene' or ·tin
ca·rot'id
ca·rous'al
ca·rouse'
·roused'
·rous'ing

car′ou·sel′
car′pen·ter
car′pen·try
car′pet
car′pet·bag′ger
car′pet·ing
carp′ing
car′port′
car′ri·age
car′ri·er
car′ries
　(*form of* carry;
　SEE caries)
car′ri·on
car′rot
　(*vegetable;* SEE
　carat, caret)
car′rou·sel′
car′ry
　·ried ·ry·ing
car′ry·all′
car′ry·out′
car′ry-o′ver
car′sick′
cart′age
carte′ blanche′
　cartes′ blanches′
car·tel′
car′ti·lage
car′ti·lag′i·nous
car′to·gram′
car·tog′ra·phy
car′ton
car·toon′

car·toon′ist
car′tridge
carve
　carved carv′ing
car′wash′
car′y·at′id
　·ids *or* ·i·des′
ca·sa′ba
　or cas·sa′ba
cas′bah
cas·cade′
　·cad′ed ·cad′ing
cas·car′a
case
　cased cas′ing
case′book′
case′hard′ened
ca′se·in
case′load′
case′mate′
case′ment
case′work′er
cash′-and-car′ry
cash′book′
cash′ew
cash·ier′
cash′mere
cas′ing
ca·si′no
　·nos
　(*gambling room*)
cas′ket
cas·sa′va
cas′se·role′

cas·sette′
cas·si′no
　(*card game*)
cas′sock
cas′so·war′y
　·war′ies
cast
　cast cast′ing
cas′ta·nets′
cast′a·way′
caste
　(*social class*)
cas′tel·lat′ed
cast′er
cas′ti·gate′
　·gat′ed ·gat′ing
cast′-i′ron
cas′tle
cast′off′
cas′tor
cas′trate
　·trat·ed ·trat·ing
cas·tra′tion
cas′u·al
cas′u·al·ly
cas′u·al·ty
　·ties
cas′u·ist
cas′u·is′tic
cas′u·ist·ry
cat′a·clysm
cat′a·comb′
cat′a·falque′
cat′a·lep′sy

cat'a·lep'tic
cat'a·lo'
 ·loes' or ·los'
cat'a·log' or
 ·logue'
 ·loged' or
 ·logued'
 ·log'ing or
 ·logu'ing
cat'a·log'er or
 ·logu'er
ca·tal'y·sis
 ·ses'
cat'a·lyst
cat'a·ma·ran'
cat'a·pult'
cat'a·ract'
ca·tarrh'
ca·tarrh'al
ca·tas'tro·phe
cat'a·stroph'ic
cat'a·stroph'i·
 cal·ly
cat'a·to'ni·a
cat'call'
catch
 caught catch'ing
catch'all'
catch'er
catch'ing
catch'pen'ny
 ·nies
catch'up
catch'word'

catch'y
 ·i·er ·i·est
cat'e·chism
cat'e·chize'
 ·chized' ·chiz'ing
cat'e·chu'men
cat'e·gor'i·cal
cat'e·go·rize'
 ·rized' ·riz'ing
cat'e·go'ry
 ·ries
ca'ter
cat'er-cor'nered
ca'ter·er
cat'er·pil'lar
cat'er·waul'
cat'gut'
ca·thar'sis
ca·thar'tic
ca·the'dral
cath'e·ter
cath'e·ter·ize'
 ·ized' ·iz'ing
cath'ode
cath'o·lic
Ca·thol'i·cism
cath'o·lic'i·ty
ca·thol'i·cize'
 ·cized' ·ciz'ing
cat'i'on
cat'-nap'
 -napped'
 -nap'ping
cat'nip

cat'-o'-nine'-tails'
cat's'-eye'
Cats'kill'
cat's'-paw'
cat'sup
cat'tail'
cat'ti·ly
cat'ti·ness
cat'tle
cat'tle·man
 ·men
cat'ty
 ·ti·er ·ti·est
cat'ty-cor'nered
cat'walk'
Cau·ca'sian
Cau'ca·soid'
cau'cus
cau'dal
cau'date
caul'dron
cau'li·flow'er
caulk
caus'a·ble
caus'al
caus'al·ly
cau·sal'i·ty
 ·ties
cau·sa'tion
caus'a·tive
cause
 caused caus'ing
cau'se·rie'
cause'way'

47

caus'tic
cau'ter·i·za'tion
cau'ter·ize'
 ·ized' ·iz'ing
cau'ter·y
 ·ies
cau'tion
cau'tion·ar'y
cau'tious
cav'al·cade'
cav'a·lier'
cav'al·ry
 ·ries
 (troops; SEE
Calvary)
cav'al·ry·man
 ·men
cave
 caved cav'ing
ca've·at' emp'tor
cave'-in'
cav'ern
cav'ern·ous
cav'i·ar'
cav'il
 ·iled or ·illed
 ·il·ing or ·il·ling
cav'i·ty
 ·ties
ca·vort'
cay·enne'
cease
 ceased ceas'ing
cease'-fire'

cease'less
ce'dar
cede
 ced'ed ced'ing
ce·dil'la
ceil'ing
ceil·om'e·ter
cel'e·brant
cel'e·brate'
 ·brat'ed ·brat'ing
cel'e·bra'tion
cel'e·bra'tor
ce·leb'ri·ty
 ·ties
ce·ler'i·ty
cel'e·ry
ce·les'ta
ce·les'tial
cel'i·ba·cy
cel'i·bate
cel'lar
cel'lar·et'
cel'lar·way'
cel'list
 or 'cel'list
cell'-like'
cel'lo
 or 'cel'lo
 ·los or ·li
cel'lo·phane'
cel'lu·lar
cel'lu·loid'
cel'lu·lose'
Cel'o·tex'

Cel'si·us
ce·ment'
cem'e·ter'y
 ·ies
cen'o·bite'
Ce'no·zo'ic
cen'ser
 (incense box)
cen'sor
 (prohibiter)
cen'sored
cen·so'ri·al
cen·so'ri·ous
cen'sor·ship'
cen'sur·a·ble
cen'sure
 ·sured ·sur·ing
 (blame)
cen'sus
cen'taur
cen·ta'vo
cen·te·nar'i·an
cen·te·nar'y
cen·ten'ni·al
cen·ten'ni·al·ly
cen'ter
cen'ter·board'
cen'tered
cen'ter·piece'
cen·tes'i·mal
cen·tes'i·mal·ly
cen'ti·grade'
cen'ti·gram'
cen'ti·li'ter

cen'time
cen'ti·me'ter
cen'ti·pede'
cen'tral
cen'tral·i·za'tion
cen'tral·ize'
·ized' ·iz'ing
cen·trif'u·gal
cen'tri·fuge'
cen·trip'e·tal
cen'trist
cen'tu·ple
cen·tu'ri·on
cen'tu·ry
·ries
ce·phal'ic
ce·ram'ic
ce·ram'ist or
ce·ram'i·cist
ce're·al
(grain; SEE serial)
cer'e·bel'lum
·lums or ·la
cer'e·bral
cer·e'bral·ly
cer'e·brate'
·brat'ed ·brat'ing
cer'e·bro·spi'nal
cer'e·brum
·brums or ·bra
cer'e·ment
cer'e·mo'ni·al
cer'e·mo'ni·al·ly
cer'e·mo'ni·ous

cer'e·mo'ny
·nies
ce·rise'
cer'tain
cer'tain·ly
cer'tain·ty
·ties
cer'ti·fi'a·ble
cer'ti·fi'a·bly
cer·tif'i·cate
cer·tif'i·ca'tion
cer'ti·fy'
·fied' ·fy'ing
cer'ti·o·ra'ri
cer'ti·tude'
ce·ru'le·an
ce·ru'men
cer'vi·cal
cer'vix
·vi·ces' or ·vix·es
ces·sa'tion
ces'sion
(a giving up; SEE
session)
cess'pool'
chafe
chafed chaf'ing
(rub)
chaff
(husks of grain)
chaf'finch
cha·grin'
·grined'
·grin'ing

chain'man
·men
chain'-re·act'
chain'-smoke'
chair'lift'
chair'man
·men
chair'wom'an
·wom'en
chaise longue
chaise or chaises
longues
chaise lounge
chaise lounges
chal·ced'o·ny
cha·let'
chal'ice
chalk'board'
chalk'i·ness
chalk'y
·i·er ·i·est
chal'lenge
·lenged ·leng·ing
chal'leng·er
chal'lis
cham'ber
cham'ber·lain
cham'ber·maid'
cham'bray
cha·me'le·on
cham'fer
cham'ois
·ois
·oised ·ois·ing

49

cham'o·mile'
cham·pagne'
  (*wine*)
cham·paign'
  (*open field*)
chance
  chanced
  chanc'ing
chan'cel
chan'cel·ler·y
  ·ies
chan'cel·lor
chance'-med'ley
chan'cer·y
  ·ies
chan'cre
chan'croid
chanc'y
  ·i·er ·i·est
chan'de·lier'
chan·delle'
chan'dler·y
  ·ies
Cha·nel'
change
  changed
  chang'ing
change'a·bil'i·ty
change'a·ble
change'a·bly
change'ful
change'ful·ly
change'less

change'ling
change'o·ver
change'-up'
chan'nel
  ·neled *or* ·nelled
  ·nel·ing *or*
  ·nel·ling
chan'nel·ize'
  ·ized' ·iz'ing
chan·teuse'
chan'tey *or* ·ty
  ·teys *or* ·ties
Cha'nu·kah
cha'os
cha·ot'ic
cha·ot'i·cal·ly
chap
  chapped
  chap'ping
chap'ar·ral'
cha·peau'
  ·peaus' *or*
  ·peaux'
chap'el
chap'er·on'
  or ·one'
  ·oned' ·on'ing
chap'fall'en
chap'lain
chap'let
chap'ter
char
  charred
  char'ring

char'ac·ter
char'ac·ter·is'tic
char'ac·ter·is'ti·
  cal·ly
char'ac·ter·i·
  za'tion
char'ac·ter·ize'
  ·ized' ·iz'ing
cha·rade'
char'coal'
chare
  chared char'ing
charge
  charged
  charg'ing
charge'a·ble
charge plate *or*
  charge'-a-plate'
charg'er
char'i·ly
char'i·ness
char'i·ot
char'i·ot·eer'
cha·ris'ma
char·is·mat'ic
char'i·ta·ble
char'i·ty
  ·ties
cha·ri'va·ri'
char'la·tan
charm'ing
char'nel
char'ry
  ·ri·er ·ri·est

char'ter
char·treuse'
char'wom·an
char'y
 ·i·er ·i·est
chase
 chased chas'ing
chasm
chas·sé'
 ·séd' ·sé'ing
chas'sis
 ·sis
chaste'ly
chas'ten
chas·tise'
 ·tised' ·tis'ing
chas·tise'ment
chas'ti·ty
chas'u·ble
chat
 chat'ted
 chat'ting
châ·teau'
 ·teaux' or ·teaus'
chat'e·laine'
cha·toy'ant
chat'tel
chat'ty
 ·ti·er ·ti·est
Chau'cer
chauf'fer
 (stove)
chauf'feur
 (driver)

chau·tau'qua
chau'vin·ism
chau'vin·ist
chau'vin·is'tic
chau'vin·is'ti·
 cal·ly
cheap
 (low in cost;
 SEE cheep)
cheap'en
cheat'er
check'book'
check'er·board'
check'ered
check'list' or
 check list
check'mate'
 ·mat'ed ·mat'ing
check'off'
check'out' or
 check'-out'
check'point'
check'rein'
check'room'
check'up'
Ched'dar
cheek'bone'
cheek'i·ly
cheek'i·ness
cheek'y
 ·i·er ·i·est
cheep
 (sound; SEE cheap)
cheer'ful

cheer'ful·ly
cheer'i·ly
cheer'i·ness
cheer'lead'er
cheer'less
cheer'y
 ·i·er ·i·est
cheese'burg'er
cheese'cake'
cheese'cloth'
chees'i·ness
chees'y
 ·i·er ·i·est
chee'tah
chem'i·cal
che·mise'
chem'ist
chem'is·try
 ·tries
chem'ur·gy
che·nille'
cher'ish
Cher'o·kee'
che·root'
cher'ry
 ·ries
cher'ub
 ·ubs or ·u·bim
che·ru'bic
che·ru'bi·cal·ly
cher'vil
chess'board'
chess'man'
ches'ter·field'

51

chest'nut
chev'i·ot
chev'ron
chew'y
  ·i·er ·i·est
Chi·an'ti
chi·a'ro·scu'ro
  ·ros
chic
  chic'quer
  chic'quest
chi·can'er·y
chi'chi or chi'-chi
chick'en-heart'ed
chicken pox
chic'le
chic'o·ry
chide
  chid'ed or chid,
  chid'ed or chid
  or chid'den,
  chid'ing
chief'ly
chief'tain
chif·fon'
chif·fo·nier'
chig'ger
chi'gnon
chig'oe
  ·oes
Chi·hua'hua
chil'blain'
child
  chil'dren

child'bear'ing
child'bed'
child'birth'
child'hood'
child'ish
child'like'
chil'i
  ·ies
chill'i·ness
chill'y
  ·i·er ·i·est
chime
  chimed chim'ing
chi·me'ra
chi·mer'i·cal
chim'ney
  ·neys
chim·pan·zee'
chin
  chinned
  chin'ning
chi'na·ware'
chin·chil'la
Chi·nese'
chi'no
chin'qua·pin
chintz
chip
  chipped
  chip'ping
chip'munk'
chi·rog'ra·phy
chi·rop'o·dist
chi·rop'o·dy

chi'ro·prac'tic
chi'ro·prac'tor
chir'rup
chis'el
  ·eled or ·elled
  ·el·ing or ·el·ling
chis'el·er or
  chis'el·ler
chi'-square'
chit'chat'
chit'ter·lings
chiv'al·rous
chiv'al·ry
chlor'dane
chlo'ric
chlo'ride
chlo'ri·nate'
  ·nat'ed ·nat'ing
chlo'ri·na'tion
chlo'rine
chlo'ro·form'
chlo'ro·phyll'
  or ·phyl'
chlo'rous
chlor·tet'ra·cy'·
  cline
chock'a·block'
chock'-full'
choc'o·late
choice
  choic'er choic'est
choir
  (*singers;* SEE
  quire)

52

choke
  choked chok'ing
chok'er
chol'er·a
chol'er·ic
cho·les'ter·ol'
choose
  chose cho'sen
  choos'ing
chop
  chopped
  chop'ping
chop'house'
chop'pi·ness
chop'py
  ·pi·er ·pi·est
chop'sticks'
chop su'ey
cho'ral
  (of a chorus)
cho·rale' or ·ral'
  (hymn tune)
chord
  (music; SEE cord)
chore
cho·re'a
chor'e·og'ra·pher
chor'e·o·graph'ic
chor'e·o·graph'·
  i·cal·ly
chor'e·og'ra·phy
chor'is·ter
chor'tle
  ·tled ·tling

cho'rus
cho'sen
chow'der
chow mein
chrism
chris'ten
Chris'ten·dom
Chris'tian
Chris'ti·an'i·ty
Chris'tian·ize'
  ·ized' ·iz'ing
chris'tie or ·ty
Christ'like'
Christ'mas
Christ'mas·tide'
chro·mat'ic
chro'ma·tin
chrome
chro'mic
chro'mi·um
chro'mo·some'
chron'ic
chron'i·cle
  ·cled ·cling
chron'o·log'i·cal
chro·nol'o·gy
chro·nom'e·ter
chro·nom'e·try
chrys'a·lis
chrys·an'the·
  mum
chrys'o·lite'
chrys'o·prase'
chub'bi·ness

chub'by
  ·bi·er ·bi·est
chuck'-full'
chuck'hole'
chuck'le
  ·led ·ling
chug
  chugged chug'ging
chuk'ka boot
chuk'ker or ·kar
chum'mi·ness
chum'my
  ·mi·er ·mi·est
chunk'i·ness
chunk'y
  ·i·er ·i·est
church'go'er
church'man
church'wom'an
church'yard'
churl'ish
churn
chute
chut'ney
chyle
chyme
ci·bo'ri·um
  ·ri·a
ci·ca'da
  ·das or ·dae
cic'a·trix
  ci·cat'ri·ces
cic'e·ly
Cic'er·o'

ci'der
ci·gar'
cig'a·rette'
or ·ret'
cig'a·ril'lo
·los
cil'i·a
(sing. cil'i·um)
cil'i·ar'y
cin·cho'na
Cin'cin·nat'i
cinc'ture
·tured ·tur·ing
cin'der
cin'e·ma
cin'e·mat'o·
graph'
cin'e·rar'i·um
·rar'i·a
cin'er·a'tor
cin'na·bar'
cin'na·mon
cinque'foil'
ci'pher
cir'ca
cir'cle
·cled ·cling
cir'clet
cir'cuit
cir·cu'i·tous
cir'cuit·ry
cir'cu·lar
cir'cu·lar·i·
za'tion

cir'cu·lar·ize'
·ized' ·iz'ing
cir'cu·late'
·lat'ed ·lat'ing
cir'cu·la'tion
cir'cu·la·to'ry
cir'cum·cise'
·cised' ·cis'ing
cir'cum·ci'sion
cir·cum'fer·ence
cir'cum·flex'
cir'cum·lo·
cu'tion
cir'cum·nav'i·
gate'
·gat'ed ·gat'ing
cir'cum·po'lar
cir'cum·scribe'
·scribed' ·scrib'ing
cir'cum·
scrip'tion
cir'cum·spect'
cir'cum·spec'tion
cir'cum·stance'
cir'cum·stan'tial
cir'cum·stan'ti·
ate'
·at'ed ·at'ing
cir'cum·vent'
cir'cum·ven'tion
cir'cus
cir·rho'sis
cir'ro·cu'mu·lus
cir'ro·stra'tus

cir'rus
·ri
cis·al'pine
cis·at·lan'tic
cis'tern
cit'a·del
ci·ta'tion
cite
cit'ed cit'ing
(mention; SEE
sight)
cit'i·fied'
cit'i·zen
cit'i·zen·ry
cit'i·zen·ship'
cit'rate
cit'ric
cit'ron
cit'ron·el'la
cit'rous adj.
cit'rus n.
cit'y
·ies
cit'y·scape'
cit'y-state'
civ'et
civ'ic
civ'il
ci·vil'ian
ci·vil'i·ty
·ties
civ'i·li·za'tion
civ'i·lize'
·lized' ·liz'ing

civ'il·ly
civ'vies
claim'ant
clair·voy'ance
clair·voy'ant
clam
 clammed
 clam'ming
clam'bake'
clam'ber
clam'mi·ness
clam'my
 ·mi·er ·mi·est
clam'or
clam'or·ous
clan·des'tine
clan·des'tine·ly
clan'gor
clan'gor·ous
clan'nish
clans'man
clap
 clapped
 clap'ping
clap'board
clap'per
clap'trap'
claque
clar'et
clar'i·fi·ca'tion
clar'i·fi'er
clar'i·fy'
 ·fied' ·fy'ing
clar'i·net'

clar'i·net'ist or
 clar'i·net'tist
clar'i·on
clar'i·ty
clas'sic
clas'si·cal
clas'si·cal·ly
clas'si·cism
clas'si·cist
clas'si·fi'a·ble
clas'si·fi·ca'tion
clas'si·fi'er
clas'si·fy'
 ·fied' ·fy'ing
class'mate'
class'room'
clat'ter
clause
claus'tro·
 pho'bi·a
clav'i·chord'
clav'i·cle
cla·vier'
clay'ey
 clay'i·er
 clay'i·est
clean'a·ble
clean'-cut'
clean'er
clean'hand'ed
clean'li·ly
clean'li·ness
clean'ly
 ·li·er ·li·est

clean'ness
cleanse
 cleansed
 cleans'ing
cleans'er
clean'shav'en
clean'up'
clear'ance
clear'-cut'
clear'eyed'
clear'head'ed
clear'ing·house'
clear'sight'ed
cleats
cleav'age
cleave
 cleaved or cleft
 or clove, cleaved
 or cleft or
 clo'ven,
 cleav'ing
 (to split)
cleave
 cleaved cleav'ing
 (to cling)
cleav'er
clem'en·cy
clem'ent
clere'sto'ry
 ·ries
cler'gy
 ·gies
cler'gy·man
 ·men

cler'ic
cler'i·cal
cler'i·cal·ly
cler'i·cal·ism
clev'er
clew
cli·ché'
click
cli'ent
cli'en·tele'
cliff'-dwell'ing
cliff'hang'er *or*
 cliff'-hang'er
cli·mac'ter·ic
cli·mac'tic
 (of a climax)
cli·mac'ti·cal·ly
cli'mate
cli·mat'ic
 (of climate)
cli·mat'i·cal·ly
cli·ma·tol'o·gy
cli'max
climb'er
clinch'er
cling
 clung cling'ing
clin'ic
clin'i·cal
cli·ni'cian
clink'er
cli·nom'e·ter
clip
 clipped clip'ping

clip'board'
clip'per
clique
cli'to·ris
clo·a'ca
 ·cae
cloak'room'
clob'ber
cloche
clock'wise'
clock'work'
clod'dish
clod'hop'per
clog
 clogged
 clog'ging
cloi'son·né'
clois'ter
close
 closed clos'ing
close
 clos'er clos'est
closed'-end'
close'fist'ed
close'fit'ting
close'grained'
close'-hauled'
close'ly
close'mouthed'
clos'et
close'-up'
clo'sure
clot
 clot'ted clot'ting

cloth *n.*
clothe *v.*
 clothed *or* clad
 cloth'ing
clothes'line'
clothes'pin'
clothes'press'
cloth'ier
cloth'ing
clo'ture
cloud'burst'
cloud'i·ness
cloud'y
 ·i·er ·i·est
clo'ver·leaf'
 ·leafs'
cloy'ing·ly
clown'ish
club
 clubbed
 club'bing
club'foot'
club'house'
clue
 clued clu'ing
clum'si·ly
clum'si·ness
clum'sy
 ·si·er ·si·est
clus'ter
clut'ter
coach'man
co·ad'ju·tor
co·ag'u·la·ble

56

co·ag'u·lant
co·ag'u·late'
 ·lat'ed ·lat'ing
co·ag'u·la'tion
co·ag'u·la'tor
co'a·lesce'
 ·lesced' ·lesc'ing
co'a·les'cence
co'a·les'cent
co'a·li'tion
coarse
 (*common;* SEE
 course)
coarse'grained'
coars'en
coarse'ness
coast'al
coast'er
coast guard
coast'land'
coast'line'
coat'ing
coat'tail'
co·au'thor
co·ax'i·al
coax'ing·ly
co'balt
cob'ble
 ·bled ·bling
cob'bler
cob'ble·stone'
co·bel·lig'er·ent
co'bra
cob'web'

co·caine'
 or ·cain'
coc'cus
coc'ci
coc'cyx
 coc·cy'ges
cock'a·lo'rum
cock'boat'
cock'crow'
cock'er·el
cock'eyed'
cock'i·ly
cock'i·ness
cock'ney
 ·neys
cock'pit'
cock'roach'
cocks'comb'
cock'sure'
cock'tail'
co'coa
co'co·nut'
 or co'coa·nut'
co·coon'
cod'dle
 ·dled ·dling
code
 cod'ed cod'ing
co'de·fend'ant
co'deine'
co'dex
 ·di·ces'
cod'fish'
codg'er

cod'i·cil
cod'i·fi·ca'tion
cod'i·fy'
 ·fied' ·fy'ing
co'ed·u·ca'tion
co'ef·fi'cient
co·erce'
 ·erced' ·erc'ing
co·er'cion
co·er'cive
co·e'val
co'ex·ist'ence
cof'fee·house'
cof'fee·pot'
cof'fer
cof'fer·dam'
cof'fin
co'gen·cy
co'gent
cog'i·tate'
 ·tat'ed ·tat'ing
cog'i·ta'tion
co'gnac
cog'nate
cog·ni'tion
cog'ni·tive
cog'ni·zance
cog'ni·zant
cog·no'men
 ·no'mens *or*
 ·nom'i·na
cog'wheel'
co·hab'it
co·hab'i·ta'tion

co'heir'
co·here'
  ·hered' ·her'ing
co·her'ence
co·her'ent
co·he'sion
co·he'sive·ness
co'hort
coif·fure'
coign
  (*position;* SEE
  coin, quoin)
coin
  (*metal money;*
  SEE coign, quoin)
coin'age
co'in·cide'
  ·cid'ed ·cid'ing
co·in'ci·dence
co·in'ci·dent
co·in'ci·den'tal
co·in'ci·den'tal·ly
co·i'tion
co'i·tus
col'an·der
  (*draining pan;*
  SEE calender)
cold'blood'ed
cold'heart'ed
co'le·op'ter·ous
cole'slaw'
col'ic
col'ick·y
col·i·se'um

co·li'tis
col·lab'o·rate'
  ·rat'ed ·rat'ing
col·lab'o·ra'tion
col·lab'o·ra'tor
col'lage'
col·lapse'
  ·lapsed' ·laps'ing
col·laps'i·bil'i·ty
col·laps'i·ble
col'lar
col'lar·bone'
col·late'
  ·lat'ed ·lat'ing
col·lat'er·al
col·lat'er·al·ly
col·la'tion
col·la'tor
col'league
col·lect'a·ble
  or ·i·ble
col·lec'tion
col·lec'tive·ly
col·lec'tiv·ism
col·lec'tiv·is'tic
col'lec·tiv'i·ty
col·lec'tiv·ize'
  ·ized' ·iz'ing
col·lec'tor
col'leen
col'lege
col·le'gi·al'i·ty
col·le'gi·an
col·le'giate

col·lide'
  ·lid'ed ·lid'ing
col'lie
col'li·gate'
  ·gat'ed ·gat'ing
col'li·mate'
  ·mat'ed ·mat'ing
col·lin'e·ar
col·li'sion
col·lo·ca'tion
col·lo'di·on
col'loid
col·loi'dal
col·lo'qui·al
col·lo'qui·al·ism
col·lo'qui·um
  ·qui·a *or* ·qui·ums
col'lo·quy
  ·quies
col'lo·type'
col·lude'
  ·lud'ed ·lud'ing
col·lu'sion
col·lu'sive
co·lo'cate'
  ·cat'ed ·cat'ing
co'-lo·ca'tion
co·logne'
co'lon
colo'nel
  (*officer;* SEE
  kernel)
co·lo'ni·al
col'o·nist

col'o·ni·za'tion
col'o·nize'
 ·nized' ·niz'ing
col'on·nade'
col'o·ny
 ·nies
col'o·phon'
col'or
Col'o·rad'o
col'o·rant
col'or·a'tion
col'o·ra·tu'ra
col'or-bear'er
col'or·blind'
col'or·cast'
 ·cast' or cast'ed
 ·cast'ing
col'ored
col'or·fast'
col'or·ful
col'or·less
co·los'sal
Col'os·se'um
co·los'sus
 ·los'si or
 ·los'sus·es
colt'ish
Co·lum'bi·a
col'umn
co·lum'nar
col'um·nist
co'ma
 (stupor; SEE
 comma)

com'a·tose'
com·bat'
 ·bat'ed or
 ·bat'ted
 ·bat'ing or
 ·bat'ting
com'bat·ant
com·bat'ive
comb'er
com·bin'a·ble
com·bi·na'tion
com·bine'
 ·bined' ·bin'ing
comb'ings
com·bus'ti·
 bil'i·ty
com·bus'ti·ble
com·bus'ti·bly
com·bus'tion
com·bus'tor
come
 came come
com'ing
come'back'
co·me'di·an
co·me'dic
co·me'di·enne'
come'down'
com'e·dy
 ·dies
come'li·ness
come'ly
 ·li·er ·li·est
co·mes'ti·ble

com'et
come'up'pance
com'fit
com'fort
com'fort·a·ble
com'fort·a·bly
com'fort·er
com'ic
com'i·cal
com'i·cal·ly
com'i·ty
 ·ties
com'ma
 (punctuation
 mark; SEE coma)
com·mand'
com'man·dant'
com'man·deer'
com·mand'er
com·mand'ment
com·man'do
 ·dos or ·does
com·mem'o·rate'
 ·rat'ed ·rat'ing
com·mem'o·
 ra'tion
com·mem'o·
 ra'tive
com·mence'
 ·menced'
 ·menc'ing
com·mence'·
 ment
com·mend'

59

com·mend′a·ble
com·mend′a·bly
com′men·da′tion
com·mend′a·
to′ry
com·men′su·
ra·ble
com·men′su·
ra·bly
com·men′su·rate
com′ment
com′men·tar′y
·ies
com′men·tate′
·tat′ed ·tat′ing
com′men·ta′tor
com′merce
com·mer′cial
com·mer′cial·ism
com·mer′cial·i·
za′tion
com·mer′cial·ize′
·ized′ ·iz′ing
com·min′gle
·gled ·gling
com·mis′er·ate′
·at′ed ·at′ing
com·mis′er·
a′tion
com·mis·sar′
com′mis·sar′i·at
com′mis·sar′y
·ies
com·mis′sion

com·mis′sion·er
com·mit′
·mit′ted ·mit′ting
com·mit′ment
com·mit′ta·ble
com·mit′tal
com·mit′tee
com·mit′tee·man
com·mode′
com·mo′di·ous
com·mod′i·ty
·ties
com′mo·dore′
com′mon·al′ty
·ties
com′mon·er
com′mon·ness
com′mon·place′
com′mon·weal′
com′mon·wealth′
com·mo′tion
com·mu′nal
com·mu′nal·ly
com·mu′nal·ism
com·mune′ v.
·muned′
·mun′ing
com′mune n.
com·mu′ni·ca·ble
com·mu′ni·cant
com·mu′ni·cate′
·cat′ed ·cat′ing
com·mu′ni·
ca′tion

com·mu′ni·
ca′tive
com·mu′ni·ca′tor
com·mun′ion
com·mu′ni·qué′
com′mu·nism
com′mu·nist
com′mu·nis′tic
com′mu·nis′ti·
cal·ly
com·mu′ni·ty
·ties
com′mu·nize′
·nized′ ·niz′ing
com·mut′a·ble
com′mu·tate′
·tat′ed ·tat′ing
com′mu·ta′tion
com′mu·ta′tive
com′mu·ta′tor
com·mute′
·mut′ed
·mut′ing
com·mut′er
com·pact′
com·pan′ion
com·pan′ion·
a·ble
com′pa·ny
·nies
com′pa·ra·ble
com′pa·ra·bly
com·par′a·tive
com·par′a·tive·ly

com·pare′
  ·pared′ ·par′ing
com·par′i·son
com·part′ment
com·part′men′·
  tal·ize′
  ·ized′ ·iz′ing
com′pass
com·pas′sion
com·pas′sion·ate
com·pat′i·bil′i·ty
com·pat′i·ble
com·pat′i·bly
com·pa′tri·ot
com′peer
com·pel′
  ·pelled′ ·pel′ling
com·pen′di·ous
com·pen′di·um
  ·ums or ·a
com·pen′sa·ble
com′pen·sate′
  ·sat′ed ·sat′ing
com′pen·sa′tion
com·pen′sa·tive
com·pen′sa·tor
com·pen′sa·to′ry
com·pete′
  ·pet′ed ·pet′ing
com′pe·tence
com′pe·ten·cy
com′pe·tent
com′pe·ti′tion
com·pet′i·tive

com·pet′i·tor
com′pi·la′tion
com·pile′
  ·piled′ ·pil′ing
com·pil′er
com·pla′cence
com·pla′cen·cy
com·pla′cent
  (*smug;* SEE
  complaisant)
com·plain′
com·plain′ant
com·plaint′
com·plai′sance
com·plai′sant
  (*obliging;* SEE
  complacent)
com′ple·ment
  (*completing part;*
  SEE compliment)
com′ple·
  men′ta·ry
com·plete′
  ·plet′ed ·plet′ing
com·ple′tion
com·plex′
com·plex′ion
com·plex′i·ty
  ·ties
com·pli′ance
com·pli′ant
com′pli·cate′
  ·cat′ed ·cat′ing
com′pli·ca′tion

com·plic′i·ty
com·pli′er
com′pli·ment
  (*praise;* SEE
  complement)
com′pli·men′·
  ta·ry
com′pli·men·
  tar′i·ly
com·ply′
  ·plied′ ·ply′ing
com·po′nent
com·port′ment
com·pose′
  ·posed′ ·pos′ing
com·pos′er
com·pos′ite
com′po·si′tion
com·pos′i·tor
com′pos men′tis
com′post
com·po′sure
com′pote
com·pound′ *v.*
com′pound *n.*
com′pre·hend′
com′pre·hen′si·
  ble
com′pre·hen′sion
com′pre·hen′sive
com·press′
com·pressed′
com·pres′si·ble
com·pres′sion

61

com·pres'sor
com·prise'
·prised' ·pris'ing
com'pro·mise'
·mised' ·mis'ing
comp·tom'e·ter
comp·trol'ler
com·pul'sion
com·pul'sive
com·pul'so·ri·ly
com·pul'so·ri·ness
com·pul'so·ry
com·punc'tion
com·punc'tious
com·put'a·bil'i·ty
com·put'a·ble
com'pu·ta'tion
com·pute'
·put'ed ·put'ing
com·put'er
com·put'er·i·
za'tion
com·put'er·ize'
·ized' ·iz'ing
com'rade
con·cat'e·na'tion
con·cave'
con·cav'i·ty
·ties
con·ca'vo·con·
cave'
con·ca'vo·con·
vex'
con·ceal'

con·cede'
·ced'ed ·ced'ing
con·ceit'
con·ceit'ed
con·ceiv'a·
bil'i·ty
con·ceiv'a·ble
con·ceiv'a·bly
con·ceive'
·ceived' ·ceiv'ing
con'cen·trate'
·trat'ed ·trat'ing
con'cen·tra'tion
con·cen'tric
con·cen'tri·cal·ly
con'cept
con·cep'tion
con·cep'tu·al
con·cep'tu·al·i·
za'tion
con·cep'tu·al·ize'
·ized' ·iz'ing
con·cep'tu·al·ly
con·cern'
con·cerned'
con·cern'ing
con'cert
con·cert'ed
con'cer·ti'na
con'cert·mas'ter
con·cer'to
·tos or ·ti
con·ces'sion
con·ces'sion·aire'

conch
conchs or
conch'es
con·chol'o·gy
con'ci·erge'
con·cil'i·ar
con·cil'i·ate'
·at'ed ·at'ing
con·cil'i·a·to'ry
con·cise'
con·cise'ly
con·cise'ness
con'clave
con·clude'
·clud'ed
·clud'ing
con·clu'sion
con·clu'sive
con·coct'
con·coc'tion
con·com'i·tance
con·com'i·tant
con'cord
con·cord'ance
con·cor'dat
con'course
con·crete'
con·cre'tion
con·cu·bine'
con·cu'pis·cence
con·cu'pis·cent
con·cur'
·curred'
·cur'ring

con·cur′rence
con·cur′rent
con·cus′sion
con·demn′
con·dem′na·ble
con′dem·na′tion
con·dem′na·to·ry
con·demn′er
con·den′sa·ble
  or ·si·ble
con′den·sa′tion
con·dense′
  ·densed′
  ·dens′ing
con·dens′er
con′de·scend′
con′de·scend′ing
con′de·scen′sion
con·dign′
con′di·ment
con·di′tion
con·di′tion·al
con·di′tion·al·ly
con·do′la·to·ry
con·dole′
  ·doled′ ·dol′ing
con·do′lence
con′dom
con·do·min′i·um
  ·i·ums *or* ·i·a
con′do·na′tion
con·done′
  ·doned′ ·don′ing
con′dor

con·duce′
  ·duced′ ·duc′ing
con·du′cive
con′duct′
con·duct′ance
con·duct′i·ble
con·duc′tion
con′duc·tiv′i·ty
con·duc′tor
con′duit
co′ney
  ·neys *or* ·nies
con·fab′u·late′
  ·lat′ed ·lat′ing
con·fec′tion
con·fec′tion·ar′y
  adj.
con·fec′tion·er
con·fec′tion·er′y
  n.
  ·ies
con·fed′er·a·cy
  ·cies
con·fed′er·ate′
  ·at′ed ·at′ing
con·fed′er·a′tion
con·fer′
  ·ferred′ ·fer′ring
con′fer·ee′
con′fer·ence
con′fer·en′tial
con·fer′ment
con·fer′ral
con·fess′

con·fes′sed·ly
con·fes′sion
con·fes′sion·al
con·fes′sor
con·fet′ti
con′fi·dant′ *n.*
con·fide′
  ·fid′ed ·fid′ing
con′fi·dence
con′fi·dent *adj.*
con′fi·den′tial
con′fi·den′tial·ly
con·fig′u·ra′tion
con·fin′a·ble *or*
  con·fine′a·ble
con·fine′
  ·fined′ ·fin′ing
con·fine′ment
con·firm′
con′fir·mand′
con′fir·ma′tion
con·firm′a·to·ry
con·firmed′
con′fis·cate′
  ·cat′ed ·cat′ing
con′fis·ca′tion
con′fla·gra′tion
con·flict′
con·flic′tion
con′flu·ence
con·form′
con·form′a·ble
con·form′a·bly
con·form′ance

63

con·for·ma′tion
con·form′ist
con·form′i·ty
con·found′ed
con·front′
con′fron·ta′tion
Con·fu′cius
con·fuse′
·fused′ ·fus′ing
con·fu′sion
con′fu·ta′tion
con·fute′
·fut′ed ·fut′ing
con·geal′
con·gen′ial
con·gen′ial·ly
con·ge′ni·al′i·ty
con·gen′i·tal
con·gen′i·tal·ly
con·gest′
con·ges′tion
con·glom′er·ate′
·at′ed ·at′ing
con·glom′er·a′tion
con·grat′u·late′
·lat′ed ·lat′ing
con·grat′u·
  la′tion
con·grat′u·
  la·to′ry
con′gre·gant
con′gre·gate′
·gat′ed ·gat′ing
con′gre·ga′tion

con·gres′sion·al
con′gress·man
con′gru·ence
con′gru·ent
con·gru′i·ty
con′gru·ous
con′ic
con′i·cal
con′i·cal·ly
co′ni·fer
co·nif′er·ous
con·jec′tur·al
con·jec′ture
·tured ·tur·ing
con·join′
con·joint′ly
con′ju·gal
con′ju·gal·ly
con′ju·gate′
·gat′ed ·gat′ing
con′ju·ga′tion
con·junc′tion
con·junc′tive
con·junc′ti·vi′tis
con·junc′ture
con′jure
·jured ·jur·ing
con′jur·er or ·or
con·nect′
Con·nect′i·cut
con·nec′tion
con·nec′tive
con·nec′tor
  or ·nect′er

conn′ing tower
con·niv′ance
con·nive′
·nived′ ·niv′ing
con′nois·seur′
con′no·ta′tion
con′no·ta′tive
con·note′
·not′ed ·not′ing
con·nu′bi·al
con′quer
con′quer·or
con′quest
con·quis′ta·dor
·dors or ·dores
con′science
con′sci·en′tious
con′scious
con·script′
con′se·crate′
·crat′ed ·crat′ing
con′se·cra′tion
con·sec′u·tive
con·sen′sus
con·sent′
con′se·quence′
con′se·quen′tial
con′se·quent′ly
con·ser′van·cy
con′ser·va′tion
con·ser′va·tism
con·ser′va·tive
con·ser′va·to′ry
·ries

con·serve'
 ·served'
 ·serv'ing
con·sid'er
con·sid'er·a·ble
con·sid'er·a·bly
con·sid'er·ate
con·sid'er·a'tion
con·sid'ered
con·sign'
con·sign'a·ble
con·sign·ee'
con·sign'ment
con·sign'or
 or ·er
con·sist'
con·sis'ten·cy
 ·cies
con·sis'tent
con·sis'to·ry
 ·ries
con·sol'a·ble
con·so·la'tion
con·sol'a·to'ry
con·sole'
 ·soled' ·sol'ing
con'sole
con·sol'i·date'
 ·dat'ed ·dat'ing
con·sol'i·da'tion
con·sol'i·da'tor
con·som·mé'
con'so·nance
con'so·nant

con·so·nan'tal
con'sort
con·sor'ti·um
 ·ti·a
con·spec'tus
con·spic'u·ous
con·spir'a·cy
 ·cies
con·spir'a·tor
con·spire'
 ·spired' ·spir'ing
con·sta·ble
con·stab'u·lar'y
 ·ies
con'stan·cy
con'stant
con·stel·la'tion
con·ster·na'tion
con'sti·pate'
 ·pat'ed ·pat'ing
con·sti·pa'tion
con·stit'u·en·cy
 ·cies
con·stit'u·ent
con'sti·tute'
 ·tut'ed ·tut'ing
con·sti·tu'tion
con·sti·tu'tion·al
con·sti·tu'tion·
 al'i·ty
con·sti·tu'tion·
 al·ly
con·strain'
con·straint'

con·strict'
con·stric'tion
con·stric'tor
con·stru'a·ble
con·struct'
con·struc'tion
con·struc'tive
con·struc'tor or
 con·struct'er
con·strue'
 ·strued' ·stru'ing
con'sul
con'sul·ar
con'sul·ate
con·sult'
con·sult'ant
con'sul·ta'tion
con·sul'ta·tive
con·sum'a·ble
con·sume'
 ·sumed'
 ·sum'ing
con·sum'er
con'sum·mate'
 ·mat'ed ·mat'ing
con·sum'mate·ly
con'sum·ma'tion
con'sum·ma'tor
con·sump'tion
con·sump'tive
con'tact
con·ta'gion
con·ta'gious
con·tain'er

65

con·tain′er·ize′
·ized′ ·iz′ing
con·tain′ment
con·tam′i·nant
con·tam′i·nate′
·nat′ed ·nat′ing
con·tam′i·na′tion
con·tam′i·na′tor
con·temn′
con′tem·plate′
·plat′ed
·plat′ing
con′tem·pla′tion
con′tem·pla′tive
con′tem·pla′tor
con·tem′po·
ra′ne·ous
con·tem′po·rar′y
con·tempt′
con·tempt′i·bil′·
i·ty
con·tempt′i·ble
con·tempt′i·bly
con·temp′tu·ous
con·tend′
con·tent′
con′tent
con·tent′ed·ly
con·ten′tion
con·ten′tious
con·tent′ment
con·test′
con·test′a·ble
con·test′ant

con′text
con·tex′tu·al
con′ti·gu′i·ty
con·tig′u·ous
con′ti·nence
con′ti·nent
con′ti·nen′tal
con·tin′gen·cy
·cies
con·tin′gent
con·tin′u·a·ble
con·tin′u·al
con·tin′u·ance
con·tin′u·a′tion
con·tin′ue
·ued ·u·ing
con′ti·nu′i·ty
·ties
con·tin′u·ous
con·tin′u·um
·u·a or ·u·ums
con·tort′
con·tor′tion
con′tour
con′tra·band′
con′tra·bass′
con′tra·cep′tion
con′tra·cep′tive
con′tract
con·tract′i·bil′i·ty
con·tract′i·ble
con·trac′tile
con·trac′tion
con′trac·tor

con·trac′tu·al
con·trac′tu·al·ly
con′tra·dict′
con′tra·dic′tion
con′tra·dic′to·ry
con′tra·dis·
tinc′tion
con′trail′
con·tral′to
·tos or ·ti
con′tra pun′tal
con′trar·i·ly
con′trar·i·ness
con′trar·i·wise′
con′trar·y
con·trast′
con′tra·vene′
·vened′ ·ven′ing
con′tra·ven′tion
con·trib′ute
·ut·ed ·ut·ing
con′tri·bu′tion
con·trib′u·tor
con·trib′u·to′ry
con·trite′
con·tri′tion
con·triv′a·ble
con·triv′ance
con·trive′
·trived′ ·triv′ing
con·trol′
·trolled′
·trol′ling
con·trol′la·bil′i·ty

66

con·trol'la·ble
con·trol'ler
con'tro·ver'sial
con'tro·ver'sy
 ·sies
con'tro·vert'
con'tro·vert'i·ble
con·tu·ma'cious
con·tu·ma·cy
con·tu·me'li·ous
con'tu·me·ly
con·tuse'
 ·tused' ·tus'ing
con·tu'sion
co·nun'drum
con'ur·ba'tion
con'va·lesce'
 ·lesced' ·lesc'ing
con'va·les'cence
con'va·les'cent
con·vec'tion
con·vec'tive
con·vec'tor
con·vene'
 ·vened' ·ven'ing
con·ven'ience
con·ven'ient
con'vent
con·ven'ti·cle
con·ven'tion
con·ven'tion·al
con·ven'tion·
 al'i·ty
 ·ties

con·ven'tion·
 al·ize'
 ·ized' ·iz'ing
con·ven'tion·eer'
con·verge'
 ·verged'
 ·verg'ing
con·ver'gence
con·vers'a·ble
con·ver'sant
con'ver·sa'tion
con'ver·sa'tion·al
con·verse'
 ·versed' ·vers'ing
con'verse
con·ver'sion
con·vert'
con·vert'er
 or ·ver'tor
con·vert'i·ble
con·vex'
con·vex'i·ty
con·vex'o·con·
 cave'
con·vex'o·con·
 vex'
con·vey'
con·vey'ance
con·vey'or or ·er
con·vict'
con·vic'tion
con·vince'
 ·vinced'
 ·vinc'ing

con·vin'ci·ble
con·viv'i·al
con·viv'i·al'i·ty
con'vo·ca'tion
con·voke'
 ·voked' ·vok'ing
con'vo·lut'ed
con'vo·lu'tion
con'voy
con·vulse'
 ·vulsed'
 ·vuls'ing
con·vul'sion
con·vul'sive
cook'book'
cook'ie or ·y
 ·ies
cook'out'
cool'ant
cool'head'ed
coo'lie
 (*Oriental laborer;*
 SEE coolly,
 coulee)
cool'ly
 (*in a cool manner;*
 SEE coolie,
 coulee)
co'-op
co·op'er·ate'
 or co-op'·
 ·at'ed ·at'ing
co·op'er·a'tion
 or co-op'·

co·op′er·a·tive
  or co-op′·
co-opt′
co·or′di·nate′
  or co-or′·
  ·nat′ed ·nat′ing
co·or′di·na′tor
  or co-or′·
co·part′ner
cope
 coped cop′ing
cop′i·er
co′pi·lot
co′pi·ous
cop′-out′
cop′per
cop′per·plate′
co′pra
cop′u·late′
 ·lat′ed ·lat′ing
cop′u·la′tion
cop′y
 ·ies
 ·ied ·y·ing
cop′y·cat′
cop′y·hold′er
cop′y·ist
cop′y·read′er
cop′y·right′
cop′y·writ′er
co·quet′
 ·quet′ted ·quet′ting
co′quet·ry
co·quette′

co·quet′tish
co·quille′
cor′al
cor′bel
cord
  (*string;* SEE
  chord)
cord′age
cor′date
cor′dial
cor′di·al′i·ty
 ·ties
cor′dil·le′ra
cord′ite
cor′don
cor′do·van
cor′du·roy′
cord′wood′
core
 cored cor′ing
co′re·spond′ent
  (*in law;* SEE
  correspondent)
Cor′fam
co′ri·an′der
Co·rin′thi·an
cork′screw′
cor′mo·rant
corn borer
corn bread
corn′cob′
cor′ne·a
cor′nered
cor′ner·stone′

cor′ner·wise′
cor′net′
cor·net′ist
  or ·net′tist
corn′field′
corn′flow′er
corn′husk′ing
cor′nice
corn′meal′
corn′stalk′
corn′starch′
cor′nu·co′pi·a
corn′y
 ·i·er ·i·est
co·rol′la
cor′ol·lar′y
 ·ies
co·ro′na
 ·nas *or* ·nae
cor′o·nar′y
cor′o·na′tion
cor′o·ner
cor′o·net′
cor′po·ral
cor′po·rate
cor′po·ra′tion
cor′po·ra·tive
cor·po′re·al
corps
 corps
  (*group of people*)
corpse
  (*dead body*)
corps′man

cor′pu·lence
cor′pu·lent
cor′pus
  cor′po·ra
cor′pus·cle
cor·ral′
 ·ralled′ ·ral′ling
cor·rect′
cor·rect′a·ble
cor·rec′tion
cor·rec′tive
cor·rec′tor
cor′re·late′
 ·lat′ed ·lat′ing
cor′re·la′tion
cor·rel′a·tive
cor′re·spond′
cor′re·
  spond′ence
cor′re·
  spond′ent
  (*writer;* SEE
  corespondent)
cor′ri·dor
cor′ri·gi·ble
cor′ri·gi·bly
cor·rob′o·rate′
 ·rat′ed ·rat′ing
cor·rob′o·ra′tion
cor·rob′o·ra′tive
cor·rob′o·ra′tor
cor·rode′
 ·rod′ed ·rod′ing
cor·rod′i·ble

cor·ro′sion
cor·ro′sive
cor′ru·gate′
 ·gat′ed ·gat′ing
cor′ru·ga′tion
cor·rupt′
cor·rupt′i·bil′i·ty
cor·rupt′i·ble
cor·rupt′i·bly
cor·rup′tion
cor·rup′tive
cor·sage′
cor′sair
corse′let
cor′set
cor′se·tiere′
cor·tege′ *or* ·tège′
cor′tex
 ·ti·ces′
cor′ti·cal
cor′ti·cal·ly
cor′ti·sone′
co·run′dum
cor·us·cate′
 ·cat′ed ·cat′ing
cor·vette′
co·se′cant
co′sign′
co′sign′er
co·sig′na·to·ry
 ·ries
co′sine
cos·met′ic
cos′me·ti′cian

cos′me·tol′o·gy
cos′mic
cos′mi·cal·ly
cos·mog′o·ny
cos·mog′ra·phy
cos′mo·line′
cos·mol′o·gy
cos′mo·naut′
cos·mop′o·lis
cos·mo·pol′i·tan
cos·mop′o·lite′
cos′mos
cos′mo·tron′
co′spon′sor
cost
 cost cost′ing
cost′li·ness
cost′ly
 ·li·er ·li·est
cost′-plus′
cos′tume
 ·tumed ·tum·ing
cos·tum′er
co·tan′gent
co′te·rie
co·til′lion
cot′tage
cot′ton
cou′gar
cough
cou′lee
 (*gulch;* SEE
 coolie, coolly)
cou·lomb′

coun'cil
(*legislature;* SEE
counsel)

coun'cil·man

coun'ci·lor
or ·cil·lor
(*council member;*
SEE counselor)

coun'sel
·seled *or* ·selled
·sel·ing *or*
·sel·ling
(*advice; advise;*
SEE council)

coun'se·lor
or ·sel·lor
(*adviser;* SEE
councilor)

count'down'

coun'te·nance

count'er
(*one that counts*)

coun'ter
(*opposite*)

coun'ter·act'

coun'ter·ac'tion

coun'ter·at·tack'

coun'ter·bal'·
ance

coun'ter·claim'

coun'ter·clock'·
wise

coun'ter·feit

coun'ter·foil'

coun'ter·ir'ri·
tant

coun'ter·man'

coun'ter·mand'

coun'ter·march'

coun'ter·meas'·
ure

coun'ter·move'

coun'ter·of·fen'·
sive

coun'ter·pane'

coun'ter·part'

coun'ter·plot'

coun'ter·point'

coun'ter·poise'

coun'ter·sign'

coun'ter·sink'
·sunk' ·sink'ing

coun'ter·spy'

coun'ter·weight'

count'ess

count'less

coun'tri·fied'

coun'try
·tries

coun'try·man

coun'try·side'

coun'ty
·ties

coup de grâce'

coup d'é·tat'

coupe

cou'ple
·pled ·pling

cou'pler

cou'plet

cou'pon

cour'age

cou·ra'geous

cou'ri·er

course

coursed

cours'ing
(*way; run;* SEE
coarse)

cour'te·ous

cour'te·san

cour'te·sy
·sies
(*polite act;*
SEE curtsy)

court'house'

cour'ti·er

court'li·ness

court'ly
·li·er ·li·est

court'-mar'tial

courts'-mar'tial
·tialed *or*
·tialled
·tial·ing *or*
·tial·ling

court'room'

court'yard'

cous'in

cou·ture'

cou·tu·rier'

cou·tu·rière'

70

cov′e·nant
Cov′en·try
cov′er·age
cov′er·alls′
cov′ered
cov′er·ing
cov′er·let
cov′ert
cov′er-up′
cov′et·ous
cov′ey
cow′ard
cow′ard·ice
cow′ard·li·ness
cow′ard·ly
cow′boy′
cow′catch′er
cow′er
cow′herd′
cow′hide′
·hid′ed ·hid′ing
cowled
cow′lick
cowl′ing
co′-work′er
cow′pox′
cow′rie or ·ry
·ries
cow′shed′
cox′comb′
cox′swain
coy′ly
coy·o′te
co′zi·ly

co′zi·ness
co′zy
·zies
·zi·er ·zi·est
crab
crabbed crab′bing
crab′bed
crab′bi·ness
crab′by
·bi·er ·bi·est
crack′brained′
crack′down′
cracked
crack′er
crack′ing
crack′le
·led ·ling
crack′lings
crack′up′
cra′dle
·dled ·dling
cra′dle·song′
craft′i·ly
craft′i·ness
crafts′man
craft′y
·i·er ·i·est
crag′gi·ness
crag′gy
·gi·er ·gi·est
cram
crammed
cram′ming
cramped

cram′pon
cran′ber′ry
·ries
crane
craned cran′ing
cra′ni·al
cra·ni·ol′o·gy
cra′ni·um
·ni·ums or ·ni·a
crank′case′
crank′i·ness
crank′shaft′
crank′y
·i·er ·i·est
cran′ny
·nies
crap′u·lence
crash′-land′
crass′ly
crass′ness
cra′ter
cra·vat′
crave
craved crav′ing
cra′ven
crawl′er
cray′fish′
cray′on
craze
crazed craz′ing
cra′zi·ly
cra′zi·ness
cra′zy
·zi·er ·zi·est

71

creak
(*squeak;* SEE creek)
creak'i·ness
creak'y
·i·er ·i·est
cream'er·y
·ies
cream'i·ness
cream'y
·i·er ·i·est
crease
creased
creas'ing
cre·ate'
·at'ed ·at'ing
cre·a'tion
cre·a'tive
cre·a·tiv'i·ty
cre·a'tor
crea'ture
cre'dence
cre·den'tial
cre·den'za
cred'i·bil'i·ty
cred'i·ble
cred'i·bly
cred'it·a·bil'i·ty
cred'it·a·ble
cred'it·a·bly
cred'i·tor
cre'do
·dos
cre·du'li·ty

cred'u·lous
creek
(*stream;* SEE creak)
creep
crept creep'ing
creep'i·ness
creep'y
·i·er ·i·est
cre'mate
·mat·ed ·mat·ing
cre·ma'tion
cre'ma·to·ry
·ries
cre'o·sote'
crepe *or* crêpe
cre·scen'do
·dos
cres'cent
crest'fall'en
cre'tin
cre'tonne
cre·vasse'
crev'ice
crew'el·work'
crib'bage
crick'et
cri'er
crim'i·nal
crim'i·nol'o·gy
crim'son
cringe
cringed
cring'ing

crin'kle
·kled ·kling
crin'o·line
crip'ple
·pled ·pling
crip'pler
cri'sis
·ses
crisp'er
crisp'i·ness
crisp'y
·i·er ·i·est
criss'cross'
cri·te'ri·on
·ri·a *or* ·ri·ons
crit'ic
crit'i·cal
crit'i·cal·ly
crit'i·cism
crit'i·cize'
·cized' ·ciz'ing
cri·tique'
croak
cro·chet'
·cheted'
·chet'ing
crock'er·y
croc'o·dile'
cro'cus
crois·sant'
crom'lech
cro'ny
·nies
crook'ed·ness

croon′er
crop
  cropped
  crop′ping
crop′-dust′ing
cro·quet′
  ·queted′
  ·quet′ing
  (*game*)
cro·quette′
  (*food*)
cro′sier
cross′bar′
cross′beam′
cross′bow′
cross′breed′
  ·bred′ ·breed′ing
cross′-check′
cross′-coun′try
cross′cur′rent
cross′cut′
cross′-ex·am′i·
  na′tion
cross′-ex·am′ine
cross′-eyed′
cross′-fer′ti·lize′
cross′-grained′
cross′hatch′
cross′-in′dex
cross′ing
cross′-leg′ged
cross′o′ver
cross′piece′
cross′-pur′pose

cross′-re·fer′
cross′-ref′er·ence
cross′road′
cross′ruff′
cross section
cross′-stitch′
cross′tie′
cross′-town′
cross′walk′
cross′wise′
cross′word′
crotch′et·i·ness
crotch′et·y
crou′pi·er′
crou′ton
crow′bar′
crowd′ed
crow′s′-foot′
  -feet′
crow′s′-nest′
cru′cial
cru′cial·ly
cru′ci·ble
cru′ci·fix′
cru′ci·fix′ion
cru′ci·form′
cru′ci·fy′
  ·fied′ ·fy′ing
crude′ly
cru′di·ty
  ·ties
cru′el·ly
cru′el·ty
  ·ties

cru′et
cruise
  cruised cruis′ing
cruis′er
crul′ler
crum′ble
  ·bled ·bling
crum′bly
  ·bli·er ·bli·est
crumb′y
  ·i·er ·i·est
crum′pet
crum′ple
  ·pled ·pling
crunch′i·ness
crunch′y
  ·i·er ·i·est
crup′per
cru·sade′
crush′a·ble
crus·ta′cean
crust′ed
crust′i·ness
crust′y
  ·i·er ·i·est
crux
  crux′es *or* cru′ces
cry
  cries
  cried cry′ing
cry′o·gen′ics
crypt
cryp′tic
cryp′ti·cal·ly

cryp'to·gram'
cryp'to·gram'mic
cryp'to·graph'ic
cryp'to·graph'i·
cal·ly
cryp·tog'ra·phy
crys'tal
crys'tal·line
crys'tal·liz'a·ble
crys'tal·li·za'tion
crys'tal·lize'
·lized' ·liz'ing
crys'tal·log'ra·phy
cub'by·hole'
cube
cubed cub'ing
cu'bic
cu'bi·cal
(*cube-shaped*)
cu'bi·cal·ly
cu'bi·cle
(*compartment*)
cu'bit
cuck'old
cuck'oo'
cu'cum·ber
cud'dle
·dled ·dling
cud'dly
·dli·er ·dli·est
cudg'el
·eled *or* ·elled
·el·ing *or*
·el·ling

cue
cued cu'ing
or cue'ing
(*signal;* SEE
queue)
cui·rass'
cui·sine'
cul'-de-sac'
cu'li·nar'y
cull
cul'mi·nate'
·nat'ed ·nat'ing
cul'mi·na'tion
cu·lottes'
cul'pa·bil'i·ty
cul'pa·ble
cul'pa·bly
cul'prit
cult'ist
cul'ti·va·ble
cul'ti·vate'
·vat'ed ·vat'ing
cul'ti·va'tion
cul'ti·va'tor
cul'tur·al
cul'ture
·tured ·tur·ing
cul'vert
cum'ber·some
cum'mer·bund'
cu'mu·late'
·lat'ed ·lat'ing
cu'mu·la'tive
cu'mu·lous *adj.*

cu'mu·lus *n.*
·li
cu·ne'i·form'
cun'ning·ly
cup'board
cup'ful'
·fuls'
cu·pid'i·ty
cu'po·la
cur'a·ble
cu·ra·çao'
cu'rate
cur'a·tive
cu·ra'tor
curb'stone'
cur'dle
·dled ·dling
cure
cured cur'ing
cure'-all'
cur'few
cu'rie
cu'ri·o'
·os'
cu'ri·os'i·ty
·ties
cu'ri·ous
curl'i·cue'
curl'i·ness
curl'y
·i·er ·i·est
cur·mudg'eon
cur'rant
(*fruit*)

cur′ren·cy
 ·cies
cur′rent
 (*a flowing*)
cur·ric′u·lar
cur·ric′u·lum
 ·u·la *or* ·u·lums
cur′ry
 ·ried ·ry·ing
cur′ry·comb′
curse
 cursed *or* curst
 curs′ing
cur′sive
cur′so·ri·ly
cur′so·ri·ness
cur′so·ry
cur·tail′
cur′tain
curt′ness
curt′sy
 ·sies
 ·sied ·sy·ing
 (*knee bend;*
 SEE courtesy)
cur′va·ture
curve
 curved curv′ing
cur·vi·lin′e·ar
curv′y
 ·i·er ·i·est
cush′ion
cus′pid
cus′pi·dor′

cus′tard
cus·to′di·al
cus·to′di·an
cus′to·dy
cus′tom
cus′tom·ar′i·ly
cus′tom·ar′y
cus′tom-built′
cus′tom-er
cus′tom·house′
cus′tom-made′
cut
 cut cut′ting
cu·ta′ne·ous
cut′a·way′
cut′back′
cut′i·cle
cut′lass *or* ·las
cut′ler·y
cut′let
cut′off′
cut′out′
cut′-rate′
cut′ter
cut′throat′
cy′a·nide′
cy′ber·cul′ture
cy′ber·na′tion
cy′ber·net′ics
cy′cla·mate′
cy′cle
 cy′cled cy′cling
cy′clic
cy′cli·cal

cy′clist
cy′cli·zine′
cy′clom′e·ter
cy′clone
cy′clo·pe′di·a
cy′clo·ra′ma
cy′clo·tron′
cyg′net
cyl′in·der
cy·lin′dri·cal
cym′bal
 (*brass plate;*
 SEE symbol)
cyn′ic
cyn′i·cal
cyn′i·cal·ly
cyn′i·cism
cy′no·sure′
cy′press
cyst′ic
cyst′oid
cy·tol′o·gy
cy′to·plasm
czar
Czech′o·slo·
 va′ki·a

D

dab′ble
 ·bled ·bling
dachs′hund

75

Da'cron
dac'tyl
dad'dy
·dies
da'do
·does
daf'fo·dil'
dag'ger
da·guerre'o·type'
dahl'ia
dai'ly
·lies
dain'ti·ly
dain'ti·ness
dain'ty
·ties
·ti·er ·ti·est
dai'qui·ri
dair'y
·ies
dair'y·maid'
dair'y·man
da'is
dai'sy
·sies
dal'li·ance
dal'ly
·lied ·ly·ing
Dal·ma'tian
dam
dammed
dam'ming
(*barrier;* SEE
damn)

dam'age
·aged ·ag·ing
dam'age·a·ble
dam'a·scene'
dam'ask
damn
damned
damn'ing
(*condemn;* SEE
dam)
dam'na·ble
dam'na·bly
dam·na'tion
dam'na·to'ry
damp'-dry'
-dried' -dry'ing
damp'en
damp'er
dam'sel
dance
danced danc'ing
danc'er
dan'de·li·on
dan'dle
·dled ·dling
dan'druff
dan'ger
dan'ger·ous
dan'gle
·gled ·gling
Dan'ish
dan·seuse'
dap'ple
·pled ·pling

dare
dared dar'ing
dare'dev'il
Dar·jee'ling
dark'en
dark'room'
dar'ling
Dar·win'i·an
dash'board'
das'tard·li·ness
das'tard·ly
da'ta
(*sing.* da'tum)
date
dat'ed dat'ing
daugh'ter
daugh'ter-in-law'
daugh'ters-
in-law'
daunt'less
dav'en·port'
dav'it
daw'dle
·dled ·dling
day'bed'
day'book'
day'break'
day'dream'
day letter
day'long'
day'light'
day room
day'time'
day'-to-day'

day'work'
daze
  dazed daz'ing
daz'zle
  ·zled ·zling
D'-day'
dea'con
dea'con·ess
de·ac'ti·vate'
dead'en
dead'-end'
dead'head'
dead'line'
dead'li·ness
dead'lock'
dead'ly
  ·li·er ·li·est
dead'wood'
deaf'en·ing·ly
deaf'-mute'
deal
  dealt deal'ing
deal'er·ship'
dean'er·y
  ·ies
dear'ly
dearth
death'bed'
death'blow'
death'less
death'ly
death'trap'
death'watch'
de·ba'cle

de·bar'
  ·barred' ·bar'ring
de·bark'
de'bar·ka'tion
de·base'
  ·based' ·bas'ing
de·bat'a·ble
de·bate'
  ·bat'ed ·bat'ing
de·bauch'
deb·au'chee'
de·bauch'er·y
  ·ies
de·ben'ture
de·bil'i·tate'
  ·tat'ed ·tat'ing
de·bil'i·ta'tion
de·bil'i·ty
  ·ties
deb'it
deb'o·nair'
  or ·naire'
deb'o·nair'ly
de·brief'
de·bris'
debt'or
de·bunk'
de·but'
deb'u·tante'
dec'ade
dec'a·dence
dec'a·dent
dec'a·gon'
dec'a·gram'

dec'a·he'dron
  ·drons or ·dra
de·cal'ci·fy'
  ·fied' ·fy'ing
de·cal'co·ma'ni·a
dec'a·li'ter
Dec'a·logue'
  or ·log'
dec'a·me'ter
de·camp'
de·cant'
de·cant'er
de·cap'i·tate'
  ·tat'ed ·tat'ing
de·cap'i·ta'tion
de·cath'lon
de·cay'
de·cease'
  ·ceased'
  ·ceas'ing
de·ce'dent
de·ceit'ful
de·ceiv'a·ble
de·ceive'
  ·ceived'
  ·ceiv'ing
de·cel'er·ate'
  ·at'ed ·at'ing
de·cel'er·a'tion
de·cel'er·a'tor
de·cel'er·on'
De·cem'ber
de·cen'cy
  ·cies

77

de·cen'ni·al
de'cent
(*proper;* SEE
descent, dissent)
de·cen'tral·i·
za'tion
de·cen'tral·ize'
·ized' ·iz'ing
de·cep'tion
de·cep'tive·ly
dec'i·bel
de·cide'
·cid'ed ·cid'ing
de·cid'ed·ly
de·cid'u·ous
dec'i·mal
dec'i·mal·ize'
·ized' ·iz'ing
dec'i·mal·ly
dec'i·mate'
·mat'ed ·mat'ing
de·ci'pher
de·ci'sion
de·ci'sive
deck'le
de·claim'
dec'la·ma'tion
de·clam'a·to'ry
de·clar'a·ble
dec'la·ra'tion
de·clar'a·tive
de·clare'
·clared'
·clar'ing

de·clas'si·fy'
·fied' ·fy'ing
de·clen'sion
dec'li·na'tion
de·cline'
·clined' ·clin'ing
de·cliv'i·ty
·ties
de·code'
de·cod'er
dé·col'le·tage'
dé·col'le·té'
de'com·pos'a·ble
de'com·pose'
de'com·po·si'tion
de'com·pres'sion
de'con·gest'ant
de'con·tam'i·nate'
de'con·trol'
·trolled'
·trol'ling
dé·cor' *or* de·cor'
dec'o·rate'
·rat'ed ·rat'ing
dec'o·ra'tion
dec'o·ra·tive
dec'o·ra'tor
dec'o·rous
de·co'rum
de'cou·page'
de·coy'
de·crease'
·creased'
·creas'ing

de·cree'
·creed' ·cree'ing
de·crep'it
de·crep'i·tude'
de·cre·scen'do
de·cres'cent
de·cri'al
de·cry'
·cried' ·cry'ing
de·crypt'
de·cum'bent
ded'i·cate'
·cat'ed ·cat'ing
ded'i·ca'tion
ded'i·ca·to'ry
de·duce'
·duced' ·duc'ing
de·duc'i·ble
de·duct'
de·duct'i·ble
de·duc'tion
de·duc'tive
de-em'pha·sis
de-em'pha·size'
deep'-chest'ed
deep'-dyed'
deep'freeze'
·froze' *or*
·freezed'
·fro'zen *or*
·freezed'
·freez'ing
deep'-fry'
-fried' -fry'ing

deep'-laid'
deep'-root'ed
deep'-seat'ed
deep'-set'
deer'skin'
de·es'ca·late'
de·es'ca·la'tion
de·face'
de fac'to
de·fal'cate
·cat·ed ·cat·ing
def'a·ma'tion
de·fam'a·to'ry
de·fame'
·famed'
·fam'ing
de·fault'
de·fea'sance
de·feat'
de·feat'ist
def'e·cate'
·cat·ed ·cat·ing
def'e·ca'tion
de·fect'
de·fec'tion
de·fec'tive
de·fec'tor
de·fend'
de·fend'ant
de·fense'
de·fen'si·ble
de·fen'sive
de·fer'
·ferred' ·fer'ring

def'er·ence
def'er·en'tial
de·fer'ment
de·fi'ance
de·fi'ant
de·fi'cien·cy
·cies
de·fi'cient
def'i·cit
de·fi'er
de·file'
·filed' ·fil'ing
de·fin'a·ble
de·fine'
·fined' ·fin'ing
def'i·nite
def'i·ni'tion
de·fin'i·tive
de·flate'
·flat'ed ·flat'ing
de·fla'tion
de·fla'tion·ar'y
de·fla'tor
de·flect'
de·flec'tion
de·flec'tor
de·flow'er
de·fo'li·ate'
·at'ed ·at'ing
de'for·ma'tion
de·formed'
de·form'i·ty
·ties
de·fraud'

de·fray'
de·fray'al
de·frost'
de·funct'
de·fuse'
de·fy'
·fied' ·fy'ing
dé'ga·gé'
de·gen'er·a·cy
de·gen'er·ate'
·at'ed ·at'ing
de·gen'er·a'tion
de·gen'er·a·tive
de·grad'a·ble
deg'ra·da'tion
de·grade'
·grad'ed
·grad'ing
de·gree'
de·hu·mid'i·fy'
de·hy'drate
·drat·ed ·drat·ing
de'hy·dra'tion
de·hy'dra·tor
de·ic'er
de'i·fi·ca'tion
de'i·fy'
·fied' ·fy'ing
deign
de'ism
de'i·ty
·ties
de·ject'ed
de·jec'tion

Del'a·ware'
de·lay'
de·lec'ta·ble
del'e·gate'
·gat'ed ·gat'ing
del'e·ga'tion
de·lete'
·let'ed ·let'ing
del'e·te'ri·ous
de·le'tion
delft'ware'
de·lib'er·ate
de·lib'er·ate·ly
de·lib'er·a'tion
del'i·ca·cy
·cies
del'i·cate
del'i·cate·ly
del'i·ca·tes'sen
de·li'cious
de·light'ful
de·light'ful·ly
de·lin'e·ate'
·at'ed ·at'ing
de·lin'e·a'tion
de·lin'e·a'tor
de·lin'quen·cy
de·lin'quent
de·lir'i·ous
de·lir'i·um
de·liv'er·a·ble
de·liv'er·ance
de·liv'er·y
·ies

de·lude'
·lud'ed ·lud'ing
del'uge
·uged ·ug·ing
de·lu'sion
de·lu'sive
de·luxe'
delve
delved delv'ing
de·mag'net·ize'
dem'a·gog'ic
dem'a·gog'i·cal·ly
dem'a·gogue'
or ·gog'
dem'a·gog'y
de·mand'ing
de·mar'cate
·cat·ed ·cat·ing
de'mar·ca'tion
de·mean'or
de·men'tia
de·mer'it
de·mesne'
dem'i·john'
de·mil'i·ta·rize'
de·mise'
dem'i·tasse'
de·mo'bi·lize'
de·moc'ra·cy
·cies
dem'o·crat'ic
dem'o·crat'i·cal·ly
de·moc'ra·ti·
za'tion

de·moc'ra·tize'
·tized' ·tiz'ing
de·mog'ra·phy
de·mol'ish
dem'o·li'tion
de'mon
de·mon'e·tize'
·tized' ·tiz'ing
de·mo'ni·ac'
de·mon'ic
de·mon'i·cal·ly
de·mon'stra·ble
dem'on·strate'
·strat'ed
·strat'ing
dem'on·stra'tion
de·mon'stra·tive
dem'on·stra'tor
de·mor'al·ize'
de·mote'
·mot'ed ·mot'ing
de·mo'tion
de·mount'
de·mul'cent
de·mur'
·murred'
·mur'ring
(to object)
de·mure'
(coy)
de·mur'rage
de·mur'rer
de·na'tion·al·ize'
de·nat'u·ral·ize'

80

de·na'ture
·tured ·tur·ing
de·ni'a·ble
de·ni'al
de·nier'
de·ni'er
den'im
den'i·zen
de·nom'i·nate'
·nat'ed ·nat'ing
de·nom'i·na'tion
de·nom'i·na'tor
de·no·ta'tion
de·note'
·not'ed ·not'ing
de·noue'ment
de·nounce'
·nounced'
·nounc'ing
dense
dens'er dens'est
dense'ly
den'si·ty
·ties
den'tal
den'tal·ly
den'ti·frice'
den'tin
den'tist
den'tist·ry
den'ture
de·nude'
·nud'ed ·nud'ing
de·nun'ci·a'tion

de·ny'
·nied' ·ny'ing
de·o'dor·ant
de·o'dor·ize'
·ized ·iz'ing
de·o'dor·iz'er
de·part'ed
de·part'ment
de·part'men'tal
de·part'men'tal·
ize'
·ized' ·iz'ing
de·par'ture
de·pend'a·bil'i·ty
de·pend'a·ble
de·pend'a·bly
de·pend'ence
de·pend'en·cy
·cies
de·pend'ent
de·per'son·al·ize'
de·pict'
de·pic'tion
de·pil'a·to'ry
·ries
de·plane'
de·plete'
·plet'ed ·plet'ing
de·ple'tion
de·plor'a·ble
de·plore'
·plored'
·plor'ing
de·ploy'

de·pon'ent
de·pop'u·late'
de·port'a·ble
de'por·ta'tion
de·port'ment
de·pose'
de·pos'it
de·pos'i·tar'y
·ies
dep'o·si'tion
de·pos'i·tor
de·pos'i·to'ry
·ries
de'pot
dep'ra·va'tion
(*a corrupting;*
SEE deprivation)
de·prave'
·praved'
·prav'ing
de·prav'i·ty
·ties
dep're·cate'
·cat'ed ·cat'ing
dep're·ca'tion
dep're·ca·to'ry
de·pre'ci·a·ble
de·pre'ci·ate'
·at'ed ·at'ing
de·pre'ci·a'tion
dep're·da'tion
de·pres'sant
de·pressed'
de·press'ing

de·pres'sion
de·pres'sive·ly
dep'ri·va'tion
  (*a taking away;*
  SEE depravation)
de·prive'
  ·prived' ·priv'ing
depth
dep'u·ta'tion
dep'u·tize'
  ·tized' ·tiz'ing
dep'u·ty
  ·ties
de·rail'
de·range'
  ·ranged'
  ·rang'ing
der'e·lict'
der'e·lic'tion
de·ride'
  ·rid'ed ·rid'ing
de ri·gueur'
de·ri'sion
de·ri'sive
de·riv'a·ble
der'i·va'tion
de·riv'a·tive
de·rive'
  ·rived' ·riv'ing
der'ma·tol'o·gist
der'o·ga'tion
de·rog'a·to'ri·ly
de·rog'a·to'ry
der'rick

der'ri·ère'
der'ring-do'
der'rin·ger
de·sal'i·na'tion
de·salt'
des'cant
de·scend'
de·scend'ant
de·scend'i·ble
de·scent'
  (*going down;* SEE
  decent, dissent)
de·scrib'a·ble
de·scribe'
  ·scribed'
  ·scrib'ing
de·scrip'tion
de·scrip'tive
de·scry'
  ·scried'
  ·scry'ing
des'e·crate'
  ·crat'ed ·crat'ing
des'e·cra'tion
de·seg're·gate'
  ·gat'ed ·gat'ing
de·seg're·ga'tion
de·sen'si·tize'
de·sen'si·tiz'er
de·sert'
  (*abandon;* SEE
  dessert)
des'ert
  (*dry area*)

de·ser'tion
de·serts'
  (*reward, etc.*)
de·serve'
  ·served'
  ·serv'ing
de·serv'ed·ly
des'ic·cant
des'ic·cate'
  ·cat'ed ·cat'ing
des'ic·ca'tion
de·sign'
des'ig·nate'
  ·nat'ed ·nat'ing
des'ig·na'tion
des'ig·na'tor
de·signed'
de·sign'er
de·sir'a·bil'i·ty
de·sir'a·ble
de·sir'a·bly
de·sire'
  ·sired' ·sir'ing
de·sir'ous
de·sist'
des'o·late'
  ·lat'ed ·lat'ing
des'o·la'tion
de·spair'
des'per·a'do
  ·does *or* ·dos
des'per·ate
  (*hopeless;* SEE
  disparate)

des'per·a'tion
des'pi·ca·ble
de·spise'
·spised'
·spis'ing
de·spite'
de·spoil'
de·spo'li·a'tion
de·spond'en·cy
de·spond'ent
des'pot
des·pot'ic
des·pot'i·cal·ly
des'pot·ism
des·sert'
  (*food;* SEE desert)
des·sert'spoon'
des'ti·na'tion
des'tine
·tined ·tin·ing
des'tin·y
·ies
des'ti·tute'
des'ti·tu'tion
de·stroy'er
de·struct'
de·struct'i·bil'i·ty
de·struct'i·ble
de·struc'tion
de·struc'tive
de·struc'tor
des'ue·tude'
des'ul·to·ry
de·tach'

de·tach'a·ble
de·tach'ment
de·tail'
de·tain'
de·tect'
de·tect'a·ble
  or ·i·ble
de·tec'tion
de·tec'tive
de·tec'tor
dé·tente'
de·ten'tion
de·ter'
·terred'
·ter'ring
de·ter'gent
de·te'ri·o·rate'
·rat'ed ·rat'ing
de·te'ri·o·ra'tion
de·ter'ment
de·ter'mi·na·ble
de·ter'mi·na·bly
de·ter'mi·nant
de·ter'mi·nate
de·ter'mi·na'tion
de·ter'mine
·mined ·min·ing
de·ter'min·ism
de·ter'rence
de·ter'rent
de·test'
de·test'a·ble
de·test'a·bly
de·tes·ta'tion

de·throne'
·throned'
·thron'ing
det'o·nate'
·nat'ed ·nat'ing
det'o·na'tion
det'o·na'tor
de'tour
de·tract'
de·trac'tor
det'ri·ment
det'ri·men'tal
de·tri'tus
deuce
de·val'u·a'tion
de·val'ue
dev'as·tate'
·tat'ed ·tat'ing
dev'as·ta'tion
de·vel'op·ment
de·vel'op·men'tal
de'vi·ant
de'vi·ate'
·at'ed ·at'ing
de'vi·a'tion
de·vice'
dev'il·ish
dev'il·ment
dev'il·try
·tries
de'vi·ous
de·vis'a·ble
  (*that can be devised;*
  SEE divisible)

83

de·vise'
  ·vised' ·vis'ing
de·vi'tal·ize'
de·void'
de·volve'
  ·volved'
  ·volv'ing
de·vote'
  ·vot'ed ·vot'ing
dev'o·tee'
de·vo'tion
de·vour'
de·vout'
dew'drop'
dew'lap'
dew'y
  ·i·er ·i·est
dex·ter'i·ty
dex'ter·ous
  or dex'trous
dex'trose
di'a·be'tes
di'a·bet'ic
di'a·bol'ic
di'a·bol'i·cal
di'a·bol'i·cal·ly
di'a·crit'i·cal
di'a·dem'
di'ag·nos'a·ble
di'ag·nose'
  ·nosed' ·nos'ing
di'ag·no'sis
  ·no'ses
di'ag·nos'tic

di'ag·nos'ti·cal·ly
di'ag·nos·ti'cian
di·ag'o·nal
di·ag'o·nal·ly
di'a·gram'
  ·gramed' or
  ·grammed'
  ·gram'ing or
  ·gram'ming
di'a·gram·mat'ic
di'al
  ·aled or ·alled
  ·al·ing or ·al·ling
di'a·lect'
di'a·lec'tal
di'a·lec'tic
di'a·lec·ti'cian
di·al'o·gist
di'a·logue' or
  ·log'
di·am'e·ter
di'a·met'ri·cal
di'a·met'ri·cal·ly
di'a·mond
di'a·pa'son
di'a·per
di·aph'a·nous
di'a·phragm'
di'a·rist
di'ar·rhe'a
  or ·rhoe'a
di'a·ry
  ·ries
di'a·stase'

di'a·ther'my
di'a·ton'ic
di'a·tribe'
dib'ble
  ·bled ·bling
dice
  diced dic'ing
  (sing. die or dice)
di·chot'o·mize'
  ·mized' ·miz'ing
di·chot'o·my
dick'er
dick'ey
  ·eys
Dic'ta·phone'
dic'tate
  ·tat·ed ·tat·ing
dic·ta'tion
dic'ta·tor
dic·ta·to'ri·al
dic'tion·ar'y
  ·ies
Dic'to·graph'
dic'tum
  ·tums or ·ta
di·dac'tic
di·dac'ti·cal·ly
die
  dice
  (cube)
die
  dies
  died die'ing
  (mold; stamp)

84

die
 died dy'ing
 (*stop living;*
 SEE dye)
die'-hard' *or*
 die'hard'
diel'drin
di·e·lec'tric
di·er'e·sis
 ·ses'
die'sel
die'sink·er
di'e·sis
 ·ses'
di'e·tar'y
di'e·tet'ic
di'e·tet'i·cal·ly
di'e·ti'tian
 or ·cian
dif'fer·ence
dif'fer·ent
dif'fer·en'tial
dif'fer·en'ti·ate'
 ·at'ed ·at'ing
dif'fer·en'ti·a'tion
dif'fi·cult
dif'fi·cul'ty
 ·ties
dif'fi·dence
dif'fi·dent
dif·fract'
dif·frac'tion
dif·fuse'
 ·fused' ·fus'ing

dif·fus'i·ble
dif·fu'sion
dif·fu'sive
dig
 dug dig'ging
dig'a·my
di'gest
di·gest'i·ble
di·ges'tive
dig'ger
dig'it
dig'it·al
dig'i·tal'is
dig'i·ti·grade'
dig'ni·fy'
 ·fied' ·fy'ing
dig'ni·tar'y
 ·ies
dig'ni·ty
 ·ties
di·gress'
di·gres'sion
di·lan'tin
di·lap'i·date'
 ·dat'ed ·dat'ing
di·lat'a·ble
di·late'
 ·lat'ed ·lat'ing
di·la'tion
dil'a·to'ry
di·lem'ma
dil'et·tante'
 ·tantes' *or* ·tan'ti
dil'et·tant'ish

dil'i·gence
dil'i·gent
dil'ly·dal'ly
 ·lied ·ly·ing
dil'u·ent
di·lute'
 ·lut'ed ·lut'ing
di·lu'tion
di·lu'vi·al
dim
 dim'mer
 dim'mest
 dimmed
 dim'ming
di·men'sion
di·min'ish
di·min'u·en'do
dim'i·nu'tion
di·min'u·tive
dim'i·ty
dim'out'
dim'ple
 ·pled ·pling
din
 dinned din'ning
dine
 dined din'ing
din'er
 (*person eating;*
 SEE dinner)
din·ette'
din'ghy
 ·ghies
 (*boat*)

din′gi·ness
din′gy
 ·gi·er ·gi·est
 (*not bright*)
din′ner
 (*meal;* SEE diner)
din′ner·ware′
di′no·saur′
di·oc′e·san
di′o·cese
di′o·ra′ma
di·ox′ide
dip
 dipped dip′ping
diph·the′ri·a
diph′thong
di·plo′ma
di·plo′ma·cy
 ·cies
dip′lo·mat′
 (*government
 representative*)
dip′lo·mate′
 (*doctor*)
dip′lo·mat′i·cal·ly
dip′so·ma′ni·a
di·rect′
di·rec′tion
di·rec′tive
di·rec′tor
di·rec′tor·ate
di·rec′to′ri·al
di·rec′to·ry
 ·ries

dire′ful
dirge
dir′i·gi·ble
dirn′dl
dirt′i·ness
dirt′y
 ·i·er ·i·est
dis·a·bil′i·ty
 ·ties
dis·a′ble
 ·bled ·bling
dis·a·buse′
 ·bused′ ·bus′ing
dis·ad·van′tage
dis·ad·van′ta′·
 geous
dis·af·fect′ed
dis·a·gree′
dis·a·gree′a·ble
dis·a·gree′a·bly
dis·a·gree′ment
dis·al·low′
dis·ap·pear′ance
dis·ap·point′ment
dis·ap·pro·ba′tion
dis·ap·prov′al
dis·ap·prove′
dis·ar′ma·ment
dis·arm′ing
dis·ar·range′
dis·ar·ray′
dis·as·sem′ble
dis·as·so′ci·ate′
dis·as′ter

dis·as′trous
dis·a·vow′
dis·a·vow′al
dis·band′
dis·bar′
dis·be·lief′
dis·be·lieve′
dis·be·liev′er
dis·burse′
 ·bursed′
 ·burs′ing
dis·burse′ment
disc
dis·card′
dis·cern′
dis·cern′i·ble
dis·cern′ing
dis·cern′ment
dis·charge′
dis·ci′ple
dis′ci·plin·a·ble
dis′ci·pli·nar′i·an
dis′ci·pli·nar′y
dis′ci·pline
 ·plined ·plin·ing
disc jockey
dis·claim′
dis·claim′er
dis·close′
dis·clo′sure
dis·cog′ra·phy
dis′coid
dis·col′or
dis·col′or·a′tion

86

dis·com′fit
dis·com′fi·ture
dis·com′fort
dis′com·pose′
dis′com·po′sure
dis′con·cert′
dis′con·nect′
dis·con′so·late
dis′con·tent′
dis′con·tin′u·ance
dis′con·tin′ue
dis′con·ti·nu′i·ty
dis′con·tin′u·ous
dis′co·phile′
dis′cord
dis·cord′ant
dis′co·thèque′
dis′count
dis·cour′age
·aged ·ag·ing
dis·cour′age·ment
dis′course
dis·cour′te·ous
dis·cour′te·sy
dis·cov′er
dis·cov′er·er
dis·cov′er·y
·ies
dis·cred′it
dis·creet′
(*prudent;* SEE
discrete)
dis·crep′an·cy
·cies

dis·crete′
(*separate;* SEE
discreet)
dis·cre′tion
dis·cre′tion·ar′y
dis·crim′i·nate′
·nat′ed ·nat′ing
dis·crim′i·na′tion
dis·crim′i·na·
to′ry
dis·cur′sive
dis′cus
·cus·es or dis′ci
dis·cuss′
dis·cus′sion
dis·dain′ful
dis·ease′
·eased′ ·eas′ing
dis′em·bark′
dis′em·bod′y
dis′em·bow′el
·eled or ·elled
·el·ing or
·el·ling
dis′en·chant′
dis′en·cum′ber
dis′en·gage′
dis′en·tan′gle
dis′es·tab′lish
dis·fa′vor
dis·fig′ure
dis·fig′ure·ment
dis·fran′chise
·chised ·chis·ing

dis·gorge′
dis·grace′
·graced′
·grac′ing
dis·grace′ful
dis·grun′tle
·tled ·tling
dis·guise′
·guised′
·guis′ing
dis·gust′
dis′ha·bille′
dis·har′mo·ny
dish′cloth′
dis·heart′en
di·shev′el
·eled or ·elled
·el·ing or
·el·ling
dis·hon′est
dis·hon′es·ty
dis·hon′or
dis·hon′or·a·ble
dish′pan′
dish towel
dish′wash′er
dish′wa′ter
dis·il·lu′sioned
dis′in·cli·na′tion
dis′in·cline′
dis′in·fect′
dis′in·fect′ant
dis′in·gen′u·ous
dis′in·her′it

dis·in′te·grate′
　·grat′ed
　·grat′ing
dis·in′te·gra′tion
dis·in′ter′
dis·in′ter·est·ed
dis·join′
dis·joint′
dis·junc′tion
disk
dis·like′
dis·lo·cate′
dis·lo·ca′tion
dis·lodge′
dis·loy′al
dis·loy′al·ty
dis′mal
dis′mal·ly
dis·man′tle
dis·may′
dis·mem′ber
dis·miss′
dis·miss′al
dis·mount′
dis·o·be′di·ence
dis·o·be′di·ent
dis·o·bey′
dis·or′der
dis·or′der·ly
dis·or′gan·i·za′·
　tion
dis·or′gan·ize′
dis·o′ri·ent′
dis·own′

dis·par′age
　·aged ·ag·ing
dis′pa·rate
　(*not alike*; SEE
　desperate)
dis·par′i·ty
dis·pas′sion·ate
dis·patch′
dis·patch′er
dis·pel′
　·pelled′ ·pel′ling
dis·pen′sa·bil′i·ty
dis·pen′sa·ble
dis·pen′sa·ry
　·ries
dis′pen·sa′tion
dis·pense′
　·pensed′
　·pens′ing
dis·pen′ser
dis·per′sal
dis·perse′
　·persed′ ·pers′ing
dis·pers′i·ble
dis·per′sion
dis·pir′it·ed
dis·place′
dis·place′ment
dis·play′
dis·please′
dis·pleas′ure
dis·port′
dis·pos′a·ble
dis·pos′al

dis·pose′
　·posed′ ·pos′ing
dis′po·si′tion
dis′pos·sess′
dis·proof′
dis′pro·por′tion
dis′pro·por′tion·
　ate
dis·prove′
dis·pu′ta·ble
dis·pu′tant
dis′pu·ta′tion
dis·pu·ta′tious
dis·pute′
　·put′ed ·put′ing
dis·qual′i·fi·ca′·
　tion
dis·qual′i·fy′
dis·qui′et
dis·qui′e·tude
dis′qui·si′tion
dis′re·gard′
dis′re·pair′
dis·rep′u·ta·ble
dis·rep′u·ta·bly
dis′re·pute′
dis′re·spect′ful
dis·robe′
dis·rupt′
dis·rup′tion
dis·rup′tive
dis·sat′is·fac′tion
dis·sat′is·fy′
　·fied′ ·fy′ing

dis·sect'
dis·sec'tion
dis·sec'tor
dis·sem'blance
dis·sem'ble
·bled ·bling
dis·sem'i·nate'
·nat'ed ·nat'ing
dis·sem'i·na'tion
dis·sen'sion
dis·sent'
(*disagree;* SEE
decent, descent)
dis·sen'tient
dis·sen'tious
dis·ser·ta'tion
dis·serv'ice
dis·sev'er
dis'si·dence
dis'si·dent
dis·sim'i·lar
dis·sim'i·lar'i·ty
dis·sim'i·la'tion
dis·sim'u·late'
dis'si·pate'
·pat'ed ·pat'ing
dis'si·pa'tion
dis·so'ci·ate'
·at'ed ·at'ing
dis·so'ci·a'tion
dis·sol'u·ble
dis'so·lute'
dis'so·lu'tion
dis·solv'a·ble

dis·solve'
·solved'
·solv'ing
dis·sol'vent
dis'so·nance
dis'so·nant
dis·suade'
·suad'ed
·suad'ing
dis·sua'sion
dis·sym'me·try
dis'taff
dis'tance
dis'tant
dis·taste'ful
dis·tem'per
dis·tend'
dis·ten'si·ble
dis·ten'tion *or*
dis·ten'sion
dis'tich
dis·till' *or* ·til'
·tilled' ·till'ing
dis'til·late
dis'til·la'tion
dis·till'er
dis·till'er·y
·ies
dis·tinct'
dis·tinc'tion
dis·tinc'tive
dis·tin·gué'
dis·tin'guish
dis·tin'guish·a·ble

dis·tin'guish·a·bly
dis·tort'
dis·tor'tion
dis·tract'
dis·tract'i·ble
dis·trac'tion
dis·trait'
dis·traught'
dis·tress'
dis·trib'ut·a·ble
dis·trib'ute
·ut·ed ·ut·ing
dis'tri·bu'tion
dis·trib'u·tive
dis·trib'u·tor
dis'trict
dis·trust'ful
dis·turb'
dis·turb'ance
dis·un'ion
dis·u·nite'
dis·u'ni·ty
dis·use'
ditch
dith'er
dit'to
·tos
·toed ·to·ing
dit'ty
·ties
di'u·ret'ic
di·ur'nal
di'va
di·van'

89

dive
  dived *or* dove
  dived div′ing
di·verge′
  ·verged′
  ·verg′ing
di·ver′gence
di·ver′gent
di′vers
  (*sundry*)
di·verse′
  (*different*)
di·ver′si·fi·ca′·
  tion
di·ver′si·form′
di·ver′si·fy′
  ·fied′ ·fy′ing
di·ver′sion
di·ver′sion·ar′y
di·ver′si·ty
di·vert′
di·ver′tisse·ment
di·vest′
di·vest′i·ture
di·vid′a·ble
di·vide′
  ·vid′ed ·vid′ing
div′i·dend′
div′i·na′tion
di·vine′
  ·vined′ ·vin′ing
di·vin′i·ty
  ·ties
di·vis′i·bil′i·ty

di·vis′i·ble
  (*that can be divided;*
  SEE devisable)
di·vi′sion
di·vi′sor
di·vorce′
  ·vorced′ ·vorc′ing
di·vor·cé′ *masc.*
di·vor·cée′ *or*
  ·cee′ *fem.*
div′ot
di·vulge′
  ·vulged′
  ·vulg′ing
di·vul′gence
diz′zi·ly
diz′zi·ness
diz′zy
  ·zi·er ·zi·est
  ·zied ·zy·ing
do′a·ble
dob′bin
do′cent
doc′ile
doc′ile·ly
do·cil′i·ty
dock′age
dock′et
dock′yard′
doc′tor
doc′tor·al
doc′tor·ate
doc′tri·naire′
doc′tri·nal

doc′trine
doc′u·ment
doc′u·men′tal
doc′u·men′ta·ry
  ·ries
doc′u·men·ta′tion
dod′der·ing
dodge
  dodged
  dodg′ing
dodg′y
  ·i·er ·i·est
do′er
does
doe′skin′
does′n′t
dog′catch′er
dog′ear′
dog′ged·ly
dog′ger·el
dog′gy *or* ·gie
  ·gies
  (*dog*)
do′gie *or* ·gy
  ·gies
  (*calf*)
dog′ma
  ·mas *or* ·ma·ta
dog·mat′ic
dog·mat′i·cal·ly
dog′ma·tism
dog′ma·tize′
  ·tized′ ·tiz′ing
dog′nap′

do'-good'er
dog'trot'
dog'watch'
dog'wood'
doi'ly
·lies
do'-it-your·self'
dol'ce
dol'drums
dole
doled dol'ing
dole'ful
dol'lar
dol'lop
dol'man
·mans
(robe)
dol'men
(tomb)
do'lor·ous
dol'phin
dolt'ish
do·main'
do·mes'tic
do·mes'ti·cate'
·cat'ed ·cat'ing
do'mes·tic'i·ty
·ties
dom'i·cile'
dom'i·nance
dom'i·nant
dom'i·nate'
·nat'ed ·nat'ing
dom'i·na'tion

dom'i·neer'ing
do·min'i·cal
do·min'ion
dom'i·no'
·noes' or ·nos'
don
donned don'ning
do'nate
·nat·ed ·nat·ing
do·na'tion
do·nee'
Don' Ju'an
don'key
·keys
don'ny·brook'
do'nor
do'-noth'ing
Don' Qui·xo'te
don't
doo'dle
·dled ·dling
doo'hick'ey
dooms'day'
door'bell'
do'-or-die'
door'jamb'
door'keep'er
door'knob'
door'man'
door'mat'
door'nail'
door'plate'
door'sill'
door'step'

door'stop'
door'-to-door'
door'way'
dope
doped dop'ing
dor'man·cy
dor'mant
dor'mer
dor'mi·to'ry
·ries
dor'mouse'
·mice'
dor'sal
do'ry
·ries
dos'-à-dos'
dos'age
dos'si·er'
dot
dot'ted dot'ting
dot'age
dot'ard
dote
dot'ed dot'ing
dou'ble
·bled ·bling
dou'ble-bar'reled
dou'ble-breast'ed
dou'ble-check'
dou'ble-cross'
dou'ble-date'
dou'ble-deal'ing
dou'ble-deck'er
dou'ble-edged'

dou'ble-
  en·ten'dre
dou'ble-faced'
dou'ble-head'er
dou'ble-joint'ed
dou'ble-knit'
dou'ble-park'
dou'ble-quick'
dou'ble-space'
dou'blet
dou'ble-tongued'
dou'bly
doubt
doubt'ful
doubt'ful·ly
doubt'less
douche
  douched
  douch'ing
dough
dough'i·ness
dough'nut'
dough'y
  ·i·er ·i·est
doup'pi·o'ni or
  dou'pi·o'ni
douse
  doused dous'ing
dove'cote'
dove'tail'
dow'a·ger
dow'di·ness
dow'dy
  ·di·er ·di·est

dow'el
dow'er
down'beat'
down'cast'
down'fall'
down'grade'
down'heart'ed
down'hill'
down'i·ness
down'pour'
down'range'
down'right'
down'spout'
down'stage'
down'stairs'
down'state'
down'stream'
down'swing'
down'time'
down'-to-earth'
down'town'
down'trod'den
down'turn'
down'ward
down'wash'
down'wind'
down'y
  ·i·er ·i·est
dow'ry
  ·ries
dox·ol'o·gy
doze
  dozed doz'ing
doz'en

drab
drab'ber
drab'best
draft·ee'
draft'i·ness
drafts'man
draft'y
  ·i·er ·i·est
drag
dragged
drag'ging
drag'gle
  ·gled ·gling
drag'gy
  ·gi·er ·gi·est
drag'net'
drag'o·man
  ·mans or ·men
drag'on
drag'on·fly'
  ·flies'
dra·goon'
drain'age
drain'pipe'
dra'ma
dra·mat'ic
dra·mat'i·cal·ly
dram'a·tist
dram'a·ti·za'tion
dram'a·tize'
  ·tized' ·tiz'ing
dram'a·tur'gy
drape
  draped drap'ing

92

drap'er·y
·ies
dras'tic
dras'ti·cal·ly
draughts'man
·men
draw
drew drawn
draw'ing
draw'back'
draw'bridge'
draw'ee'
draw'er
draw'knife'
·knives'
drawl
drawn'work'
draw'string'
dray'age
dray'man
dread'ful
dread'ful·ly
dread'nought'
dream'i·ly
dream'i·ness
dream'y
·i·er ·i·est
drear'i·ly
drear'i·ness
drear'y
·i·er ·i·est
dredge
dredged
dredg'ing

drenched
dress
dressed or drest
dress'ing
dress'er
dress'i·ly
dress'i·ness
dress'ing-down'
dress'mak'er
dress'y
·i·er ·i·est
drib'ble
·bled ·bling
drib'let
dri'er or dry'er
drift'wood'
drill'mas'ter
drill press
drink
drank drunk
drink'ing
drink'a·ble
drip
dripped or dript
drip'ping
drip'-dry'
drive
drove driv'en
driv'ing
drive'-in'
driv'el
·eled or ·elled
·el·ing or
·el·ling

driv'er
drive'way'
driz'zle
·zled ·zling
driz'zly
droll'er·y
·ies
drol'ly
drom'e·dar'y
·ies
drone
droned dron'ing
droop'i·ly
droop'i·ness
droop'y
·i·er ·i·est
drop
dropped
drop'ping
drop'cloth'
drop'-forge'
-forged'
-forg'ing
drop'let
drop'out'
drop'per
dross
drought
or drouth
dro'ver
drown
drowse
drowsed
drows'ing

drow'si·ly
drow'si·ness
drow'sy
·si·er ·si·est
drub
drubbed
drub'bing
drudge
drudged
drudg'ing
drudg'er·y
drug
drugged
drug'ging
drug'gist
drug'store'
drum
drummed
drum'ming
drum'beat'
drum'head'
drum'mer
drum'stick'
drunk'ard
drunk'en·ness
drunk·o'me·ter
drupe'let
dry
dri'er dri'est
dried dry'ing
dry'as·dust'
dry'-clean'
dry cleaner
dry cleaning

dry'er
dry'-eyed'
dry ice
dry'ly or dri'ly
dry'ness
du'al
(of two; SEE duel)
du'al·ism
du'al·is'tic
du'al·ly
du'al-pur'pose
dub
dubbed dub'bing
du·bi'e·ty
du'bi·ous
du'cal
duc'at
duch'ess
duch'y
·ies
duck'ling
duck'pins'
duc'tile
duct'less
dudg'eon
due bill
du'el
·eled or ·elled
·el·ing or
·el·ling
(fight; SEE dual)
du·et'
duf'fel or ·fle
dug'out'

dul'cet
dul'ci·mer
dull'ard
dull'ness
dul'ly
(in a dull manner)
du'ly
(as due)
dumb'bell'
dumb'found' or
·dum'found'
dumb'ly
dumb'wait'er
dum'dum'
dum'my
·mies
dump'i·ness
dump'ling
dump'y
·i·er ·i·est
dun
dunned
dun'ning
dun'der·head'
dun'ga·ree'
dun'geon
dung'hill'
dun'nage
du'o
du'os or du'i
du'o·dec'i·mal
du'o·de'nal
du'o·logue'
du·op'o·ly

du'o·tone'
du'o·type'
dupe
  duped dup'ing
du'ple
du'plex
du'pli·cate'
  ·cat'ed ·cat'ing
du'pli·ca'tion
du'pli·ca'tor
du·plic'i·ty
  ·ties
du'ra·bil'i·ty
du'ra·ble
du'ra·bly
dur'ance
du·ra'tion
du·ress'
dur'ing
du'rum
dusk'i·ness
dusk'y
  ·i·er ·i·est
dust'i·ness
dust'pan'
dust'y
  ·i·er ·i·est
du'te·ous
du'ti·a·ble
du'ti·ful
du'ti·ful·ly
du'ty
  ·ties
du'ty-free'

dwarf
  dwarfs *or*
  dwarves
dwell
  dwelt *or* dwelled
  dwell'ing
dwin'dle
  ·dled ·dling
dy'ad
dyb'buk
dye
  dyed dye'ing
  (*color;* SEE die)
dyed'-in-the-wool'
dy'er
dye'stuff'
dy·nam'ic
dy·nam'i·cal·ly
dy'na·mism
dy'na·mite'
  ·mit'ed ·mit'ing
dy'na·mo'
  ·mos'
dy'na·mom'e·ter
dy'na·mo'tor
dy'nas·ty
  ·ties
dyne
dy·nel'
dys'en·ter'y
dys·func'tion
dys·pep'si·a
dys·pep'tic
dys'tro·phy

E

ea'ger
ea'gle
ea'gle-eyed'
ear'ache'
ear'drum'
ear'ly
  ·li·er ·li·est
ear'mark'
ear'muffs'
ear'nest
earn'ings
ear'phone'
ear'plug'
ear'ring'
ear'shot'
earth'en·ware'
earth'i·ness
earth'ly
earth'quake'
earth'shak'ing
earth'ward
earth'y
  ·i·er ·i·est
ear'wax'
ease
  eased eas'ing
ea'sel
ease'ment
eas'i·ly

eas'i·ness
east'er·ly
east'ern
east'ward
eas'y
 ·i·er ·i·est
eas'y·go'ing
eat
 ate eat'en
 eat'ing
eat'a·ble
eaves'drop'
ebb tide
eb'on·y
e·bul'lient
e·bul·li'tion
ec·cen'tric
ec·cen'tri·cal·ly
ec'cen·tric'i·ty
 ·ties
ec·cle'si·as'ti·cal
ech'e·lon'
ech'o
 ·oes
e·cho'ic
é·clair'
é·clat'
ec·lec'tic
ec·lec'ti·cism
e·clipse'
 ·clipsed'
 ·clips'ing
e·clip'tic
ec'o·log'i·cal

ec'o·log'i·cal·ly
e·col'o·gist
e·col'o·gy
e'co·nom'ic
e'co·nom'i·cal
e'co·nom'i·cal·ly
e·con'o·mist
e·con'o·mize'
 ·mized' ·miz'ing
e·con'o·my
 ·mies
e'co·sys'tem
e'co·tone'
ec'ru
ec'sta·sy
 ·sies
ec·stat'ic
ec·stat'i·cal·ly
ec'u·men'i·cal
ec'ze·ma
ed'dy
 ·dies
e'del·weiss'
e·de'ma
 ·mas or ·ma·ta
edge
 edged edg'ing
edge'ways'
edge'wise'
edg'i·ly
edg'i·ness
edg'y
 ·i·er ·i·est
ed'i·bil'i·ty

ed'i·ble
e'dict
ed'i·fi·ca'tion
ed'i·fice
ed'i·fy'
 ·fied' ·fy'ing
e·di'tion
 (*form of book;* SEE addition)
ed'i·tor
ed'i·to'ri·al
ed'i·to'ri·al·ize'
 ·ized' ·iz'ing
ed'i·to'ri·al·ly
ed'u·ca·bil'i·ty
ed'u·ca·ble
ed'u·cate'
 ·cat'ed ·cat'ing
ed'u·ca'tion
ed'u·ca'tive
ed'u·ca'tor
e·duce'
 ·duced' ·duc'ing
e·duc'i·ble
ee'rie or ·ry
 ·ri·er ·ri·est
ee'ri·ly
ee'ri·ness
ef·face'
 ·faced' ·fac'ing
ef·face'a·ble
ef·fect'
 (*result;* SEE affect)

ef·fec'tive
(*having effect;*
SEE affective)

ef·fec'tu·al

ef·fec'tu·ate'
·at'ed ·at'ing

ef·fem'i·na·cy

ef·fem'i·nate

ef'fer·ent

ef'fer·vesce'
·vesced'
·vesc'ing

ef'fer·ves'cence

ef'fer·ves'cent

ef·fete'

ef'fi·ca'cious

ef'fi·ca·cy

ef·fi'cien·cy

ef·fi'cient

ef'fi·gy
·gies

ef'flo·resce'
·resced'
·resc'ing

ef'flo·res'cence

ef'flu·ence

ef'flu·ent
(*flowing;* SEE
affluent)

ef·flu'vi·um
·vi·a *or* ·vi·ums

ef'fort

ef·fron'ter·y
·ies

ef·ful'gence

ef·fu'sion

ef·fu'sive

e·gal'i·tar'i·an

egg'nog'

egg'shell'

e'go

e'go·cen'tric

e'go·cen'tri·cal·ly

e'go·ism

e'go·ist

e'go·ma'ni·a

e'go·tism

e'go·tist

e'go·tis'tic

e'go·tis'ti·cal·ly

e·gre'gious

e'gress

e'gret

ei'der·down'

ei·det'ic

eight'een'

eighth

eight'i·eth

eight'y
·ies

ei'ther

ei'ther-or'

e·jac'u·late'
·lat'ed ·lat'ing

e·jac'u·la'tion

e·jac'u·la'tor

e·ject'

e·jec'tion

e·jec'tor

eke
eked ek'ing

e·kis'tics

e·kis'ti·cal

e·lab'o·rate'
·rat'ed ·rat'ing

e·lab'o·rate·ly

e·lab'o·ra'tion

e·lapse'
·lapsed'
·laps'ing

e·las'tic

e·las'tic'i·ty

e·las'ti·cize'
·cized' ·ciz'ing

e·late'
·lat'ed ·lat'ing

e·la'tion

el'bow·room'

eld'er·ly

eld'est

e·lec'tion

e·lec'tion·eer'

e·lec'tive

e·lec'tor

e·lec'tor·al

e·lec'tor·ate

e·lec'tric

e·lec'tri·cal

e·lec'tri·cal·ly

e·lec'tri'cian

e·lec'tric'i·ty

e·lec'tri·fi·ca'tion

e·lec'tri·fy'
  ·fied' ·fy'ing
e·lec'tro·cute'
  ·cut'ed ·cut'ing
e·lec'tro·cu'tion
e·lec'trode
e·lec'trol'y·sis
e·lec'tro·lyte'
e·lec'tro·lyt'ic
e·lec'tro·lyze'
  ·lyzed' ·lyz'ing
e·lec'tro·mag'net
e·lec'trom'e·ter
e·lec'tro·mo'tive
e·lec'tron
e·lec'tron'ic
e·lec'tron'i·cal·ly
e·lec'tro·plate'
e·lec'tro·scope'
e·lec'tro·stat'ics
e·lec'tro·ther'a·py
e·lec'tro·type'
e·lec'tro·typ'y
el'ee·mos'y·nar'y
el'e·gance
el'e·gant
el'e·gi'ac
el'e·gize'
  ·gized' ·giz'ing
el'e·gy
  ·gies
el'e·ment
el'e·men'tal
el'e·men'ta·ri·ness

el'e·men'ta·ry
  (*basic;* SEE
  alimentary)
el'e·phant .
el'e·phan·ti'a·sis
el'e·phan'tine
El'eu·sin'i·an
el'e·vate'
  ·vat'ed ·vat'ing
el'e·va'tion
el'e·va'tor
e·lev'enth
elf
  elves
elf'in
e·lic'it
  (*draw forth;*
  SEE illicit)
e·lide'
  ·lid'ed ·lid'ing
el'i·gi·bil'i·ty
el'i·gi·ble
el'i·gi·bly
e·lim'i·nate'
  ·nat'ed ·nat'ing
e·lim'i·na'tion
e·li'sion
e·lite' *or* é·lite'
e·lix'ir
E·liz'a·be'than
el·lipse'
el·lip'sis
  ·ses
el·lip'ti·cal

el·lip'ti·cal·ly
el'o·cu'tion
e·lon'gate
  ·gat'ed ·gat'ing
e·lon'ga'tion
e·lope'
  ·loped' ·lop'ing
e·lope'ment
el'o·quence
el'o·quent
else'where'
e·lu'ci·date'
  ·dat'ed ·dat'ing
e·lu'ci·da'tion
e·lude'
  ·lud'ed ·lud'ing
  (*escape;* SEE
  allude)
e·lu'sion
  (*an escape;* SEE
  allusion, illusion)
e·lu'sive
  (*hard to grasp;*
  SEE allusive,
  illusive)
e·ma'ci·ate'
  ·at'ed ·at'ing
e·ma'ci·a'tion
em'a·nate'
  ·nat'ed ·nat'ing
em'a·na'tion
e·man'ci·pate'
  ·pat'ed ·pat'ing
e·man'ci·pa'tion

e·man'ci·pa'tor
e·mas'cu·late'
 ·lat'ed ·lat'ing
e·mas'cu·la'tion
e·mas'cu·la'tor
em·balm'
em·bank'ment
em·bar'go
 ·goes
 ·goed ·go·ing
em·bark'
em'bar·ka'tion
em·bar'rass
em·bar'rass·ment
em'bas·sy
 ·sies
em·bat'tle
 ·tled ·tling
em·bed'
em·bel'lish
em'ber
em·bez'zle
 ·zled ·zling
em·bez'zler
em·bla'zon
em'blem
em'blem·at'ic
em·bod'i·ment
em·bod'y
 ·ied ·y·ing
em·bold'en
em'bo·lism
em'bo·lus
 ·li

em·boss'
em'bou·chure'
em·brace'
 ·braced'
 ·brac'ing
em·brace'a·ble
em·bra'sure
em·broi'der
em·broi'der·y
 ·ies
em·broil'
em'bry·o'
 ·os'
em'bry·ol'o·gy
em'bry·on'ic
em·cee'
 ·ceed' ·cee'ing
e·mend'
 (*to correct;*
 SEE amend)
e'men·da'tion
em'er·ald
e·merge'
 ·merged'
 ·merg'ing
 (*appear;* SEE
 immerge)
e·mer'gence
e·mer'gen·cy
 ·cies
e·mer'i·tus
em'er·y
e·met'ic
em'i·grant

em'i·grate'
 ·grat'ed
 ·grat'ing
em'i·gra'tion
em'i·nence
em'i·nent
 (*prominent;* SEE
 imminent)
em'is·sar'y
 ·ies
e·mis'sion
e·mit'
 ·mit'ted
 ·mit'ting
e·mol'li·ent
e·mol'u·ment
e·mo'tion·al
e·mo'tion·al·ize'
 ·ized' ·iz'ing
em·path'ic
em'pa·thize'
 ·thized' ·thiz'ing
em'pa·thy
em'pen·nage'
em'per·or
em'pha·sis
 ·ses'
em'pha·size'
 ·sized' ·siz'ing
em·phat'ic
em'phy·se'ma
em'pire
em·pir'i·cal
em·pir'i·cism

em·place'ment
em·ploy'
em·ploy'a·ble
em·ploy'ee
em·ploy'er
em·ploy'ment
em·po'ri·um
 ·ri·ums *or* ·ri·a
em·pow'er
em'press
emp'ti·ly
emp'ti·ness
emp'ty
 ·ti·er ·ti·est
 ·ties
 ·tied ·ty·ing
emp'ty-hand'ed
emp'ty-head'ed
em'u·late'
 ·lat'ed ·lat'ing
em'u·la'tion
em'u·lous
e·mul'si·fi·ca'tion
e·mul'si·fi'er
e·mul'si·fy'
 ·fied' ·fy'ing
e·mul'sion
en·a'ble
 ·bled ·bling
en·act'ment
en·am'el
 ·eled *or* ·elled
 ·el·ing *or*
 ·el·ling

en·am'el·ware'
en·am'ored
en·camp'ment
en·case'
 ·cased' ·cas'ing
en·caus'tic
en·ceph'a·li'tis
en·chant'ment
en·chi·la'da
en·cir'cle
en'clave
en·close'
 ·closed'
 ·clos'ing
en·clo'sure
en·code'
en·co'mi·ast'
en·co'mi·um
 ·ums *or* ·a
en·com'pass
en'core
en·coun'ter
en·cour'age
 ·aged ·ag·ing
en·cour'age·ment
en·croach'
en·cum'ber
en·cum'brance
en·cyc'li·cal
en·cy'clo·pe'di·a
 or ·pae'di·a
en·dan'ger
en·dear'
en·dear'ment

en·deav'or
en·dem'ic
end'ing
en'dive
end'less
end'most'
en'do·crine'
en·dog'a·my
en'do·me'tri·um
en·dorse'
 ·dorsed'
 ·dors'ing
en·dor·see'
en·dorse'ment
en·dors'er
en·dow'
en·dow'ment
end'pa'per
en·dur'a·ble
en·dur'a·bly
en·dur'ance
en·dure'
 ·dured' ·dur'ing
end'ways'
en'e·ma
en'e·my
 ·mies
en'er·get'ic
en'er·get'i·cal·ly
en'er·gize'
 ·gized' ·giz'ing
en'er·giz'er
en'er·gy
 ·gies

en'er·vate'
·vat'ed ·vat'ing
en·fee'ble
·bled ·bling
en'fi·lade'
·lad'ed ·lad'ing
en·fold'
en·force'
·forced'
·forc'ing
en·force'a·ble
en·fran'chise
en·gage'
·gaged' ·gag'ing
en·gage'ment
en·gen'der
en'gine
en'gi·neer'
Eng'lish
en·gorge'
·gorged' ·gorg'ing
en·grave'
·graved'
·grav'ing
en·grav'er
en·gross'
en·gulf'
en·hance'
·hanced'
·hanc'ing
e·nig'ma
e·nig·mat'ic
e·nig·mat'i·cal·ly
en·join'

en·joy'a·ble
en·joy'a·bly
en·joy'ment
en·kin'dle
·dled ·dling
en·lace'
en·large'
·larged'
·larg'ing
en·large'ment
en·larg'er
en·light'en
en·light'en·ment
en·list'
en·list'ment
en·liv'en
en masse
en·mesh'
en'mi·ty
·ties
en·no'ble
·bled ·bling
en'nui
e·nor'mi·ty
·ties
e·nor'mous
e·nough'
en·plane'
en·rage'
en·rap'ture
·tured ·tur·ing
en·rich'
en·roll' or ·rol'
·rolled' ·roll'ing

en·roll'ee'
en·roll'ment or
en·rol'ment
en route'
en·sconce'
·sconced'
·sconc'ing
en·sem'ble
en·shrine'
·shrined'
·shrin'ing
en'sign
en·slave'
en·snare'
en·snarl'
en·sue'
·sued' ·su'ing
en·sure'
en·tail'
en·tan'gle
en·tente'
en'ter·prise'
en'ter·pris'ing
en'ter·tain'
en·thrall' or
en·thral'
·thralled'
·thrall'ing
en·throne'
en·thuse'
·thused'
·thus'ing
en·thu'si·asm
en·thu'si·as'tic

en·thu'si·as'ti·
  cal·ly
en·tice'
  ·ticed' ·tic'ing
en·tice'ment
en·tire'
en·tire'ly
en·tire'ty
  ·ties
en·ti'tle
  ·tled ·tling
en'ti·ty
  ·ties
en·tomb'
en'to·mol'o·gy
  (*insect study;* SEE
  etymology)
en·tou·rage'
en·tr'acte'
en'trails
en·train'
en'trance
en'trance
  ·tranced'
  ·tranc'ing
en'trant
en·trap'
en·treat'
en·treat'y
  ·ies
en'tree or ·trée
en·trench'ment
en'tre·pre·neur'
en·trust'

en'try
  ·tries
en·twine'
e·nu'mer·ate'
  ·at'ed ·at'ing
e·nu'mer·a'tion
e·nu'mer·a'tor
e·nun'ci·ate'
  ·at'ed ·at'ing
  (*pronounce;* SEE
  annunciate)
e·nun'ci·a'tion
e·nun'ci·a'tor
en·vel'op v.
en've·lope' n.
en·ven'om
en'vi·a·ble
en'vi·a·bly
en'vi·ous
en·vi'ron·ment
en·vi'ron·men'tal
en·vi'rons
en·vis'age
  ·aged ·ag·ing
en·vi'sion
en'voy
en'vy
  ·vies
  ·vied ·vy·ing
en'zyme
e'o·lith'ic
e'on
ep'au·let' or
  ·lette'

e·pergne'
e·phem'er·al
ep'ic
  (*poem;* SEE
  epoch)
ep'i·cen'ter
ep'i·cure'
ep'i·cu·re'an
ep'i·dem'ic
ep'i·der'mis
ep'i·glot'tis
ep'i·gram'
ep'i·gram·mat'ic
ep'i·gram·mat'i·
  cal·ly
ep'i·graph'
ep'i·graph'ic
ep'i·graph'i·cal·ly
ep'i·lep'sy
ep'i·lep'tic
ep'i·logue' or
  ·log'
E·piph'a·ny
e·pis'co·pal
E·pis'co·pa'li·an
ep'i·sode'
ep'i·sod'ic
ep'i·sod'i·cal·ly
e·pis'tle
e·pis'to·lar'y
ep'i·taph
ep'i·the'li·al
ep'i·the'li·um
  ·li·ums or ·li·a

ep'i·thet'
e·pit'o·me
e·pit'o·mize'
  ·mized' ·miz'ing
ep'och
  (*period;* SEE epic)
ep'och·al
ep'o·nym'
ep·ox'y
ep'si·lon'
eq'ua·bil'i·ty
eq'ua·ble
eq'ua·bly
e'qual
  ·qualed *or*
  ·qualled
  ·qual·ing *or*
  ·qual·ling
e·qual'i·tar'i·an
e·qual'i·ty
  ·ties
e'qual·i·za'tion
e'qual·ize'
  ·ized' ·iz'ing
e'qual·ly
e'qua·nim'i·ty
e·quate'
  ·quat'ed
  ·quat'ing
e·qua'tion
e·qua'tor
e'qua·to'ri·al
eq'uer·ry
  ·ries

e·ques'tri·an
e·ques'tri·enne'
e'qui·an'gu·lar
e'qui·dis'tant
e'qui·lat'er·al
e·quil'i·brant
e·quil'i·brate'
  ·brat'ed ·brat'ing
e'qui·lib'ri·um
  ·ri·ums *or* ·ri·a
e'quine
e'qui·noc'tial
e'qui·nox'
e·quip'
  ·quipped'
  ·quip'ping
eq'ui·page
e·quip'ment
e'qui·poise'
e·qui·pol'lent
eq'ui·ta·ble
eq'ui·ta·bly
eq'ui·ty
  ·ties
e·quiv'a·lence
e·quiv'a·lent
e·quiv'o·cal
e·quiv'o·cal·ly
e·quiv'o·cate'
  ·cat'ed ·cat'ing
e·quiv'o·ca'tion
e·quiv'o·ca'tor
e'ra
e·rad'i·ca·ble

e·rad'i·cate'
  ·cat'ed ·cat'ing
e·rad'i·ca'tion
e·rad'i·ca'tor
e·ras'a·ble
e·rase'
  ·rased' ·ras'ing
e·ras'er
e·ra'sure
e·rect'
e·rec'tile
e·rec'tion
e·rec'tor
erg
er'go
er·gos'ter·ol'
er'got
er'mine
e·rode'
  ·rod'ed ·rod'ing
e·rog'e·nous
e·ro'sion
e·ro'sive
e·rot'ic
e·rot'i·ca
e·rot'i·cal·ly
e·rot'i·cism
er'o·tism
e·ro'to·gen'ic
err
er'ran·cy
  ·cies
er'rand
er'rant

er·ra′ta
  (*sing.* er·ra′tum)
er·rat′ic
er·rat′i·cal·ly
er·ro′ne·ous
er′ror
er′satz
erst′while′
e·ruct′
e·ruc′tate
 ·tat·ed ·tat·ing
e·ruc·ta′tion
er′u·dite′
er′u·di′tion
e·rupt′
e·rupt′i·ble
e·rup′tion
e·rup′tive
e·ryth′ro·my′cin
es′ca·drille′
es′ca·lade′
 ·lad′ed ·lad′ing
es′ca·late′
 ·lat′ed ·lat′ing
es′ca·la′tion
es′ca·la′tor
es·cal′lop *or* ·op
es′ca·pade′
es·cape′
 ·caped′ ·cap′ing
es·cap′ee′
es·cape′ment
es·cap′ism
es·cap′ist

es′ca·role′
es·carp′ment
es′cha·rot′ic
es′cha·tol′o·gy
es·cheat′
es·chew′
es·chew′al
es′cort
es′cri·toire′
es′crow
es′cu·lent
es·cutch′eon
Es′ki·mo′
 ·mos′ *or* ·mo′
e·soph′a·gus
 ·a·gi′
es′o·ter′ic
es′o·ter′i·cal·ly
es′pa·drille′
es·pal′ier
es·pe′cial
es·pe′cial·ly
Es′pe·ran′to
es′pi·o·nage′
es′pla·nade′
es·pous′al
es·pouse′
 ·poused′ ·pous′ing
es·pres′so
 ·sos
es·prit′ de corps′
es·py′
 ·pied′ ·py′ing
es′quire

es·say′
 (*try;* SEE assay)
es′say·ist
es′sence
es·sen′tial
es·sen′ti·al′i·ty
es·sen′tial·ly
es·tab′lish
es·tab′lish·ment
es·tate′
es·teem′
es′thete
es·thet′ic
es·thet′i·cal·ly
es·thet′i·cism
es′ti·ma·ble
es′ti·mate′
 ·mat′ed ·mat′ing
es′ti·ma′tion
es′ti·ma′tor
es′ti·val
es′ti·vate′
 ·vat′ed ·vat′ing
es·trange′
 ·tranged′
 ·trang′ing
es·trange′ment
es′tro·gen
es′trous *adj.*
es′trus *n.*
es·tu·ar′i·al
es′tu·ar′y
 ·ies
et cet′er·a

et·cet′er·as
etch′ing
e·ter′nal
e·ter′nal·ly
e·ter′ni·ty
·ties
e′ther
e·the′re·al
e·the′re·al·ize′
·ized′ ·iz′ing
e′ther·ize′
·ized′ ·iz′ing
eth′i·cal
eth′i·cal·ly
eth′ics
eth′nic
eth′ni·cal·ly
eth′no·cen′tri·
cal·ly
eth′no·cen′trism
eth·nog′ra·phy
eth′no·log′i·cal
eth·nol′o·gy
e′thos
eth′yl
e·ti·ol′o·gy
et′i·quette
é′tude
et′y·mo·log′i·cal
et′y·mol′o·gy
·gies
(*word study;* SEE
entomology)
et′y·mon′

eu′ca·lyp′tus
·tus·es *or* ·ti
Eu′cha·rist
eu′chre
eu·gen′i·cal·ly
eu·gen′ics
eu′lo·gize′
·gized′ ·giz′ing
eu′lo·gy
·gies
eu′nuch
eu′phe·mism
eu′phe·mis′tic
eu′phe·mis′ti·
cal·ly
eu′phe·mize′
·mized′ ·miz′ing
eu·phon′ic
eu·pho′ni·ous
eu·pho′ni·um
eu′pho·ny
·nies
eu·pho′ri·a
eu·phor′ic
eu′phu·ism
eu′phu·is′tic
Eur·a′sian
Eur′a·tom′
eu·re′ka
Eu′ro·crat′
Eu′ro·dol′lars
Eu′ro·pe′an
eu·ryth′mics
eu·ryth′my

Eu·sta′chi·an
eu′tha·na′si·a
e·vac′u·ate′
·at′ed ·at′ing
e·vac′u·a′tion
e·vac′u·ee′
e·vade′
·vad′ed ·vad′ing
e·val′u·ate′
·at′ed ·at′ing
e·val′u·a′tion
ev′a·nesce′
·nesced′ ·nesc′ing
ev′a·nes′cence
ev′a·nes′cent
e·van·gel′i·cal
e·van·gel′i·cal·ly
e·van′gel·ism
e·van′gel·ist
e·van′gel·is′tic
e·van′gel·ize′
·ized′ ·iz′ing
e·vap′o·rate′
·rat′ed ·rat′ing
e·vap′o·ra′tion
e·va′sion
e·va′sive
e′ven-hand′ed
eve′ning
e′ven·ness
e·vent′
e′ven-tem′pered
e·vent′ful
e·ven′tu·al

e·ven·tu·al′i·ty
·ties
e·ven′tu·al·ly
e·ven′tu·ate′
·at′ed ·at′ing
ev′er·glade′
ev′er·green′
ev′er·last′ing
ev′er·more′
e·vert′
ev′er·y·bod′y
ev′er·y·day′
ev′er·y·one
ev′er·y·thing′
ev′er·y·where′
e·vict′
e·vic′tion
ev′i·dence
·denced ·denc·ing
ev′i·dent
ev′i·den′tial
e′vil·do′er
e′vil·ly
e′vil·mind′ed
e·vince′
·vinced′
·vinc′ing
e·vin′ci·ble
e·vis′cer·ate′
·at′ed ·at′ing
e·vis′cer·a′tion
ev′o·ca′tion
e·voke′
·voked′ ·vok′ing

ev′o·lu′tion
ev′o·lu′tion·ar′y
ev′o·lu′tion·ist
e·volve′
·volved′ ·volv′ing
ewe
(*sheep;* SEE yew)
ew′er
ex·ac′er·bate′
·bat′ed ·bat′ing
ex·ac′er·ba′tion
ex·act′
ex·act′ing
ex·ac′tion
ex·ac′ti·tude′
ex·act′ly
ex·ag′ger·ate′
·at′ed ·at′ing
ex·ag′ger·a′tion
ex·ag′ger·a′tor
ex·alt′
ex′al·ta′tion
ex·am′i·na′tion
ex·am′ine
·ined ·in·ing
ex·am′in·er
ex·am′ple
ex·as′per·ate′
·at′ed ·at′ing
ex·as′per·a′tion
ex′ ca·the′dra
ex′ca·vate′
·vat′ed ·vat′ing
ex·ca·va′tion

ex′ca·va′tor
ex·ceed′
(*surpass;* SEE
accede)
ex·ceed′ing·ly
ex·cel′
·celled′ ·cel′ling
ex′cel·lence
ex′cel·len·cy
·cies
ex′cel·lent
ex·cel′si·or
ex·cept′
(*omit;* SEE accept)
ex·cept′ed
(*left out;* SEE
accepted)
ex·cep′tion
ex·cep′tion·a·ble
ex·cep′tion·al
ex·cep′tion·al·ly
ex·cerpt′
ex·cess′
(*surplus;* SEE
access)
ex·ces′sive
ex·ces′sive·ly
ex·change′
·changed′
·chang′ing
ex·change′·
a·bil′i·ty
ex·change′a·ble
ex·cheq′uer

106

ex·cis'a·ble
ex·cise'
ex·cise'
 ·cised' ·cis'ing
ex·ci'sion
ex·cit'a·bil'i·ty
ex·cit'a·ble
ex·cit'a·bly
ex·ci·ta'tion
ex·cite'
 ·cit'ed ·cit'ing
ex·cite'ment
ex·claim'
ex'cla·ma'tion
ex·clam'a·to'ry
ex'clave
ex·clud'a·ble
ex·clude'
 ·clud'ed
 ·clud'ing
ex·clu'sion
ex·clu'sive
ex·clu·siv'i·ty
ex·com·mu'ni·
 cate'
 ·cat'ed ·cat'ing
ex·co'ri·ate'
 ·at'ed ·at'ing
ex·co'ri·a'tion
ex'cre·ment
ex·cres'cence
ex·crete'
 ·cret'ed
 ·cret'ing

ex·cre'tion
ex'cre·to'ry
ex·cru'ci·ate'
 ·at'ed ·at'ing
ex'cul·pate'
 ·pat'ed ·pat'ing
ex'cul·pa'tion
ex·cur'sion
ex·cus'a·ble
ex·cus'a·bly
ex·cuse'
 ·cused' ·cus'ing
ex'e·cra·ble
ex'e·crate'
 ·crat'ed
 ·crat'ing
ex'e·cra'tion
ex'e·cute'
 ·cut'ed ·cut'ing
ex'e·cu'tion
ex'e·cu'tion·er
ex·ec'u·tive
ex·ec'u·tor
ex'e·ge'sis
ex·em'plar
ex·em'pla·ri·ly
ex·em'pla·ri·ness
ex·em'pla·ry
ex·em'pli·fi·
 ca'tion
ex·em'pli·fy'
 ·fied' ·fy'ing
ex·empt'
ex·emp'tion

ex'er·cis'a·ble
ex'er·cise'
 ·cised' ·cis'ing
 (use; SEE exorcise)
ex·ert'
ex·er'tion
ex'e·unt
ex'ha·la'tion
ex·hale'
 ·haled' ·hal'ing
ex·haust'
ex·haust'i·ble
ex·haus'tion
ex·haus'tive
ex·hib'it
ex'hi·bi'tion
ex'hi·bi'tion·ism
ex·hib'i·tor
ex·hil'a·rant
ex·hil'a·rate'
 ·rat'ed ·rat'ing
ex·hil'a·ra'tion
ex·hort'
ex'hor·ta'tion
ex'hu·ma'tion
ex·hume'
 ·humed'
 ·hum'ing
ex'i·gen·cy
 ·cies
ex'i·gent
ex'ile
ex·ist'
ex·ist'ence

ex·ist′ent
ex′is·ten′tial
ex·is·ten′tial·ism
ex′it
ex′o·dus
ex′ of·fi′ci·o′
ex·og′a·my
ex·on′er·ate′
 ·at′ed ·at′ing
ex·on′er·a′tion
ex·o′ra·ble
ex·or′bi·tance
ex·or′bi·tant
ex·or′cise′ or
 ·cize′
 ·cised′ or ·cized′
 ·cis′ing or ·ciz′ing
 (expel; SEE
 exercise)
ex′or·cism
ex·o·ter′ic
ex·ot′ic
ex·ot′i·ca
ex·ot′i·cal·ly
ex·pand′
ex·panse′
ex·pan′si·ble
ex·pan′sion
ex·pan′sive
ex·pa′ti·ate′
 ·at′ed ·at′ing
ex·pa′ti·a′tion
ex·pa′tri·ate′
 ·at′ed ·at′ing

ex·pa′tri·a′tion
ex·pect′
ex·pect′an·cy
ex·pect′ant
ex′pec·ta′tion
ex·pec′to·rant
ex·pec′to·rate′
 ·rat′ed ·rat′ing
ex·pec′to·ra′tion
ex·pe′di·ence
ex·pe′di·en·cy
 ·cies
ex·pe′di·ent
ex′pe·dite′
 ·dit′ed ·dit′ing
ex′pe·dit′er
ex′pe·di′tion
ex′pe·di′tion·ar′y
ex′pe·di′tious
ex·pel′
 ·pelled′ ·pel′ling
ex·pel′la·ble
ex′pel·lee′
ex·pend′
ex·pend′a·bil′i·ty
ex·pend′a·ble
ex·pend′i·ture
ex·pense′
ex·pen′sive
ex·pen′sive·ly
ex·pe′ri·ence
 ·enced ·enc·ing
ex·pe′ri·en′tial
ex·per′i·ment

ex·per′i·men′tal
ex·per′i·men·
 ta′tion
ex′pert
ex′pert·ise′
ex′pi·a·ble
ex′pi·ate′
 ·at′ed ·at′ing
ex′pi·a′tion
ex′pi·a′tor
ex′pi·ra′tion
ex·pir′a·to·ry
ex·pire′
 ·pired′ ·pir′ing
ex·plain′a·ble
ex′pla·na′tion
ex·plan′a·to′ry
ex·ple′tive
ex′pli·ca·ble
ex′pli·cate′
 ·cat′ed ·cat′ing
ex′pli·ca′tion
ex·plic′it
ex·plod′a·ble
ex·plode′
 ·plod′ed
 ·plod′ing
ex′ploit
ex′ploi·ta′tion
ex′plo·ra′tion
ex·plor′a·to′ry
ex·plore′
 ·plored′
 ·plor′ing

ex·plor′er
ex·plo′sion
ex·plo′sive
ex·po′nent
ex′po·nen′tial
ex·port′
ex′por·ta′tion
ex·pose′
·posed′ ·pos′ing
ex′po·sé′
ex′po·si′tion
ex·pos′i·tor
ex·pos′i·to·ry
ex post fac′to
ex·pos′tu·late′
·lat′ed ·lat′ing
ex·pos′tu·la′tion
ex·pos′tu·la′tor
ex·po′sure
ex·pound′
ex·press′
ex·press′age
ex·press′i·ble
ex·pres′sion
ex·pres′sion·ism
ex·pres′sion·
   is′tic
ex·pres′sive
ex·press′man
ex·press′way
ex·pro′pri·ate′
·at′ed ·at′ing
ex·pro′pri·a′tion
ex·pul′sion

ex·punge′
·punged′
·pung′ing
ex′pur·gate′
·gat′ed ·gat′ing
ex′pur·ga′tion
ex′qui·site
ex′tant
(*existing;* SEE
extent)
ex·tem′po·ra′ne·
   ous
ex·tem′po·re
ex·tem′po·rize′
·rized′ ·riz′ing
ex·tend′
ex·ten′si·ble
ex·ten′sion
ex·ten′sive
ex·tent′
(*scope;* SEE extant)
ex·ten′u·ate′
·at′ed ·at′ing
ex·ten′u·a′tion
ex·te′ri·or
ex·ter′mi·nate′
·nat′ed ·nat′ing
ex·ter′mi·na′tion
ex·ter′mi·na′tor
ex·ter′nal
ex·ter′nal·ize′
·ized′ ·iz′ing
ex·tinct′
ex·tinc′tion

ex·tin′guish
ex′tir·pate′
·pat′ed ·pat′ing
ex′tir·pa′tion
ex·tol′ *or* ·toll′
·tolled′ ·tol′ling
ex·tort′
ex·tor′tion
ex·tor′tion·ate
ex·tor′tion·er
ex·tor′tion·ist
ex′tra
ex·tract′a·ble
or ·i·ble
ex·trac′tion
ex·trac′tor
ex′tra·cur·ric′u·
   lar
ex′tra·dit′a·ble
ex′tra·dite′
·dit′ed ·dit′ing
ex′tra·di′tion
ex′tra·le′gal
ex′tra·mar′i·tal
ex′tra·mu′ral
ex·tra′ne·ous
ex·traor′di·
   nar′i·ly
ex·traor′di·
   nar′y
ex·trap′o·late′
·lat′ed ·lat′ing
ex′tra·sen′so·ry

ex'tra·ter'ri·
·to'ri·al
ex·trav'a·gance
ex·trav'a·gant
ex·trav'a·gan'za
ex'tra·ve·hic'u·lar
ex·treme'
ex·treme'ly
ex·trem'ism
ex·trem'ist
ex·trem'i·ty
·ties
ex'tri·cate'
·cat'ed ·cat'ing
ex·tri·ca'tion
ex·trin'sic
ex·trin'si·cal·ly
ex'tro·ver'sion
ex'tro·vert'
ex·trude'
·trud'ed
·trud'ing
ex·tru'sion
ex·u'ber·ance
ex·u'ber·ant
ex'u·da'tion
ex·ude'
·ud'ed ·ud'ing
ex·ult'
ex·ult'ant
ex'ul·ta'tion
ex'urb'
ex·ur'ban·ite'
ex·ur'bi·a

eye
eyed eye'ing
or ey'ing
eye'ball'
eye'brow'
eye'-catch'er
eye'cup'
eye'ful'
eye'glass'
eye'hole'
eye'lash'
eye'let
(*hole;* SEE islet)
eye'lid'
eye liner
eye'-o'pen·er
eye'piece'
eye shadow
eye'shot'
eye'sight'
eye'sore'
eye'strain'
eye'tooth'
eye'wash'
eye'wink'
eye'wit'ness

F

fa'ble
·bled ·bling
fab'ric

fab'ri·cate'
·cat'ed ·cat'ing
fab'ri·ca'tion
fab'ri·ca'tor
Fab'ri·koid'
fab'u·lous
fa·çade' *or* ·cade'
face
faced fac'ing
face'plate'
face'-sav'ing
fac'et
fa·ce'tious
fa'cial
fac'ile
fa·cil'i·tate'
·tat'ed ·tat'ing
fa·cil'i·ta'tion
fa·cil'i·ty
·ties
fac·sim'i·le
·led ·le·ing
fac'tion
fac'tious
fac·ti'tious
(*artificial;* SEE
fictitious)
fac'tor
fac·to'ri·al
fac'to·ry
·ries
fac·to'tum
fac'tu·al
fac'tu·al·ly

fac'ul·ty
 ·ties

fad'dish

fad'dism

fade
 fad'ed fad'ing

fade'-in'

fade'-out'

fag
 fagged
 fag'ging

fag'ot·ing

Fahr'en·heit'

fail'-safe'

fail'ure

faint
 (*weak;* SEE feint)

faint'heart'ed

fair'ground'

fair'ly

fair'-mind'ed

fair'-spo'ken

fair'-trade'

fair'way'

fair'-weath'er

fair'y
 ·ies

fair'y·land'

faith'ful

faith'ful·ly

faith'less

fake
 faked fak'ing

fak'er
 (*fraud*)

fa·kir'
 (*Moslem beggar*)

fal'cate

fal'con

fal'con·ry

fall
 fell fall'en
 fall'ing

fal·la'cious

fal'la·cy
 ·cies

fal'li·bil'i·ty

fal'li·ble

fal'li·bly

fall'ing-out'

fall'off'

fall'out'

fal'low

false
 fals'er fals'est

false'heart'ed

false'hood'

fal·set'to

fal'si·fi·ca'tion

fal'si·fi'er

fal'si·fy'
 ·fied' ·fy'ing

fal'si·ty
 ·ties

fal'ter

fa·mil'ial

fa·mil'iar

fa·mil'i·ar'i·ty
 ·ties

fa·mil'iar·i·
 za'tion

fa·mil'iar·ize'
 ·ized' ·iz'ing

fam'i·ly
 ·lies

fam'ine

fam'ish

fa'mous

fan
 fanned fan'ning

fa·nat'ic

fa·nat'i·cal·ly

fa·nat'i·cism

fan'ci·ful

fan'cy
 ·cies
 ·ci·er ·ci·est
 ·cied ·cy·ing

fan'cy-free'

fan'cy·work'

fan'fare'

fan'light'

fan'tail'

fan·ta'si·a

fan'ta·size'
 ·sized' ·siz'ing

fan·tas'tic

fan·tas'ti·cal·ly

fan'ta·sy
 ·sies
 ·sied ·sy·ing

far
  far′ther
  far′thest
far′ad
far′a·day′
far′a·way′
farce
  farced farc′ing
far′ci·cal
far′ci·cal·ly
fare
  fared far′ing
fare′well′
far′fetched′
far′-flung′
fa·ri′na
far′i·na′ceous
farm′hand′
farm′house′
farm′stead′
farm′yard′
far′o
far′-off′
far′-out′
far′-reach′ing
far′row
far′see′ing
far′sight′ed
far′ther
far′thing
fas′ces
fas′ci·cle
fas′ci·nate′
  ·nat′ed ·nat′ing

fas′ci·na′tion
fas′ci·na′tor
fas′cism
fas′cist
fash′ion
fash′ion·a·ble
fash′ion·a·bly
fast′back′
fas′ten
fas′ten·er
fas′ten·ing
fas·tid′i·ous
fat
  fat′ter fat′test
  fat′ted fat′ting
fa′tal
fa′tal·ism
fa′tal·ist
fa′tal·is′tic
fa′tal·is′ti·cal·ly
fa·tal′i·ty
  ·ties
fa′tal·ly
fate′ful
fa′ther·hood′
fa′ther-in-law′
  fa′thers-
  in-law′
fa′ther·land′
fa′ther·less
fa′ther·li·ness
fa′ther·ly
fath′om
fath′om·a·ble

fath′om·less
fat′i·ga·ble
fa·tigue′
  ·tigued′
  ·tigu′ing
fat′-sol′u·ble
fat′ten
fat′ti·ness
fat′ty
  ·ti·er ·ti·est
fa·tu′i·ty
  ·ties
fat′u·ous
fat′-wit′ted
fau′cet
fault′find′ing
fault′i·ness
fault′less
fault′y
  ·i·er ·i·est
faun
  (*deity;* SEE fawn)
fau′na
  ·nas or ·nae
faux′ pas′
  faux′ pas′
fa′vor·a·ble
fa′vor·a·bly
fa′vored
fa′vor·ite
fa′vor·it·ism
fawn
  (*deer; act ser-*
  vilely; SEE faun)

faze
 fazed faz'ing
 (*disturb;* SEE
 phase)
fe'al·ty
fear'ful
fear'ful·ly
fear'less
fear'some
fea'si·bil'i·ty
fea'si·ble
fea'si·bly
feast
feat
 (*deed;* SEE feet)
feath'er·bed'
feath'er·
 bed'ding
feath'er·
 brain'
feath'ered
feath'er·edge'
feath'er·i·ness
feath'er·stitch'
feath'er·weight'
feath'er·y
fea'ture
 ·tured ·tur·ing
fea'ture-length'
feb'ri·fuge'
fe'brile
Feb'ru·ar'y
fe'cal
fe'ces

feck'less
fe'cund
fe'cun·date'
 ·dat·ed ·dat·ing
fe·cun'di·ty
fed'er·al
fed'er·al·ism
fed'er·al·i·
 za'tion
fed'er·al·ize'
 ·ized ·iz'ing
fed'er·ate'
 ·at·ed ·at·ing
fed'er·a'tion
fe·do'ra
fee'ble
 ·bler ·blest
fee'ble·mind'ed
feed
 fed feed'ing
feed'back'
feel
 felt feel'ing
fee'-split'ting
feet
 (*pl. of* foot;
 SEE feat)
feign
feint
 (*pretense;* SEE
 faint)
fe·lic'i·tate'
 ·tat·ed ·tat·ing
fe·lic'i·ta'tion

fe·lic'i·tous
fe·lic'i·ty
 ·ties
fe'line
fel'low·ship'
fel'on
fe·lo'ni·ous
fel'o·ny
 ·nies
fe·luc'ca
fe'male
fem'i·nine
fem'i·nin'i·ty
fem'i·nism
fem'i·nize'
 ·nized' ·niz'ing
femme fa·tale'
 femmes fa·tales'
fence
 fenced fenc'ing
fend'er
fen'es·tra'tion
fen'nel
fer'ment
fer'men·ta'tion
fern
fe·ro'cious
fe·roc'i·ty
fer'ret
fer'ri·age
Fer'ris wheel
fer'rule
 (*metal ring;*
 SEE ferule)

113

fer'ry
·ries
·ried ·ry·ing
fer'ry·boat'
fer'tile
fer·til'i·ty
fer'til·iz'a·ble
fer'til·i·za'tion
fer'til·ize'
·ized' ·iz'ing
fer'til·iz'er
fer'ule
(*stick;* SEE
ferrule)
fer'vent
fer'vid
fer'vor
fes'cue
fes'tal
fes'ter
fes'ti·val
fes'tive
fes·tiv'i·ty
·ties
fes·toon'
fe'tal
fetch'ing
fete *or* fête
fet'ed *or* fêt'ed
fet'ing *or* fêt'ing
fe'ti·cide'
fet'id
fet'ish
fet'ish·ism

fet'lock'
fet'ter
fet'tle
fet'tuc·ci'ne
fe'tus
·tus·es
feu'dal
feu'dal·ism
feu'dal·is'tic
fe'ver·ish
fez
fez'zes
fi'an·cé' *masc.*
fi'an·cée' *fem.*
fi·as'co
·coes *or* ·cos
fi'at
fib
fibbed fib'bing
fib'ber
fi'ber *or* ·bre
fi'ber·board'
Fi'ber·glas'
fi'bril·la'tion
fi'broid
fi'brous
fib'u·la
·lae *or* ·las
fick'le
fic'tion·al·ize'
·ized' ·iz'ing
fic·ti'tious
(*imaginary;* SEE
factitious)

fid'dle
·dled ·dling
fi·del'i·ty
·ties
fidg'et
fidg'et·i·ness
fidg'et·y
fi·du'ci·ar'y
·ies
field'er
field'-strip'
field'-test'
field'work'
fiend'ish
fierce
fierc'er
fierc'est
fierce'ly
fi'er·i·ness
fi'er·y
·i·er ·i·est
fi·es'ta
fif'teen'
fif'ti·eth
fif'ty
·ties
fight
fought
fight'ing
fig'ment
fig'u·ra'tion
fig'u·ra·tive
fig'ure
·ured ·ur·ing

fig'ure·head'
fig'u·rine'
fil'a·ment
fil'lar
fil'bert
file
  filed fil'ing
fi·let' mi·gnon'
fil'i·al
fil'i·a'tion
fil'i·bus'ter
fil'i·gree'
  ·greed'
  ·gree'ing
fil'ings
Fil'i·pi'no
  ·nos
fil'let
fill'-in'
fill'ing
fil'lip
fil'ly
  ·lies
film'strip'
film'y
  ·i·er ·i·est
fil'ter
  (*strainer;* SEE
  philter)
fil'ter·a·ble
filth'i·ly
filth'i·ness
filth'y
  ·i·er ·i·est

fil'trate
  ·trat·ed ·trat·ing
fin'a·ble
fi·na'gle
  ·gled ·gling
fi·na'le
fi'nal·ist
fi·nal'i·ty
fi'nal·ize'
  ·ized' ·iz'ing
fi'nal·ly
fi·nance'
  ·nanced'
  ·nanc'ing
fi·nan'cial
fi·nan'cial·ly
fin'an·cier'
find
  found find'ing
find'er
fine
  fin'er fin'est
  fined fin'ing
fine'-cut'
fine'-drawn'
fine'-grained'
fine'ly
fine'ness
fin'er·y
  ·ies
fine'spun'
fi·nesse'
  ·nessed'
  ·ness'ing

fine'-toothed'
fin'ger·board'
fin'gered
fin'ger·nail'
fin'ger·print'
finger tip
fin'i·al
fin'i·cal
fin'ick·i·ness
fin'ick·y
fi'nis
fin'ish
fin'ished
fi'nite
fin'nan had'die
fiord
fir
  (*tree;* SEE fur)
fire
  fired fir'ing
fire'arm'
fire'ball'
fire'boat'
fire'bomb'
fire'box'
fire'brand'
fire'break'
fire'brick'
fire'bug'
fire'clay'
fire'crack'er
fire'-cure'
fire'damp'
fire'dog'

fire'-eat'er
fire escape
fire'fly'
· ·flies'
fire'man
fire'place'
fire'plug'
fire'pow'er
fire'proof'
fire'side'
fire'trap'
fire'wa'ter
fire'wood'
fire'works'
fir'kin
fir'ma·ment
firm'ly
first'born'
first'-class'
first'hand'
first'ly
first'-rate'
firth
fis'cal
fis'cal·ly
fish'bowl'
fish'er·man
fish'er·y
· ·ies
fish'hook'
fish'i·ness
fish'mon'ger
fish'plate'
fish'pond'

fish'tail'
fish'wife'
fish'y
· ·i·er ·i·est
fis'sion
fis'sion·a·ble
fis'sure
· ·sured ·sur·ing
fist'i·cuffs'
fis'tu·lous
fit
fit'ted fit'ting
fit'ter fit'test
fit'ful
fit'ful·ly
fit'ness
five'fold'
fix'ate
· ·at·ed ·at·ing
fix·a'tion
fix'a·tive
fixed
fix'ed·ly
fix'ture
fiz'zle
· ·zled ·zling
fjord
flab'ber·gast'
flab'bi·ness
flab'by
· ·bi·er ·bi·est
flac'cid
flac·cid'i·ty
fla·con'

flag
flagged
flag'ging
flag'el·lant
flag'el·late'
· ·lat'ed ·lat'ing
flag'el·la'tion
fla·gel'lum
· ·la or ·lums
flag'eo·let'
flag'on
flag'pole'
fla'gran·cy
fla'grant
flag'ship'
flag'stone'
flag'-wav'ing
flail
flair
(knack; SEE flare)
flake
flaked flak'ing
flak'i·ness
flak'y
· ·i·er ·i·est
flam·bé'
flam'beau
· ·beaux or ·beaus
flam·boy'ance
flam·boy'ant
flame
flamed flam'ing
fla·men'co
· ·cos

116

flame'out'
flame'proof'
fla·min'go
·gos *or* ·goes
flam'ma·bil'i·ty
flam'ma·ble
flange
flanged
flang'ing
flank
flan'nel
flan'nel·ette'
flan'nel-mouthed'
flap
flapped
flap'ping
flap'jack'
flap'per
flare
flared flar'ing
(*blaze;* SEE flair)
flare'-up'
flash'back'
flash'bulb'
flash'card'
flash'cube'
flash'i·ly
flash'i·ness
flash'light'
flash'y
·i·er ·i·est
flat
flat'ter flat'test
flat'ted flat'ting

flat'boat'
flat'car'
flat'fish'
flat'-foot'ed
flat'i·ron
flat'ten
flat'ter
flat'ter·y
flat'u·lent
flat'ware'
flat'work'
flaunt
flau'tist
fla'vor·ful
fla'vor·ing
fla'vor·less
flaw'less
flax'en
flax'seed'
flea'-bit'ten
fledg'ling
flee
fled flee'ing
fleece
fleeced fleec'ing
fleec'i·ness
fleec'y
·i·er ·i·est
fleet'ing
flesh'-col'ored
flesh'i·ness
flesh'pots'
flesh'y
·i·er ·i·est

fleur'-de-lis'
fleurs'-de-lis'
flex'i·bil'i·ty
flex'i·ble
flex'i·bly
flick'er
flied
(*only in baseball*)
fli'er *or* fly'er
flight'i·ness
flight'less
flight'y
·i·er ·i·est
flim'si·ly
flim'si·ness
flim'sy
·si·er ·si·est
flinch'ing·ly
fling
flung fling'ing
flint'lock'
flint'y
·i·er ·i·est
flip
flipped flip'ping
flip'pan·cy
·cies
flip'pant
flip'per
flir·ta'tion
flir·ta'tious
flit
flit'ted flit'ting
float'er

float'ing
floc'cu·late'
· lat'ed ·lat'ing
floc'cu·lent
floe
(*ice;* SEE flow)
flog
flogged
flog'ging
flood'gate'
flood'light'
· light'ed *or* ·lit'
· light'ing
floor'ing
floor'walk'er
flop
flopped
flop'ping
flo'ra
· ras *or* ·rae
flo'ral
flo·res'cence
(*blooming;* SEE
fluorescence)
flo·res'cent
flo'ret
flo'ri·cul'ture
flor'id
Flor'i·da
flo·rid'i·ty
flor'in
flo'rist
floss'y
· i·er ·i·est

118

flo·ta'tion
flo·til'la
flot'sam
flounce
flounced
flounc'ing
floun'der
flour'ish
flout
flow
(*glide;* SEE floe)
flow'ered
flow'er·i·ness
flow'er·pot'
flow'er·y
· i·er ·i·est
flu
(*influenza*)
fluc'tu·ate'
· at'ed ·at'ing
flue
(*pipe*)
flu'en·cy
flu'ent
fluf'fi·ness
fluf'fy
· fi·er ·fi·est
flu'id
flu·id'i·ty
flun'ky
· kies
flu'o·resce'
· resced'
· resc'ing

flu'o·res'cence
(*light;* SEE
florescence)
flu'o·res'cent
fluor'i·date'
· dat'ed ·dat'ing
fluor'i·da'tion
fluor'i·nate'
· nat'ed ·nat'ing
fluor'o·scope'
flu'o·ros'co·py
flur'ry
· ries
· ried ·ry·ing
flus'ter
flute
flut'ed flut'ing
flut'ist
flut'ter
flu'vi·al
fly
flies
flew flown
fly'ing
fly'a·ble
fly'a·way'
fly'-by-night'
fly'catch'er
fly'leaf'
· leaves'
fly'pa'per
fly'speck'
fly'trap'
fly'weight'

fly'wheel'
foam'i·ness
foam'y
 ·i·er ·i·est
fo'cal
fo'cal·ize'
 ·ized' ·iz'ing
fo'cus
 ·cus·es or ·ci
 ·cused or ·cussed
 ·cus·ing or
 ·cus·sing
fod'der
fog
 fogged fog'ging
fog'bound'
fog'gi·ly
fog'gi·ness
fog'gy
 ·gi·er ·gi·est
fog'horn'
fo'gy or fo'gey
 ·gies or ·geys
foi'ble
foist
fold'a·way'
fold'er
fo'li·age
fo'li·ate'
 ·at'ed ·at'ing
fo'li·a'tion
fo'li·o'
 ·os', ·oed' ·o'ing
folk'lore'

folk'way'
fol'li·cle
fol'low·er
fol'low-through'
fol'low-up'
fol'ly
 ·lies
fo·ment'
fo'men·ta'tion
fon'dant
fon'dle
 ·dled ·dling
fond'ness
fon·due'
food'stuff'
fool'har'di·ness
fool'har'dy
fool'ish·ness
fool'proof'
fools'cap'
foot
 feet
foot'age
foot'ball'
foot'bridge'
foot'-can'dle
foot'fall'
foot'hold'
foot'ing
foot'lights'
foot'lock'er
foot'loose'
foot'note'
foot'path'

foot'-pound'
foot'print'
foot'race'
foot'rest'
foot'sore'
foot'step'
foot'stool'
foot'-ton'
foot'wear'
foot'work'
fop'pish
for'age
for'ay
for·bear'
 ·bore' ·borne'
 ·bear'ing
 (*abstain;* SEE
 forebear)
for·bear'ance
for·bid'
 ·bade' or ·bad'
 ·bid'den
 ·bid'ding
force
 forced forc'ing
force'ful
for'ceps
 ·ceps
for'ci·ble
for'ci·bly
fore'arm'
fore'bear'
 (*ancestor;* SEE
 forbear)

fore·bode′
  ·bod′ed ·bod′ing
fore′cast′
  ·cast′ or ·cast′ed
  ·cast′ing
fore′cas′tle
fore·close′
fore·clo′sure
fore·doom′
fore′fa′ther
fore′fin′ger
fore′foot′
fore·go′
  ·went′ ·gone′
  ·go′ing
  (*precede;* SEE
  forgo)
fore′go′ing
fore′ground′
fore′hand′
fore·hand′ed
fore′head
for′eign
for′eign-born′
for′eign·er
fore′knowl′edge
fore′leg′
fore′lock′
fore′man
fore′most′
fore′named′
fore′noon′
fo·ren′sic
fo·ren′si·cal·ly

fore′or·dain′
fore′paw′
fore′play′
fore′quar′ter
fore′run′ner
fore′sail′
fore·see′
  ·saw′ ·seen′
  ·see′ing
fore·see′a·ble
fore·se′er
fore·shad′ow
fore·short′en
fore·show′
  ·showed′,
  ·shown′ or
  ·showed′,
  ·show′ing
fore′sight′
fore′skin′
for′est
fore·stall′
for′est·a′tion
for′est·er
for′est·ry
fore′taste′
fore·tell′
  ·told′ ·tell′ing
fore′thought′
for·ev′er
fore·warn′
fore′word′
  (*preface;* SEE
  forward)

for′feit
for′fei·ture
forge
  forged forg′ing
forg′er
forg′er·y
  ·ies
for·get′
  ·got′, ·got′ten
  or ·got′,
  ·get′ting
for·get′ful
for·get′-me-not′
for·get′ta·ble
for·giv′a·ble
for·give′
  ·gave′ ·giv′en
  ·giv′ing
for·give′ness
for·go′ or fore·
  ·went′ ·gone′
  ·go′ing
  (*do without;*
  SEE forego)
forked
fork′lift′
for·lorn′
for′mal
form·al′de·hyde′
for·mal′i·ty
  ·ties
for′mal·i·za′tion
for′mal·ize′
  ·ized′ ·iz′ing

for'mal·ly
for'mat
for·ma'tion
form'a·tive
for'mer
For·mi'ca
for'mi·da·ble
for'mi·da·bly
form'less
for'mu·la
·las or ·lae'
for'mu·late'
·lat'ed ·lat'ing
for'mu·la'tion
for'ni·cate'
·cat'ed ·cat'ing
for'ni·ca'tion
for'ni·ca'tor
for·sake'
·sook' ·sak'en
·sak'ing
for·swear'
·swore' ·sworn'
·swear'ing
for·syth'i·a
fort
(*fortified place*)
forte
(*special skill*)
forth'com'ing
forth'right'
forth'with'
for'ti·eth
for'ti·fi·ca'tion

for'ti·fi'er
for'ti·fy'
·fied' ·fy'ing
for'ti·tude'
for'tress
for·tu'i·tous
for·tu'i·ty
·ties
for'tu·nate
for'tune
for'tune·tell'er
for'ty
·ties
fo'rum
·rums or ·ra
for'ward
(*to the front;*
SEE foreword)
fos'sil
fos'ter
foul
(*filthy;* SEE fowl)
fou·lard'
foul'mouthed'
foun·da'tion
foun'der *v.*
found'er *n.*
found'ling
found'ry
·ries
foun'tain
foun'tain·head'
four'-flush'er
four'fold'

four'-foot'ed
Four'-H' club *or*
4'-H' club
four'-in-hand'
four'-post'er
four'score'
four'some
four'square'
four'-star'
four'teen'
fourth
fourth'-class'
four'-way'
fowl
(*bird;* SEE foul)
fox'hole'
fox'hound'
fox'i·ly
fox'i·ness
fox'y
·i·er ·i·est
foy'er
fra'cas
frac'tion
frac'tious
frac'ture
·tured ·tur·ing
frag'ile
fra·gil'i·ty
frag'ment
frag·men'tal·ly
frag'men·tar'y
fra'grance
fra'grant

frail'ty
·ties
frame
framed
fram'ing
frame'-up'
frame'work'
franc
(*coin;* SEE frank)
fran'chise
·chised ·chis·ing
fran'gi·bil'i·ty
fran'gi·ble
frank
(*free;* SEE franc)
frank'furt·er
frank'in·cense'
fran'tic
fran'ti·cal·ly
frap·pé'
fra·ter'nal
fra·ter'nal·ly
fra·ter'ni·ty
·ties
frat'er·ni·za'tion
frat'er·nize'
·nized' ·niz'ing
frat'ri·cide'
fraud'u·lence
fraud'u·lent
fraught
freak'ish
freck'le
·led ·ling

free
fre'er fre'est
freed free'ing
free'bie *or* ·by
·bies
free'born'
freed'man
free'dom
free'-for-all'
free'-form'
free'hand'
free'-lance'
free'load'er
free'man
Free'ma'son
free'-spo'ken
free'-stand'ing
free'stone'
free'think'er
free'way'
free'wheel'ing
freez'a·ble
freeze
froze fro'zen
freez'ing
(*become ice;* SEE
frieze)
freeze'-dry'
-dried' -dry'ing
freez'er
freight'age
freight'er
French cuff
French doors

French fry
French fries
French toast
fre·net'ic
fre·net'i·cal·ly
fren'zy
·zies
·zied ·zy·ing
fre'quen·cy
·cies
fre'quent
fres'co
·coes *or* ·cos
fresh'en
fresh'et
fresh'man
fresh'wa'ter
fret
fret'ted
fret'ting
fret'ful
fret'ful·ly
fret'work'
Freud'i·an
fri'a·bil'i·ty
fri'a·ble
fri'ar
fric'as·see'
·seed' ·see'ing
fric'tion
Fri'day
friend'li·ness
friend'ly
·li·er ·li·est

friend′ship
frieze
 (*in architecture;*
 SEE freeze)
frig′ate
fright′ened
fright′ful
frig′id
fri·gid′i·ty
frill′y
 ·i·er ·i·est
fringe
 fringed
 fring′ing
frip′per·y
 ·ies
Fris′bee
fri·sé′
frisk′i·ness
frisk′y
 ·i·er ·i·est
frit′ter
fri·vol′i·ty
 ·ties
friv′o·lous
friz′zi·ness
frog′man′
frol′ic
 ·icked ·ick·ing
frol′ick·er
frol′ic·some
front′age
fron′tal
fron·tier′

fron·tiers′man
fron′tis·piece′
front′let
frost′bite′
 ·bit′ ·bit′ten
 ·bit′ing
frost′i·ly
frost′i·ness
frost′ing
frost′y
 ·i·er ·i·est
froth′i·ly
froth′i·ness
froth′y
 ·i·er ·i·est
fro′ward
frown
frow′zi·ness
frow′zy
 ·zi·er ·zi·est
fro′zen
fruc′ti·fy′
 ·fied′ ·fy′ing
fru′gal
fru·gal′i·ty
fru′gal·ly
fruit′cake′
fruit′ful
fruit′i·ness
fru·i′tion
fruit′less
fruit′wood′
fruit′y
 ·i·er ·i·est

frump′ish
frus′trate
 ·trat·ed ·trat·ing
frus·tra′tion
frus′tum
 ·tums or ·ta
fry
 fried fry′ing
fry′er or fri′er
f′-stop′
fuch′sia
fudge
 fudged
 fudg′ing
fu′el
 ·eled or ·elled
 ·el·ing or ·el·ling
fuel cell
fu′gi·tive
fugue
ful′crum
 ·crums or ·cra
ful·fill′ or ·fil′
 ·filled′ ·fill′ing
ful·fill′ment
 or ·fil′ment
full′back′
full′-blood′ed
full′-blown′
full′-bod′ied
full′-dress′
full′er's earth
full′-faced′
full′-fash′ioned

full'-fledged'
full'-length'
full'-scale'
full'-time'
full'y
ful'mi·nate'
·nat'ed ·nat'ing
ful'some
fum'ble
·bled ·bling
fume
fumed fum'ing
fu'mi·gant
fu'mi·gate'
·gat'ed ·gat'ing
fu'mi·ga'tion
fu'mi·ga'tor
func'tion·al
func'tion·al·ly
func'tion·ar'y
·ar'ies
fun'da·men'tal
fun'da·men'tal·
ism
fun'da·men'tal·ly
fund'-rais'er
fu'ner·al
fu·ne're·al
fun'gi·cid'al
fun'gi·cide'
fun'gous *adj.*
fun'gus *n.*
·gi *or* ·gus·es
fu·nic'u·lar

fun'nel
·neled *or* ·nelled
·nel·ing *or*
·nel·ling
fun'ni·ness
fun'ny
·ni·er ·ni·est
fur
furred fur'ring
(*hair;* SEE fir)
fur'be·low'
fur'bish
fu'ri·ous
fur'long
fur'lough
fur'nace
fur'nish·ings
fur'ni·ture
fu'ror
fur'ri·er
fur'ri·ness
fur'row
fur'ry
·ri·er ·ri·est
fur'ther
fur'ther·ance
fur'ther·more'
fur'ther·most'
fur'thest
fur'tive
fu'ry
·ries
fuse
fused fus'ing

fu'se·lage'
fu'si·bil'i·ty
fu'si·ble
fu'sil·lade'
·lad'ed ·lad'ing
fu'sion
fuss'i·ness
fuss'y
·i·er ·i·est
fus'tian
fust'y
·i·er ·i·est
fu'tile
fu'tile·ly
fu·til'i·ty
fu'ture
fu·tu'ri·ty
·ties
fuzz'i·ly
fuzz'i·ness
fuzz'y
·i·er ·i·est

G

gab'ar·dine'
ga'ble
gad'a·bout'
gadg'et
gag
gagged
gag'ging

gage
  (*pledge;* SEE
  gauge)
gag'gle
gag'man'
gai'e·ty
gai'ly
gain'er
gain'ful
gain'ful·ly
gain'li·ness
gain'ly
  ·li·er ·li·est
gain'say'
  ·said' ·say'ing
gait
  (*way of walking;*
  SEE gate)
gai'ter
ga'la
Gal'a·had'
gal'ax·y
  ·ies
gal'lant
gal'lant·ry
  ·ries
gal'le·on
gal'ler·y
  ·ies
  ·ied ·y·ing
gal'ley
  ·leys
gall'ing
gal'li·vant'

gal'lon
gal'lop
gal'lows
  ·lows·es *or* ·lows
gall'stone'
ga·lore'
ga·losh'
  or ·loshe'
ga·lumph'
gal·van'ic
gal'va·nism
gal'va·ni·za'tion
gal'va·nize'
  ·nized' ·niz'ing
gal·va·nom'e·ter
gam'bit
gam'ble
  ·bled ·bling
  (*risk;* SEE
  gambol)
gam'bler
gam'bol
  ·boled *or* ·bolled
  ·bol·ing *or*
  ·bol·ling
  (*frolic;* SEE
  gamble)
gam'brel
game'cock'
game'keep'er
games'man·ship'
gam'in
gam'i·ness
gam'ma

gam'ut
gam'y
  ·i·er ·i·est
gan'der
Gan'dhi·ism
ga'nef *or* ·nof
gang'land'
gan'gling
gan'gli·on
  ·gli·a *or* ·gli·ons
gang'plank'
gan'grene
gan'gre·nous
gang'ster
gang'way'
gant'let
gan'try
  ·tries
gap
  gapped
  gap'ping
gape
  gaped gap'ing
ga·rage'
  ·raged' ·rag'ing
gar'bage
gar'ble
  ·bled ·bling
gar·çon'
  ·çons'
gar'den·er
gar·de'ni·a
Gar·gan'tu·an *or*
  gar·gan'tu·an

gar'gle
·gled ·gling

gar'goyle

gar'ish

gar'land

gar'lic

gar'lick·y

gar'ment

gar'ner

gar'net

gar'nish

gar'nish·ee'
·eed' ·ee'ing

gar'nish·ment

gar'ret

gar'ri·son

gar·rote'
·rot'ed or
·rot'ted
·rot'ing or
·rot'ting

gar·ru'li·ty

gar'ru·lous

gar'ter

gas
gassed
gas'sing

gas'e·ous

gas'ket

gas'light'

gas'o·line' or
·lene'

gas'sy
·si·er ·si·est

gas'tric

gas'tro·nome'

gas'tro·nom'i·cal

gas·tron'o·my

gate
(*door;* SEE gait)

gate'way'

gath'er·ing

gauche
(*lacking grace;*
SEE gouache)

gau·che·rie'

gaud'i·ly

gaud'i·ness

gaud'y
·i·er ·i·est

gauge
gauged
gaug'ing
(*measure;* SEE
gage)

gauge'a·ble

gaunt

gaunt'let

gauze

gauz'y
·i·er ·i·est

gav'el

gawk'i·ness

gawk'y
·i·er ·i·est

gay'ly

gaze
gazed gaz'ing

ga·ze'bo
·bos or ·boes

ga·zelle'

ga·zette'

gaz'et·teer'

gear'box'

gear'shift'

gear'wheel'

Gei'ger

gei'sha
·sha or ·shas

gel
gelled gel'ling

gel'a·tin or ·tine

ge·lat'i·nize'
·nized' ·niz'ing

ge·lat'i·nous

geld
geld'ed or gelt
geld'ing

gel'id

ge·lid'i·ty

gem'i·nate'
·nat'ed ·nat'ing

Gem'i·ni'

gen'darme

gen'der

ge'ne·a·log'i·cal

ge'ne·al'o·gy
·gies

gen'er·al

gen'er·al'i·ty
·ties

gen'er·al·i·za'tion

gen'er·al·ize'
 ·ized' ·iz'ing
gen'er·al·ly
gen'er·ate'
 ·at'ed ·at'ing
gen'er·a'tion
gen'er·a'tor
ge·ner'ic
ge·ner'i·cal·ly
gen'er·os'i·ty
 ·ties
gen'er·ous
gen'e·sis
 ·ses'
ge·net'ic
ge·net'i·cal·ly
ge'nial
ge'ni·al'i·ty
ge'nial·ly
ge'nie
gen'i·tal
ge'nius
gen'o·cide'
gen'o·type'
gen're
gen·teel'
gen·teel'ly
gen'tile
gen·til'i·ty
gen'tle
 ·tler ·tlest
gen'tle·man
gen'tle·man·ly
gen'tle·wom'an

gen'tly
gen'try
gen'u·flect'
gen'u·ine
gen'u·ine·ly
ge'nus
 gen'er·a
ge'o·cen'tric
ge·og'ra·pher
ge'o·graph'i·cal
ge·og'ra·phy
 ·phies
ge'o·log'ic
ge'o·log'i·cal·ly
ge·ol'o·gist
ge·ol'o·gy
 ·gies
ge'o·met'ric
ge'o·met'ri·cal·ly
ge·om'e·try
 ·tries
ge'o·phys'i·cal
ge'o·phys'i·cist
ge'o·phys'ics
ge'o·po·lit'i·cal
ge'o·pol'i·tics
Geor'gia
ge'o·stat'ics
ge·ot'ro·pism
ge·ra'ni·um
ger'bil or ·bille
ger'i·at'rics
ger·mane'
ger'mi·cid'al

ger'mi·cide'
ger'mi·nate'
 ·nat'ed ·nat'ing
ger'mi·na'tion
ger'on·tol'o·gy
ger'ry·man'der
ger'und
Ge·stalt'
ges'tate
 ·tat·ed ·tat·ing
ges·ta'tion
ges·tic'u·late'
 ·lat'ed ·lat'ing
ges·tic'u·la'tion
ges·tic'u·la'tor
ges'ture
 ·tured ·tur·ing
get
 got, got or
 got'ten,
 get'ting
get'a·way'
get'-to·geth'er
gew'gaw
gey'ser
ghast'li·ness
ghast'ly
 ·li·er ·li·est
gher'kin
ghet'to
 ·tos or ·toes
ghet'to·ize'
 ·ized' ·iz'ing
ghil'lie

127

ghost'li·ness
ghost'ly
·li·er ·li·est
ghost'write'
ghost'writ'er
ghoul'ish
gi'ant
gib'ber·ish
gib'bet
gib'bon
gib·bos'i·ty
·ties
gib'bous
gibe
gibed gib'ing
(*taunt;* SEE jibe)
gib'let
gid'di·ly
gid'di·ness
gid'dy
·di·er ·di·est
gift'ed
gift'-wrap'
-wrapped'
-wrap'ping
gig
gigged gig'ging
gi·gan'tic
gi·gan'ti·cal·ly
gi·gan'tism
gig'gle
·gled ·gling
gig'o·lo'
·los'

gild
gild'ed *or* gilt
gild'ing
(*coat with gold;*
SEE guild)
gilt
(*gold;* SEE guilt)
gilt'-edged'
gim'bals
gim'crack'
gim'let
gim'mick
gin'ger
gin'ger·bread'
ging'ham
gi·raffe'
gird
gird'ed *or* girt
gird'ing
gird'er
gir'dle
·dled ·dling
girl'ish
gist
give
gave giv'en
giv'ing
give'a·way'
giz'zard
gla·cé'
·céed' ·cé'ing
gla'cial
gla'ci·ate'
·at'ed ·at'ing

gla'cier
glad
glad'der
glad'dest
glad'den
glad'i·a'tor
glad'i·o'lus *or* ·la
·lus·es *or* ·li, ·las
glad'some
glair
(*glaze;* SEE glare)
glam'or·ize'
·ized' ·iz'ing
glam'or·ous
glam'our *or* ·or
glance
glanced
glanc'ing
glan'du·lar
glare
glared glar'ing
(*strong light;*
SEE glair)
glar'i·ness
glar'y
·i·er ·i·est
glass'ful'
·fuls'
glass·ine'
glass'i·ness
glass'ware'
glass'y
·i·er ·i·est
glau·co'ma

glaze
  glazed glaz′ing
gla′zier
glean′ings
glee′ful
glee′ful·ly
glib
  glib′ber
  glib′best
glib′ly
glide
  glid′ed glid′ing
glid′er
glim′mer
glimpse
  glimpsed
  glimps′ing
glis·sade′
  ·sad′ed ·sad′ing
glis′ten
glit′ter
glit′ter·y
gloam′ing
gloat
glob′al
globe′-trot′ter
glob′u·lar
glob′ule
glock′en·spiel′
gloom′i·ly
gloom′i·ness
gloom′y
  ·i·er ·i·est
glo′ri·fi·ca′tion

glo′ri·fy′
  ·fied′ ·fy′ing
glo′ri·ous
glo′ry
  ·ries
  ·ried ·ry·ing
glos′sa·ry
  ·ries
gloss′i·ness
gloss′y
  ·i·er ·i·est
  ·ies
glot′tal
glove
  gloved glov′ing
glow′er
glow′ing·ly
glow′worm′
glu′cose
glue
  glued glu′ing
glue′y
  glu′i·er
  glu′i·est
glum′ly
glut
  glut′ted
  glut′ting
glu′ten
glu′ten·ous
  (having gluten)
glu′ti·nous
  (gluey)
glut′ton

glut′ton·ous
  (greedy)
glut′ton·y
glyc′er·in or ·ine
gnarled
gnash
gnat
gnaw
  gnawed
  gnaw′ing
gneiss
gnoc′chi
gnome
gno′mic
gno′mon
gnos′tic
gnu
go
  went gone
  go′ing
goad
go′-a·head′
goal′keep′er
goat·ee′
gob′ble
  ·bled ·bling
gob′ble·dy·gook′
go′-be·tween′
gob′let
gob′lin
god′child′
god′daugh′ter
god′dess
god′fa′ther

God'-giv'en
god'li·ness
god'ly
·li·er ·li·est
god'moth'er
god'par'ent
god'send'
god'son'
God'speed'
go'-get'ter
gog'gle
·gled ·gling
go'-go'
goi'ter or ·tre
gold'en
gold'-filled'
gold'fish'
gold leaf
gold'smith'
golf'er
gon'do·la
gon'do·lier'
gon'or·rhe'a
or ·rhoe'a
good
bet'ter best
good'bye' or
good'-bye'
·byes' or -byes'
good'-for-
noth'ing
good'-heart'ed
good'-hu'mored
good'-look'ing

good'ly
·li·er ·li·est
good'-na'tured
good night
good'-sized'
good'-tem'pered
good'y
·ies
goo'ey
goo'i·er goo'i·est
goo'gol
goose
geese
goose'neck'
goose'-step'
go'pher
gore
gorged gorg'ing
gorge
gorged gorg'ing
gor'geous
go·ril'la
(ape; SEE guerrilla)
gor'i·ness
gor'mand·ize'
·ized· ·iz'ing
gor'y
·i·er ·i·est
gos'hawk'
gos'ling
gos'pel
gos'sa·mer
gos'sip
got'ten

gouache
(painting; SEE
gauche)
gouge
gouged
goug'ing
gou'lash
gourd
gour'mand
gour'met
gout
gov'ern·ess
gov'ern·ment
gov'ern·men'tal
gov'er·nor
grab
grabbed
grab'bing
grace'ful
grace'ful·ly
grace'less
gra'cious
gra'date
·dat·ed ·dat·ing
gra·da'tion
grade
grad'ed grad'ing
grad'u·al
grad'u·ate'
·at'ed ·at'ing
grad·u·a'tion
graf·fi'ti
(sing. graf·fi'to)
graft'er

gra′ham
grain′i·ness
grain′y
 ·i·er ·i·est
gram′mar
gram·mar′i·an
gram·mat′i·cal
gran′a·ry
 ·ries
grand′aunt′
grand′child′
grand′daugh′ter
gran′deur
grand′fa′ther
gran·dil′o·quent
gran′di·ose′
grand′moth′er
grand′neph′ew
grand′niece′
grand′par′ent
grand′son′
grand′stand′
grand′un′cle
gran′ite
gran′ite·ware′
grant·ee′
grant′-in-aid′
 grants′-in-aid′
grant′or
gran′u·lar
gran′u·late′
 ·lat′ed ·lat′ing
gran′ule
grape′fruit′

grape′vine′
graph′ic
graph′i·cal·ly
graph′ite
graph·ol′o·gy
grap′nel
grap′ple
 ·pled ·pling
grap′pler
grasp′ing
grass′hop′per
grass′y
 ·i·er ·i·est
grate
 grat′ed grat′ing
grate′ful
grate′ful·ly
grat′i·fi·ca′tion
grat′i·fy′
 ·fied′ ·fy′ing
gra′tis
grat′i·tude
gra·tu′i·tous
gra·tu′i·ty
 ·ties
grave
 graved, grav′en
 or graved,
 grav′ing
 (carve out)
grave
 graved grav′ing
 (clean the hull)
grave′clothes′

grav′el
 ·eled or ·elled
 ·el·ing or ·el·ling
grav′el·ly
grave′ly
grave′side′
grave′stone′
grave′yard′
grav′i·tate′
 ·tat′ed ·tat′ing
grav′i·ta′tion
grav′i·ty
 ·ties
gra′vy
 ·vies
gray
gray′-head′ed
graze
 grazed graz′ing
grease
 greased
 greas′ing
grease′paint′
greas′i·ness
greas′y
 ·i·er ·i·est
great′-aunt′
great′coat′
great′-grand′child′
great′-grand′par′·
 ent
great′ly
great′-neph′ew
great′ness

great'-niece'
great'-un'cle
greed'i·ly
greed'i·ness
greed'y
 ·i·er ·i·est
Greek'-let'ter
green'back'
green'er·y
green'-eyed'
green'gage'
green'horn'
green'house'
green'room'
green'sward'
greet'ing
gre·gar'i·ous
grem'lin
gre·nade'
gren'a·dier'
gren'a·dine'
grey'hound' *or*
 gray'·
grid'dle
 ·dled ·dling
grid'dle·cake'
grid'i'ron
grief'-strick'en
griev'ance
grieve
 grieved
 griev'ing
 griev'ous
grif'fin

grill
 (*broiler grid*)
grille
 (*open grating*)
grill'room'
grim
 grim'mer
 grim'mest
gri·mace'
 ·maced'
 ·mac'ing
grime
 grimed grim'ing
grim'i·ly
grim'i·ness
grim'y
 ·i·er ·i·est
grin
 grinned
 grin'ning
grind
 ground
 grind'ing
grind'stone'
grip
 gripped *or* gript
 grip'ping
 (*hold*)
gripe
 griped grip'ing
 (*distress*)
grippe
 (*influenza*)
gris'li·ness

gris'ly
 ·li·er ·li·est
 (*horrid*)
gris'tle
gris'tly
 (*of gristle*)
grist'mill'
grit
 grit'ted
 grit'ting
 grit'ti·ness
grit'ty
 ·ti·er ·ti·est
griz'zly bear
groan'ing
gro'cer·y
 ·ies
grog'gi·ly
grog'gi·ness
grog'gy
 ·gi·er ·gi·est
groin
grom'met
groom
groove
 grooved
 groov'ing
groov'y
 ·i·er ·i·est
grope
 groped grop'ing
gros'grain'
gross'ly
gross'ness

gro·tesque'
gro·tesque'ly
grot'to
·toes or ·tos
grouch'i·ly
grouch'i·ness
grouch'y
·i·er ·i·est
ground'less
grounds'keep'er
ground'speed'
ground'work'
group
grout
grove
grov'el
·eled or ·elled
·el·ing or ·el·ling
grow
grew grown
grow'ing
growl'er
grown'-up'
growth
grub
grubbed
grub'bing
grub'bi·ness
grub'by
·bi·er ·bi·est
grub'stake'
grudge
grudged
grudg'ing

gru'el
gru'el·ing or
gru'el·ling
grue'some
grue'some·ly
gruff'ly
grum'ble
·bled ·bling
grum'bler
grum'bly
grump'i·ness
grump'y
·i·er ·i·est
grun'ion
grunt
Gru·yère'
G'-string'
G'-suit'
guar'an·tee'
·teed' ·tee'ing
guar'an·tor'
guar'an·ty
·ties
·tied ·ty·ing
guard'ed
guard'house'
guard'i·an
guard'rail'
guard'room'
guards'man
gua'va
gu'ber·na·to'ri·al
Guern'sey
·seys

guer·ril'la or gue·
(soldier; SEE
gorilla)
guess'work'
guest
guid'a·ble
guid'ance
guide
guid'ed
guid'ing
guide'book'
guide'line'
guide'post'
guild
(union; SEE gild)
guilds'man
guile'ful
guile'less
guil'lo·tine'
·tined' ·tin'ing
guilt
(blame; SEE gilt)
guilt'i·ly
guilt'i·ness
guilt'y
·i·er ·i·est
guin'ea pig
guise
gui·tar'
gui·tar'ist
gulch
gul'let
gul'li·bil'i·ty
gul'li·ble

gul'li·bly
gul'ly
·lies
gum'drop'
gum'mi·ness
gum'my
·mi·er ·mi·est
gun
gunned
gun'ning
gun'cot'ton
gun'fire'
gung'-ho'
gun'lock'
gun'man
gun'ner·y
gun'ny·sack'
gun'play'
gun'point'
gun'pow'der
gun'run'ning
gun'shot'
gun'-shy'
gun'smith'
gun'stock'
gup'py
·pies
gur'gle
·gled ·gling
gu'ru
gush'er
gush'i·ness
gush'y
·i·er ·i·est

gus'set
gus'ta·to'ry
gus'to
gust'y
·i·er ·i·est
gut
gut'ted
gut'ting
gut'ta-per'cha
gut'ter·snipe'
gut'tur·al
guy
guz'zle
·zled ·zling
guz'zler
gym·na'si·um
·si·ums or ·si·a
gym'nast
gym·nas'tics
gym'no·sperm'
gyn'e·col'o·gist
gyn'e·col'o·gy
gyp
gypped gyp'ping
gyp'sum
Gyp'sy
·sies
gy'rate
·rat·ed ·rat·ing
gy·ra'tion
gy'ro·com'pass
gy'ro·scope'
gy'ro·scop'ic
gy'ro·sta'bi·liz'er

H

ha'be·as cor'pus
hab'er·dash'er·y
·ies
ha·bil'i·tate'
·tat'ed ·tat'ing
hab'it
hab'it·a·ble
hab'i·tat'
hab'i·ta'tion
hab'it-form'ing
ha·bit'u·al
ha·bit'u·ate'
·at'ed ·at'ing
hab'i·tude'
ha·bit'u·é'
ha'ci·en'da
hack'ney
·neys
hack'neyed
hack'saw'
had'dock
hag'gard
hag'gle
·gled ·gling
hai'ku
·ku
hail
(*ice;* SEE hale)
hail'stone'

hail'storm'
hair'breadth'
hair'cut'
hair'do'
hair'dress'er
hair'i·ness
hair'line'
hair'piece'
hair'-rais'ing
hair'split'ting
hair'spring'
hair'y
  ·i·er ·i·est
hal'cy·on
hale
  haled hal'ing
  (healthy; force;
  SEE hail)
half
  halves
half'back'
half'-baked'
half'-breed'
half'-caste'
half'-cocked'
half'heart'ed
half'-hour'
half'-mast'
half'-moon'
half'tone'
half'track'
half'-truth'
half'way'
half'-wit'ted

hal'i·but
hal'i·to'sis
hal'le·lu'jah
  or ·iah
hall'mark'
hal'lowed
Hal'low·een'
hal·lu'ci·nate'
  ·nat·ed ·nat·ing
hal·lu'ci·na'tion
hal·lu'ci·na·to'ry
hal·lu'ci·no·gen
hall'way'
ha'lo
  ·los or ·loes
hal'ter
halt'ing·ly
ha·lutz'
  ha'lutz·im'
halve
  halved halv'ing
hal'yard
ham'burg·er
ham'let
ham'mer
ham'mer·head'
ham'mock
ham'per
ham'ster
ham'string'
hand'bag'
hand'ball'
hand'bar'row
hand'bill'

hand'book'
hand'breadth'
hand'clasp'
hand'cuff'
hand'ful'
  ·fuls'
hand'gun'
hand'i·cap'
  ·capped'
  ·cap'ping
hand'i·craft'
hand'i·ly
hand'i·ness'
hand'i·work'
hand'ker·chief
  ·chiefs
han'dle
  ·dled ·dling
han'dle·bar'
hand'ler
hand'made'
hand'-me-down'
hand'out'
hand'picked'
hand'rail'
hand'saw'
hand'sel
  ·seled or ·selled
  ·sel·ing or ·sel·ling
hand'set'
hand'shake'
hands'-off'
hand'some
hand'spring'

135

hand′stand′
hand′-to-hand′
hand′-to-mouth′
hand′work′
hand′writ′ing
hand′y
 ·i·er ·i·est
han′dy·man′
hang
 hung hang′ing
 (*suspend*)
hang
 hanged hang′ing
 (*put to death*)
hang′ar
 (*aircraft shed*)
hang′dog′
hang′er
 (*garment holder*)
hang′er-on′
 hang′ers-on′
hang′man
hang′nail′
hang′o′ver
hang′-up′
hank′er
han′ky-pan′ky
han′som (cab)
Ha′nu·ka′
hap′haz′ard
hap′less
hap′pen
hap′pen·stance′
hap′pi·ly

hap′pi·ness
hap′py
 ·pi·er ·pi·est
hap′py-go-luck′y
ha′ra-ki′ri
ha·rangue′
 ·rangued′
 ·rangu′ing
ha·rangu′er
har·ass′
har′bin·ger
har′bor
hard′back′
hard′-bit′ten
hard′-boiled′
hard′-bound′
hard′-core′
hard′-cov′er
hard′en
hard′fist′ed
hard′goods′
hard′head′ed
hard′heart′ed
har′di·hood′
har′di·ly
har′di·ness
hard′ly
hard′pan′
hard′-shell′
hard′ship′
hard′tack′
hard′top′
hard′ware′
hard′wood′

har′dy
 ·di·er ·di·est
hare′brained′
hare′lip′
ha′rem
har′le·quin
harm′ful
harm′less
har·mon′ic
har·mon′i·ca
har·mo′ni·ous
har′mo·nize′
 ·nized′ ·niz′ing
har′mo·ny
har′ness
harp′ist
har·poon′
harp′si·chord′
har′py
 ·pies
har′ri·er
har′row
har′row·ing
har′ry
 ·ried ·ry·ing
harsh′ness
har′te·beest′
har′um-scar′um
har′vest·er
has′-been′
ha′sen·pfef′fer
hash′ish *or* ·eesh
has′sle
 ·sled ·sling

has'sock
haste
has'ten
hast'i·ly
hast'i·ness
hast'y
 ·i·er ·i·est
hat'band'
hatch'er·y
 ·ies
hatch'et
hatch'ing
hatch'way'
hate
 hat'ed hat'ing
hate'a·ble
hate'ful
hat'rack'
ha'tred
hat'ter
haugh'ti·ly
haugh'ti·ness
haugh'ty
 ·ti·er ·ti·est
haul'age
haunch
haunt'ed
haunt'ing
hau·teur'
have
 had hav'ing
have'lock
ha'ven
have'-not'

hav'er·sack'
hav'oc
Ha·wai'i
Ha·wai'ian
hawk
hawk'-eyed'
hawk'ish
haw'ser
hay fever
hay'field'
hay'loft'
hay'ride'
haz'ard
haz'ard·ous
haze
 hazed haz'ing
ha'zel·nut'
ha'zi·ly
ha'zi·ness
ha'zy
 ·zi·er ·zi·est
H'-bomb'
head'ache'
head'board'
head'cheese'
head'dress'
head'first'
head'gear'
head'hunt'er
head'i·ly
head'i·ness
head'land
head'less
head'light'

head'line'
head'long'
head'man
head'mas'ter
head'mis'tress
head'-on'
head'phone'
head'piece'
head'quar'ters
head'rest'
head'room'
head'set'
head'stand'
head start
head'stock'
head'strong'
head'wait'er
head'wa'ters
head'way'
head wind
head'y
 ·i·er ·i·est
heal
 (*cure;* SEE heel)
health'ful
health'i·ly
health'i·ness
health'y
 ·i·er ·i·est
heap
hear
 heard hear'ing
hear'ken
hear'say'

hearse
heart'ache'
heart'beat'
heart'break'
heart'bro'ken
heart'burn'
heart'en
heart'felt'
hearth'stone'
heart'i·ly
heart'i·ness
heart'less
heart'-rend'ing
heart'sick'
heart'strings'
heart'-to-heart'
heart'warm'ing
heart'y
 ·i·er ·i·est
heat'ed·ly
heat'er
heath
hea'then
heath'er
heat'stroke'
heave
 heaved *or* hove
 heav'ing
heav'en·ly
heav'en·ward
heav'i·ly
heav'i·ness
heav'y
 ·i·er ·i·est

138

heav'y-du'ty
heav'y-hand'ed
heav'y-heart'ed
heav'y·set'
heav'y·weight'
He·bra'ic
He'brew
heck'le
 ·led ·ling
hec'tic
hec'ti·cal·ly
hec'to·graph'
hedge
 hedged
 hedg'ing
hedge'hop'
he'do·nism
he'do·nis'tic
heed'ful
heed'less
heel
 (*foot part;*
 SEE heal)
heft'y
 ·i·er ·i·est
heif'er
height
height'en
hei'nous
heir
 (*inheritor;* SEE
 air)
heir'ess
heir'loom'

hel'i·cal
hel'i·cop'ter
he'li·o·graph'
he'li·o·trope'
hel'i·port'
he'li·um
he'lix
 ·lix·es *or* ·li·ces'
hel'lion
hel·lo'
 ·los'
 ·loed' ·lo'ing
hel'met
helms'man
help'ful
help'ful·ly
help'less
hel'ter-skel'ter
hem
 hemmed
 hem'ming
he'ma·tol'o·gy
hem'i·sphere'
hem'i·spher'i·cal
hem'line'
he'mo·glo'bin
he'mo·phil'i·a
hem'or·rhage
 ·rhaged
 ·rhag·ing
hem'or·rhoid'
hem'stitch'
hence'forth'
hench'man

hen'na
  ·naed ·na·ing
hen'ner·y
  ·ies
hen'pecked'
hen'ry
  ·rys or ·ries
he·pat'ic
hep'a·ti'tis
hep'ta·gon'
her'ald
he·ral'dic
her'ald·ry
her·ba'ceous
her'bi·cide'
her'bi·vore'
her·biv'o·rous
herds'man
here'a·bout'
here·af'ter
here'by'
he·red'i·tar'y
he·red'i·ty
  ·ties
here·in'
here'in·af'ter
here's
her'e·sy
  ·sies
her'e·tic
he·ret'i·cal
here'to·fore'
here·with'
her'it·a·ble

her'it·age
her·maph'ro·dite'
her·met'i·cal·ly
her'mit
her'ni·a
  ·as or ·ae'
her'ni·ate'
  ·at'ed ·at'ing
he'ro
  ·roes
he·ro'ic
he·ro'i·cal·ly
her'o·in
  (narcotic)
her'o·ine
  (female hero)
her'o·ism
her'pes
her'ring·bone'
her·self'
hes'i·tan·cy
  ·cies
hes'i·tant
hes'i·tate'
  ·tat'ed ·tat'ing
hes'i·ta'tion
het'er·o·dox'
het'er·o·dox'y
  ·ies
het'er·o·dyne'
  ·dyned' ·dyn'ing
het'er·o·ge·ne'i·ty
  ·ties
het'er·o·ge'ne·ous

het'er·o·nym'
het'er·o·sex'u·al
heu·ris'tic
heu·ris'ti·cal·ly
hew
  hewed, hewed or
  hewn, hew'ing
  (chop; SEE hue)
hex'a·gon'
hex·ag'o·nal
hex'a·he'dron
  ·drons or ·dra
hey'day'
H'-hour'
hi·a'tus
  ·tus·es or ·tus
hi·ba'chi
hi'ber·nate'
  ·nat'ed ·nat'ing
hi'ber·na'tion
hi'ber·na'tor
hi·bis'cus
hic'cup or ·cough
  ·cuped or ·cupped
  ·cup·ing or
  ·cup·ping
hick'o·ry
  ·ries
hide
  hid, hid'den or
  hid, hid'ing
hide'a·way'
hide'bound'
hid'e·ous

hide′-out′
hie
  hied, hie′ing
  or hy′ing
hi·er·ar′chi·cal
hi′er·ar′chy
  ·chies
hi′er·o·glyph′ic
hi′-fi′
high′ball′
high′born′
high′boy′
high′bred′
high′brow′
high′chair′
high′-class′
high′er-up′
high′fa·lu′tin
high′-flown′
high′-grade′
high′hand′ed
high′-keyed′
high′land-er
high′-lev′el
high′light′
high′ly
high′-mind′ed
high′-pitched′
high′-pow′ered
high′-pres′sure
high′-priced′
high′-rise′
high′-sound′ing
high′-spir′it·ed

high′-strung′
high′-ten′sion
high′-test′
high′-toned′
high′way′
hi′jack′
hike
  hiked hik′ing
hi·lar′i·ous
hi·lar′i·ty
hill′i·ness
hill′ock
hill′side′
hill′y
  ·i·er ·i·est
him·self′
hind
  hind′er,
  hind′most′ *or*
  hind′er·most′
hin′der
hin′drance
hind′sight′
hinge
  hinged hing′ing
hin′ter·land′
hip′bone′
hip′pie
hip′po·drome′
hip′po·pot′a·mus
  ·mus·es *or* ·mi
hir′a·ble *or* hire′·
hire
  hired hir′ing

hire′ling
hiss′ing
his′ta·mine′
his·tol′o·gy
his·to′ri·an
his·tor′i·cal
his·tor′i·cal·ly
his′to·ry
  ·ries
his′tri·on′ic
hit
  hit hit′ting
hit′-and-run′
hitch′hike′
hith′er·to′
hit′-or-miss′
hives
hoard
  (*reserve;* SEE
  horde)
hoar′frost′
hoar′i·ness
hoarse
hoar′y
  ·i·er ·i·est
hob′ble
  ·bled ·bling
hob′by
  ·bies
hob′by·horse′
hob′gob′lin
hob′nail′
hob′nob′
  ·nobbed′ ·nob′bing

ho'bo
·bos *or* ·boes
hock'ey
ho'cus-po'cus
hodge'podge'
hoe
hoed hoe'ing
hoe'down'
hog'gish
hogs'head'
hog'tie'
·tied', ·ty'ing
or ·tie'ing
hog'wash'
hoi' pol·loi'
hoist
hold
held hold'ing
hold'out'
hold'o'ver
hold'up'
hole
holed hol'ing
hole'y
(*with holes;* SEE
holy, wholly)
hol'i·day'
ho'li·ly
ho'li·ness
hol'lan·daise'
hol'low
hol'lo·ware'
hol'ly
·lies

hol'ly·hock'
hol'o·caust'
ho·log'ra·phy
Hol'stein
hol'ster
ho'ly
·li·er ·li·est
·lies
(*sacred;* SEE
holey, wholly)
hom'age
hom'burg
home
homed hom'ing
home'bod'y
home'bred'
home'-brew'
home'com'ing
home'-grown'
home'land'
home'less
home'li·ness
home'ly
·li·er ·li·est
(*plain;* SEE
homey)
home'made'
home'mak'er
home'own'er
home'sick'
home'spun'
home'stead'
home'stretch'
home'ward

home'work'
home'y
hom'i·er
hom'i·est
(*cozy;* SEE
homely)
home'y·ness
hom'i·ci'dal
hom'i·cide'
hom'i·let'ics
hom'i·ly
·lies
hom'i·ny
ho'mo·ge·ne'i·ty
ho'mo·ge'ne·ous
ho·mog'e·nize'
·nized' ·niz'ing
hom'o·graph'
ho·mol'o·gous
hom'o·nym'
hom'o·phone'
Ho'mo sa'pi·ens'
ho'mo·sex'u·al
ho'mo·sex'u·
al'i·ty
hone
honed hon'ing
hon'est
hon'es·ty
hon'ey
·eys, ·eyed *or*
·ied, ·ey·ing
hon'ey·bee'
hon'ey·comb'

141

hon′ey·dew′
hon′ey·moon′
hon′ey·suck′le
hon′or·a·ble
hon′o·ra′ri·um
  ·ri·ums *or* ·ri·a
hon′or·ar′y
hon′or·if′ic
hood′ed
hood′lum
hood′wink′
hoof
hoof′beat′
hook′ah *or* ·a
hook′up′
hook′y
hoo′li·gan
hoop′la
hoot′en·an′ny
  ·nies
hop
  hopped hop′ping
hope
  hoped hop′ing
hope′ful
hope′ful·ly
hope′less
hop′per
horde
  hord′ed hord′ing
  (*crowd;* SEE
  hoard)
hore′hound′
ho·ri′zon

hor′i·zon′tal
hor·mo′nal
hor′mone
hor′net
horn′i·ness
horn′pipe′
horn′y
  ·i·er ·i·est
ho·rol′o·gy
hor′o·scope′
hor·ren′dous
hor′ri·ble
hor′ri·bly
hor′rid
hor′ri·fy′
  ·fied′ ·fy′ing
hor′ror
hors′ d′oeu′vre
  ·vres
horse′back′
horse′fly′
  ·flies′
horse′hair′
horse′hide′
horse′laugh′
horse′man
horse′play′
horse′pow′er
horse′rad′ish
horse′shoe′
  ·shoed′ ·shoe′ing
horse′tail′
horse′whip′
horse′wom′an

hors′i·ness
hors′y
  ·i·er ·i·est
hor′ta·to′ry
hor′ti·cul′ture
hor′ti·cul′tur·ist
ho·san′na
hose
  hosed hos′ing
ho′sier·y
hos′pice
hos′pi·ta·ble
hos′pi·ta·bly
hos′pi·tal
hos′pi·tal′i·ty
  ·ties
hos′pi·tal·i·za′tion
hos′pi·tal·ize′
  ·ized′ ·iz′ing
hos′tage
hos′tel
  (*inn;* SEE hostile)
hos′tel·ry
  ·ries
host′ess
hos′tile
  (*unfriendly;* SEE
  hostel)
hos′tile·ly
hos·til′i·ty
  ·ties
hos′tler
hot
  hot′ter hot′test

hot'bed'
hot'-blood'ed
hot'box'
ho·tel'
ho'tel·ier'
hot'foot'
·foots'
hot'head'ed
hot'house'
hot'-tem'pered
hound'ed
hour'glass'
hour'ly
house
  housed hous'ing
house'boat'
house'break'
  ·broke' ·bro'ken
  ·break'ing
house'clean'ing
house'dress'
house'coat'
house'fly'
  ·flies'
house'ful'
house'hold'
house'keep'er
house'lights'
house'maid'
house'man'
house'moth'er
house organ
house party
house'-rais'ing

house'warm'ing
house'wife'
  ·wives'
house'work'
hous'ing
hov'el
  ·eled or ·elled
  ·el·ing or ·el·ling
hov'er
how'dah
how·ev'er
how'itz·er
howl'ing
how'so·ev'er
how'-to'
hoy'den
hua·ra'ches
hub'bub'
hub'cap'
huck'le·ber'ry
  ·ries
huck'ster
hud'dle
  ·dled ·dling
hue
  (color; SEE hew)
huff'i·ly
huff'i·ness
huff'y
  ·i·er ·i·est
hug
  hugged hug'ging
huge'ness
hulk'ing

hul'la·ba·loo'
hum
  hummed
  hum'ming
hu'man
hu·mane'
hu'man·ism
hu'man·is'tic
hu'man·is'ti·cal·ly
hu·man'i·tar'i·an
hu·man'i·ty
  ·ties
hu'man·ize'
  ·ized' ·iz'ing
hu'man·kind'
hu'man·ly
hu'man·ness
hu'man·oid'
hum'ble
  ·bler ·blest
  ·bled ·bling
hum'bly
hum'bug'
hum'drum'
hu·mec'tant
hu'mer·us
  ·mer·i'
  (bone; SEE
  humorous)
hu'mid
hu·mid'i·fi·ca'tion
hu·mid'i·fi'er
hu·mid'i·fy'
  ·fied' ·fy'ing

143

hu·mid'i·ty
hu'mi·dor'
hu·mil'i·ate'
 ·at'ed ·at'ing
hu·mil'i·a'tion
hu·mil'i·ty
hum'ming·bird'
hum'mock
hu'mor
hu'mor·esque'
hu'mor·ist
hu'mor·ous
 (*funny;* SEE
 humerus)
hump'back'
hu'mus
hunch'back'
hun'dred·fold'
hun'dredth
hun'dred·weight'
hun'ger
hun'gri·ly
hun'gri·ness
hun'gry
 ·gri·er ·gri·est
hunt'er
hunt'ress
hunts'man
hur'dle
 ·dled ·dling
 (*barrier;* SEE
 hurtle)
hur'dy-gur'dy
hurl'er

hurl'y-burl'y
hur·rah'
hur'ri·cane'
hur'ried·ly
hur'ry
 ·ried ·ry·ing
hurt
 hurt hurt'ing
hurt'ful
hur'tle
 ·tled ·tling
 (*rush;* SEE hurdle)
hus'band
hus'band·ry
hush'-hush'
husk'i·ly
husk'i·ness
hus'ky
 ·kies
 (*dog*)
husk'y
 ·i·er ·i·est, ·ies
 (*hoarse; robust*)
hus'sy
 ·sies
hus'tle
 ·tled ·tling
hus'tler
hy'a·cinth'
hy'brid
hy'brid·ize'
 ·ized' ·iz'ing
hy·dran'ge·a
hy'drant

hy'drate
 ·drat·ed ·drat·ing
hy'dra·tor
hy·drau'lic
hy'dro·chlo'ric
hy'dro·dy·nam'ics
hy'dro·e·lec'tric
hy'dro·foil'
hy'dro·gen
hy'dro·gen·ate'
 ·at'ed ·at'ing
hy'dro·gen·a'tion
hy'dro·ki·net'ics
hy·drol'o·gy
hy·drol'y·sis
hy'dro·lyt'ic
hy·dro·me·
 chan'ics
hy·drom'e·ter
hy'dro·naut'
hy'dro·pho'bi·a
hy'dro·plane'
hy'dro·pon'ics
hy'dro·ski'
hy'dro·stat'ics
hy'dro·ther'a·py
hy'drous
hy·e'na
hy'giene
hy'gi·en'ic
hy'gi·en'i·cal·ly
hy'gi·en·ist
hy·grom'e·ter
hy'gro·scope'

hy'men
hy'me·ne'al
hymn
hym'nal
hym·nol'o·gy
hy'per·a·cid'i·ty
hy'per·ac'tive
hy·per'bo·la
  (*curve*)
hy·per'bo·le
  (*exaggeration*)
hy'per·bol'ic
hy'per·crit'i·cal
  (*too critical;* SEE
  hypocritical)
hy'per·sen'si·tive
hy'per·son'ic
hy'per·ten'sion
hy'per·ven'ti·
  la'tion
hy'phen
hy'phen·ate'
  ·at'ed ·at'ing
hy'phen·a'tion
hyp·no'sis
  ·ses
hyp·not'ic
hyp·not'i·cal·ly
hyp'no·tism
hyp'no·tiz'a·ble
hyp'no·tize'
  ·tized' ·tiz'ing
hy'po·chon'dri·a
hy'po·chon'dri·ac'

hy'po·chon·
  dri'a·cal
hy'po·chon·
  dri'a·sis
hy·poc'ri·sy
  ·sies
hyp'o·crite
hyp'o·crit'i·cal
  (*deceitful;* SEE
  hypercritical)
hy'po·der'mic
hy·pot'e·nuse'
hy·poth'e·cate'
  ·cat'ed ·cat'ing
hy·poth'e·sis
  ·ses'
hy·poth'e·size'
  ·sized' ·siz'ing
hy'po·thet'i·cal
hy'po·thet'i·cal·ly
hys'ter·ec'to·my
  ·mies
hys·te'ri·a
hys·ter'ic
hys·ter'i·cal
hys·ter'i·cal·ly

I

i·am'bic
ice
iced ic'ing

ice'berg'
ice'bound'
ice'box'
ice'break'er
ice'cap'
ice cream
ice field
ice'house'
ice'man'
ice milk
ich'thy·ol'o·gy
i'ci·cle
i'ci·ly
i'ci·ness
ic'ing
i'con
i·con'ic
i·con'o·clast'
i'cy
  i'ci·er i'ci·est
I'da·ho'
i·de'a
i·de'al
i·de'al·ism
i·de'al·ist
i'de·al·is'tic
i·de·al·is'ti·cal·ly
i·de'al·i·za'tion
i·de'al·ize'
  ·ized' ·iz'ing
i·de'al·ly
i'de·ate'
  ·at'ed ·at'ing
i'de·a'tion

i·den'ti·cal
i·den'ti·cal·ly
i·den'ti·fi'a·ble
i·den'ti·fi·ca'tion
i·den'ti·fi'er
i·den'ti·fy'
 ·fied' ·fy'ing
i·den'ti·ty
 ·ties
id'e·o·gram'
id'e·o·graph'ic
i'de·o·log'i·cal
i'de·o·log'i·cal·ly
i'de·ol'o·gist
i'de·ol'o·gize'
 ·gized' ·giz'ing
i'de·ol'o·gy
 ·gies
id'i·o·cy
id'i·om
id'i·o·mat'ic
id'i·o·mat'i·cal·ly
id'i·o·syn'cra·sy
 ·sies
id'i·o·syn·crat'ic
id'i·ot
id'i·ot'ic
id'i·ot'i·cal·ly
i'dle
 i'dler i'dlest
 i'dled i'dling
 (*not active;* SEE
 idol, idyll)
i'dle·ness

i'dler
i'dly
i'dol
 (*image worshiped;*
 SEE idle, idyll)
i·dol'a·ter
i·dol'a·trous
i·dol'a·try
i'dol·ize'
 ·ized' ·iz'ing
i'dyll *or* i'dyl
 (*pastoral poem;*
 SEE idle, idol)
i·dyl'lic
ig'loo
 ·loos
ig'ne·ous
ig·nit'a·ble
 or ·i·ble
ig·nite'
 ·nit'ed ·nit'ing
ig·ni'tion
ig·no'ble
ig'no·min'i·ous
ig'no·min'y
 ·ies
ig'no·ra'mus
ig'no·rance
ig'no·rant
ig·nore'
 ·nored' ·nor'ing
i·gua'na
il'e·um
 (*intestine*)

il'i·um
 (*bone*)
ill
 worse worst
ill'-ad·vised'
ill'-be'ing
ill'-bod'ing
ill'-bred'
ill'-con·sid'ered
ill'-dis·posed'
il·le'gal
il'le·gal'i·ty
 ·ties
il·le'gal·ly
il'leg·i·bil'i·ty
il·leg'i·ble
il·leg'i·bly
il'le·git'i·ma·cy
 ·cies
il'le·git'i·mate
il'le·git'i·mate·ly
ill'-fat'ed
ill'-fa'vored
ill'-found'ed
ill'-got'ten
ill'-hu'mored
il·lib'er·al
il·lic'it
 (*unlawful;* SEE
 elicit)
il·lim'it·a·ble
il·lim'it·a·bly
Il'li·nois'
il·lit'er·a·cy

il·lit'er·ate
il·lit'er·ate·ly
ill'-man'nered
ill'-na'tured
ill'ness
il·log'i·cal
il·log'i·cal·ly
ill'-sort'ed
ill'-spent'
ill'-starred'
ill'-suit'ed
ill'-tem'pered
ill'-timed'
ill'-treat'
il·lu'mi·nate'
·nat'ed ·nat'ing
il·lu'mi·na'tion
il·lu'mi·na'tor
ill'-us'age
ill'-use'
il·lu'sion
(*false idea;* SEE
allusion, elusion)
il·lu'sive
(*deceptive;* SEE
allusive, elusive)
il·lu'so·ri·ly
il·lu'so·ri·ness
il·lu'so·ry
il'lus·trate'
·trat'ed ·trat'ing
il'lus·tra'tion
il·lus'tra·tive
il'lus·tra'tor

il·lus'tri·ous
im'age
·aged ·ag·ing
im'age·ry
·ries
i·mag'i·na·ble
i·mag'i·na·bly
i·mag'i·nar'i·ness
i·mag'i·nar'y
i·mag'i·na'tion
i·mag'i·na·tive
i·mag'ine
·ined ·in·ing
im'ag·ism
im·bal'ance
im'be·cile
im'be·cil'ic
im'be·cil'i·ty
·ties
im·bibe'
·bibed' ·bib'ing
im·bib'er
im'bri·cate'
·cat'ed ·cat'ing
im'bri·ca'tion
im·bro'glio
·glios
im·brue'
·brued' ·bru'ing
im·bue'
·bued' ·bu'ing
im'i·ta·ble
im'i·tate'
·tat'ed ·tat'ing

im'i·ta'tion
im'i·ta'tive
im'i·ta'tor
im·mac'u·late
im'ma·nent
(*inherent;* SEE
imminent)
im·ma·te'ri·al
im·ma·ture'
im·ma·tu'ri·ty
im·meas'ur·a·ble
im·me'di·a·cy
im·me'di·ate
im·me'di·ate·ly
im'me·mo'ri·al
im·mense'
im·mense'ly
im·men'si·ty
im·merge'
·merged'
·merg'ing
(*plunge;* SEE
emerge)
im·mer'gence
im·merse'
·mersed'
·mers'ing
im·mers'i·ble
im·mer'sion
im'mi·grant
im'mi·grate'
·grat'ed ·grat'ing
im'mi·gra'tion
im'mi·nence

im'mi·nent
(*impending;* SEE
eminent,
immanent)
im·mis'ci·ble
im·mit'i·ga·ble
im·mo'bile
im·mo·bil'i·ty
im·mo'bi·li·
za'tion
im·mo'bi·lize'
·lized' ·liz'ing
im·mod'er·ate
im·mod'er·a'tion
im·mod'est
im·mod'es·ty
im'mo·late'
·lat'ed ·lat'ing
im'mo·la'tion
im·mor'al
im'mo·ral'i·ty
·ties
im·mor'tal
im'mor·tal'i·ty
im·mor'tal·i·
za'tion
im·mor'tal·ize'
·ized' ·iz'ing
im·mov'a·bil'i·ty
im·mov'a·ble
im·mune'
im·mu'ni·ty
·ties
im'mu·ni·za'tion

im'mu·nize'
·nized' ·niz'ing
im'mu·nol'o·gy
im·mure'
·mured' ·mur'ing
im·mu'ta·bil'i·ty
im·mu'ta·ble
im·mu'ta·bly
im·pact'ed
im·pac'tion
im·pair'
im·pale'
·paled' ·pal'ing
im'pal·pa·bil'i·ty
im·pal'pa·ble
im·pan'el
·eled *or* ·elled
·el·ing *or* ·el·ling
im·part'
im·part'a·ble
im·par'tial
im'par·ti·al'i·ty
im·part'i·ble
im·pas'sa·bil'i·ty
im·pass'a·ble
(*not passable;*
SEE impassible)
im'passe
im·pas'si·bil'i·ty
im·pas'si·ble
(*unfeeling;* SEE
impassable)
im·pas'sioned
im·pas'sive

im·pas·siv'i·ty
im·pa'tience
im·pa'tient
im·peach'
im·peach'a·ble
im·pec'ca·bil'i·ty
im·pec'ca·ble
im·pec'ca·bly
im'pe·cu'ni·
os'i·ty
im'pe·cu'ni·ous
im·ped'ance
im·pede'
·ped'ed ·ped'ing
im·ped'i·ment
im·ped'i·men'ta
im·pel'
·pelled' ·pel'ling
im·pel'lent
im·pel'ler
im·pend'
im·pend'ing
im·pen'e·tra·
bil'i·ty
im·pen'e·tra·ble
im·pen'i·tence
im·pen'i·tent
im·per'a·tive
im'per·cep'ti·ble
im'per·cep'ti·bly
im·per'fect
im'per·fec'tion
im·per'fo·rate
im·pe'ri·al

im·pe′ri·al·ism
im·pe′ri·al·is′tic
im·pe′ri·al·ly
im·per′il
im·pe′ri·ous
im·per′ish·a·ble
im·per′ma·nent
im·per′me·a·ble
im′per·mis′si·ble
im·per′son·al
im·per′son·al′i·ty
im·per′son·al·ize′
im·per′son·ate′
·at′ed ·at′ing
im·per′son·a′tion
im·per′son·a′tor
im·per′ti·nence
im·per′ti·nent
im′per·turb′a·
bil′i·ty
im′per·turb′a·ble
im·per′vi·ous
im·pe·ti′go
im·pet′u·os′i·ty
im·pet′u·ous
im′pe·tus
im·pi′e·ty
·ties
im·pinge′
·pinged′ ·ping′ing
im·pinge′ment
im′pi·ous
imp′ish
im·pla′ca·ble

im·plant′
im′plan·ta′tion
im·plau′si·ble
im′ple·ment
im′ple·men′tal
im′ple·men·ta′tion
im′pli·cate′
·cat′ed ·cat′ing
im′pli·ca′tion
im′pli·ca′tive
im·plic′it
im·plode′
·plod′ed ·plod′ing
im·plore′
·plored′ ·plor′ing
im·plo′sion
im·ply′
·plied′ ·ply′ing
im·po·lite′
im·pol′i·tic
im·pon′der·a·ble
im·port′
im·port′a·ble
im·por′tance
im·por′tant
im′por·ta′tion
im·port′er
im·por′tu·nate
im′por·tune′
·tuned′ ·tun′ing
im′por·tu′ni·ty
·ties
im·pose′
·posed′ ·pos′ing

im′po·si′tion
im·pos′si·bil′i·ty
·ties
im·pos′si·ble
im′post
im·pos′tor
(deceiver)
im·pos′ture
(deception)
im′po·tence
im′po·tent
im·pound′
im·pov′er·ish
im·prac′ti·ca·
bil′i·ty
im·prac′ti·ca·ble
im·prac′ti·cal
im′pre·cate′
·cat′ed ·cat′ing
im′pre·ca′tion
im′pre·cise′
im·preg′na·bil′i·ty
im·preg′na·ble
im·preg′nate
·nat·ed ·nat·ing
im′preg·na′tion
im′pre·sa′ri·o
·ri·os
im′pre·scrip′ti·ble
im·press′
im·press′i·ble
im·pres′sion
im·pres′sion·a·ble
im·pres′sion·a·bly

im·pres′sion·ism
im·pres′sive
im·pres′sive·ly
im·pri′ma′tur
im·print′
im·pris′on
im·prob′a·ble
im·promp′tu
im·prop′er
im′pro·pri′e·ty
·ties
im·prov′a·ble
im·prove′
·proved′ ·prov′ing
im·prove′ment
im·prov′i·dent
im·prov′i·sa′tion
im′pro·vise′
·vised′ ·vis′ing
im·pru′dence
im·pru′dent
im′pu·dence
im′pu·dent
im·pugn′
im·pugn′a·ble
im′pulse
im·pul′sion
im·pul′sive
im·pul′sive·ly
im·pu′ni·ty
im·pure′
im·pu′ri·ty
·ties
im·put′a·bil′i·ty

im·put′a·ble
im′pu·ta′tion
im·put′a·tive
im·pute′
·put′ed ·put′ing
in′a·bil′i·ty
in′ac·ces′si·ble
in·ac′cu·ra·cy
·cies
in·ac′cu·rate
in·ac′tion
in·ac′ti·vate′
·vat′ed ·vat′ing
in·ac′ti·va′tion
in·ac′tive
in′ac·tiv′i·ty
in·ad′e·qua·cy
·cies
in·ad′e·quate
in′ad·mis′si·ble
in′ad·vert′ence
in′ad·vert′ent
in′ad·vis′a·bil′i·ty
in′ad·vis′a·ble
in·al′ien·a·ble
in·al′ter·a·ble
in·ane′
in·an′i·mate
in·an′i·ty
·ties
in·ap′pli·ca·ble
in′ap·pre′ci·a·ble
in′ap·proach′a·ble
in′ap·pro′pri·ate

in′ar·tic′u·late
in′ar·tis′tic
in′as·much′ as
in′at·ten′tion
in′at·ten′tive
in·au′di·ble
in·au′gu·ral
in·au′gu·rate′
·rat′ed ·rat′ing
in′aus·pi′cious
in′board′
in′born′
in′bred′
·bred′ ·breed′ing
in·cal′cu·la·ble
in·cal′cu·la·bly
in′can·des′cence
in′can·des′cent
in′can·ta′tion
in′ca·pa·bil′i·ty
in·ca′pa·ble
in·ca·pac′i·tate′
·tat′ed ·tat′ing
in·ca·pac′i·ta′tion
in·ca·pac′i·ty
in·car′cer·ate′
·at′ed ·at′ing
in·car′cer·a′tion
in·car′nate
·nat·ed ·nat·ing
in′car·na′tion
in·cau′tioᴜs
in·cen′di·ar′y
·ies

in'cense
in·cense'
·censed' ·cens'ing
in·cen'tive
in·cep'tion
in·cep'tive
in·cer'ti·tude'
in·ces'sant
in'cest
in·ces'tu·ous
in·cho'ate
in'ci·dence
in'ci·dent
in'ci·den'tal
in'ci·den'tal·ly
in·cin'er·ate'
·at'ed ·at'ing
in·cin'er·a'tion
in·cin'er·a'tor
in·cip'i·ence
in·cip'i·ent
in·cise'
·cised' ·cis'ing
in·ci'sion
in·ci'sive
in·ci'sor
in·cite'
·cit'ed ·cit'ing
in·cit'er
in'ci·vil'i·ty
·ties
in·clem'en·cy
in·clem'ent
in·clin'a·ble

in·cli·na'tion
in·cline'
·clined' ·clin'ing
in'cli·nom'e·ter
in·clude'
·clud'ed
·clud'ing
in·clu'sion
in·clu'sive
in·co·er'ci·ble
in·cog·ni'to
·tos
in·cog'ni·zance
in·cog'ni·zant
in'co·her'ence
in'co·her'ent
in'com·bus'ti·ble
in'come
in'com'ing
in·com·men'su·
ra·ble
in·com·men'su·
rate
in·com·mode'
·mod'ed ·mod'ing
in'com·mo'di·ous
in'com·mu'ni·
ca·ble
in'com·mu'ni·
ca'do
in·com'pa·ra·ble
in'com·pat'i·
bil'i·ty
·ties

in'com·pat'i·ble
in·com'pe·tence
in·com'pe·tent
in'com·plete'
in'com·pre·
hen'si·ble
in'com·press'i·ble
in'com·put'a·ble
in'con·ceiv'a·ble
in'con·clu'sive
in·con'dite
in'con·form'i·ty
in·con'gru·ent
in·con·gru'i·ty
·ties
in·con'gru·ous
in·con'se·
quen'tial
in'con·sid'er·a·ble
in'con·sid'er·ate
in'con·sid'er·
ate·ly
in'con·sid'er·
a'tion
in'con·sis'ten·cy
·cies
in'con·sis'tent
in'con·sol'a·ble
in'con·spic'u·ous
in·con'stan·cy
in·con'stant
in'con·sum'a·ble
in'con·test'a·ble
in·con'ti·nent

151

in·con·trol'la·ble
in·con·tro·vert'i·ble
in·con·ven'ience
in·con·ven'ient
in·con·vert'i·ble
in'co·or'di·nate
in·cor'po·rate'
 ·rat'ed ·rat'ing
in·cor·po·ra'tion
in·cor'po·ra'tor
in·cor·po're·al
in·cor·rect'
in·cor'ri·gi·bil'i·ty
in·cor'ri·gi·ble
in·cor'ri·gi·bly
in·cor·rupt'
in·cor·rupt'i·ble
in·creas'a·ble
in·crease'
 ·creased'
 ·creas'ing
in·creas'ing·ly
in·cred'i·bil'i·ty
in·cred'i·ble
in·cred'i·bly
in·cre·du'li·ty
in·cred'u·lous
in'cre·ment
in'cre·men'tal
in·crim'i·nate'
 ·nat'ed ·nat'ing
in·crim'i·na'tion
in·crim'i·na·to'ry

in·crust'
in·crus·ta'tion
in'cu·bate'
 ·bat'ed ·bat'ing
in·cu·ba'tion
in'cu·ba·tor
in·cul'cate
 ·cat·ed ·cat·ing
in'cul·ca'tion
in·culp'a·ble
in'cul·pa'tion
in·cum'ben·cy
 ·cies
in·cum'bent
in·cu·nab'u·la
in·cur'
 ·curred'
 ·cur'ring
in·cur·a·bil'i·ty
in·cur'a·ble
in·cur'a·bly
in·cu'ri·ous
in·cur'sion
in·debt'ed
in·de'cen·cy
 ·cies
in·de'cent
in·de·ci'pher·
 a·ble
in·de·ci'sion
in·de·ci'sive
in·de·clin'a·ble
in·dec'o·rous
in·de·co'rum

in·deed'
in·de·fat'i·ga·ble
in·de·fat'i·ga·bly
in·de·fea'si·ble
in·de·fect'i·ble
in·de·fen'si·ble
in·de·fin'a·ble
in·def'i·nite
in·del'i·ble
in·del'i·bly
in·del'i·ca·cy
 ·cies
in·del'i·cate
in·dem'ni·fi·
 ca'tion
in·dem'ni·fy'
 ·fied' ·fy'ing
in·dem'ni·ty
 ·ties
in·dent'
in'den·ta'tion
in·den'tion
in·den'ture
 ·tured ·tur·ing
in·de·pend'ence
in·de·pend'ent
in'-depth'
in·de·scrib'a·ble
in·de·scrib'a·bly
in·de·struct'i·ble
in·de·ter'mi·na·
 ble
in·de·ter'mi·na·cy
in·de·ter'mi·nate

in'de·ter'mi·
  na'tion
in'dex
  ·dex·es *or* ·di·ces'
In'di·an'a
in'di·cate'
  ·cat'ed ·cat'ing
in'di·ca'tion
in·dic'a·tive
in'di·ca'tor
in·dict'
  (*accuse formally;*
  SEE indite)
in·dict'a·ble
in·dict'ment
in·dif'fer·ence
in·dif'fer·ent
in'di·gence
in·dig'e·nous
in'di·gent
in·di·gest'i·ble
in'di·ges'tion
in·dig'nant
in'dig·na'tion
in·dig'ni·ty
  ·ties
in'di·go'
in'di·rect'
in'di·rec'tion
in'dis·cern'i·ble
in'dis·creet'
  (*lacking prudence*)
in'dis·crete'
  (*not separated*)

in'dis·cre'tion
  (*indiscreet act*)
in'dis·crim'i·nate
in'dis·pen'sa·ble
in'dis·pose'
in'dis·po·si'tion
in'dis·pu'ta·ble
in'dis·sol'u·ble
in'dis·tinct'
in'dis·tinc'tive
in'dis·tin'guish·
  a·ble
in·dite'
  ·dit'ed ·dit'ing
  (*write;* SEE indict)
in'di·vid'u·al
in'di·vid'u·al·ism
in'di·vid'u·al·
  is'tic
in'di·vid'u·al'i·ty
in'di·vid'u·al·ize'
  ·ized' ·iz'ing
in'di·vid'u·al·ly
in'di·vid'u·ate'
  ·at'ed ·at'ing
in'di·vis'i·bil'i·ty
in'di·vis'i·ble
in·doc'tri·nate'
  ·nat'ed ·nat'ing
in·doc'tri·na'tion
in·doc'tri·na'tor
in'do·lence
in'do·lent
in·dom'i·ta·ble

in·dom'i·ta·bly
in'door'
in'doors'
in·dorse'
  ·dorsed'
  ·dors'ing
in·du'bi·ta·ble
in·du'bi·ta·bly
in·duce'
  ·duced' ·duc'ing
in·duce'ment
in·duct'
in·duct'ance
in·duct'ee'
in·duc'tile
in·duc'tion
in·duc'tive
in·duc'tor
in·dulge'
  ·dulged'
  ·dulg'ing
in·dul'gence
in·dul'gent
in'du·rate'
  ·rat'ed ·rat'ing
in'du·ra'tion
in·dus'tri·al
in·dus'tri·al·ism
in·dus'tri·al·ist
in·dus'tri·al·i·
  za'tion
in·dus'tri·al·ize'
  ·ized' ·iz'ing
in·dus'tri·ous

153

in'dus·try
 ·tries

in·e'bri·ate'
 ·at'ed ·at'ing

in·e'bri·a'tion

in·e·bri'e·ty

in·ed'i·ble

in·ed'u·ca·ble

in·ef'fa·ble

in·ef'fa·bly

in'ef·face'a·ble

in'ef·fec'tive

in'ef·fec'tu·al

in'ef·fi·ca'cious

in·ef'fi·ca·cy

in'ef·fi'cien·cy

in'ef·fi'cient

in'e·las'tic

in'e·las·tic'i·ty

in·el'e·gance

in·el'e·gant

in·el'i·gi·bil'i·ty

in·el'i·gi·ble

in'e·luc'ta·ble

in'e·lud'i·ble

in·ept'

in·ept'i·tude'

in'e·qual'i·ty
 ·ties

in·eq'ui·ta·ble

in·eq'ui·ty
 ·ties
 (*unfairness;*
 SEE iniquity)

in·e·rad'i·ca·ble

in·er'ra·ble

in·er'rant

in·ert'

in·er'tia

in'es·cap'a·ble

in'es·cap'a·bly

in'es·sen'tial

in·es'ti·ma·ble

in·ev'i·ta·bil'i·ty

in·ev'i·ta·ble

in·ev'i·ta·bly

in·ex·act'

in·ex·cus'a·ble

in'ex·haust'i·ble

in·ex'o·ra·ble

in'ex·pe'di·ent

in'ex·pen'sive

in'ex·pe'ri·ence

in·ex'pert

in·ex'pi·a·ble

in·ex'pli·ca·ble

in·ex'pli·ca·bly

in'ex·press'i·ble

in'ex·press'i·bly

in'ex·pres'sive

in'ex·ten'si·ble

in'ex·tin'guish·a·
 ble

in·ex'tri·ca·ble

in·ex'tri·ca·bly

in'fal·li·bil'i·ty

in·fal'li·ble

in·fal'li·bly

in'fa·mous

in'fa·my
 ·mies

in'fan·cy
 ·cies

in'fant

in·fan'ti·cide'

in'fan·tile'

in'fan·ti·lism

in'fan·try
 ·tries

in'fan·try·man

in·fat'u·ate'
 ·at'ed ·at'ing

in·fat'u·a'tion

in·fect'

in·fec'tion

in·fec'tious

in·fec'tive

in·fec'tor

in'fe·lic'i·tous

in'fe·lic'i·ty
 ·ties

in·fer'
 ·ferred'
 ·fer'ring

in·fer'a·ble

in'fer·ence

in'fer·en'tial

in·fe'ri·or

in·fe'ri·or'i·ty

in·fer'nal

in·fer'no
 ·nos

in·fer′tile
in·fest′
in′fi·del
in′fi·del′i·ty
 ·ties
in′field′
in′fil′trate
 ·trat·ed ·trat·ing
in′fil·tra′tion
in′fil·tra′tor
in′fi·nite
in′fi·nite·ly
in·fin·i·tes′i·mal
in·fin′i·tive
in·fin′i·ty
 ·ties
in·firm′
in·fir′ma·ry
 ·ries
in·fir′mi·ty
 ·ties
in·flame′
 ·flamed′
 ·flam′ing
in·flam′ma·ble
in′flam·ma′tion
in·flam′ma·to′ry
in·flat′a·ble
in·flate′
 ·flat′ed
 ·flat′ing
in·fla′tion
in·fla′tion·ar′y
in·flec′tion

in·flex′i·ble
in·flex′i·bly
in·flict′
in·flic′tion
in′-flight′
in′flow′
in′flu·ence
 ·enced ·enc·ing
in′flu·en′tial
in′flu·en′za
in′flux′
in·form′
in·for′mal
in′for·mal′i·ty
in·form′ant
in′for·ma′tion
in·form′a·tive
in·form′er
in·frac′tion
in·fran′gi·ble
in′fra·red′
in·fre′quent
in·fringe′
in·fringe′ment
in·fu′ri·ate′
 ·at·ed ·at·ing
in·fuse′
 ·fused′ ·fus′ing
in·fu′sion
in·gen′ious
 (clever; SEE
 ingenuous)
in′gé·nue′
in′ge·nu′i·ty

in·gen′u·ous
 (frank; SEE
 ingenious)
in·gest′
in·ges′tion
in·glo′ri·ous
in′got
in·grained′
in′grate
in·gra′ti·ate′
 ·at·ed ·at·ing
in·grat′i·tude′
in·gre′di·ent
in′gress
in′-group′
in′grown′
in·hab′it
in·hab′it·a·ble
in·hab′it·ant
in·hal′ant
in′ha·la′tion
in·hale′
 ·haled′ ·hal′ing
in·hal′er
in′har·mon′ic
in′har·mo′ni·ous
in·here′
 ·hered′ ·her′ing
in·her′ence
in·her′ent
in·her′it
in·her′it·a·ble
in·her′it·ance
in·her′i·tor

in·hib'it
in'hi·bi'tion
in·hib'i·tive
in·hib'i·tor
in·hos'pi·ta·ble
in'hos·pi·tal'i·ty
in'-house'
in·hu'man
in·hu·mane'
in·hu·man'i·ty
·ties
in·im'i·cal
in·im'i·ta·ble
in·iq'ui·tous
in·iq'ui·ty
·ties
(*wickedness*;
SEE inequity)
in·i'tial
·tialed *or* ·tialled
·tial·ing *or* ·tial·ling
in·i'tial·ly
in·i'ti·ate'
·at'ed ·at'ing
in·i'ti·a'tion
in·i'ti·a·tive
in·i'ti·a'tor
in·ject'
in·jec'tion
in·jec'tor
in'ju·di'cious
in·junc'tion
in'jure
·jured ·jur·ing

in·ju'ri·ous
in'ju·ry
·ries
in·jus'tice
ink'blot'
ink'ling
ink'y
·i·er ·i·est
in'laid'
in'land
in'-law'
in'lay'
·laid' ·lay'ing
·lays'
in'let
in'mate'
in me·mo'ri·am
in'most'
in'nards
in·nate'
in'ner·most'
in'ner·spring'
in·ner'vate
·vat·ed ·vat·ing
in'ning
inn'keep'er
in'no·cence
in'no·cent
in·noc'u·ous
in'no·vate'
·vat'ed ·vat'ing
in'no·va'tion
in'no·va'tive
in'no·va'tor

in'nu·en'do
·does *or* ·dos
in·nu'mer·a·ble
in·oc'u·late'
·lat'ed ·lat'ing
in·oc'u·la'tion
in'of·fen'sive
in·op'er·a·ble
in·op'er·a·tive
in·op'por·tune'
in·or'di·nate
in'or·gan'ic
in'pa'tient
in'put'
in'quest
in·qui'e·tude'
in·quire'
·quired'
·quir'ing
in'quir·y
·ies
in'qui·si'tion
in·quis'i·tive
in·quis'i·tor
in'road'
in·sane'
in·san'i·tar'y
in·san'i·ty
in·sa'ti·a·ble
in·scribe'
·scribed'
·scrib'ing
in·scrip'tion
in·scru'ta·bil'i·ty

in·scru'ta·ble
in'seam'
in'sect
in·sec'ti·cide'
in·se·cure'
in·se·cu'ri·ty
in·sem'i·nate'
 ·nat'ed ·nat'ing
in·sem'i·na'tion
in·sen'sate
in·sen'si·bil'i·ty
in·sen'si·ble
in·sen'si·tive
in·sen'si·tiv'i·ty
in·sep'a·ra·ble
in·sert'
in·ser'tion
in'-ser'vice
in'side'
in·sid'i·ous
in'sight'
in·sig'ni·a
in·sig·nif'i·cance
in·sig·nif'i·cant
in·sin·cere'
in·sin·cere'ly
in·sin·cer'i·ty
in·sin'u·ate'
 ·at'ed ·at'ing
in·sin'u·a'tion
in·sip'id
in'si·pid'i·ty
in·sist'
in·sist'ence

in·sist'ent
in'so·bri'e·ty
in'so·far'
in'sole'
in'so·lence
in'so·lent
in·sol'u·ble
in·sol'vent
in·som'ni·a
in·sou'ci·ance
in·sou'ci·ant
in·spect'
in·spec'tion
in·spec'tor
in'spi·ra'tion
in·spire'
 ·spired' ·spir'ing
in·spir'it
in'sta·bil'i·ty
in·stall' or ·stal'
 ·stalled' ·stall'ing
in·stal·la'tion
in·stall'ment
 or ·stal'ment
in'stance
in'stant
in·stan·ta'ne·ous
in·stan'ter
in·state'
 ·stat'ed ·stat'ing
in·stead'
in'step'
in'sti·gate'
 ·gat'ed ·gat'ing

in'sti·ga'tion
in'sti·ga'tor
in·still' or ·stil'
 ·stilled' ·still'ing
in'stinct
in·stinc'tive
in'sti·tute'
 ·tut'ed ·tut'ing
in'sti·tu'tion
in'sti·tu'tion·al·
 ize'
 ·ized' ·iz'ing
in·struct'
in·struc'tion
in·struc'tive
in·struc'tor
in'stru·ment
in'stru·men'tal
in'stru·men·
 tal'i·ty
in'stru·men·
 ta'tion
in·sub·or'di·nate
in·sub·or'di·
 na'tion
in'sub·stan'tial
in·suf'fer·a·ble
in·suf·fi'cien·cy
 ·cies
in·suf·fi'cient
in'su·lar
in'su·late'
 ·lat'ed ·lat'ing
in'su·la'tion

in·su·la·tor
in·su·lin
in·sult′
in·su′per·a·ble
in′sup·port′a·ble
in′sup·press′i·ble
in·sur′a·bil′i·ty
in·sur′a·ble
in·sur′ance
in·sure′
 ·sured′ ·sur′ing
in·sur′er
in·sur′gence
in·sur′gent
in′sur·mount′a·
 ble
in′sur·rec′tion
in·tact′
in·tagl′io
 ·ios
in′take′
in·tan′gi·ble
in′te·ger
in′te·gral
in′te·grate′
 ·grat′ed ·grat′ing
in′te·gra′tion
in·teg′ri·ty
in·teg′u·ment
in′tel·lect′
in′tel·lec′tu·al
in′tel·lec′tu·al·ize′
 ·ized′ ·iz′ing
in′tel·lec′tu·al·ly

in·tel′li·gence
in·tel′li·gent
in·tel′li·gent′si·a
in·tel′li·gi·bil′i·ty
in·tel′li·gi·ble
in·tel′li·gi·bly
In′tel·sat′
in·tem′per·ance
in·tem′per·ate
in·tend′
in·tend′ant
in·tense′
in·tense′ly
in·ten′si·fi·ca′tion
in·ten′si·fy′
 ·fied′ ·fy′ing
in·ten′si·ty
in·ten′sive
in·tent′
in·ten′tion
in·ten′tion·al
in·ten′tion·al·ly
in·ter′
 ·terred′ ·ter′ring
in′ter·act′
in′ter·ac′tion
in′ter·breed′
 ·bred′ ·breed′ing
in′ter·cede′
 ·ced′ed ·ced′ing
in′ter·cept′
in′ter·cep′tion
in′ter·cep′tor
in′ter·ces′sion

in′ter·change′
in′ter·change′a·
 ble
in′ter·com′
in′ter·com·mu′ni·
 cate′
in′ter·con·nect′
in′ter·course′
in′ter·de·nom′i·
 na′tion·al
in′ter·de·part′·
 men′tal
in′ter·de·pend′·
 ence
in′ter·dict′
in′ter·dis′ci·
 pli·nar′y
in′ter·est
in′ter·est·ed
in′ter·faith′
in′ter·fere′
 ·fered′ ·fer′ing
in′ter·fer′ence
in′ter·fer′on
in′ter·im
in·te′ri·or
in′ter·ject′
in′ter·jec′tion
in′ter·lace′
in′ter·leaf′
 ·leaves′
in′ter·leave′
 ·leaved′
 ·leav′ing

in'ter·lin'e·ar
in'ter·lin'ing
in'ter·lock'
in'ter·lo·cu'tion
in'ter·loc'u·tor
in'ter·loc'u·to'ry
in'ter·lope'
·loped' ·lop'ing
in'ter·lop'er
in'ter·lude'
in'ter·mar'riage
in'ter·mar'ry
in'ter·me'di·ar'y
·ar'ies
in'ter·me'di·ate
in·ter'ment
in'ter·mez'zo
·zos *or* ·zi
in·ter'mi·na·ble
in'ter·min'gle
in'ter·mis'sion
in'ter·mit'tent
in'tern
(*doctor*)
in·tern'
(*detain*)
in·ter'nal
in·ter'nal·ize'
·ized' ·iz'ing
in·ter'nal·ly
in'ter·na'tion·al
in'ter·ne'cine
in'tern·ee'
in'ter·nist

in·tern'ment
in'tern·ship'
in'ter·of'fice
in'ter·pen'e·
trate'
in'ter·per'son·al
in'ter·phone'
in'ter·plan'e·
tar'y
in'ter·play'
in·ter'po·late'
·lat'ed ·lat'ing
in'ter·po·la'tion
in'ter·pose'
in·ter'pret
in·ter'pre·ta'tion
in·ter'pret·er
in'ter·ra'cial
in'ter·re·late'
in'ter·re·la'tion
in·ter'ro·gate'
·gat'ed ·gat'ing
in·ter'ro·ga'tion
in·ter'rog'a·tive
in·ter'rog'a·tor
in·ter'rog'a·to'ry
in'ter·rupt'
in'ter·rup'tion
in'ter·scho·las'tic
in'ter·sect'
in'ter·sec'tion
in'ter·sperse'
·spersed'
·spers'ing

in'ter·sper'sion
in'ter·state'
in'ter·stel'lar
in·ter'stice
·stic·es
in'ter·twine'
in'ter·ur'ban
in'ter·val
in'ter·vene'
·vened' ·ven'ing
in'ter·ven'tion
in'ter·view'
in'ter·view'er
in'ter·weave'
·wove' ·wov'en
·weav'ing
in·tes'tate
in·tes'tin·al
in·tes'tine
in'ti·ma·cy
·cies
in'ti·mate
in'ti·ma'tion
in·tim'i·date'
·dat'ed ·dat'ing
in·tim'i·da'tion
in·tol'er·a·ble
in·tol'er·ance
in·tol'er·ant
in'to·na'tion
in·tone'
in·tox'i·cant
in·tox'i·cate'
·cat'ed ·cat'ing

in·tox'i·ca'tion
in·trac'ta·ble
in'tra·mu'ral
in'tra·mus·cu·lar
in·tran'si·gent
in·tran'si·tive
in'tra·state'
in'tra·u'ter·ine
in'tra·ve'nous
in·trep'id
in'tre·pid'i·ty
in'tri·ca·cy
·cies
in'tri·cate
in·trigue'
·trigued'
·trigu'ing
in·trin'sic
in'tro·duce'
·duced' ·duc'ing
in'tro·duc'tion
in'tro·duc'to·ry
in'tro·spec'tion
in'tro·spec'tive
in'tro·ver'sion
in'tro·vert'
in·trude'
·trud'ed
·trud'ing
in·trud'er
in·tru'sion
in·tru'sive
in·tu·i'tion
in·tu'i·tive

in'un·date'
·dat'ed ·dat'ing
in'un·da'tion
in·ure'
·ured' ·ur'ing
in·vade'
·vad'ed ·vad'ing
in·vad'er
in'va·lid
in·val'id
in·val'i·date'
·dat'ed ·dat'ing
in·val'i·da'tion
in·val'u·a·ble
in·val'u·a·bly
in·var'i·a·ble
in·var'i·a·bly
in·va'sion
in·vec'tive
in·veigh'
in·vei'gle
·gled ·gling
in·vent'
in·ven'tion
in·ven'tive
in·ven'tor
in'ven·to'ry
·ries, ·ried ·ry·ing
in·verse'
in·ver'sion
in·vert'
in·ver'te·brate
in·vert'i·ble
in·vest'

in·ves'ti·gate'
·gat'ed ·gat'ing
in·ves'ti·ga'tion
in·ves'ti·ga'tor
in·ves'ti·ture
in·vest'ment
in·vet'er·ate
in·vi'a·ble
in·vid'i·ous
in·vig'or·ate'
·at'ed ·at'ing
in·vin'ci·bil'i·ty
in·vin'ci·ble
in·vin'ci·bly
in·vi'o·la·ble
in·vi'o·late
in·vis'i·ble
in'vi·ta'tion
in·vite'
·vit'ed ·vit'ing
in'vo·ca'tion
in'voice
·voiced ·voic·ing
in·voke'
·voked' ·vok'ing
in·vol'un·tar'i·ly
in·vol'un·tar'y
in'vo·lute'
in·volve'
·volved'
·volv'ing
in·vul'ner·a·ble
in'ward
i'o·dine'

i'on
i'on·i·za'tion
i'on·ize'
  ·ized' ·iz'ing
i·on'o·sphere'
i·o'ta
I'o·wa
ip'e·cac'
ip'so fac'to
i·ras'ci·bil'i·ty
i·ras'ci·ble
i·rate'
ire'ful·ly
ir'i·des'cence
ir'i·des'cent
irk'some
i'ron·bound'
i'ron·clad'
i·ron'i·cal
i·ron'i·cal·ly
i'ron·stone'
i'ron·work'
i'ro·ny
  ·nies
ir·ra'di·ate'
ir·ra'di·a'tion
ir·ra'tion·al
ir·ra'tion·al'i·ty
ir·ra'tion·al·ly
ir're·claim'a·ble
ir'rec'on·cil'a·ble
ir're·cov'er·a·ble
ir're·deem'a·ble
ir're·duc'i·ble

ir·ref'u·ta·ble
ir·reg'u·lar
ir·reg'u·lar'i·ty
  ·ties
ir·rel'e·vant
ir're·li'gious
ir're·me'di·a·ble
ir're·mis'si·ble
ir're·mov'a·ble
ir·rep'a·ra·ble
ir're·place'a·ble
ir're·press'i·ble
ir're·proach'a·ble
ir're·sist'i·ble
ir·res'o·lute'
ir're·spec'tive
ir're·spon'si·ble
ir're·triev'a·ble
ir·rev'er·ence
ir·rev'er·ent
ir're·vers'i·ble
ir·rev'o·ca·ble
ir'ri·ga·ble
ir'ri·gate'
  ·gat'ed ·gat'ing
ir'ri·ga'tion
ir'ri·ta·bil'i·ty
ir'ri·ta·ble
ir'ri·ta·bly
ir'ri·tant
ir'ri·tate'
  ·tat'ed ·tat'ing
ir'ri·ta'tion
ir·rupt'

ir·rup'tion
i'sin·glass'
is'land
isle
  (*island;* SEE aisle)
is'let
  (*small island;*
  SEE eyelet)
is'n't
i'so·bar'
i'so·late'
  ·lat'ed ·lat'ing
i'so·la'tion
i'so·la'tion·ist
i'so·mer
i'so·met'ric
i'so·met'ri·cal·ly
i·sos'ce·les'
i'so·therm'
i'so·tope'
i'so·trop'ic
Is'ra·el
Is·rae'li
is'su·ance
is'sue
  ·sued ·su·ing
isth'mus
  ·mus·es *or* ·mi
i·tal'ic
i·tal'i·cize'
  ·cized' ·ciz'ing
itch'i·ness
itch'y
  ·i·er ·i·est

i'tem·ize'
 ·ized' ·iz'ing
it'er·ate'
 ·at'ed ·at'ing
it'er·a'tion
i·tin'er·ant
i·tin'er·ar'y
 ·ies
i·tin'er·ate'
 ·at'ed ·at'ing
its
 (of it)
it's
 (it is)
it·self'
I've
i'vied
i'vo·ry
 ·ries
i'vy
 i'vies

J

jab
 jabbed jab'bing
jab'ber
ja·bot'
ja'cinth
jack'al
jack'a·napes'
jack'ass'

jack'boot'
jack'et
jack'ham'mer
jack'-in-the-box'
 -box'es
jack'knife'
 ·knives'
 ·knifed' ·knif'ing
jack'-of-all'-
 trades'
 jacks'-
jack'-o'-lan'tern
 ·terns
jack'pot'
jack'screw'
jack'straw'
Jac·quard'
jade
 jad'ed jad'ing
jag'ged
jag'uar
jai' a·lai'
jail'bird'
jail'er or ·or
jal'ou·sie'
 (door; SEE
 jealousy)
jam
 jammed
 jam'ming
jam'ba·lay'a
jam'bo·ree'
jan'gle
 ·gled ·gling

jan'i·tor
Jan'u·ar'y
 ·ar'ies
ja·pan'
 ·panned'
 ·pan'ning
jar
 jarred jar'ring
jar'di·niere'
jar'gon
jas'mine
jas'per
ja'to or JA'TO
jaun'dice
 ·diced ·dic·ing
jaun'ti·ly
jaun'ti·ness
jaun'ty
 ·ti·er ·ti·est
jav'e·lin
jaw'bone'
jaw'break'er
Jay'cee'
jay'walk'er
jazz'i·ness
jazz'y
 ·i·er ·i·est
jeal'ous
jeal'ous·y
 ·ies
 (envy; SEE
 jalousie)
jeans
jeer'ing·ly

je·june′
jel′li·fy′
 ·fied′ ·fy′ing
jel′ly
 ·lies, ·lied ·ly·ing
jel′ly·fish′
jel′ly·roll′
jen′ny
 ·nies
jeop′ard·ize′
 ·ized′ ·iz′ing
jeop′ard·y
je·quir′i·ty
 ·ties
jer′e·mi′ad
jerk′i·ly
jer′kin
jerk′i·ness
jerk′wa′ter
jerk′y
 ·i·er ·i·est
 (*moving fitfully*)
jer′ky
 (*dried beef*)
Jer′sey
 ·seys
 (*dairy cattle*)
jer′sey
 ·seys
 (*cloth; shirt*)
jest′er
jet
 jet′ted jet′ting
jet′-black′

jet′lin′er
jet′port′
jet′-pro·pelled′
jet′sam
jet stream
jet′ti·son
jet′ty
 ·ties, ·tied ·ty·ing
jew′el
 ·eled *or* ·elled
 ·el·ing *or* ·el·ling
jew′el·er *or*
 ·el·ler
jew′el·ry
Jew′ish
Jew′ry
 ·ries
jew′s′-harp′ *or*
 jews′′-harp′
Jez′e·bel
jib
 jibbed jib′bing
jibe
 jibed jib′ing
 (*nautical; agree;*
 SEE gibe)
jig′ger
jig′gle
 ·gled ·gling
jig′saw′
Jim′-Crow′
jim′my
 ·mies
 ·mied ·my·ing

jin′gle
 ·gled ·gling
jin′go
 ·goes
jin′go·ism
jin′go·is′ti·cal·ly
jin·ni′
 jinn
jin·rik′i·sha
jinx
jit′ney
 ·neys
jit′ter·y
job
 jobbed job′bing
job′ber
jock′ey
 ·eys
 ·eyed ·ey·ing
jock′strap′
jo·cose′
jo·cos′i·ty
 ·ties
joc′u·lar
joc′u·lar′i·ty
joc′und
jo·cun′di·ty
jodh′purs
jog
 jogged jog′ging
jog′ger
jog′gle
 ·gled ·gling
john′ny·cake′

163

join'er
joint'ly
join'ture
joist
joke
  joked jok'ing
jol'li·ness
jol'li·ty
jol'ly
  ·li·er ·li·est
jon'quil
jos'tle
  ·tled ·tling
jot
  jot'ted jot'ting
jounce
  jounced
  jounc'ing
jour'nal
jour'nal·ese'
jour'nal·ism
jour'nal·is'tic
jour'ney
  ·neys
  ·neyed ·ney·ing
jour'ney·man
joust
jo'vi·al
jo'vi·al'i·ty
jo'vi·al·ly
jowl
joy'ful
joy'less
joy'ous

ju'bi·lant
ju'bi·la'tion
ju'bi·lee'
Ju·da'i·ca
Ju'da·ism
judge
  judged judg'ing
judg'ment or
  judge'·
ju'di·ca·to'ry
  ·ries
ju·di'cial
ju·di'ci·ar'y
  ·ies
ju·di'cious
ju'do
jug
  jugged jug'ging
jug'ger·naut'
jug'gle
  ·gled ·gling
jug'u·lar
juice
  juiced juic'ing
juic'er
juic'i·ly
juic'i·ness
juic'y
  ·i·er ·i·est
ju·jit'su or
ju·jut'su
ju'jube
juke'box'
ju'lep

ju'li·enne'
Ju·ly'
  ·lies'
jum'ble
  ·bled ·bling
jum'bo
jump'er
jump'i·ness
jump'y
  ·i·er ·i·est
junc'tion
junc'ture
June
jun'gle
jun'ior
jun·ior'i·ty
ju'ni·per
jun'ket
junk'man'
jun'ta
jun'to
  ·tos
ju·rid'i·cal
ju·rid'i·cal·ly
ju'ris·dic'tion
ju'ris·pru'dence
ju'rist
ju·ris'tic
ju'ror
ju'ry
  ·ries
ju'ry·man
jus'tice
jus'ti·fi'a·ble

jus'ti·fi'a·bly
jus'ti·fi·ca'tion
jus'ti·fy'
 ·fied' ·fy'ing
just'ly
jut
 jut'ted jut'ting
jute
ju'ven·ile
jux'ta·pose'
 ·posed' ·pos'ing
jux'ta·po·si'tion

K

Ka·bu'ki
kaf'fee·klatsch'
kai'ser
ka·lei'do·scope'
ka·lei'do·scop'ic
kal'so·mine'
ka'mi·ka'ze
kan'ga·roo'
Kan'sas
ka'o·lin
ka'pok
ka·put'
kar'a·kul
kar'at
ka·ra'te
ka'sha
ka'ty·did'

katz'en·jam'mer
kay'ak
ka·zoo'
ke·bab'
kedge
 kedged kedg'ing
keel'haul'
keel'son
keen'ness
keep
 kept keep'ing
keep'sake'
keg'ler
ke'loid
kempt
ken'nel
 ·neled or ·nelled
 ·nel·ing or
 ·nel·ling
Ken·tuck'y
ker'a·tin
ker'chief
ker'mis or ·mess
ker'nel
 (grain; SEE
 colonel)
ker'o·sene' or
 ·sine'
ker'sey
 ·seys
ketch'up
ke'tone
ket'tle
ket'tle·drum'

key
 keys
 keyed key'ing
 (lock; SEE quay)
key'board'
key club
key'hole'
key'note'
key punch
key'stone'
key'way'
kha'ki
kib'ble
kib·butz'
 kib'but·zim'
kib'itz·er
kick'off'
kid'nap
 ·napped' or
 ·naped'
 ·nap'ping or
 ·nap'ing
kid'nap'per or
 kid'nap·er
kid'ney
 ·neys
kill'er
kill'-joy'
kiln
kil'o·gram'
kil'o·hertz'
 ·hertz'
kil'o·li'ter
ki·lo'me·ter

kil′o·volt′
kil′o·watt′
kil′o·watt′-hour′
kil′ter
ki·mo′no
·nos
kin′der·gar′ten
kin′der·gart′ner
kind′heart′ed
kin′dle
·dled ·dling
kind′li·ness
kind′ly
·li·er ·li·est
kin′dred
kin′e·mat′ics
kin′e·scope′
ki·ne′sics
kin′es·thet′ic
ki·net′ic
kin′folk′
king′bolt′
king′dom
king′fish′
king′li·ness
king′ly
·li·er ·li·est
king′pin′
king post
king′-size′
kink′i·ness
kink′y
·i·er ·i·est
kin′ship′

kins′man
ki′osk
kis′met
kitch′en
kitch′en·ette′
kitch′en·ware′
kit′ten
kit′ty
·ties
kit′ty-cor′nered
klax′on
Klee′nex
klep′to·ma′ni·ac
klieg light
knack
knack′wurst′
knap′sack′
knave
(rogue; SEE nave)
knav′er·y
knav′ish
knead
(press; SEE need)
knee
kneed knee′ing
knee′cap′
knee′-deep′
knee′-high′
knee′hole′
kneel
knelt or kneeled
kneel′ing
knee′pad′
knell

knick′er·bock′ers
knick′knack′
knife
knives
knifed knif′ing
knife′-edge′
knight
(rank; SEE night)
knight′hood′
knit
knit′ted or knit
knit′ting
knit′ter
knob′by
·bi·er ·bi·est
knock′a·bout′
knock′down′
knock′-kneed′
knock′out′
knoll
knot
knot′ted
knot′ting
knot′hole′
knot′ty
·ti·er ·ti·est
know
knew known
know′ing
know′a·ble
know′-how′
know′-it-all′
knowl′edge
knowl′edge·a·ble

knowl'edge·a·bly
knuck'le
 ·led ·ling
knurled
ko·a'la
ko'di·ak' bear
kohl·ra'bi
 ·bies
Ko·ran'
ko'sher
kow'tow'
ku'chen
ku'dos
küm'mel
kum'quat
kwa'shi·or'kor

L

la'bel
 ·beled or ·belled
 ·bel·ing or
 ·bel·ling
la'bi·al
la'bile
la'bor
lab'o·ra·to'ry
 ·ries
la'bor·er
la·bo'ri·ous
la'bor-sav'ing
lab'y·rinth'

lab'y·rin'thine
lace
 laced lac'ing
lac'er·ate'
 ·at'ed ·at'ing
lac'er·a'tion
lace'work'
lach'ry·mose'
lac'i·ness
lack·a·dai'si·cal
lack'ey
 ·eys
lack'lus·ter
la·con'ic
la·con'i·cal·ly
lac'quer
la·crosse'
lac'tate
 ·tat·ed ·tat·ing
lac·ta'tion
lac'te·al
lac'tic
lac'tose
la·cu'na
 ·nas or ·nae
lac'y
 ·i·er ·i·est
lad'der
lad'en
lad'ing
la'dle
 ·dled ·dling
la'dy
 ·dies

la'dy·bug'
la'dy·fin'ger
la'dy·like'
la'dy·ship'
lag
 lagged lag'ging
la'ger
lag'gard
la·gniappe'
la·goon'
lair
 (den; SEE layer)
lais'sez faire'
la'i·ty
la'ma
 (monk; SEE llama)
la'ma·ser'y
 ·ies
lam·baste'
 ·bast'ed ·bast'ing
lam'bent
lamb'kin
lam'bre·quin
lamb'skin'
lame
 (crippled)
la·mé'
 (fabric)
la·ment'
lam'en·ta·ble
lam'en·ta'tion
lam'i·nate'
 ·nat'ed ·nat'ing
lam'i·na'tion

lamp'black'
lam·poon'
lamp'post'
lance
  lanced lanc'ing
lan'dau
land'fill'
land'hold'er
land'ing
land'la'dy
land'locked'
land'lord'
land'lub'ber
land'mark'
land'own'er
land'scape'
  ·scaped'
  ·scap'ing
land'slide'
lands'man
lan'guage
lan'guid
lan'guish
lan'guor
lan'guor·ous
lank'i·ness
lank'ness
lank'y
  ·i·er ·i·est
lan'o·lin
lan'tern
lan'yard
lap
  lapped lap'ping

la·pel'
lap'i·dar'y
  ·ies
lap'in
lap'is laz'u·li'
lapse
  lapsed laps'ing
lar'ce·nous
lar'ce·ny
lard'er
large
  larg'er larg'est
large'ly
large'-scale'
lar'gess or ·gesse
lar'i·at
lar'va
  ·vae or ·vas
la·ryn'ge·al
lar'yn·gi'tis
lar'ynx
  lar'ynx·es or
  la·ryn'ges
la·sa'gna
las·civ'i·ous
lase
  lased las'ing
  (*emit laser light;*
  SEE laze)
la'ser
lash'ing
las'si·tude'
las'so
  ·sos or ·soes

last'-ditch'
Las'tex
last'ing
latch'key'
latch'string'
late
  lat'er or lat'ter
  lat'est or last
la·teen'
late'ly
la'ten·cy
la'tent
lat'er·al
la'tex
  lat'i·ces' or
  la'tex·es
lath
  (*wood strip*)
lathe
  lathed lath'ing
  (*machine*)
lath'er
lath'ing
lat'i·tude'
lat'ke
  ·kes
la·trine'
lat'ter-day'
lat'tice
  ·ticed ·tic·ing
lat'tice·work'
laud'a·ble
laud'a·bly
laud'a·to'ry

laugh'a·ble
laugh'ing·stock'
laugh'ter
laun'der
laun'dress
laun'dro·mat'
laun'dry
·dries
laun'dry·man
lau're·ate
lau'rel
la'va
la·va'bo
·boes
lav'a·liere'
lav'a·to'ry
·ries
lav'en·der
lav'ish
law'-a·bid'ing
law'break'er
law'ful
law'ful·ly
law'giv'er
law'less
law'mak'er
lawn mower
law'suit'
law'yer
lax'a·tive
lax'i·ty
lay
  laid lay'ing
  (*put;* SEE lie)

lay'er
  (*stratum;* SEE
  lair)
lay·ette'
lay'man
lay'off'
lay'out'
lay'o·ver
laze
  lazed laz'ing
  (*loaf;* SEE lase)
la'zi·ly
la'zi·ness
la'zy
  ·zi·er ·zi·est
leach
  (*filter;* SEE leech)
lead
  led lead'ing
lead'en
lead'er·ship'
lead'-in'
lead'off'
leaf
  leaves
leaf'let
leaf'y
  ·i·er ·i·est
league
  leagued
  leagu'ing
leagu'er
leak
  (*escape;* SEE leek)

leak'age
leak'y
  ·i·er ·i·est
lean
  leaned *or* leant
  lean'ing
lean
  (*thin;* SEE lien)
lean'ness
lean'-to'
  -tos'
leap
  leaped *or* leapt
  leap'ing
leap'frog'
  ·frogged'
  ·frog'ging
learn
  learned *or* learnt
  learn'ing
learn'ed *adj.*
leas'a·ble
lease
  leased leas'ing
lease'-back'
lease'hold'er
least
leath'er
leath'er·ette'
leath'er·i·ness
leath'er·y
leave
  left leav'ing
  (*let stay*)

169

leave
  leaved leav′ing
  (*bear leaves*)
leav′en·ing
leave′-tak·ing
lech′er·ous
lec′i·thin
lec′tern
lec′ture
  ·tured ·tur·ing
ledge
ledg′er
leech
  (*worm;* SEE
  leach)
leek
  (*vegetable;* SEE
  leak)
leer′y
  ·i·er ·i·est
lee′ward
lee′way′
left′-hand′ed
left′ist
left′o′ver
left′-wing′er
leg
  legged leg′ging
leg′a·cy
  ·cies
le′gal·ese′
le·gal′i·ty
  ·ties
le′gal·i·za′tion

le′gal·ize′
  ·ized′ ·iz′ing
le′gal·ly
leg′a·tee′
le·ga′tion
le·ga′to
leg′end
leg′end·ar′y
leg′er·de·main′
leg′gi·ness
leg′gy
  ·gi·er ·gi·est
leg′i·bil′i·ty
leg′i·ble
leg′i·bly
le′gion
le′gion·naire′
leg′is·late′
  ·lat′ed ·lat′ing
leg′is·la′tion
leg′is·la′tive
leg′is·la′tor
leg′is·la′ture
le·git′i·ma·cy
le·git′i·mate
le·git′i·mize′
  ·mized′ ·miz′ing
leg′man′
leg′room′
leg′ume
lei
lei′sure
lei′sure·ly
lem′on·ade′

lend
  lent lend′ing
length′en
length′i·ness
length′wise′
length′y
  ·i·er ·i·est
le′ni·en·cy
le′ni·ent
len′i·tive
len′i·ty
lens
len′til
  (*pea;* SEE lintel)
leop′ard
le′o·tard′
lep′er
lep′re·chaun′
lep′ro·sy
lep′rous
les′bi·an
le′sion
les·see′
less′en
  (*make less*)
less′er
  (*smaller*)
les′son
  (*instruction*)
les′sor
  (*one who leases*)
let
  let let′ting
let′down′

le'thal
le·thar'gic
le·thar'gi·cal·ly
leth'ar·gize'
·gized' ·giz'ing
leth'ar·gy
let'tered
let'ter·head'
let'ter·per'fect
let'ter·press'
let'tuce
let'up'
leu·ke'mi·a
lev'ee
·eed ·ee·ing
(embankment;
SEE levy)
lev'el
·eled or ·elled
·el·ing or ·el·ling
lev'el·head'ed
lev'el·ly
lev'er·age
lev'i·a·ble
lev'i·er
le'vis
lev'i·tate'
·tat'ed ·tat'ing
lev'i·ta'tion
lev'i·ty
lev'y
·ies, ·ied ·y·ing
(tax; SEE levee)
lewd'ness

lex'i·cog'ra·pher
lex'i·con
li·a·bil'i·ty
·ties
li'a·ble
(likely; SEE libel)
li'ai·son'
li'ar
(one who tells
lies; SEE lyre)
li·ba'tion
li'bel
·beled or ·belled
·bel·ing or
·bel·ling
(defame; SEE
liable)
li'bel·ous or
·bel·lous
lib'er·al
lib'er·al'i·ty
lib'er·al·ize'
·ized' ·iz'ing
lib'er·ate'
·at'ed ·at'ing
lib'er·a'tion
lib'er·a'tor
lib'er·tar'i·an
lib'er·tine'
lib'er·ty
·ties
li·bid'i·nous
li·bi'do
li·brar'i·an

li'brar'y
·ies
li·bret'tist
li·bret'to
·tos or ·ti
Lib'ri·um
li'cense
·censed ·cens·ing
li·cen'tious
li'chen
lic'it
lic'o·rice
lie
lay lain ly'ing
(to rest; SEE lay)
lie
lied ly'ing
(tell falsehood;
SEE lye)
li'en
(claim; SEE lean)
lieu
lieu·ten'an·cy
lieu·ten'ant
life
lives
life belt
life'blood'
life'boat'
life buoy
life'-giv'ing
life'guard'
life'less
life'like'

171

life'line'
life'long'
life'sav'er
life'-size'
life'time'
life'work'
lift'off'
lig'a·ment
lig'a·ture
·tured ·tur·ing
light
light'ed *or* lit
light'ing
light'en
·ened ·en·ing
(*make light or less heavy;* SEE lightning)
light'face'
light'-fin'gered
light'-foot'ed
light'-hand'ed
light'head'ed
light'heart'ed
light'house'
light'ly
light'-mind'ed
light'ning
(*flash of light;* SEE lighten)
light'weight'
light'-year'
lig'ne·ous
lig'nite
lik'a·ble *or* like'·

like
liked lik'ing
like'li·hood'
like'ly
like'-mind'ed
lik'en
like'ness
like'wise'
li'lac
Lil'li·pu'tian
lil'y
·ies
lil'y-liv'ered
lil'y-white'
limb
(*branch;* SEE limn)
lim'ber
lim'bo
lime
limed lim'ing
lime'light'
lim'er·ick
lime'stone'
lim'it·a·ble
lim'i·ta'tion
lim'it·ed
limn
(*draw;* SEE limb)
lim'ou·sine'
lim'pid
limp'ness
lin'age *or* line'·
(*number of lines;* SEE lineage)

linch'pin'
Lin'coln
lin'den
line
lined lin'ing
lin'e·age
(*ancestry;* SEE linage)
lin'e·al
lin'e·a·ment
(*feature;* SEE liniment)
lin'e·ar
line'man
lin'en
lin'er
lines'man
line'up'
lin'ger
lin'ge·rie'
lin'go
·goes
lin'gual
lin'guist
lin·guis'tics
lin'i·ment
(*medication;* SEE lineament)
lin'ing
link'age
links
(*golf course;* SEE lynx)
li·no'le·um

lin'o·type'
lin'seed'
lin'sey-wool'sey
lin'tel
　(*beam;* SEE lentil)
li'on·ess
li'on·heart'ed
lip'-read'
　-read' -read'ing
lip'stick'
lip'-sync'
liq'ue·fac'tion
liq'ue·fi'a·ble
liq'ue·fi'er
liq'ue·fy'
　·fied' ·fy'ing
li·ques'cent
li·queur'
liq'uid
liq'ui·date'
　·dat'ed ·dat'ing
liq'ui·da'tion
liq'ui·da'tor
liq'uor
lisle
lisp'ing·ly
lis'some *or* ·som
lis'ten
list'less
lit'a·ny
　·nies
li'tchi nut
li'ter
lit'er·a·cy

lit'er·al
　(*exact;* SEE
　littoral)
lit'er·al·ly
lit'er·ar'y
lit'er·ate
lit'er·a·ture
lithe'ly
lith'o·graph'
li·thog'ra·pher
li·thog'ra·phy
lith'o·sphere'
lit'i·ga·ble
lit'i·gant
lit'i·gate'
　·gat'ed ·gat'ing
lit'i·ga'tion
lit'mus
li'to·tes
lit'ter
lit'ter·bug'
lit'tle
　lit'tler *or* less *or*
　less'er, lit'tlest
　or least
lit'to·ral
　(*shore;* SEE
　literal)
li·tur'gi·cal
lit'ur·gy
　·gies
liv'a·ble *or* live'·
live
　lived liv'ing

live'li·hood'
live'li·ness
live'long'
live'ly
　·li·er ·li·est
liv'en
liv'er·wurst'
liv'er·y
　·ies
live'stock'
liv'id
liz'ard
lla'ma
　(*animal;* SEE
　lama)
load
　(*burden;* SEE lode)
load'stone'
loaf
　loaves
loaf'er
loam'y
　·i·er ·i·est
loan
　(*something lent;*
　SEE lone)
loath
　(*unwilling*)
loathe
　loathed loath'ing
　(*detest*)
loath'some
lob
　lobbed lob'bing

173

lob'by
·bies
·bied ·by·ing
lob'by·ist
lobe
lob'ster
lo'cal
lo·cale'
lo'cal·ism
lo·cal'i·ty
·ties
lo'cal·ize'
·ized' ·iz'ing
lo'cal·ly
lo'cate
·cat·ed ·cat·ing
lo·ca'tion
lock'er
lock'et
lock'out'
lock'smith'
lo'co·mo'tion
lo'co·mo'tive
lo'co·weed'
lo'cus
·ci
lo'cust
lo·cu'tion
lode
(*ore;* SEE load)
lode'stone'
lodge
lodged lodg'ing
(*house;* SEE loge)

lodg'er
lodg'ment
loft'i·ly
loft'i·ness
loft'y
·i·er ·i·est
log
logged log'ging
log'a·rithm
loge
(*theater box;*
SEE lodge)
log'ger·head'
log'gi·a
·gi·as
log'ic
log'i·cal
log'i·cal·ly
lo·gi'cian
lo·gis'tics
log'o·gram'
log'o·griph'
log'or·rhe'a
lo'gy
·gi·er ·gi·est
loin'cloth'
loi'ter
lol'li·pop' *or* ·ly·
lone
(*solitary;*
SEE loan)
lone'li·ness
lone'ly
·li·er ·li·est

lone'some
long'-dis'tance
long'-drawn'
lon·gev'i·ty
long'hand'
lon'gi·tude'
lon'gi·tu'di·nal
long'-lived'
long'-play'ing
long'-range'
long'-run'
long'shore'man
long'stand'ing
long'-suf'fer·ing
long'-term'
long'-wind'ed
look'er-on'
look'ers-on'
look'out'
loop'hole'
loose
loosed loos'ing
(*free;* SEE
lose, loss)
loose'-joint'ed
loose'-leaf'
loose'ly
loos'en
loose'-tongued'
lop
lopped lop'ping
lope
loped lop'ing
lop'sid'ed

lo·qua'cious
lo·quac'i·ty
lor·do'sis
lor·gnette'
lor'ry
  ·ries
lose
  lost los'ing
  (*mislay;* SEE
  loose, loss)
los'er
loss
  (*thing lost;* SEE
  loose, lose)
Lo·thar'i·o'
lo'tion
lot'ter·y
  ·ies
loud'mouthed'
loud'speak'er
Lou·i'si·an'a
lounge
  lounged
  loung'ing
louse
  lice
lout'ish
lou'ver
lov'a·ble *or*
  love'·
love
  loved lov'ing
love'li·ness
love'lorn'

love'ly
  ·li·er ·li·est
lov'ing·kind'ness
low'boy'
low'bred'
low'brow'
low'-cost'
low'-down'
low'er
low'er·class'man
low'-grade'
low'-key'
low'-lev'el
low'li·ness
low'ly
  ·li·er ·li·est
low'-mind'ed
low'-necked'
low'-pitched'
low'-spir'it·ed
lox
loy'al
loy'al·ly
loy'al·ty
  ·ties
loz'enge
lu·au'
lu'bri·cant
lu'bri·cate'
  ·cat'ed ·cat'ing
lu'bri·ca'tion
lu'bri·ca'tor
lu'cid
lu·cid'i·ty

luck'i·ly
luck'i·ness
luck'y
  ·i·er ·i·est
lu'cra·tive
lu'cre
lu'cu·bra'tion
lu'di·crous
lug'gage
lu·gu'bri·ous
luke'warm'
lull'a·by'
  ·bies'
lum'bar
  (*of the loins*)
lum'ber
  (*timber*)
lum'ber·jack'
lum'ber·yard'
lu'men
  ·mi·na *or* ·mens
lu'mi·nar'y
  ·ies
lu'mi·nes'cent
lu'mi·nous
lump'i·ness
lump'y
  ·i·er ·i·est
lu'na·cy
lu'nar
lu'na·tic
lunch'eon
lunge
  lunged lung'ing

lu'pine
lure
  lured lur'ing
lu'rid
lurk'ing
lus'cious
lush'ness
lus'ter
lust'i·ness
lus'trous
lust'y
  ·i·er ·i·est
lux·u'ri·ance
lux·u'ri·ant
lux·u'ri·ate'
  ·at'ed ·at'ing
lux·u'ri·ous
lux'u·ry
  ·ries
ly·ce'um
lye
  (alkaline sub-
  stance; SEE lie)
ly'ing-in'
lym·phat'ic
lynch'ing
lynx
  (animal; SEE links)
ly'on·naise'
lyre
  (harp; SEE liar)
lyr'ic
lyr'i·cal
lyr'i·cist

176

M

ma·ca'bre
mac·ad'am
mac·ad'am·ize'
  ·ized' ·iz'ing
mac·a·ro'ni
mac·a·roon'
mac'er·ate'
  ·at'ed ·at'ing
ma·che'te
Mach'i·a·vel'li·an
mach'i·nate'
  ·nat'ed ·nat'ing
mach'i·na'tion
ma·chine'
  ·chined'
  ·chin'ing
ma·chin'er·y
ma·chin'ist
mack'er·el
mack'i·naw'
mack'in·tosh'
  (coat; SEE
  McIntosh)
mac'ra·mé'
mac'ro·bi·ot'ics
mac'ro·cosm
ma'cron
mac'u·la
  ·lae

mad
  mad'der
  mad'dest
mad'am
mad'ame
  mes·dames'
mad'cap'
mad'den·ing
Ma·deir'a
ma'de·moi·selle'
made'-to-or'der
made'-up'
mad'house'
mad'man'
ma'dras
mad'ri·gal
mad'wom'an
mael'strom
ma·es'tro
  ·tros or ·tri
Ma'fi·a or Maf'·
mag'a·zine'
ma·gen'ta
mag'got
mag'ic
mag'i·cal·ly
ma·gi'cian
mag·is·te'ri·al
mag'is·trate'
mag·na·nim'i·ty
mag·nan'i·mous
mag'nate
  (influential
  person)

mag·ne′sia
mag′net
  (*iron attracter*)
mag·net′ic
mag·net′i·cal·ly
mag′net·ism
mag′net·ize′
 ·ized′ ·iz′ing
mag·ne′to
 ·tos
mag′ni·fi·ca′tion
mag·nif′i·cence
mag·nif′i·cent
mag′ni·fi′er
mag′ni·fy′
 ·fied′ ·fy′ing
mag·nil′o·quent
mag′ni·tude′
mag·no′li·a
mag′num
mag′pie′
ma′ha·ra′jah *or*
 ·ra′ja
ma′ha·ra′ni *or*
 ·ra′nee
ma·hat′ma
mah′-jongg′
ma·hog′a·ny
maid′en
maid′ser′vant
mail′box′
mail′man′
maim
Maine

main′land′
main′line′
main′ly
main′spring′
main′stream′
main·tain′
main′te·nance
maî′tre d′hô·tel′
maize
 (*corn;* SEE maze)
ma·jes′tic
ma·jes′ti·cal·ly
maj′es·ty
 ·ties
ma·jol′i·ca
ma′jor
ma′jor-do′mo
 ·mos
ma·jor′i·ty
 ·ties
ma·jus′cule
make
 made mak′ing
make′-be·lieve′
make′shift′
make′up′
mal′a·dapt′ed
mal′ad·just′ed
mal′ad·min′is·ter
mal′a·droit′
mal′a·dy
 ·dies
ma·laise′
mal′a·prop·ism

mal′ap·ro·pos′
ma·lar′i·a
mal′con·tent′
mal de mer′
mal′e·dic′tion
mal′e·fac′tion
mal′e·fac′tor
ma·lef′i·cent
male′ness
ma·lev′o·lence
ma·lev′o·lent
mal·fea′sance
mal′for·ma′tion
mal·formed′
mal·func′tion
mal′ice
ma·li′cious
ma·lign′
ma·lig′nan·cy
ma·lig′nant
ma·lig′ni·ty
 ·ties
ma·lin′ger
ma·lin′ger·er
mall
 (*promenade;* SEE
 maul)
mal′lard
mal′le·a·bil′i·ty
mal′le·a·ble
mal′let
malm′sey
mal′nu·tri′tion
mal′oc·clu′sion

177

mal·o'dor·ous
mal·prac'tice
malt'ose
mal·treat'
mam'mal
mam·ma'li·an
mam'ma·ry
mam'mon
mam'moth
man
 men, manned
 man'ning
man'a·cle
 ·cled ·cling
man'age
 ·aged ·ag·ing
man'age·a·ble
man'age·ment
man'ag·er
man'a·ge'ri·al
ma·ña'na
man'-child'
 men'-chil'dren
man·da'mus
man'da·rin
man'date
 ·dat·ed ·dat·ing
man'da·to'ry
man'di·ble
man'do·lin'
man'drel or ·dril
 (metal spindle)
man'drill
 (baboon)

man'-eat'er
ma·nège'
 (horsemanship;
 SEE ménage)
ma·neu'ver
ma·neu'ver·a·ble
man'ful·ly
man'ga·nese'
mange
man'ger
man'gi·ness
man'gle
 ·gled ·gling
man'go
 ·goes or ·gos
man'grove
man'gy
 ·gi·er ·gi·est
man'han'dle
Man·hat'tan
man'hole'
man'hood'
man'-hour'
man'hunt'
ma'ni·a
ma'ni·ac'
ma·ni'a·cal
man'ic
man'i·cot'ti
man'i·cure'
 ·cured' ·cur'ing
man'i·cur'ist
man'i·fest'
man'i·fes·ta'tion

man'i·fes'to
 ·toes
man'i·fold'
man'i·kin
Ma·ni'la
ma·nip'u·late'
 ·lat'ed ·lat'ing
ma·nip'u·la'tion
ma·nip'u·la'tive
ma·nip'u·la'tor
man'kind'
man'li·ness
man'ly
 ·li·er ·li·est
man'-made'
man'na
man'ne·quin
man'ner
 (way; SEE manor)
man'ner·ism
man'ner·ly
man'nish
man'-of-war'
 men'-of-war'
ma·nom'e·ter
man'or
 (residence;
 SEE manner)
man'pow'er
man'sard
man'ser'vant
 men'ser'vants
man'sion
man'-sized'

178

man′slaugh′ter
man′teau
 ·teaus
man′tel
 (*fireplace fac-
 ing;* SEE mantle)
man′tel·et
man′tel·piece′
man·til′la
man′tis
 ·tis·es *or* ·tes
man′tle
 ·tled ·tling
 (*cloak;* SEE
 mantel)
man′tu·a
man′u·al
man′u·fac′to·ry
 ·ries
man′u·fac′ture
 ·tured ·tur·ing
man′u·fac′tur·er
ma·nure′
 ·nured′ ·nur′ing
man′u·script′
man′y
 more most
man′y-sid′ed
map
 mapped
 map′ping
ma′ple
mar
 marred mar′ring

mar′a·bou′
ma·ra′ca
mar′a·schi′no
ma·ras′mus
mar′a·thon′
ma·raud′
mar′ble
 ·bled ·bling
mar′ble·ize′
 ·ized′ ·iz′ing
mar′ca·site′
mar·cel′
 ·celled′ ·cel′ling
March
mar′chion·ess
Mar′di gras′
mare’s′-nest′
mare’s′-tail′
mar′ga·rine
mar′gin
mar′gin·al
mar′gin·al·ly
mar′i·gold′
ma·ri·jua′na *or*
 ·hua′na
ma·rim′ba
ma·ri′na
mar′i·nade′
 ·nad′ed ·nad′ing
mar′i·nate′
 ·nat′ed ·nat′ing
ma·rine′
mar′i·ner
mar′i·o·nette′

mar′i·tal
 (*of marriage;*
 SEE martial)
mar′i·time′
mar′jo·ram
mark′down′
marked
mark′ed·ly
mar′ket·a·bil′i·ty
mar′ket·a·ble
mar′ket·place′
marks′man
mark′up′
mar′lin
 (*fish*)
mar′line
 (*cord*)
mar′line·spike′
mar′ma·lade′
mar′mo·set′
mar′mot
ma·roon′
mar·quee′
mar′quess
mar′que·try
mar′quis
mar·quise′
mar′qui·sette′
mar′riage
mar′riage·a·ble
mar′row
mar′row·bone′
mar′ry
 ·ried ·ry·ing

Mar·sa′la
mar′shal
  ·shaled *or*
  ·shalled
  ·shal·ing *or*
  ·shal·ling
marsh′mal′low
mar·su′pi·al
mar·su′pi·um
  ·pi·a
mar′ten
  (*animal;* SEE
  martin)
mar′tial
  (*military;* SEE
  marital)
Mar′tian
mar′tin
  (*bird;* SEE marten)
mar′ti·net′
mar′tin·gale′
mar·ti′ni
  ·nis
mar′tyr
mar′tyr·dom
mar′tyr·ize′
  ·ized′ ·iz′ing
mar′vel
  ·veled *or* ·velled
  ·vel·ing *or*
  ·vel·ling
mar′vel·ous
Marx′ism
Mar′y·land

mar′zi·pan′
mas·ca′ra
  ·raed ·ra·ing
mas′con′
mas′cot
mas′cu·line
mas′cu·lin′i·ty
ma′ser
mash′ie
mask
  (*cover;* SEE
  masque)
masked
mas′och·ism
mas′och·is′tic
mas′och·is′ti·
  cal·ly
ma′son
Ma′son·ite′
ma′son·ry
masque
  (*masked ball;* SEE
  mask)
mas′quer·ade′
  ·ad′ed ·ad′ing
Mas′sa·chu′setts
mas′sa·cre
  ·cred ·cring
mas·sage′
  ·saged′ ·sag′ing
mas·seur′
mas·seuse′
mas′sive
mas′ter·ful

mas′ter·ly
mas′ter·mind′
mas′ter·piece′
mas′ter·y
  ·ies
mast′head′
mas′tic
mas′ti·cate′
  ·cat′ed ·cat′ing
mas′ti·ca′tion
mas′tiff
mas′to·don′
mas′toid
mas′tur·bate′
  ·bat′ed ·bat′ing
mas′tur·ba′tion
mat
  mat′ted
  mat′ting
mat′a·dor′
match′box′
match′less
match′lock′
match′mak′er
mate
  mat′ed mat′ing
ma′te·las·sé′
ma·te′ri·al
  (*of matter;*
  SEE materiel)
ma·te′ri·al·ism
ma·te′ri·al·is′tic
ma·te′ri·al·ize′
  ·ized′ ·iz′ing

ma·te′ri·al·ly
ma·te′ri·el′
  or ·té′ri·el′
  (equipment;
  SEE material)
ma·ter′nal
ma·ter′ni·ty
math′e·mat′i·cal
math′e·ma·ti′cian
math′e·mat′ics
mat′i·nee′
  or ·i·née′
ma′tri·arch′
ma′tri·ar′chal
ma′tri·ar′chy
  ·chies
ma′tri·cide′
ma·tric′u·lant
ma·tric′u·late′
  ·lat′ed ·lat′ing
ma·tric′u·la′tion
mat′ri·mo′ni·al
mat′ri·mo′ny
ma′trix
  ·tri·ces′ or ·trix·es
ma′tron
ma′tron·li·ness
ma′tron·ly
mat′ter
mat′ter-of-fact′
mat′tock
mat′tress
mat′u·rate′
  ·rat′ed ·rat′ing

mat′u·ra′tion
ma·ture′
  ·tured′ ·tur′ing
ma·ture′ly
ma·tu′ri·ty
mat′zo
  ·zot or ·zoth
  or ·zos
maud′lin
maul
  (mallet; injure;
  SEE mall)
maun′der
mau·so·le′um
  ·le′ums or ·le′a
mauve
mav′er·ick
mawk′ish
max·il′la
max′il·lar′y
max′im
max′i·mal
max′i·mize′
  ·mized′ ·miz′ing
max′i·mum
  ·mums or ·ma
May
may′be
May′day′
may′hem
may′on·naise′
may′or
may′or·al·ty
  ·ties

May′pole′
maze
  (labyrinth; SEE
  maize)
maz′el tov′
Mc′In·tosh′
  (apple; SEE
  mackintosh)
mead′ow
mea′ger
meal′time′
meal′y
  ·i·er ·i·est
meal′y-mouthed′
mean v.
  meant mean′ing
mean adj., n.
  (middle; low;
  SEE mien)
me·an′der
mean′ing·ful
mean′ing·less
mean′ness
mean′time′
mean′while′
mea′sles
mea′sly
  ·sli·er ·sli·est
meas′ur·a·bil′i·ty
meas′ur·a·ble
meas′ur·a·bly
meas′ure
  ·ured ·ur·ing
meas′ure·less

181

meas′ure·ment
meas′ur·er
meat
  (*flesh;* SEE
  meet, mete)
meat′i·ness
me·a′tus
meat′y
  ·i·er ·i·est
me·chan′ic
me·chan′i·cal
mech′a·ni′cian
me·chan′ics
mech′a·nism
mech′a·ni·za′tion
mech′a·nize′
  ·nized′ ·niz′ing
med′al
  (*award;*
  SEE meddle)
med′al·ist
me·dal′lion
med′dle
  ·dled ·dling
  (*interfere;*
  SEE meddle)
med′dler
med′dle·some
me′di·a
  (*sing.* medium)
me′di·al
me′di·an
me′di·ate′
  ·at′ed ·at′ing

me′di·a′tion
me′di·a′tor
Med′i·caid′
med′i·cal
Med′i·care′
med′i·cate′
  ·cat′ed ·cat′ing
med′i·ca′tion
me·dic′i·nal
med′i·cine
me′di·e′val
  or ·ae′val
me′di·o′cre
me′di·oc′ri·ty
  ·ties
med′i·tate′
  ·tat′ed ·tat′ing
med′i·ta′tion
med′i·ta′tor
Med′i·ter·ra′ne·an
me′di·um
  ·di·ums *or* ·di·a
med′ley
  ·leys
meer′schaum
meet
  met meet′ing
  (*come upon;* SEE
  meat, mete)
meg′a·death′
meg′a·hertz′
meg′a·lo·ma′ni·a
meg′a·lop′o·lis
meg′a·phone′

meg′a·ton′
mel′an·cho′li·a
mel′an·chol′ic
mel′an·chol′y
mé′lange′
mel′a·nin
me′lee *or* mê′lée
mel′io·rate′
  ·rat′ed ·rat′ing
mel′io·ra′tion
mel·lif′lu·ous
mel′low
me·lo′de·on
me·lod′ic
me·lo′di·ous
mel′o·dra′ma
mel′o·dra·mat′ic
mel′o·dy
  ·dies
mel′on
melt′a·ble
mel′ton
mem′ber·ship′
mem′brane
mem′bra·nous
me·men′to
  ·tos *or* ·toes
mem′oir
mem′o·ra·bil′i·a
mem′o·ra·ble
mem′o·ra·bly
mem′o·ran′dum
  ·dums *or* ·da
me·mo′ri·al

me·mo′ri·al·ize′
·ized′ ·iz′ing
mem′o·ri·za′tion
mem′o·rize′
·rized′ ·riz′ing
mem′o·ry
·ries
men′ace
·aced ·ac′ing
mé·nage′ or me·
(household; SEE
manège)
me·nag′er·ie
men·da′cious
men·dac′i·ty
Men·de′li·an
men′di·cant
me′ni·al
men′in·gi′tis
me·nis′cus
·cus·es or ·ci
Men′non·ite′
men′o·pause′
men′ses
men′stru·al
men′stru·ate′
·at′ed
·at′ing
men′stru·a′tion
men′sur·a·ble
men′su·ra′tion
mens′wear′
men′tal
men·tal′i·ty

men′thol
men′tho·lat′ed
men′tion
men′tor
men′u
·us
me·phit′ic
me·pro′ba·mate′
mer′can·tile
mer′can·til·ism
mer′ce·nar′y
·nar′ies
mer′cer·ize′
·ized′ ·iz′ing
mer′chan·dise′
·dised′ ·dis′ing
mer′chan·dis′er
mer′chant
mer′ci·ful
mer′ci·ful·ly
mer′ci·less
mer·cu′ri·al
mer·cu′ro·
chrome′
mer′cu·ry
mer′cy
·cies
mere
mer′est
mere′ly
mer·en′gue
(dance; SEE
meringue)
mer′e·tri′cious

merge
merged merg′ing
merg′er
me·rid′i·an
me·ringue′
(pie topping;
SEE merengue)
me·ri′no
·nos
mer′it
mer′i·to′ri·ous
mer′maid′
mer′ri·ly
mer′ri·ment
mer′ri·ness
mer′ry
·ri·er ·ri·est
mer′ry-an′drew
mer′ry-go-round′
mer′ry·mak′ing
Mer·thi′o·late′
me′sa
mé·sal′li·ance
mes·cal′
mes′ca·line′
mes′dames′
mes′de·moi·selles′
me·shu′ga
mesh′work′
mes′mer·ism
mes′mer·ize′
·ized′ ·iz′ing
mes′on
mes′sage

183

mes'sen·ger
mes·si'ah
mes'sieurs
mess'i·ly
mess'i·ness
mess'y
·i·er ·i·est
met'a·bol'ic
me·tab'o·lism
me·tab'o·lize'
·lized' ·liz'ing
met'al
·aled or ·alled
·al·ing or ·al·ling
(*mineral;* SEE
mettle)
me·tal'lic
met'al·lur'gi·cal
met'al·lur'gist
met'al·lur'gy
met'al·work'
met'a·mor'phic
met'a·mor'phism
met'a·mor'phose
·phosed ·phos·ing
met'a·mor'pho·sis
·ses
met'a·phor'
met'a·phor'i·cal
met'a·phor'i·
cal·ly
met'a·phys'i·cal
met'a·phys'ics
met'a·tar'sal

me·tath'e·sis
·ses'
mete
met'ed met'ing
(*allot;* SEE meat,
meet)
me'te·or
me'te·or'ic
me'te·or·ite'
me'te·or·oid'
me'te·or·o·
log'i·cal
me'te·or·ol'o·gist
me'te·or·ol'o·gy
me'ter
meth'a·done'
meth'ane
meth'a·nol'
meth'e·drine'
meth'od
me·thod'i·cal
me·thod'i·cal·ly
Meth'od·ist
meth'od·ize'
·ized' ·iz'ing
meth'od·ol'o·gy
me·tic'u·lous
mé·tier'
me·ton'y·my
met'ric
met'ri·cal
met'ro·nome'
me·trop'o·lis
met'ro·pol'i·tan

met'tle
(*spirit;* SEE metal)
mez'za·nine'
mez'zo-so·pra'no
·nos or ·ni
mez'zo·tint'
mi·as'ma
·mas or ·ma·ta
mi'ca
Mich'i·gan
mi'cro·bar'
mi'crobe
mi·cro'bic
mi'cro·cop'y
mi'cro·cosm
mi'cro·dot'
mi'cro·fiche'
mi'cro·film'
mi'cro·groove'
mi·crom'e·ter
mi'cro·or'gan·
ism
mi'cro·phone'
mi'cro·print'
mi'cro·read'er
mi'cro·scope'
mi'cro·scop'ic
mi'cro·scop'i·
cal·ly
mi'cro·wave'
mid'air'
mid'cult'
mid'day'
mid'dle

mid'dle-aged'
mid'dle·brow'
mid'dle-class'
mid'dle·man'
mid'dle-of-the-
  road'
mid'dle-sized'
mid'dle·weight'
mid'dling
mid'dy
  ·dies
midg'et
mid'i·ron
mid'land
mid'night'
mid'point'
mid'riff
mid'ship'man
midst
mid'stream'
mid'sum'mer
mid'term'
mid'-Vic·to'ri·an
mid'way'
mid'week'
Mid'west'
Mid'west'ern·er
mid'wife'
  ·wives'
mid'win'ter
mid'year'
mien
  (*manner;* SEE
  mean)

miffed
might
  (*power;* SEE mite)
might'i·ly
might'i·ness
might'y
  ·i·er ·i·est
mi'gnon
mi'graine
mi'grant
mi'grate
  ·grat·ed ·grat·ing
mi·gra'tion
mi'gra·to·ry
mi·ka'do
  ·dos
mi·la'dy
mil'dew'
mild'ly
mile'age
mile'post'
mile'stone'
mi·lieu'
mil'i·tan·cy
mil'i·tant
mil'i·tar'i·ly
mil'i·ta·rism
mil'i·ta·ris'tic
mil'i·ta·ri·za'tion
mil'i·ta·rize'
  ·rized' ·riz'ing
mil'i·tar'y
mil'i·tate'
  ·tat'ed ·tat'ing

mi·li'tia
milk'i·ness
milk'maid'
milk'man'
milk'shake'
milk'shed'
milk'sop'
milk toast
  (*food;* SEE
  milquetoast)
milk'weed'
milk'y
  ·i·er ·i·est
mill'age
mill'dam'
milled
mil·len'ni·um
  ·ni·ums *or* ·ni·a
mill'er
mil'let
mil'liard
mil'li·bar'
mil'li·gram'
mil'li·li'ter
mil'li·me'ter
mill'line'
mil'li·ner
mil'li·ner'y
mill'ing
mil'lion
mil'lion·aire'
mil'lionth
mil'li·pede'
mill'pond'

mill′race′
mill′stone′
mill′stream′
mill wheel
mill′work′
mill′wright′
milque′toast′
　(*timid person;*
　SEE milk toast)
Mil·wau′kee
mime
　mimed mim′ing
mim′e·o·graph′
mim′er
mi·met′ic
mim′ic
　·icked ·ick·ing
mim′ick·er
mim′ic·ry
mi·mo′sa
min′a·ret′
min′a·to′ry
mince
　minced minc′ing
mince′meat′
mind′ful
mind′less
mind reader
mine
　mined min′ing
mine′lay′er
min′er
　(*mine worker;*
　SEE minor)

min′er·al
min′er·al·i·za′tion
min′er·al·ize′
　·ized′ ·iz′ing
min′er·al′o·gist
min′er·al′o·gy
mi′ne·stro′ne
min′gle
　·gled ·gling
min′i·a·ture
min′i·a·tur′i·
　za′tion
min′i·a·tur·ize′
　·ized′ ·iz′ing
min′i·bus′
min′i·fi·ca′tion
min′i·fy′
　·fied′ ·fy′ing
min′im
min′i·mal
min′i·mal·ly
min′i·mize′
　·mized′ ·miz′ing
min′i·mum
　·mums or ·ma
min′ion
　(*deputy;* SEE
　minyan)
min′i·skirt′
min′is·ter
　(*diplomat; clergy-
　man;* SEE minster)
min′is·te′ri·al
min′is·trant

min′is·tra′tion
min′is·try
　·tries
min′i·track′
min′i·ver
Min′ne·ap′o·lis
min′ne·sing′er
Min′ne·so′ta
min′now
mi′nor
　(*lesser;* SEE
　miner)
mi·nor′i·ty
　·ties
min′ster
　(*church;* SEE
　minister)
min′strel
mint′age
min′u·end′
min′u·et′
mi′nus
mi·nus′cule
min′ute *n.*
mi·nute′ *adj.*
mi·nute′ly
min′ute·man′
mi·nu′ti·ae′
　(*sing.* mi·nu′ti·a)
minx
min·yan′
　min′ya·nim′
　(*group;* SEE
　minion)

mir'a·cle
mi·rac'u·lous
mi·rage'
mire
  mired mir'ing
mir'ror
mirth'ful
mirth'less
mir'y
  ·i·er ·i·est
mis'ad·ven'ture
mis'ad·vise'
mis'al·li'ance
mis'al·ly'
mis'an·thrope'
mis'an·throp'ic
mis·an'thro·py
mis'ap·pli·ca'tion
mis'ap·ply'
mis'ap·pre·hend'
mis'ap·pre·
  hen'sion
mis'ap·pro'pri·ate'
mis'be·got'ten
mis'be·have'
mis'be·hav'ior
mis'be·lief'
mis'be·lieve'
mis·cal'cu·late'
mis'cal·cu·la'tion
mis·car'riage
mis·car'ry
mis·cast'
mis·ce·ge·na'tion

mis'cel·la'ne·a
mis'cel·la'ne·ous
mis'cel·la'ny
  ·nies
mis·chance'
mis'chief
mis'chief-mak'er
mis'chie·vous
mis'ci·bil'i·ty
mis'ci·ble
mis'con·ceive'
mis'con·cep'tion
mis·con'duct
mis'con·
  struc'tion
mis'con·strue'
mis·count'
mis'cre·ant
mis·cue'
mis·date'
mis·deal'
  ·dealt' ·deal'ing
mis·deed'
mis'de·mean'or
mis'di·rect'
mi'ser
mi'ser·a·ble
mi'ser·a·bly
mi'ser·ly
mis'er·y
  ·ies
mis·es'ti·mate'
mis·fea'sance
mis·file'

mis·fire'
mis'fit'
mis·for'tune
mis·giv'ing
mis·gov'ern
mis·guid'ance
mis·guide'
mis·han'dle
mis'hap
mish'mash'
mis'in·form'
mis'in·for·ma'tion
mis'in·ter'pret
mis·judge'
mis·judg'ment
  or ·judge'ment
mis·lay'
  ·laid' ·lay'ing
mis·lead'
  ·led' ·lead'ing
mis·man'age
mis·man'age·
  ment
mis·match'
mis·mate'
mis·no'mer
mi·sog'a·mist
mi·sog'a·my
mi·sog'y·nist
mi·sog'y·ny
mis·place'
mis·print'
mis·pri'sion
mis'pro·nounce'

187

mis·pro·nun·ci·
  a'tion
mis·quo·ta'tion
mis·quote'
mis·read'
  ·read' ·read'ing
mis·rep·re·sent'
mis·rep·re·sen·
  ta'tion
mis·rule'
Miss
  Miss'es
mis'sal
  (*book;* SEE
  missile, missive)
mis·shape'
mis·shap'en
mis'sile
  (*weapon;* SEE
  missal, missive)
mis'sion
mis'sion·ar'y
Mis·sis·sip'pi
mis'sive
  (*letter;* SEE
  missal, missile)
Mis·sou'ri
mis·speak'
  ·spoke' ·spo'ken
  ·speak'ing
mis·spell'
  ·spelled' *or*
  ·spelt'
  ·spell'ing

mis·spend'
  ·spent'
  ·spend'ing
mis·state'
mis·state'ment
mis·step'
mis·take'
  ·took' ·tak'en
  ·tak'ing
mist'i·ly
mist'i·ness
mis'tle·toe'
mis'tral
mis·treat'ment
mis'tress
mis·tri'al
mis·trust'
mist'y
  ·i·er ·i·est
mis·un·der·stand'
  ·stood' ·stand'ing
mis·us'age
mis·use'
mis·val'ue
mis·write'
  ·wrote' ·writ'ten
  ·writ'ing
mite
  (*arachnid; tiny*
  thing; SEE might)
mi'ter
mit'i·ga·ble
mit'i·gate'
  ·gat'ed ·gat'ing

mit'i·ga'tion
mit'i·ga'tor
mi'tral
mitt
mit'ten
mix
  mixed *or* mixt
  mix'ing
mix'er
mix'ture
mix'-up'
miz'zen·mast
mne·mon'ic
moan'ing
moat
  (*ditch;* SEE mote)
mob
  mobbed
  mob'bing
mo'bile
mo·bil'i·ty
mo'bi·liz'a·ble
mo'bi·li·za'tion
mo'bi·lize'
  ·lized' ·liz'ing
mob·oc'ra·cy
  ·cies
moc'ca·sin
mo'cha
mock'er·y
  ·ies
mock'-he·ro'ic
mock'ing·bird'
mock'-up'

mod′a·cryl′ic
mod′al
  (of a mode)
mod′el
  ·eled or ·elled
  ·el·ing or ·el·ling
  (copy)
mod′er·ate′
  ·at′ed ·at′ing
mod′er·ate·ly
mod′er·a′tion
mod′er·a′tor
mod′ern
mod′ern·ism
mod′ern·is′tic
mo·der′ni·ty
mod′ern·i·za′tion
mod′ern·ize′
  ·ized′ ·iz′ing
mod′ern·ness
mod′est
mod′es·ty
mod′i·cum
mod′i·fi·ca′tion
mod′i·fi′er
mod′i·fy′
  ·fied′ ·fy′ing
mod′ish
mo·diste′
mod′u·lar
mod′u·late′
  ·lat′ed ·lat′ing
mod′u·la′tion
mod′u·la′tor

mod′ule
mo′gul
mo′hair
moi′e·ty
  ·ties
moire
moi·ré′
mois′ten
moist′ness
mois′ture
mois′tur·ize′
  ·ized′ ·iz′ing
mo′lar
mo·las′ses
mold′board′
mold′er
mold′i·ness
mold′ing
mold′y
  ·i·er ·i·est
mole
mo·lec′u·lar
mol′e·cule′
mole′hill′
mole′skin′
mo·lest′
mo′les·ta′tion
mol′li·fy′
  ·fied′ ·fy′ing
mol′lusk
mol′ly·cod′dle
  ·dled ·dling
molt
mol′ten

mo·lyb′de·num
mo′ment
mo′men·tar′i·ly
mo′men·tar′y
mo·men′tous
mo·men′tum
  ·tums or ·ta
mom′ism
mo·nan′drous
mon′arch
mo·nar′chal
mon′ar·chism
mon′ar·chy
  ·chies
mon′as·ter′y
  ·ies
mo·nas′tic
mo·nas′ti·cism
mon·au′ral
Mon′day
mon′e·tar′y
mon′e·tize′
  ·tized′ ·tiz′ing
mon′ey
  ·eys or ·ies
mon′ey·bag′
mon′ey-chang′er
mon′eyed
mon′ey-grub′ber
mon′ey·lend′er
mon′ey·mak′er
mon′ger
Mon′gol·ism
Mon′gol·oid′

189

mon′goose
· goos·es
mon′grel
mo·ni′tion
mon′i·tor
mon′i·to′ry
· ries
monk
mon′key
· keys
monk's cloth
mon′o·chro·
mat′ic
mon′o·chrome′
mon′o·cle
mon′o·coque′
mo·noc′u·lar
mon′o·dra′ma
mo·nog′a·mist
mo·nog′a·mous
mo·nog′a·my
mon′o·gram′
· grammed′
· gram′ming
mon′o·graph′
mo·nog′y·ny
mon′o·lith′
mon′o·logue′
or · log′
mon′o·logu·ist or
mo·nol′o·gist
mon′o·ma′ni·a
mon′o·met′al·lism
mon′o·nu′cle·o′sis

mon′o·plane′
mo·nop′o·list
mo·nop′o·lis′tic
mo·nop′o·li·
za′tion
mo·nop′o·lize′
· lized′ · liz′ing
mo·nop′o·ly
· lies
mon′o·rail′
mon′o·syl·lab′ic
mon′o·syl′la·ble
mon′o·the′ism
mon′o·the·is′tic
mon′o·tone′
mo·not′o·nous
mo·not′o·ny
mon′o·type′
mon·ox′ide
Mon′sei·gneur′
Mes′sei·gneurs′
mon·sieur′
mes′sieurs
Mon·si′gnor
mon·soon′
mon′ster
mon·stros′i·ty
· ties
mon′strous
mon·tage′
· taged′ · tag′ing
Mon·tan′a
month′ly
· lies

mon′u·ment
mon′u·men′tal
mood′i·ly
mood′i·ness
mood′y
· i·er · i·est
moon′beam′
moon′-faced′
moon′light′
moon′light′ing
moon′lit′
moon′port′
moon′rise′
moon′set′
moon′shine′
moon′shot′
moon′stone′
moon′struck′
moor′age
moor′ing
moose
moose
(*deer;* SEE
mouse, mousse)
moot
(*debatable;*
SEE mute)
mop
mopped
mop′ping
mope
moped mop′ing
mop′pet
mop′-up′

mo·raine'
mor'al
mo·rale'
mor'al·ist
mor'al·is'tic
mor'al·is'ti·cal·ly
mo·ral'i·ty
mor'al·ize'
  ·ized' ·iz'ing
mor'al·ly
mo·rass'
mor'a·to'ri·um
  ·ri·ums or ·ri·a
mor'bid
mor·bid'i·ty
mor'dant
  (corrosive)
mor'dent
  (musical term)
more·o'ver
mo'res
mor'ga·nat'ic
morgue
mor'i·bund'
mor'i·bun'di·ty
Mor'mon
morn'ing
  (part of day;
  SEE mourning)
mo·roc'co
mo'ron
mo·ron'ic
mo·rose'
mor'phine

mor·phol'o·gy
mor'sel
mor'tal
mor·tal'i·ty
mor'tal·ly
mor'tar
mor'tar·board'
mort'gage
  ·gaged ·gag·ing
mort'ga·gee'
mort'ga·gor
mor·ti'cian
mor'ti·fi·ca'tion
mor'ti·fy'
  ·fied' ·fy'ing
mor'tise
  ·tised ·tis·ing
mor'tu·ar'y
  ·ies
mo·sa'ic
  ·icked ·ick·ing
mosque
mos·qui'to
  ·toes or ·tos
moss'back'
moss'i·ness
moss'y
  ·i·er ·i·est
most'ly
mote
  (speck; SEE moat)
mo·tel'
moth'ball'
moth'-eat'en

moth'er·hood'
moth'er-in-law'
  moth'ers-in-law'
moth'er·land'
moth'er·li·ness
moth'er·ly
moth'er-of-pearl'
moth'proof'
mo·tif'
mo'tile
mo·til'i·ty
mo'tion·less
mo'ti·vate'
  ·vat'ed ·vat'ing
mo'ti·va'tion
mo'ti·va'tor
mo'tive
mot'ley
mo'tor·bike'
mo'tor·boat'
mo'tor·bus'
mo'tor·cade'
mo'tor·cy'cle
mo'tor·drome'
mo'tor·ist
mo'tor·ize'
  ·ized' ·iz'ing
mo'tor·man
mot'tle
  ·tled ·tling
mot'to
  ·toes or ·tos
mou·lage'
mound

moun'tain
moun'tain·eer'
moun'tain·ous
moun'te·bank'
mourn'ful
mourn'ing
  (*grieving;*
  SEE morning)
mouse
  mice
  moused mous'ing
  (*rodent;* SEE
  moose, mousse)
mous'er
mouse'trap'
mous'i·ness
mousse
  (*food;* SEE
  moose, mouse)
mousse·line'
  de soie'
mous'y
  ·i·er ·i·est
mouth'ful'
  ·fuls'
mouth'part'
mouth'piece'
mouth'-to-mouth'
mouth'wash'
mouth'wa·ter·ing
mou'ton'
  (*fur;* SEE mutton)
mov'a·ble
  or move'·

mov'a·bly
move
  moved mov'ing
move'ment
mov'ie
mov'ie·go·er'
mov'i·o'la
mow
  mowed, mowed
  or mown,
  mow'ing
moz'za·rel'la
Mr.
  Messrs.
Mrs.
  Mmes.
mu'ci·lage
mu'ci·lag'i·nous
muck'rake'
mu'cous *adj.*
mu'cus *n.*
mud'der
mud'di·ness
mud'dle
  ·dled ·dling
mud'dler
mud'dy
  ·di·er ·di·est
mud'sling'ing
Muen'ster
mu·ez'zin
muf'fin
muf'fle
  ·fled ·fling

muf'fler
muf'ti
mug
  mugged
  mug'ging
mug'gi·ness
mug'gy
  ·gi·er ·gi·est
mug'wump'
muk'luk'
mu·lat'to
  ·toes
mul'ber'ry
  ·ries
mulch
mulct
mul'ish
mul'li·ga·taw'ny
mul'lion
mul'ti·col'ored
mul'ti·far'i·ous
mul'ti·form'
mul'ti·lat'er·al
mul'ti·ple
mul'ti·plex'
mul'ti·pli'a·ble
mul'ti·pli·cand'
mul'ti·pli·ca'tion
mul'ti·plic'i·ty
mul'ti·pli'er
mul'ti·ply'
  ·plied' ·ply'ing
mul'ti·tude'
mul'ti·tu'di·nous

mul·ti·ver′si·ty
mum′ble
 ·bled ·bling
mum′bler
mum′mer·y
mum′mi·fy′
 ·fied′ ·fy′ing
mum′my
 ·mies
munch
mun·dane′
mu·nic′i·pal
mu·nic′i·pal′i·ty
 ·ties
mu·nic′i·pal·ize′
 ·ized′ ·iz′ing
mu·nif′i·cence
mu·nif′i·cent
mu·ni′tion
mu′ral
mur′der·er
mur′der·ous
murk′i·ly
murk′i·ness
murk′y
 ·i·er ·i·est
mur′mur
mur′mur·er
mus′ca·dine
mus′ca·tel′
mus′cle
 ·cled ·cling
 (*body part*;
 SEE mussel)

mus′cle-bound′
mus′cu·lar
mus′cu·la′ture
muse
 mused mus′ing
mu·sette′
mu·se′um
mush′i·ness
mush′room
mush′y
 ·i·er ·i·est
mu′sic
mu′si·cal *adj.*
mu′si·cale′ *n.*
mu·si′cian
mu′si·col′o·gist
mu′si·col′o·gy
mus′kel·lunge′
mus′ket
musk′i·ness
musk′mel′on
musk′rat′
musk′y
 ·i·er ·i·est
mus′lin
mus′sel
 (*shellfish*;
 SEE muscle)
mus·tache′
 or mous·
mus′tang
mus′tard
mus′ter
mus′ti·ness

mus′ty
 ·ti·er ·ti·est
mu·ta·bil′i·ty
mu′ta·ble
mu′tant
mu′tate
 ·tat·ed ·tat·ing
mu·ta′tion
mute
 mut′ed mut′ing
 (*silent*; SEE moot)
mu′ti·late′
 ·lat′ed ·lat′ing
mu′ti·la′tion
mu′ti·neer′
mu′ti·nous
mu′ti·ny
 ·nies
 ·nied ·ny·ing
mut′ter
mut′ton
 (*food*; SEE
 mouton)
mu′tu·al
mu′tu·al′i·ty
mu′tu·al·ly
muu′muu
Mu′zak
muz′zle
 ·zled ·zling
my′e·li′tis
my′e·lo·gram′
my′lar
my′na *or* ·nah

my·o'pi·a
my·op'ic
myr'i·ad
myr'i·a·pod'
myr'mi·don'
myrrh
myr'tle
my·self'
mys·te'ri·ous
mys'ter·y
·ies
mys'tic
mys'ti·cal
mys'ti·cal·ly
mys'ti·cism
mys'ti·fi·ca'tion
mys'ti·fy'
·fied' ·fy'ing
mys·tique'
myth'i·cal
myth'o·log'i·cal
my·thol'o·gize'
·gized' ·giz'ing
my·thol'o·gy
·gies
myth'os

N

nab
nabbed nab'bing
na·celle'

na'cre
na'cre·ous
na'dir
nag
nagged nag'ging
nail'head'
nain'sook
na·ive' *or* ·ïve'
na·ive·te' *or* ·ïve·
na'ked·ness
nam'by-pam'by
·bies
name
named nam'ing
name'a·ble
or nam'·
name'-drop'per
name'less
name'ly
name'plate'
name'sake'
nan·keen' *or* ·kin'
nap
napped nap'ping
na'palm
na'per·y
naph'tha
naph'tha·lene'
nap'kin
na·po'le·on
nap'per
nar·cis'sism
nar'cis·sist
nar'cis·sis'tic

nar·cis'sus
nar'co·lep'sy
nar·co'sis
nar·cot'ic
nar'co·tism
nar'rate
·rat·ed ·rat·ing
nar·ra'tion
nar'ra·tive
nar'ra·tor
nar'row-mind'ed
nar'whal
na'sal
na·sal'i·ty
na'sal·ize'
·ized' ·iz'ing
nas'cent
nas'ti·ly
nas'ti·ness
na·stur'tium
nas'ty
·ti·er ·ti·est
na'tal
na'tant
na·ta·to'ri·um
·ri·ums *or* ·ri·a
na·ta·to'ry
na'tion
na'tion·al
na'tion·al·ism
na'tion·al·is'ti·
cal·ly
na'tion·al'i·ty
·ties

na'tion·al·i·za'tion
na'tion·al·ize'
·ized' ·iz'ing
na'tion·al·ly
na'tion·wide'
na'tive
na'tive-born'
na·tiv'i·ty
·ties
nat'ti·ly
nat'ty
·ti·er ·ti·est
nat'u·ral
nat'u·ral·ism
nat'u·ral·ist
nat'u·ral·is'tic
nat'u·ral·i·za'tion
nat'u·ral·ize'
·ized' ·iz'ing
nat'u·ral·ly
na'ture
naug'a·hyde'
naught
naugh'ti·ly
naugh'ti·ness
naugh'ty
·ti·er ·ti·est
nau'se·a
nau'se·ate'
·at'ed ·at'ing
nau'seous
nau'ti·cal
nau'ti·lus
·lus·es *or* ·li'

na'val
(*of a navy*)
nave
(*part of a church;*
SEE knave)
na'vel
(*umbilicus*)
nav'i·cert
nav'i·ga·ble
nav'i·gate'
·gat'ed ·gat'ing
nav'i·ga'tion
nav'i·ga'tor
na'vy
·vies
nay
(*no;* SEE nee,
neigh)
Ne·an'der·thal'
near'by'
near'ly
near'sight'ed
neat'ly
neat'ness
neb'bish
Ne·bras'ka
neb'u·la
·lae' *or* ·las
neb'u·lar
neb·u·los'i·ty
neb'u·lous
nec'es·sar'i·ly
nec'es·sar'y
·ies

ne·ces'si·tate'
·tat'ed ·tat'ing
ne·ces'si·tous
ne·ces'si·ty
·ties
neck'er·chief
neck'lace
neck'line'
neck'piece'
neck'tie'
neck'wear'
ne·crol'o·gy
·gies
nec'ro·man'cy
nec'tar
nec'tar·ine'
nee *or* née
(*born;* SEE nay,
neigh)
need
(*require;* SEE
knead)
need'ful
need'i·ness
nee'dle
·dled ·dling
nee'dle·like'
nee'dle·point'
nee'dler
need'less
nee'dle·work'
need'n't
need'y
·i·er ·i·est

ne'er'-do-well'
ne·far'i·ous
ne·gate'
  ·gat'ed ·gat'ing
ne·ga'tion
neg'a·tive
neg'a·tiv·ism
neg·lect'
neg·lect'ful
neg'li·gee'
neg'li·gence
neg'li·gent
neg'li·gi·ble
neg'li·gi·bly
ne·go'ti·a·bil'i·ty
ne·go'ti·a·ble
ne·go'ti·ate'
  ·at'ed ·at'ing
ne·go'ti·a'tion
ne·go'ti·a'tor
Ne'gro
  ·groes
Ne'groid
neigh
  (*whinny;* SEE
  nay, nee)
neigh'bor
neigh'bor·hood'
neigh'bor·li·ness
neigh'bor·ly
nei'ther
  (*not either;*
  SEE nether)
nem'a·tode'

nem'e·sis
  ·ses'
ne'o·clas'sic
ne'o·lith'ic
ne·ol'o·gism
ne'o·my'cin
ne'on
ne'o·phyte'
ne'o·plasm
ne'o·prene'
ne·pen'the
neph'ew
ne·phri'tis
nep'o·tism
Nep'tune'
nerve
  nerved nerv'ing
nerve'-rack'ing
  or -wrack'·
nerv'ous
nerv'y
  ·i·er ·i·est
nes'ci·ent
nes'tle
  ·tled ·tling
nest'ling
  (*young bird*)
net
  net'ted net'ting
neth'er
  (*lower;* SEE
  neither)
net'tle
  ·tled ·tling

net'work'
Neuf'châ·tel'
neu'ral
neu·ral'gia
neu'ras·the'ni·a
neu·ri'tis
neu'ro·log'i·cal
neu·rol'o·gist
neu·rol'o·gy
neu·ro'sis
  ·ses
neu·rot'ic
neu'ter
neu'tral
neu·tral'i·ty
neu'tral·i·za'tion
neu'tral·ize'
  ·ized' ·iz'ing
neu'tral·iz'er
neu·tri'no
neu'tron
Ne·vad'a
nev'er·more'
nev'er·the·less'
ne'vus
  ·vi
new'born'
new'com'er
new'el
new'fan'gled
new'-fash'ioned
New'found·land'
New Hamp'shire
New Jer'sey

new'ly·wed'
New Mex'i·co
news'boy'
news'cast'
news'deal'er
news'let'ter
news'man'
news'pa'per
new'speak'
news'print'
news'reel'
news'stand'
news'wor'thy
New York
next'-door'
nex'us
·us·es *or* nex'us
ni'a·cin
Ni·ag'a·ra
nib'ble
·bled ·bling
nib'lick
nice
nic'er nic'est
nice'ly
ni'ce·ty
·ties
niche
(*recess*)
nick
(*notch*)
nick'el
·eled *or* ·elled
·el·ing *or* ·el·ling

nick'el·o'de·on
nick'name'
nic'o·tine'
nic'o·tin'ism
nic'ti·tate'
·tat'ed ·tat'ing
niece
nig'gard·ly
nig'gling
night
(*darkness;* SEE
knight)
night'cap'
night'club'
night'dress'
night'fall'
night'gown'
night'in·gale'
night'long'
night'ly
night'mare'
night'mar'ish
night'shirt'
night'time'
ni'hil·ism
ni'hil·is'tic
nim'ble
·bler ·blest
nim'bly
nim'bus
·bi *or* ·bus·es
nin'com·poop'
nine'fold'
nine'pins'

nine'teen'
nine'ti·eth
nine'ty
·ties
nin'ny
·nies
ni'non
ninth
nip
nipped nip'ping
nip'per
nip'pi·ness
nip'ple
nip'py
·pi·er ·pi·est
nip'-up'
nir·va'na
ni'sei
·sei *or* ·seis
nit'-pick'ing
ni'tro·gen
ni'tro·glyc'er·in
or ·er·ine
nit'ty-grit'ty
no·bil'i·ty
no'ble
·bler ·blest
no'ble·man
no'bly
no'bod'y
·ies
noc·tur'nal
noc·tur'nal·ly
noc'turne

197

noc'u·ous
nod
  nod'ded nod'ding
nod'al
node
nod'u·lar
nod'ule
no·el' *or* ·ël'
nog'gin
no'-hit'ter
noise
  noised nois'ing
noise'less
noise'mak·er
nois'i·ly
nois'i·ness
noi'some
nois'y
  ·i·er ·i·est
no'mad
no·mad'ic
nom' de plume'
  noms' de plume'
no'men·cla'ture
nom'i·nal
nom'i·nal·ly
nom'i·nate'
  ·nat'ed ·nat'ing
nom'i·na'tion
nom'i·na·tive
nom'i·na'tor
nom'i·nee'
non'a·ge·nar'i·an
non'-book'

nonce
non'cha·lance'
non'cha·lant'
non·com'bat·ant
non·com·mit'tal
non com'pos
  men'tis
non'con·form'ist
non'co·op'er·a'·
  tion
non'de·script'
non·en'ti·ty
  ·ties
non·es·sen'tial
none'such'
none'the·less'
non·ex·ist'ent
non·fea'sance
non'he'ro
non·nu'cle·ar
no-non'sense
non'pa·reil'
non·par'ti·san
non·plus'
  ·plused' *or*
  ·plussed'
  ·plus'ing *or*
  ·plus'sing
non·prof'it
non·sched'uled
non·sec·tar'i·an
non'sense
non·sen'si·cal
non·sen'si·cal·ly

non' se'qui·tur
non'-sked'
non'skid'
non'stop'
non·sup·port'
non·un'ion
non·vi'o·lence
noo'dle
noon'day'
no one
noon'time'
noose
  noosed noos'ing
no'-par'
nor'mal
nor'mal·cy
nor·mal'i·ty
nor'mal·ize'
  ·ized' ·iz'ing
nor'mal·ly
north'bound'
North Car'o·li'na
North Da·ko'ta
north'east'
north'east'er·ly
north'east'ern
north'er·ly
north'ern
north'ward
north'west'
north'west'er·ly
north'west'ern
nose
  nosed nos'ing

nose′bleed′
nose cone
nose′-dive′
  -dived′ -div′ing
nose′gay′
nose′piece′
no′-show′
nos·tal′gia
nos·tal′gic
nos′tril
nos′trum
no′ta·ble
no′ta·bly
no′ta·ri·za′tion
no′ta·rize′
  ·rized′ ·riz′ing
no′ta·ry public
  no′ta·ries public
  or no′ta·ry publics
no·ta′tion
notched
note
  not′ed not′ing
note′book′
note′wor′thy
noth′ing·ness
no′tice
  ·ticed ·tic·ing
no′tice·a·ble
no′tice·a·bly
no′ti·fi′a·ble
no′ti·fi·ca′tion
no′ti·fy′
  ·fied′ ·fy′ing

no′tion
no′to·ri′e·ty
no·to′ri·ous
no′-trump′
not′with·stand′ing
nou′gat
nought
nour′ish·ment
nou′veau riche′
  nou′veaux riches′
no′va
  ·vas or ·vae
nov′el
nov′el·ette′
nov′el·ist
no·vel′la
nov′el·ty
  ·ties
No·vem′ber
nov′ice
no·vi′ti·ate
now′a·days′
no′where′
no′wise′
nox′ious
noz′zle
nu′ance
nub′bi·ness
nub′by
  ·bi·er ·bi·est
nu′bile
nu′cle·ar
nu′cle·ate′
  ·at′ed ·at′ing

nu·cle·on′ics
nu′cle·us
  ·cle·i′ or
  ·cle·us·es
nude
nudge
  nudged nudg′ing
nud′ist
nu′di·ty
nu′ga·to′ry
nug′get
nui′sance
nul′li·fi·ca′tion
nul′li·fy′
  ·fied′ ·fy′ing
num′ber
num′ber·less
numb′ly
numb′ness
nu′mer·a·ble
nu′mer·al
nu′mer·ate′
  ·at′ed ·at′ing
nu′mer·a′tion
nu′mer·a′tor
nu·mer′i·cal
nu′mer·ol′o·gy
nu′mer·ous
nu′mis·mat′ic
nu·mis′ma·tist
num′skull′
nun′ner·y
  ·ies
nup′tial

199

nurse
  nursed nurs'ing
nurse'maid'
nurs'er·y
  ·ies
nur'ture
  ·tured ·tur·ing
nut'crack'er
nut'gall'
nut'meat'
nut'meg'
nut'pick'
nu'tri·a
nu'tri·ent
nu'tri·ment
nu·tri'tion
nu·tri'tious
nu'tri·tive
nut'shell'
nuz'zle
  ·zled ·zling
ny'lon
nymph
nym'pho·
  ma'ni·ac'

O

oaf'ish
oa'kum
oar
  (*pole;* SEE ore)

oar'lock'
oars'man
o·a'sis
  ·ses
oath
oat'meal'
ob'bli·ga'to
  ·tos *or* ·ti
ob'du·ra·cy
ob'du·rate
o·be'di·ence
o·be'di·ent
o·bei'sance
o·bei'sant
ob'e·lisk'
o·bese'
o·be'si·ty
o·bey'
ob'fus·cate'
  ·cat'ed ·cat'ing
ob'i·ter dic'tum
  ob'i·ter dic'ta
o·bit'u·ar'y
  ·ies
ob'ject
ob·jec'tion
ob·jec'tion·a·ble
ob·jec'tion·a·bly
ob·jec'tive
ob·jec'tive·ly
ob'jec·tiv'i·ty
ob·jec'tor
ob'jet d'art'
  ob'jets d'art'

ob'jur·gate'
  ·gat'ed ·gat'ing
ob'jur·ga'tion
ob·la'tion
ob'li·gate'
  ·gat'ed ·gat'ing
ob'li·ga'tion
ob·lig'a·to'ry
o·blige'
  o·bliged'
  o·blig'ing
ob·lique'
ob·lique'ly
ob·liq'ui·ty
ob·lit'er·ate'
  ·at'ed ·at'ing
ob·lit'er·a'tion
ob·lit'er·a'tor
ob·liv'i·on
ob·liv'i·ous
ob'long
ob'lo·quy
  ·quies
ob·nox'ious
o'boe
o'bo·ist
ob·scene'
ob·scen'i·ty
  ·ties
ob·scure'
  ·scured' ·scur'ing
ob·scure'ly
ob·scu'ri·ty
  ·ties

ob'se·quies
ob·se'qui·ous
ob·serv'a·ble
ob·serv'ance
ob·serv'ant
ob·ser·va'tion
ob·serv'a·to'ry
·ries
ob·serve'
·served' ·serv'ing
ob·serv'er
ob·sess'
ob·ses'sion
ob·ses'sive
ob·sid'i·an
ob'so·lesce'
·lesced' ·lesc'ing
ob'so·les'cence
ob'so·les'cent
ob'so·lete'
ob'sta·cle
ob·stet'ric
ob·stet'ri·cal
ob'ste·tri'cian
ob'sti·na·cy
·cies
ob'sti·nate
ob'sti·nate·ly
ob·strep'er·ous
ob·struct'
ob·struc'tion
ob·struc'tion·ist
ob·struc'tive
ob·tain'

ob·trude'
·trud'ed
·trud'ing
ob·tru'sion
ob·tru'sive
ob·tru'sive·ly
ob·tuse'
ob·verse'
ob·vert'
ob'vi·ate'
·at'ed ·at'ing
ob'vi·ous
ob'vi·ous·ly
oc'a·ri'na
oc·ca'sion
oc·ca'sion·al
oc·ca'sion·al·ly
Oc'ci·dent
Oc'ci·den'tal
oc·cip'i·tal
oc·clude'
·clud'ed
·clud'ing
oc·clu'sion
oc·cult'
oc·cul·ta'tion
oc·cult'ism
oc'cu·pan·cy
·cies
oc'cu·pant
oc'cu·pa'tion
oc'cu·pa'tion·al·ly
oc'cu·py'
·pied' ·py'ing

oc·cur'
·curred'
·cur'ring
oc·cur'rence
o'cean
o'cean·go'ing
o'ce·an'ic
o'ce·a·nog'ra·phy
o'ce·an·ol'o·gy
o'ce·lot'
o'cher or o'chre
o'·clock'
oc'ta·gon'
oc·tag'o·nal
oc·ta·he'dron
oc'tane
oc·tan'gu·lar
oc'tave
oc·ta'vo
·vos
oc·tet' or ·tette'
Oc·to'ber
oc'to·ge·nar'i·an
oc'to·pus
·pus·es or ·pi'
or oc·top'o·des'
oc'tu·ple
oc'u·lar
oc'u·list
odd'i·ty
·ties
odd'ly
odds'-on'
o'di·ous

o'di·um
o·dom'e·ter
o'dor
o'dor·if'er·ous
o'dor·ous
Od'ys·sey
of'fal
off'beat'
off'-col'or
of·fend'
of·fense'
of·fen'sive
of'fer
of'fer·ing
of'fer·to·ry
·ries
off'hand'
off'hand'ed·ly
of'fice
of'fice·hold'er
of'fi·cer
of·fi'cial·ese'
of·fi'cial
of·fi'ci·ate'
·at'ed ·at'ing
of·fi'ci·a'tion
of·fi'ci·a'tor
of·fi'cious
off'ing
off'-key'
off'-lim'its
off'-line'
off'print'
off'set'

off'shoot'
off'shore'
off'side'
off'spring'
·spring' or
·springs'
off'stage'
off'-white'
of'ten
of'ten·times'
o'gle
o'gled o'gling
o'gre
o'gre·ish or
o'grish
O·hi'o
ohm'me'ter
oil'cloth'
oil'i·ness
oil'pa'per
oil'skin'
oil'stone'
oil'y
·i·er ·i·est
oint'ment
OK or O.K.
OK's or O.K.'s
OK'd or O.K.'d
OK'ing or O.K.'ing
O'kla·ho'ma
old'-fash'ioned
old'ish
old'-line'
old'ster

old'-tim'er
old'-world'
o'le·o'
o'le·o·mar'ga·
rine or ·rin
ol·fac'tion
ol·fac'to·ry
·ries
ol'i·garch'
ol'i·gar'chy
·chies
ol'i·gop'o·ly
·lies
ol'ive
O·lym'pic
o·me'ga
om'e·let or
·lette
o'men
om'i·nous
o·mis'si·ble
o·mis'sion
o·mit'
o·mit'ted
o·mit'ting
om'ni·bus'
om'ni·far'i·ous
om·nip'o·tence
om·nip'o·tent
om'ni·pres'ence
om'ni·pres'ent
om'ni·range'
om·nis'cience
om·nis'cient

om·niv′o·rous
once′-o′ver
on′com·ing
one′ness
on′er·ous
one′self′
one′-sid′ed
one′-time′
one′-track′
one′-up′
 -upped′
 -up′ping
one′-up′man·ship′
one′-way′
on′go·ing
on′ion·skin′
on′-line′
on′look′er
on′ly
on′o·mat′o·poe′ia
on′rush′
on′set′
on′shore′
on′side′
on′slaught′
o′nus
on′ward
on′yx
oo′long
ooze
 oozed ooz′ing
oo′zi·ness
oo′zy
 ·zi·er ·zi·est

o·pac′i·ty
o′pal
o′pal·es′cent
o·paque′
o′pen-and-shut′
o′pen-end′
o′pen-end′ed
o′pen·er
o′pen-eyed′
o′pen·hand′ed
o′pen·heart′ed
o′pen·hearth′
o′pen·ly
o′pen·mind′ed
o′pen-mouthed′
o′pen·ness
o′pen·work′
op′er·a
op′er·a·ble
op′er·ate′
 ·at′ed ·at′ing
op′er·at′ic
op′er·a′tion
op′er·a′tion·al
op′er·a′tion·al·ly
op′er·a′tive
op′er·a′tor
op′er·et′ta
oph′thal·mol′o·
 gist
oph′thal·mol′o·gy
oph·thal′mo·
 scope′
o′pi·ate

o·pin′ion
o·pin′ion·at′ed
o·pin′ion·a′tive
o′pi·um
o·pos′sum
op·po′nent
op′por·tune′
op′por·tun′ism
op′por·tun′ist
op′por·tu′ni·ty
 ·ties
op·pos′a·ble
op·pose′
 ·posed′ ·pos′ing
op·pos′er
op′po·site
op′po·si′tion
op·press′
op·pres′sion
op·pres′sive
op·pres′sive·ly
op·pres′sor
op·pro′bri·ous
op·pro′bri·um
op′tic
op′ti·cal
op·ti′cian
op′ti·mal
op′ti·mism
op′ti·mist
op′ti·mis′tic
op′ti·mis′ti·cal·ly
op′ti·mize′
 ·mized′ ·miz′ing

op'ti·mum
  ·mums or ·ma
op'tion
op'tion·al
op'tion·al·ly
op·tom'e·trist
op·tom'e·try
op'u·lence
op'u·lent
o'pus
  op'er·a or
  o'pus·es
or'a·cle
  (wise person;
  SEE auricle)
o·rac'u·lar
o'ral
  (of the mouth;
  SEE aural)
o'ral·ly
or'ange
or'ange·ade'
or'ange·wood'
o·rang'u·tan'
o·ra'tion
or'a·tor
or'a·tor'i·cal
or'a·to'ri·o'
  ·os'
or'a·to'ry
  ·ries
or·bic'u·lar
or'bit
or'chard

or'ches·tra
or·ches'tral
or'ches·trate'
  ·trat'ed ·trat'ing
or'ches·tra'tion
or'chid
or·dain'
or·deal'
or'der
or'der·li·ness
or'der·ly
  ·lies
or'di·nal
or'di·nance
  (law; SEE
  ordnance)
or'di·nar'i·ly
or'di·nar'y
  ·ies
or'di·nate
or'di·na'tion
ord'nance
  (artillery; SEE
  ordinance)
or'dure
ore
  (mineral; SEE oar)
o·reg'a·no
Or'e·gon
or'gan
or'gan·dy or ·die
or·gan'ic
or·gan'i·cal·ly
or'gan·ism

or'gan·ist
or'gan·iz'a·ble
or'gan·i·za'tion
or'gan·ize'
  ·ized' ·iz'ing
or'gan·iz'er
or·gan'za
or'gasm
or·gas'mic
or·gi·as'tic
or'gy
  ·gies
O'ri·ent n.
o'ri·ent' v.
O'ri·en'tal
o'ri·en·tate'
  ·tat'ed ·tat'ing
o'ri·en·ta'tion
or'i·fice
or'i·ga'mi
or'i·gin
o·rig'i·nal
o·rig'i·nal'i·ty
o·rig'i·nal·ly
o·rig'i·nate'
  ·nat'ed ·nat'ing
o·rig'i·na'tion
o·rig'i·na'tor
o'ri·ole'
or'lon
or'na·ment
or'na·men'tal
or'na·men·ta'tion
or·nate'

or·nate′ly
or′ni·thol′o·gy
o′ro·tund′
or′phan·age
or′thi·con′
or′tho·don′tics
or′tho·don′tist
or′tho·dox′
or′tho·dox′y
·ies
or·thog′ra·phy
or′tho·pe′dics
or′tho·pe′dist
os′cil·late′
·lat′ed ·lat′ing
(*fluctuate;* SEE
osculate)
os′cil·la′tion
os′cil·la′tor
os·cil′lo·scope′
os′cu·late′
·lat′ed ·lat′ing
(*kiss;* SEE
oscillate)
os·mo′sis
os′prey
·preys
os′si·fy′
·fied′ ·fy′ing
os·ten′si·ble
os·ten′si·bly
os·ten′sive
os·ten′sive·ly
os′ten·ta′tion

os′ten·ta′tious
os′te·o·path′
os′te·op′a·thy
os′tra·cism
os′tra·cize′
·cized′ ·ciz′ing
os′trich
oth′er-di·rect′ed
oth′er·wise′
o′ti·ose′
ot′ter
ot′to·man
·mans
ought
(*be obliged;* SEE
aught)
our·self′
our·selves′
oust′er
out′-and-out′
out′bid′
·bid′ ·bid′ding
out′board′
out′bound′
out′break′
out′build′ing
out′burst′
out′cast′
out′class′
out′come′
out′crop′
out′cry′
·cries′
out′dat′ed

out′dis′tance
·tanced ·tanc·ing
out′do′
·did′ ·done′
·do′ing
out′door′
out′doors′
out′er·most′
out′er space
out′er·wear′
out′face′
out′field′er
out′fit′
out′fit′ter
out′flank′
out′flow′
out′go′
·went′ ·gone′
·go′ing
out′go′
·goes′
out′go′ing
out′-group′
out′grow′
·grew′ ·grown′
·grow′ing
out′growth′
out′guess′
out′house′
out′ing
out′land′er
out·land′ish
out·last′
out′law′

205

out'law·ry
·ries
out'lay'
·laid' ·lay'ing
out'let'
out'li·er
out'line'
out'live'
out'look'
out'ly'ing
out'man'
out'ma·neu'ver
out'mod'ed
out'most'
out'num'ber
out'-of-date'
out'-of-doors'
out'-of-pock'et
out'-of-the-way'
out'-of-town'er
out'pa'tient
out'post'
out'pour'ing
out'put'
out'rage'
out·ra'geous
out'rank'
out'reach'
out'ride'
·rode' ·rid'den
·rid'ing
out'rid'er
out'rig'ger
out'right'

out'run'
·ran' ·run'
·run'ning
out'sell'
·sold' ·sell'ing
out'set'
out'shine'
·shone' ·shin'ing
out'side'
out'sid'er
out'sit'
·sat' ·sit'ting
out'size'
out'skirts'
out'smart'
out'speak'
·spoke' ·spo'ken
·speak'ing
out'spo'ken·ness
out'spread'
·spread'
·spread'ing
out'stand'ing
out'stare'
out'sta'tion
out'stay'
out'stretch'
out'strip'
out'talk'
out'think'
·thought'
·think'ing
out'vote'
out'ward

out'wear'
·wore' ·worn'
·wear'ing
out'weigh'
out'wit'
·wit'ted
·wit'ting
out'work'
o'val
o'val·ly
o·var'i·an
o'va·ry
·ries
o·va'tion
ov'en
o'ver·age
o'ver·all'
o'ver·alls'
o'ver·awe'
·awed' ·aw'ing
o'ver·bal'ance
o'ver·bear'
·bore' ·borne'
·bear'ing
o'ver·bid'
·bid' ·bid'ding
o'ver·bite'
o'ver·blouse'
o'ver·board'
o'ver·cap'i·tal·
ize'
o'ver·cast'
o'ver·charge'
o'ver·coat'

o'ver·come'
 ·came' ·come'
 ·com'ing
o'ver·com'pen·
 sate'
o'ver·con'fi·dent
o'ver·crowd'ed
o'ver·do'
 ·did' ·done'
 ·do'ing
o'ver·dose'
o'ver·draft'
o'ver·draw'
 ·drew' ·drawn'
 ·draw'ing
o'ver·dress'
o'ver·drive'
o'ver·due'
o'ver·flight'
o'ver·flow'
o'ver·fly'
 ·flew' ·flown'
 ·fly'ing
o'ver·gar'ment
o'ver·glaze'
o'ver·grow'
 ·grew' ·grown'
 ·grow'ing
o'ver·hand'
o'ver·hang'
 ·hung'
 ·hang'ing
o'ver·haul'
o'ver·head'

o'ver·hear'
 ·heard'
 ·hear'ing
o'ver·heat'
o'ver·in·dul'·
 gence
o'ver·is'sue
o'ver·joy'
o'ver·lad'en
o'ver·lap'
o'ver·lay'
 ·laid' ·lay'ing
o'ver·leap'
o'ver·lie'
 ·lay' ·lain'
 ·ly'ing
o'ver·load'
o'ver·look'
o'ver·ly
o'ver·nice'
o'ver·night'
o'ver·pass'
o'ver·pay'
 ·paid' ·pay'ing
o'ver·pop'u·late'
o'ver·pow'er
o'ver·pro·duce'
o'ver·pro·tect'
o'ver·rate'
o'ver·reach'
o'ver·ride'
 ·rode' ·rid'den
 ·rid'ing
o'ver·rule'

o'ver·run'
 ·ran' ·run'
 ·run'ning
o'ver·seas'
o'ver·see'
 ·saw' ·seen'
 ·see'ing
o'ver·se'er
o'ver·sell'
 ·sold' ·sell'ing
o'ver·sexed'
o'ver·shad'ow
o'ver·shoe'
o'ver·shoot'
 ·shot' ·shoot'ing
o'ver·sight'
o'ver·sim'pli·fy'
o'ver·size'
o'ver·skirt'
o'ver·slaugh'
o'ver·sleep'
 ·slept' ·sleep'ing
o'ver·spend'
 ·spent' ·spend'ing
o'ver·spread'
o'ver·state'
o'ver·stay'
o'ver·step'
o'ver·stock'
o'ver·strung'
o'ver·stuff'
o'ver·sub·scribe'
o'ver·sup·ply'
o·vert'

o'ver·take'
  ·took' ·tak'en
  ·tak'ing
o'ver·tax'
o'ver-the-count'er
o'ver·throw'
  ·threw' ·thrown'
  ·throw'ing
o'ver·time'
o'ver·tone'
o'ver·ture
o'ver·use'
o'ver·view'
o'ver·ween'ing
o'ver·weight'
o'ver·whelm'
o'ver·wind'
  ·wound' ·wind'ing
o'ver·work'
o'ver·write'
  ·wrote' ·writ'ten
  ·writ'ing
o'ver·wrought'
o·vip'a·rous
o'void
o'vu·late'
  ·lat'ed ·lat'ing
o'vu·la'tion
o'vule
o'vum
  o'va
owe
  owed ow'ing
owl'ish

own'er·ship'
ox
  ox'en
ox'blood'
ox'bow'
ox'ford
ox'i·da'tion
ox'i·dize'
  ·dized' ·diz'ing
ox'tail'
ox'y·gen
ox'y·gen·ate'
  ·at'ed ·at'ing
ox'y·gen·a'tion
ox'y·mo'ron
  ·mo'ra
ox'y·tet'ra·cy'·
  cline
oys'ter
o'zone

P

pab'lum
pace
  paced pac'ing
pace'mak'er
pach'y·derm'
pach'y·san'dra
pac'i·fi'a·ble
pa·cif'ic
pac'i·fi·ca'tion

pac'i·fi'er
pac'i·fism
pac'i·fy'
  ·fied' ·fy'ing
pack'age
  ·aged ·ag·ing
pack'et
pack'ing
pack'sad'dle
pack'thread'
pact
pad
  pad'ded
  pad'ding
pad'dle
  ·dled ·dling
pad'dock
pad'dy
  ·dies
  (*rice;* SEE patty)
pad'lock'
pa'dre
  ·dres
pae'an
  (*song;* SEE peon)
pa'gan
page
  paged pag'ing
pag'eant
pag'eant·ry
  ·ries
page'boy'
pag'i·nate'
  ·nat'ed ·nat'ing

pag·i·na'tion
pa·go'da
pail
 (*bucket;* SEE
 pale)
pail'ful'
 ·fuls'
pain
 (*hurt;* SEE pane)
pain'ful
pain'less
pains'tak'ing
paint'brush'
paint'er
pair
 (*two;* SEE pare,
 pear)
pais'ley
pa·ja'mas
pal'ace
pal'an·quin'
pal'at·a·ble
pal'at·a·bly
pal'a·tal
pal'ate
 (*roof of mouth;*
 SEE palette, pallet)
pa·la'tial
pal'a·tine'
pa·lav'er
pale
 paled pal'ing
 (*white;* SEE pail)
pale'face'

pale'ly
pa'le·o·lith'ic
pa'le·on·tol'o·gy
pal'ette
 (*paint board;* SEE
 palate, pallet)
pal'in·drome'
pal'ing
pal'i·sade'
pall
 palled pall'ing
pal·la'di·um
pall'bear'er
pal'let
 (*tool; bed;* SEE
 palate, palette)
pal'li·ate'
 ·at'ed ·at'ing
pal'li·a'tive
pal'lid
pall'-mall'
 (*game;* SEE
 pell-mell)
pal'lor
palm
pal·met'to
 ·tos *or* ·toes
palm'is·try
pal'o·mi'no
 ·nos
pal'pa·ble
pal'pa·bly
pal'pate
 ·pat·ed ·pat·ing

pal'pi·tate'
 ·tat'ed ·tat'ing
pal'pi·ta'tion
pal'sy
 ·sied ·sy·ing
pal'tri·ness
pal'try
 ·tri·er ·tri·est
 (*trifling;*
 SEE poultry)
pam'pas
pam'per
pam'phlet
pam'phlet·eer'
pan
 panned pan'ning
pan·a·ce'a
pa·nache'
Pan'-A·mer'i·can
pan·a·tel'a
pan'cake'
pan'chro·mat'ic
pan'cre·as
pan'cre·at'ic
pan·dem'ic
pan'de·mo'ni·um
pan'der
pan·dow'dy
 ·dies
pane
 (*window;* SEE
 pain)
pan'e·gyr'ic
pan'e·gyr'i·cal

pan′el
  ·eled *or* ·elled
  ·el·ing *or* ·el·ling
pan′el·ist
pan′-fry′
  -fried′ -fry′ing
pan′han′dle
pan′ic
  ·icked ·ick·ing
pan′ic·al·ly
pan′ick·y
pan′ic-strick′en
panne
pan′nier
pan′o·ply
  ·plies
pan′o·ra′ma
pan′o·ram′ic
pan′o·ram′i·cal·ly
pan′ta·loons′
pant′dress′
pan′the·ism
pan′the·is′tic
pan′the·on′
pan′ther
pant′ies
pan′to·graph
pan′to·mime′
  ·mimed′
  ·mim′ing
pan′to·mim′ic
pan′to·mim′ist
pan′try
  ·tries

pant′suit′ *or*
  pants suit
pant′y hose
pa′pa·cy
  ·cies
pa′pal
pa′paw
pa·pa′ya
pa′per·back′
pa′per·bound′
pa′per·hang′er
pa′per·weight′
pa′per·y
pa′pier-mâ·ché′
pa·poose′
pa·pri′ka
pap′ule
pa·py′rus
  ·ri *or* ·rus·es
par
  parred par′ring
par′a·ble
pa·rab′o·la
par′a·bol′ic
par′a·bol′i·cal·ly
par′a·chute′
  ·chut′ed
  ·chut′ing
par′a·chut′ist
pa·rade′
  ·rad′ed ·rad′ing
par′a·digm′
par′a·dise′
par′a·dox′

par′a·dox′i·cal
par′a·dox′i·cal·ly
par′af·fin
par′a·gon′
par′a·graph′
par′a·keet′
par′al·lax′
par′al·lel′
  ·leled′ *or* ·lelled′
  ·lel′ing *or*
  ·lel′ling
par′al·lel·ism′
par′al·lel′o·gram′
pa·ral′y·sis
par′a·lyt′ic
par′a·lyze′
  ·lyzed′ ·lyz′ing
par′a·me′ci·um
  ·ci·a
par′a·med′ic
par′a·med′i·cal
pa·ram′e·ter
  (*math. term;* SEE
  perimeter)
par′a·mount′
par′a·mour′
par′a·noi′a
par′a·noi′ac
par′a·noid′
par′a·pet
par′a·pher·na′li·a
par′a·phrase′
  ·phrased′
  ·phras′ing

par'a·ple'gi·a
par'a·ple'gic
par'a·prax'is
·es
par'a·psy·chol'o·
gy
par'a·res'cue
par'a·sail'
par'a·site'
par'a·sit'ic
par'a·sol'
par'a·troops'
par'boil'
par'buck·le
par'cel
·celed *or* ·celled
·cel·ing *or*
·cel·ling
parch'ment
par'don·a·ble
par'don·a·bly
pare
pared par'ing
(*trim;* SEE pair,
pear)
par'e·gor'ic
par'ent
par'ent·age
pa·ren'tal
pa·ren'the·sis
·ses'
pa·ren'the·size'
·sized' ·siz'ing
par'en·thet'i·cal

par'ent·hood'
pa·re'sis
par'e·ve
par ex'cel·lence'
par·fait'
par·he'li·on
·li·a
pa·ri'ah
pa·ri'e·tal
par'i·mu'tu·el
par'ish
pa·rish'ion·er
par'i·ty
·ties
par'ka
park'way'
parl'ance
par'lay
(*bet*)
par'ley
(*confer*)
par'lia·ment
par'lia·men·
tar'i·an
par'lia·men'ta·ry
par'lor
pa·ro'chi·al
par'o·dist
par'o·dy
·dies
·died ·dy·ing
pa·role'
·roled' ·rol'ing
pa·rol·ee'

pa·rot'id
par·ox·ysm
par·ox·ys'mal
par·quet'
·queted'
·quet'ing
par'quet·ry
par'ra·keet'
par'ri·ci'dal
par'ri·cide'
par'rot
par'ry
·ries
·ried ·ry·ing
par'sec'
par'si·mo'ni·ous
par'si·mo'ny
pars'ley
pars'nip
par'son
par'son·age
par·take'
·took' ·tak'en
·tak'ing
par·terre'
par'the·no·gen'e·
sis
par'tial
par'ti·al'i·ty
par'tial·ly
par'ti·ble
par·tic'i·pant
par·tic'i·pate'
·pat'ed ·pat'ing

par·tic'i·pa'tion
par·tic'i·pa'tor
par'ti·cip'i·al
par'ti·ci·ple
par'ti·cle
par'ti·col'ored
par·tic'u·lar
par·tic'u·lar'i·ty
·ties
par·tic'u·lar·ize'
·ized' ·iz'ing
par·tic'u·lar·ly
par'ti·san
par·ti'tion
part'ner
part'ner·ship'
par'tridge
part'-time'
par·tu'ri·ent
par'tu·ri'tion
par'ty
·ties
par've·nu'
·nus'
pas'chal
pass'a·ble
pass'a·bly
pas'sage
pas'sage·way'
pass'book'
pas·sé'
passed
(*pp. of* pass;
SEE past)

pas'sen·ger
passe'-par·tout'
pass'er-by'
pass'ers-by'
pas'sion
pas'sion·ate
pas'sion·ate·ly
pas'sive
pas'sive·ly
pas·siv'i·ty
pass'key'
Pass'o'ver
pass'port'
pass'-through'
pass'word'
past
(*gone by; over;*
SEE passed)
paste
past'ed past'ing
paste'board'
pas·tel'
pas'teur·i·za'tion
pas'teur·ize'
·ized' ·iz'ing
pas·tille'
pas'time'
past'i·ness
pas'tor
pas'to·ral
pas'tor·ate
pas·tra'mi
pas'try
·tries

pas'ture
·tured ·tur·ing
past'y
·i·er ·i·est
pat
pat'ted pat'ting
patch'work'
patch'y
·i·er ·i·est
pâ·té' de foie'
gras'
pa·tel'la
·las *or* ·lae
pat'ent
pat'ent·ee'
pa·ter'nal
pa·ter'nal·is'tic
pa·ter'ni·ty
pa·thet'ic
pa·thet'i·cal·ly
path'find'er
path'o·gen'ic
path'o·log'i·cal
pa·thol'o·gy
·gies
pa'thos
pa'tience
pa'tient
pat'i·na
pa'ti·o'
·os'
pa·tis'se·rie'
pat'ois
·ois

pa'tri·arch'
pa'tri·ar'chal
pa'tri·ar'chy
 ·chies
pa·tri'cian
pat'ri·cide'
pat'ri·mo'ny
 ·nies
pa'tri·ot
pa'tri·ot'ic
pa'tri·ot'i·cal·ly
pa'tri·ot·ism
pa·trol'
 ·trolled'
 ·trol'ling
pa·trol'man
pa'tron
pa'tron·age'
pa'tron·ize'
 ·ized' ·iz'ing
pat'ro·nym'ic
pat'ter
pat'tern·mak'er
pat'ty
 ·ties
 (*cake;* SEE paddy)
pau'ci·ty
paunch'i·ness
paunch'y
pau'per
pause
 paused paus'ing
pave
 paved pav'ing

pave'ment
pa·vil'ion
pawn'bro'ker
pawn'shop'
pay
 paid pay'ing
pay'a·ble
pay'check'
pay'day'
pay·ee'
pay'load'
pay'mas'ter
pay'ment
pay'off'
pay'roll'
peace
 (*harmony;*
 SEE piece)
peace'a·ble
peace'a·bly
peace'ful
peace'ful·ly
peace'mak'er
peace pipe
peace'time'
peach
pea'cock'
peak
 (*highest point;*
 SEE peek, pique)
peaked
 (*pointed*)
peak'ed
 (*thin and drawn*)

peal
 (*sound;* SEE peel)
pea'nut
pear
 (*fruit;* SEE pair,
 pare)
pearl
 (*gem;* SEE purl)
pearl'y
 ·i·er ·i·est
pear'-shaped'
peas'ant
peas'ant·ry
peat moss
peau' de soie'
peb'ble
 ·bled ·bling
peb'bly
 ·bli·er ·bli·est
pe·can'
pec'ca·dil'lo
 ·loes *or* ·los
pec'cant
peck
pec'tin
pec'to·ral
pec'u·late'
 ·lat'ed ·lat'ing
pec'u·la'tion
pec'u·la'tor
pe·cul'iar
pe·cul'i·ar'i·ty
 ·ties
pe·cu'ni·ar'i·ly

pe·cu'ni·ar'y
ped'a·gog'ic
ped'a·gogue'
  or ·gog'
ped'a·go'gy
ped'al
  ·aled or ·alled
  ·al·ing or
  ·al·ling
  (foot lever; SEE
  peddle)
ped'ant
pe·dan'tic
pe·dan'ti·cal·ly
ped'ant·ry
  ·ries
ped'dle
  ·dled ·dling
  (sell; SEE pedal)
ped'dler
ped'es·tal
pe·des'tri·an
pe'di·a·tri'cian
pe'di·at'rics
ped'i·cure'
ped'i·gree'
ped'i·greed'
ped'i·ment
pe·dom'e·ter
peek
  (look; SEE
  peak, pique)
peel
  (skin; SEE peal)

peep'hole'
peer
  (equal; look;
  SEE pier)
peer group
peer'less
peeve
  peeved peev'ing
pee'vish
peg
  pegged peg'ging
peg'board'
peign·oir'
pe'jo·ra'tion
pe'jo·ra·tive
Pe'king·ese'
pe'koe
pel'i·can
pel·la'gra
pel'let
pell'-mell'
  (without order;
  SEE pall-mall)
pel·lu'cid
pel'vic
pel'vis
pem'mi·can
pen
  penned or pent
  pen'ning
  (enclose)
pen
  penned pen'ning
  (write with pen)

pe'nal
pe'nal·i·za'tion
pe'nal·ize'
  ·ized' ·iz'ing
pen'al·ty
  ·ties
pen'ance
pen'chant
pen'cil
  ·ciled or ·cilled
  ·cil·ing or
  ·cil·ling
pend'ant or
  ·ent n.
pend'ent or
  ·ant adj.
pend'ing
pen'du·lous
pen'du·lum
pen'e·tra·bil'i·ty
pen'e·tra·ble
pen'e·tra·bly
pen'e·trate'
  ·trat'ed ·trat'ing
pen'e·tra'tion
pen'e·trom'e·ter
pen'guin
pen'hold'er
pen'i·cil'lin
pen·in'su·la
pen·in'su·lar
pe'nis
  ·nis·es or ·nes
pen'i·tence

pen'i·tent
pen'i·ten'tial
pen'i·ten'tia·ry
·ries
pen'knife'
·knives'
pen'light' or ·lite'
pen'man·ship'
pen name
pen'nant
pen'non
Penn'syl·va'ni·a
pen'ny
·nies
pen'ny ante
pen'ny·weight'
pen'ny·wise'
pen'ny·worth'
pe'no·log'i·cal
pe·nol'o·gist
pe·nol'o·gy
pen'sion
pen'sion·ar'y
·ies
pen'sive
pen'sive·ly
pen'stock'
pen'ta·gon'
pen·tag'o·nal
pen·ta·he'dral
pen·ta·he'dron
·drons or ·dra
pen·tam'e·ter
Pen'ta·teuch'

pen·tath'lon
Pen'te·cost'
pent'house'
pen·tom'ic
pent'-up'
pe·nu'che or ·chi
pe'nult
pe·nul'ti·mate
pe·num'bra
·brae or ·bras
pe·nu'ri·ous
pen'u·ry
pe'on
(laborer; SEE
paean)
pe'on·age
pe'o·ny
·nies
peo'ple
·pled ·pling
pep'lum
·lums or ·la
pep'per-and-salt'
pep'per·corn'
pep'per·i·ness
pep'per·mint'
pep'per·o'ni
·nis or ·ni
pep'per·y
·i·er ·i·est
pep'pi·ly
pep'pi·ness
pep'py
·pi·er ·pi·est

pep'sin
pep'tic
per·am'bu·late'
·lat'ed ·lat'ing
per·am'bu·la'tion
per·am'bu·la'tor
per an'num
per·cale'
per cap'i·ta
per·ceiv'a·ble
per·ceiv'a·bly
per·ceive'
·ceived' ·ceiv'ing
per·cent' or
per cent
per·cent'age
per·cen'tile
per'cept
per·cep'ti·ble
per·cep'ti·bly
per·cep'tion
per·cep'tive
per·cep'tive·ly
per·cep'tu·al
per·chance'
Per'che·ron'
per·cip'i·ent
per'co·late'
·lat'ed ·lat'ing
per'co·la'tion
per'co·la'tor
per·cus'sion
per·cus'sive
per di'em

215

per·di′tion
per·du′ or ·due′
per·dur′a·ble
per′e·gri·nate′
·nat′ed ·nat′ing
per′e·gri·na′tion
per·emp′to·ri·ly
per·emp′to·ri·ness
per·emp′to·ry
per·en′ni·al
per′fect
per·fect′i·bil′i·ty
per·fect′i·ble
per·fec′tion
per·fec′tion·ism
per·fec′to
·tos
per·fid′i·ous
per′fi·dy
·dies
per′fo·rate′
·rat′ed ·rat′ing
per′fo·ra′tion
per′fo·ra′tor
per·force′
per·form′
per·form′ance
per·fume′
·fumed′ ·fum′ing
per·fume′ n.
per·fum′er
per·func′to·ri·ly
per·func′to·ry
per′go·la

per·haps′
per′i·gee′
per′i·he′li·on
·li·ons or ·li·a
per′il
·iled or ·illed
·il·ing or ·il·ling
per′il·ous
per′i·lune′
pe·rim′e·ter
(boundary; SEE
parameter)
pe′ri·od
pe′ri·od′ic
pe′ri·od′i·cal
pe′ri·od′i·cal·ly
pe′ri·o·dic′i·ty
per′i·pa·tet′ic
pe·riph′er·al
pe·riph′er·y
·ies
pe·riph′ra·sis
per′i·phras′tic
pe·rique′
per′i·scope′
per′i·scop′ic
per′ish
per′ish·a·bil′i·ty
per′ish·a·ble
per′i·stal′sis
per′i·style′
per′i·to·ni′tis
per′jure
·jured ·jur·ing

per′jur·er
per′ju·ry
·ries
perk′i·ness
perk′y
·i·er ·i·est
per′ma·frost′
perm′al·loy
per′ma·nence
per′ma·nent
per′me·a·bil′i·ty
per′me·a·ble
per′me·ate′
·at′ed ·at′ing
per′me·a′tion
per·mis′si·bil′i·ty
per·mis′si·ble
per·mis′si·bly
per·mis′sion
per·mis′sive
per·mis′sive·ly
per·mit′
·mit′ted
·mit′ting
per·mut′a·ble
per′mu·ta′tion
per·ni′cious
per·nod′
per′o·rate′
·rat′ed ·rat′ing
per′o·ra′tion
per·ox′ide
·id·ed ·id·ing
per·pen·dic′u·lar

216

per'pe·trate'
·trat'ed ·trat'ing

per'pe·tra'tion

per'pe·tra'tor

per·pet'u·al

per·pet'u·al·ly

per·pet'u·ate'
·at'ed ·at'ing

per·pet'u·a'tion

per·pet'u·a'tor

per'pe·tu'i·ty
·ties

per·plex'

per·plexed'

per·plex'ed·ly

per·plex'i·ty
·ties

per'qui·site
(*privilege;* SEE
prerequisite)

per se

per'se·cute'
·cut'ed ·cut'ing
(*harass;* SEE
prosecute)

per'se·cu'tion

per'se·cu'tor

per'se·ver'ance

per'se·vere'
·vered' ·ver'ing

per·si·flage'

per·sim'mon

per·sist'

per·sist'ence

per·sist'ent

per'son

per'son·a·ble

per'son·age

per'son·al
(*private;* SEE
personnel)

per'son·al'i·ty
·ties

per'son·al·ize'
·ized' ·iz'ing

per'son·al·ly

per'son·ate'
·at'ed ·at'ing

per·son·a'tion

per·son·a'tor

per·son'i·fi·
ca'tion

per·son'i·fy'
·fied' ·fy'ing

per·son·nel'
(*employees;* SEE
personal)

per·spec'tive
(*view;* SEE
prospective)

per'spi·ca'cious

per'spi·cac'i·ty

per'spi·cu'i·ty

per·spic'u·ous

per'spi·ra'tion

per·spir'a·to·ry

per·spire'
·spired' ·spir'ing

per·suad'a·ble

per·suade'
·suad'ed
·suad'ing

per·sua'si·bil'i·ty

per·sua'sion

per·sua'sive

per·tain'

per'ti·na'cious

per'ti·nac'i·ty

per'ti·nence

per'ti·nent

pert'ly

per·turb'

per'tur·ba'tion

pe·rus'al

pe·ruse'
·rused' ·rus'ing

per·vade'
·vad'ed ·vad'ing

per·va'sion

per·va'sive

per·verse'

per·verse'ly

per·ver'sion

per·ver'si·ty

per·vert'

per'vi·ous

Pe'sach

pe'so
·sos

pes'si·mism

pes'si·mist

pes'si·mis'tic

pes'si·mis'ti·
  cal·ly
pes'ter
pest'hole'
pes'ti·cide'
pes'ti·lence
pes'ti·lent
pes'ti·len'tial
pes'tle
  ·tled ·tling
pet
  pet'ted pet'ting
pet'al
pet'al·like'
pet'cock'
pe·tite'
pe'tit four'
  pe'tits fours'
  or pe'tit fours'
pe·ti'tion
pet'it jury
pe·tit' mal'
pet'it point
pe'tri dish
pet'ri·fac'tion
pet'ri·fy'
  ·fied' ·fy'ing
pet'ro·la'tum
pe·tro'le·um
pet'ti·coat'
pet'ti·fog'
  ·fogged'
  ·fog'ging
pet'ti·fog'ger

pet'ti·ly
pet'ti·ness
pet'ti·pants'
pet'tish
pet'ty
  ·ti·er ·ti·est
pet'u·lance
pet'u·lant
pew'ter
pha'e·ton
pha'lanx
  ·lanx·es or
  pha·lan'ges
phal'lic
phal'lus
  ·li or ·lus·es
phan'tasm
phan'tom
phar'i·sa'ic
phar'i·see'
phar'ma·ceu'ti·cal
phar'ma·cist
phar'ma·col'o·gy
phar'ma·co·pe'ia
phar'ma·cy
  ·cies
phar'ynx
  ·ynx·es or
  pha·ryn'ges
phase
  phased phas'ing
  (stage; SEE faze)
phase'-out'
pheas'ant

phe'no·bar'bi·tal'
phe·nom'e·nal
phe·nom'e·nal·ly
phe·nom'e·non'
  ·na or ·nons'
phi'al
Phil'a·del'phi·a
phi·lan'der·er
phil'an·throp'ic
phi·lan'thro·pist
phi·lan'thro·py
  ·pies
phil'a·tel'ic
phi·lat'e·list
phi·lat'e·ly
phil'har·mon'ic
Phil'ip·pine'
Phil'is·tine'
phil'o·den'dron
phil'o·log'i·cal
phi·lol'o·gist
phi·lol'o·gy
phi·los'o·pher
phil'o·soph'ic
phil'o·soph'i·
  cal·ly
phi·los'o·phize'
  ·phized' ·phiz'ing
phi·los'o·phy
  ·phies
phil'ter
  (potion; SEE
  filter)
phle·bi'tis

phlegm
phleg·mat′ic
phlox
pho′bi·a
pho′bic
phoe′be
Phoe′nix
phone
  phoned phon′ing
pho′neme
pho·net′ic
pho·net′i·cal·ly
pho·ne·ti′cian
phon′ics
pho′ni·ness
pho′no·graph′
pho·nol′o·gy
pho′ny
  ·ni·er ·ni·est
  ·nies
phos′phate
phos′pho·
  res′cence
phos′pho·res′cent
pho′to·chron′o·
  graph
pho′to·cop′i·er
pho′to·cop′y
  ·ies
  ·ied ·y·ing
pho′to·e·lec′tric
pho′to·en·grave′
  ·graved′
  ·grav′ing

pho′to·flash′
pho′to·flood′
pho′to·gen′ic
pho′to·graph′
pho·tog′ra·pher
pho′to·graph′ic
pho′to·graph′i·
  cal·ly
pho·tog′ra·phy
pho′to·gra·vure′
pho′to·lith′o·
  graph
pho′to·li·thog′ra·
  phy
pho′to·map′
pho·tom′e·ter
pho′to·met′ric
pho·tom′e·try
pho′to·mon·tage′
pho′to·mu′ral
pho′to-off′set′
pho′to·sen′si·tive
pho′to·stat′
  ·stat′ed or
  ·stat′ted
  ·stat′ing or
  ·stat′ting
pho′to·stat′ic
pho′to·syn′the·sis
phras′al
phras′al·ly
phrase
  phrased
  phras′ing

phra′se·ol′o·gy
  ·gies
phre·net′ic
phre·nol′o·gy
phy·lac′ter·y
  ·ies
phy′lum
  ·la
phys′ic
  ·icked ·ick·ing
phys′i·cal
phys′i·cal·ly
phy·si′cian
phys′i·cist
phys′ics
phys′i·og′no·my
phys′i·og′ra·phy
phys′i·o·log′i·cal
phys′i·ol′o·gy
phys′i·o·ther′a·
  pist
phys′i·o·ther′a·py
phy·sique′
pi
  pied
  pie′ing or pi′ing
  (jumble; SEE pie)
pi
  (Greek letter;
  SEE pie)
pi·a·nis′si·mo′
pi·an′ist
pi·an′o
  ·os

pi·a·no'la
pi·az'za
pi'ca
pic'a·dor'
pic'a·resque'
pic'a·yune'
Pic'ca·dil'ly
pic'ca·lil'li
pic'co·lo'
 ·los'
pick'ax' *or* ·axe'
pick'er·el
pick'et
pick'le
 ·led ·ling
pick'pock'et
pick'up'
pic'nic
 ·nicked
 ·nick·ing
pic'nick·er
pi'cot
 ·coted ·cot·ing
pic'to·graph'
pic·to'ri·al
pic·to'ri·al·ly
pic'ture
 ·tured ·tur·ing
pic'tur·esque'
pid'dle
 ·dled ·dling
pidg'in English
pie
 (*food;* SEE pi)

pie'bald'
piece
 pieced piec'ing
 (*part;* SEE peace)
pièce de ré·sis·
 tance'
piece'-dyed'
piece'meal'
piece'work'
pied'mont
pier
 (*structure;* SEE
  peer)
pierce
 pierced
 pierc'ing
pier glass
pi'e·tism
pi'e·ty
 ·ties
pi'geon
pi'geon·hole'
 ·holed' ·hol'ing
pi'geon-toed'
pig'gish
pig'gy·back'
pig'head'ed
pig iron
pig'let
pig'ment
pig'men·ta'tion
pi·gno'li·a
pig'pen'
pig'skin'

pig'sty'
 ·sties'
pig'tail'
pi·laf' *or* ·laff'
pi·las'ter
pile
 piled pil'ing
pi'le·ous
pile'up'
pil'fer
pil'fer·age
pil'grim
pil'grim·age
pil'lage
 ·laged ·lag·ing
pil'lar
pill'box'
pil'lion
pil'lo·ry
 ·ries
 ·ried ·ry·ing
pil'low
pil'low·case'
pi'lose
pi'lot
pi'lot·house'
Pil'sener *or*
 Pil'sner
pi·men'to *or*
 ·mien'·
 ·tos
pim'ple
pim'ply
pin'a·fore'

220

pi·ña′ta
pin′ball′
pince′-nez′
pin′cers
pinch′beck′
pinch′-hit′
·hit′ ·hit′ting
pin′cush′ion
pine
pined pin′ing
pine′ap′ple
pin′feath′er
ping′-pong′
pin′head′
pin′hole′
pin′ion
pink′eye′
pin′na·cle
·cled ·cling
(acme)
pi′noch′le or
·noc′·
(game)
pin′point′
pin stripe
pin′to
·tos
pint′-size′
pin′up′
pin′wale′
pin′wheel′
pin′worm′
pi′o·neer′
pi′ous

pipe
piped pip′ing
pipe′ful′
·fuls′
pipe′line′
pip′er
pipe′stem′
pi·pette′ or ·pet′
·pet′ted ·pet′ting
pip′pin
pi′quan·cy
pi′quant
pique
piqued piqu′ing
(offend; SEE
peak, peek)
pi·qué′ or ·que′
(fabric)
pi′ra·cy
pi·ra′nha
pi′rate
·rat·ed ·rat·ing
pir′ou·ette′
·et′ted ·et′ting
pis′ca·to′ri·al
pis′ci·cul′ture
pis·ta′chi·o′
·os′
pis′til
(part of plant)
pis′tol
·toled or ·tolled
·tol·ing or ·tol·ling
(firearm)

pis′tol-whip′
pis′ton
pit
pit′ted pit′ting
pitch′-black′
pitch′blende′
pitch′-dark′
pitch′er·ful′
·fuls′
pitch′fork′
pitch pipe
pit′e·ous
pit′fall′
pith′i·ness
pith′y
·i·er ·i·est
pit′i·a·ble
pit′i·ful
pit′i·less
pit′tance
Pitts′burgh
pi·tu′i·tar′y
pit′y
·ies, ·ied ·y·ing
piv′ot
piv′ot·al
pix′ie or ·y
·ies
piz′za
piz′ze·ri′a
piz′zi·ca′to
plac′a·bil′i·ty
plac′a·ble
plac′a·bly

221

plac‹ard
pla‹cate
·cat·ed ·cat·ing
place
placed plac‹ing
pla·ce‹bo
·bos or ·boes
place‹ment
pla·cen‹ta
·tas or ·tae
plac‹er
plac‹id
pla·cid‹i·ty
plack‹et
pla‹gia·rism
pla‹gia·rize‹
·rized‹ ·riz‹ing
pla‹gia·ry
·ries
plague
plagued
plagu‹ing
plagu‹er
plaid
plain
(clear; simple;
SEE plane)
plain‹ness
plains‹man
plain‹song‹
plain‹-spo‹ken
plain‹tiff
plain‹tive
plain‹tive·ly

plait
(pleat; braid;
SEE plate)
plan
planned
plan‹ning
plane
planed plan‹ing
(level; SEE plain)
plan‹et
plan‹e·tar‹i·um
·i·ums or ·i·a
plan‹e·tar‹y
plan‹e·tes‹i·mal
plan‹et·oid‹
plank‹ing
plank‹ton
plan‹ner
plan‹tain
plan‹tar
(of the sole)
plan·ta‹tion
plant‹er
(one that plants)
plan‹ti·grade‹
plaque
plas‹ma
plas‹ter
plas‹ter·board‹
plas‹ter·er
plas‹tic
plas‹ti·cal·ly
plas‹ti·cine
plas·tic‹i·ty

plas‹ti·cize‹
·cized‹ ·ciz‹ing
plat
plat‹ted
plat‹ting
(map)
plate
plat‹ed plat‹ing
(dish; SEE plait)
pla·teau‹
·teaus‹ or
·teaux‹
plate‹ful‹
·fuls‹
plat‹en
plat‹form‹
plat‹i·num
plat‹i·tude
plat‹i·tu‹di·nous
pla·ton‹ic
pla·ton‹i·cal·ly
pla·toon‹
plat‹ter
plau‹dit
plau‹si·bil‹i·ty
plau‹si·ble
plau‹si·bly
play‹back‹
play‹bill‹
play‹boy‹
play‹-by-play‹
play‹ful·ly
play‹go‹er
play‹ground‹

play'house'
play'mate'
play'-off'
play'pen'
play'room'
play'thing'
play'wright'
pla'za
plea
plead
  plead'ed or plead
  plead'ing
pleas'ant
pleas'ant·ry
  ·ries
please
  pleased
  pleas'ing
pleas'ur·a·ble
pleas'ur·a·bly
pleas'ure
pleat
ple·be'ian
pleb'i·scite'
plec'trum
  ·trums or ·tra
pledge
  pledged
  pledg'ing
pledg·ee'
ple'na·ry
plen'i·po·ten'ti·
  ar'y
  ·ies

plen'i·tude'
plen'te·ous
plen'ti·ful
plen'ti·ful·ly
plen'ty
ple'num
  ·nums or ·nu
ple'o·nasm
pleth'o·ra
pleu'ral
  (of the pleura;
  SEE plural)
pleu'ri·sy
Plex'i·glas'
pli'a·bil'i·ty
pli'a·ble
pli'an·cy
pli'ant
pli'ers
plight
plis·sé' or ·se'
plod
  plod'ded
  plod'ding
plop
  plopped
  plop'ping
plot
  plot'ted
  plot'ting
plow'share'
pluck'i·ness
pluck'y
  ·i·er ·i·est

plug
  plugged
  plug'ging
plum
  (fruit)
plum'age
plumb
  (lead weight)
plumb'er
plumb'ing
plume
  plumed
plum'ing
plum'met
plu'mose
plump'ness
plun'der
plunge
  plunged
  plung'ing
plung'er
plu·per'fect
plu'ral
  (more than one;
  SEE pleural)
plu'ral·ism
plu'ral·is'tic
plu·ral'i·ty
  ·ties
plu'ral·ize'
  ·ized' ·iz'ing
plush'i·ness
plush'y
  ·i·er ·i·est

plu·toc'ra·cy
·cies
plu'to·crat'
plu'to·crat'ic
plu·to'ni·um
plu'vi·al
ply
plies
plied ply'ing
ply'wood'
pneu·mat'ic
pneu·mo'ni·a
poached
poach'er
pock'et·book'
(*purse*)
pocket book
(*small book*)
pock'et·ful'
·fuls'
pock'et·knife'
·knives'
pock'et-size'
pock'mark'
po·di'a·trist
po·di'a·try
po'di·um
·di·a *or* ·di·ums
po'em
po·et'ic
po·et'i·cal·ly
po'et·ry
po·go'ni·a
po'go stick

po·grom'
poign'an·cy
poign'ant
poin·set'ti·a
point'-blank'
point'ed·ly
point'er
point'less
poise
poised pois'ing
poi'son·ous
poke
poked pok'ing
pok'er
pok'i·ness
pok'y
·i·er ·i·est
po'lar
po·lar'i·ty
po'lar·i·za'tion
po'lar·ize'
·ized' ·iz'ing
pole
poled pol'ing
(*rod;* SEE poll)
pole'ax' *or* ·axe'
po·lem'ic
po·lem'i·cist
pole'star'
pole'-vault' *v.*
po·lice'
·liced' ·lic'ing
po·lice'man
po·lice'wom'an

pol'i·clin'ic
(*outpatient clinic;*
SEE polyclinic)
pol'i·cy
·cies
pol'i·cy·hold'er
po'li·o·my'e·li'tis
pol'ish
po·lite'ly
po·lite'ness
pol'i·tic
·ticked ·tick·ing
po·lit'i·cal
po·lit'i·cal·ly
(*in a political
manner*)
pol'i·ti'cian
pol'i·tic·ly
(*shrewdly*)
po·lit'i·co'
·cos'
pol'i·tics
pol'i·ty
·ties
pol'ka
pol'ka dot
poll
(*vote;* SEE pole)
poll'ee'
pol'len
pol'li·nate'
·nat'ed ·nat'ing
pol'li·na'tion
pol'li·wog'

224

poll′ster
poll tax
pol·lu′tant
pol·lute′
 ·lut′ed ·lut′ing
pol·lu′tion
pol′ter·geist′
pol·troon′
pol′y·an′drous
pol′y·an′dry
pol′y·clin′ic
 (*hospital;* SEE
 policlinic)
pol′y·es′ter
pol′y·eth′yl·ene′
po·lyg′a·mous
po·lyg′a·my
pol′y·glot′
pol′y·gon′
pol′y·graph′
po·lyg′y·ny
pol′y·mer
pol′y·sty′rene
pol′y·syl·lab′ic
pol′y·syl′la·ble
pol′y·tech′nic
pol′y·the·ism
pol′y·un·sat′u·
 rat′ed
pom′ace
 (*pulp;* SEE
 pumice)
po·ma′ceous
po·made′

pome′gran′ate
pom′mel
 ·meled *or*
 ·melled
 ·mel·ing *or*
 ·mel·ling
pom′pa·dour′
pom′pa·no′
Pom·pei′i
pom′pon′
pom·pos′i·ty
pom′pous
pon′cho
 ·chos
pon′der
pon′der·a·ble
pon′der·ous
pon·gee′
pon′iard
pon′tiff
pon·tif′i·cal
pon·tif′i·cate′
 ·cat′ed ·cat′ing
pon·toon′
po′ny
 ·nies
po′ny·tail′
poo′dle
pooh′-pooh′
pool′room′
poor′house′
pop
 popped pop′ping
pop′corn′

pop′eyed′
pop′lar
 (*tree;* SEE
 popular)
pop′lin
pop′o′ver
pop′per
pop′pet
pop′py
 ·pies
pop′u·lace
 (*the masses;*
 SEE populous)
pop′u·lar
 (*liked by many;*
 SEE poplar)
pop′u·lar′i·ty
pop′u·lar·i·
 za′tion
pop′u·lar·ize′
 ·ized′ ·iz′ing
pop′u·late′
 ·lat′ed ·lat′ing
pop′u·la′tion
pop′u·lous
 (*full of people;*
 SEE populace)
por′ce·lain
por′cu·pine′
pore
 pored por′ing
 (*ponder; tiny*
 opening; SEE
 pour)

pork'er
por'no·graph'ic
por·nog'ra·phy
po·ros'i·ty
po'rous
por'phy·ry
 ·ries
por'poise
por'ridge
por'rin·ger
port'a·bil'i·ty
por'ta·ble
por'tage
 ·taged ·tag·ing
por'tal
port·cul'lis
por·tend'
por'tent
por·ten'tous
por'ter
por'ter·house'
port·fo'li·o'
 ·os'
port'hole'
por'ti·co'
 ·coes' or ·cos'
por·tiere'
por'tion
port'li·ness
port'ly
 ·li·er ·li·est
port·man'teau
 ·teaus or ·teaux
por'trait

por'trai·ture
por·tray'
por·tray'al
Por'tu·guese'
por'tu·lac'a
pose
 posed pos'ing
posh
po·si'tion
pos'i·tive
pos'i·tive·ly
pos'i·tiv·ism
pos'e
pos·sess'
pos·sessed'
pos·ses'sion
pos·ses'sive
pos·ses'sor
pos·si·bil'i·ty
 ·ties
pos'si·ble
pos'si·bly
post'age
post'al
post'box'
post card
post'date'
post'er
pos·te'ri·or
pos·ter'i·ty
post'grad'u·ate
post'haste'
post'hu·mous
post'hyp·not'ic

pos·til'ion
post'man
post'mark'
post'mas'ter
post'mis'tress
post'-mor'tem
post'na'tal
post'paid'
post·pon'a·ble
post·pone'
 ·poned' ·pon'ing
post·pone'ment
post'script'
pos'tu·late'
 ·lat'ed ·lat'ing
pos'tu·la'tion
pos'tu·la'tor
pos'tur·al
pos'ture
 ·tured ·tur·ing
post'war'
pot
 pot'ted pot'ting
po'ta·ble
po·ta'tion
po·ta'to
 ·toes
pot'bel'lied
pot'bel'ly
 ·lies
pot'boil'er
po'ten·cy
po'tent
po'ten·tate'

po·ten'tial
po·ten'ti·al'i·ty
 ·ties
po·ten'tial·ly
po'tent·ly
poth'er
pot'hold'er
pot'hole'
pot'hook'
po'tion
pot'latch'
pot'luck'
pot'pour·ri'
pot'sherd'
pot'shot'
pot'tage
pot'ter·y
 ·ies
pouch'i·ness
poul'tice
poul'try
 (fowls; SEE
 paltry)
pounce
 pounced
 pounc'ing
pound'-fool'ish
pour
 (flow; SEE pore)
pout
pov'er·ty
pow'der·y
 ·i·er ·i·est
pow'er·ful

pow'er·ful·ly
pow'er·house'
pow'er·less
pow'wow'
pox
prac'ti·ca·bil'i·ty
prac'ti·ca·ble
prac'ti·ca·bly
prac'ti·cal
prac'ti·cal'i·ty
 ·ties
prac'ti·cal·ly
prac'tice
 ·ticed ·tic·ing
prac'tic·er
prac'ti·cum
prac·ti'tion·er
prag·mat'ic
prag·mat'i·cal·ly
prag'ma·tism
prag'ma·tist
prai'rie
praise
 praised
 prais'ing
praise'wor'thy
pra'line
prance
 pranced
 pranc'ing
prank'ish
prate
 prat'ed
 prat'ing

prat'tle
 ·tled ·tling
pray
 (implore; SEE
 prey)
pray'er
 (one who prays)
prayer
 (an entreaty)
preach'er
pre'am'ble
pre'ar·range'
 ·ranged'
 ·rang'ing
pre'ar·range'ment
preb'end
pre·can'cel
pre·car'i·ous
pre·cau'tion
pre·cau'tion·ar'y
pre·cede'
 ·ced'ed ·ced'ing
 (come before;
 SEE proceed)
prec'e·dence
 (priority)
prec'e·dent
 (example)
pre'-cen'sor
pre'cept
pre·cep'tor
pre·ces'sion
 (a going before;
 SEE procession)

227

pre·ces′sion·al
pre′cinct
pre·ci·os′i·ty
pre′cious
prec′i·pice
pre·cip′i·tate′
·tat′ed ·tat′ing
pre·cip′i·ta′tion
pre·cip′i·tous
pré·cis′
·cis′
(*abstract*)
pre·cise′
(*definite*)
pre·cise′ly
pre·ci′sion
pre·clude′
·clud′ed
·clud′ing
pre·clu′sion
pre·co′cious
pre′cog·ni′tion
pre′con·ceive′
pre′con·cep′tion
pre′con′scious
pre·cur′sor
pre·cur′so·ry
pre·da′cious
pre·date′
pred′a·tor
pred′a·to′ry
pre′de·cease′
pred′e·ces′sor
pre·des′ti·na′tion

pre·des′tine
·tined ·tin·ing
pre·de·ter′mine
pred′i·ca·bil′i·ty
pred′i·ca·ble
pre·dic′a·ment
pred′i·cate′
·cat′ed ·cat′ing
pred′i·ca′tion
pre·dict′
pre·dict′a·ble
pre·dic′tion
pre·dic′tive
pre·dic′tor
pre′di·gest′
pre′di·lec′tion
pre′dis·pose′
pre′dis·po·si′tion
pre·dom′i·nant
pre·dom′i·nate′
pre·em′i·nence
pre·em′i·nent
pre·empt′
pre·emp′tion
pre·emp′tive
pre·emp′tor
pre′es·tab′lish
pre′ex·ist′
pre′ex·ist′ence
pre′fab′
pre·fab′ri·cate′
pref′ace
·aced ·ac·ing
pref′a·to′ry

pre′fect
pre′fec·ture
pre·fer′
·ferred′ ·fer′ring
pref′er·a·ble
pref′er·a·bly
pref′er·ence
pref′er·en′tial
pre·fer′ment
pre·fig·u·ra′tion
pre·fig′ur·a·tive
pre·fig′ure
pre′fix′
pre′flight′
preg′na·ble
preg′nan·cy
·cies
preg′nant
pre·hen′sile
pre′his·tor′ic
pre·judge′
pre·judg′ment *or*
·judge′·
prej′u·dice
·diced ·dic·ing
prej′u·di′cial
prel′a·cy
prel′ate
pre·lim′i·nar′y
·ies
prel′ude
pre·mar′i·tal
pre′ma·ture′
pre′ma·ture′ly

pre·med'i·cal
pre·med'i·tate'
pre·mier'
  (*chief*)
pre·mière'
  ·mièred'
  ·mièr'ing
  (*first showing*)
prem'ise
  ·ised ·is·ing
pre'mi·um
pre·mo·ni'tion
pre·mon'i·to'ry
pre·na'tal
pre·oc'cu·pan·cy
pre·oc'cu·pa'tion
pre·oc'cu·py'
  ·pied' ·py'ing
pre'or·dain'
pre·pack'age
pre·paid'
prep'a·ra'tion
pre·par'a·tive
pre·par'a·to'ry
pre·pare'
  ·pared' ·par'ing
pre·par'ed·ness
pre·pay'
  ·paid' ·pay'ing
pre·pay'ment
pre·pon'der·ance
pre·pon'der·ant
pre·pon'der·ate'
  ·at'ed ·at'ing

prep'o·si'tion
pre'pos·sess'
pre'pos·sess'ing
pre·pos'ter·ous
pre're·cord'
pre·req'ui·site
  (*requirement;* SEE
  perquisite)
pre·rog'a·tive
pre·sage'
  ·saged' ·sag'ing
pres'by·ter
Pres'by·te'ri·an
pre'school'
pre'sci·ence
pre'sci·ent
pre·scribe'
  ·scribed'
  ·scrib'ing
  (*order;* SEE
  proscribe)
pre·scrip'tion
pre·scrip'tive
pres'ence
pres'ent
pre·sent'a·ble
pre'sen·ta'tion
pres'ent-day'
pre·sen'ti·ment
  (*premonition*)
pre·sent'ment
  (*presentation*)
pre·serv'a·ble
pres'er·va'tion

pre·serv'a·tive
pre·serve'
  ·served'
  ·serv'ing
pre·set'
pre'-shrunk'
pre·side'
  ·sid'ed ·sid'ing
pres'i·den·cy
  ·cies
pres'i·dent
pres'i·dent-e·lect'
pres'i·den'tial
pre·sid'i·um
  ·i·a *or* ·i·ums
pre·sig'ni·fy'
press box
press'ing
press'man
pres'sure
  ·sured ·sur·ing
pres'sur·ize'
  ·ized' ·iz'ing
press'work'
pres'ti·dig'i·ta'tor
pres·tige'
pres·ti'gious
pre'stressed'
pre·sum'a·ble
pre·sume'
  ·sumed'
  ·sum'ing
pre·sump'tion
pre·sump'tive

pre·sump′tu·ous
pre·sup·pose′
pre·sup·po·si′tion
pre·tend′
pre·tend′er
pre·tense′
pre·ten′sion
pre·ten′tious
pre·ter·nat′u·ral
pre′text
pre′tri′al
pret′ti·fy′
·fied′ ·fy′ing
pret′ti·ly
pret′ti·ness
pret′ty
·ti·er ·ti·est
·tied ·ty·ing
pret′zel
pre·vail′
pre·vail′ing
prev′a·lence
prev′a·lent
pre·var′i·cate′
·cat′ed ·cat′ing
pre·var′i·ca′tion
pre·var′i·ca′tor
pre·ven′ient
pre·vent′
pre·vent′a·ble or
·i·ble
pre·ven′tion
pre·ven′tive or
·vent′a·tive

pre′view
pre′vi·ous
pre·vi′sion
pre′war′
prey
(victim; SEE
pray)
pri′a·pism
price
priced pric′ing
price′less
prick′le
·led ·ling
prick′li·ness
prick′ly
·li·er ·li·est
pride
prid′ed prid′ing
pri′er
(one who pries;
SEE prior)
priest′ess
priest′hood
priest′ly
·li·er ·li·est
prig′gish
prim
prim′mer
prim′mest
pri′ma·cy
pri′ma don′na
pri′ma fa′ci·e′
pri′mal
pri·ma′ri·ly

pri′ma·ry
·ries
pri′mate
prime
primed prim′ing
prim′er
pri·me′val
prim′i·tive
prim′i·tive·ly
prim′i·tiv·ism
pri′mo·gen′i·tor
pri′mo·gen′i·ture
pri·mor′di·al
primp
prim′rose′
prince′ling
prince′ly
·li·er ·li·est
prin′cess
prin′ci·pal
(chief; SEE
principle)
prin′ci·pal′i·ty
·ties
prin′ci·pal·ly
prin′ci·ple
(basic rule; SEE
principal)
prin′ci·pled
print′a·ble
print′out′
pri′or
(previous; SEE
prier)

pri·or·ess
pri·or'i·ty
 ·ties
pri'o·ry
 ·ries
prism
pris·mat'ic
pris'on
pris'on·er
pris'tine
pri'va·cy
pri'vate
pri'va·teer'
pri·va'tion
priv'et
priv'i·lege
 ·leged ·leg·ing
priv'y
 ·ies
prize
 prized priz'ing
prize'fight'
prob'a·bil'i·ty
prob'a·ble
prob'a·bly
pro'bate
 ·bat·ed ·bat·ing
pro·ba'tion
pro·ba'tion·ar'y
pro·ba'tion·er
pro'ba·tive
probe
 probed prob'ing
prob'i·ty

prob'lem
prob'lem·at'ic
pro·bos'cis
 ·cis·es or ·ci·des'
pro·ce'dur·al
pro·ce'dure
pro·ceed'
 (*go on;* SEE
 precede)
pro'ceeds
proc'ess
pro·ces'sion
 (*parade;* SEE
 precession)
pro·ces'sion·al
proc'es·sor *or*
 proc'ess·er
pro·claim'
proc'la·ma'tion
pro·cliv'i·ty
 ·ties
pro·cras'ti·nate'
 ·nat·ed ·nat·ing
pro·cras'ti·na'tion
pro·cras'ti·na'tor
pro'cre·ant
pro'cre·ate'
 ·at·ed ·at·ing
pro'cre·a'tor
proc·tol'o·gy
proc'tor
proc'to·scope'
pro·cum'bent
pro·cur'a·ble

proc'u·ra'tor
pro·cure'
 ·cured' ·cur'ing
pro·cure'ment
prod
prod'ded
prod'ding
prod'i·gal
prod'i·gal'i·ty
pro·di'gious
prod'i·gy
 ·gies
 (*genius;* SEE
 protégé)
pro·duce'
 ·duced'
 ·duc'ing
pro·duc'er
pro·duc'i·ble
prod'uct
pro·duc'tion
pro·duc'tive
pro·duc'tive·ly
pro'duc·tiv'i·ty
prof'a·na'tion
pro·fane'
 ·faned' ·fan'ing
pro·fane'ly
pro·fan'i·ty
 ·ties
pro·fess'
pro·fessed'
pro·fess'ed·ly
pro·fes'sion

pro·fes′sion·al·ly
pro·fes′sor
pro·fes′so·ri·al
pro·fes′so·ri·ate
prof′fer
pro·fi′cien·cy
pro·fi′cient
pro′file
·filed ·fil·ing
prof′it
(*gain;* SEE
prophet)
prof′it·a·ble
prof′it·a·bly
prof′i·teer′
prof′li·ga·cy
prof′li·gate
pro·found′
pro·fun′di·ty
·ties
pro·fuse′
pro·fuse′ly
pro·fu′sion
pro·gen′i·tor
prog′e·ny
·nies
prog′na·thous
prog·no′sis
·ses
prog·nos′tic
prog·nos′ti·cate′
·cat·ed ·cat·ing
prog·nos′ti·
ca′tion

prog·nos′ti·ca′tor
pro′gram
·grammed
or ·gramed
·gram·ming
or ·gram·ing
pro′gram·mat′ic
pro′gram·mer
or ·gram·er
prog′ress
pro·gres′sion
pro·gres′sive
pro·gres′siv·ism
pro·hib′it
pro′hi·bi′tion
pro·hib′i·tive
pro·hib′i·to′ry
proj′ect
pro·jec′tile
pro·jec′tion
pro·jec′tive
pro·jec′tor
pro·lep′sis
·ses
pro′le·tar′i·an
pro′le·tar′i·at
pro·lif′er·ate′
·at′ed ·at′ing
pro·lif′ic
pro·lix′
pro·lix′i·ty
pro·loc′u·tor
pro′logue
pro·long′

pro·lon′gate
·gat·ed ·gat·ing
pro′lon·ga′tion
prom′e·nade′
·nad′ed
·nad′ing
prom′i·nence
prom′i·nent
prom′is·cu′i·ty
·ties
pro·mis′cu·ous
prom′ise
·ised ·is·ing
prom′is·so′ry
prom′on·to′ry
·ries
pro·mot′a·ble
pro·mote′
·mot′ed ·mot′ing
pro·mot′er
pro·mo′tion
prompt′er
promp′ti·tude′
prompt′ly
prom′ul·gate′
·gat′ed ·gat′ing
prom′ul·ga′tion
prom′ul·ga′tor
prone
pronged
pro′noun
pro·nounce′
·nounced′
·nounc′ing

pro·nounce′a·ble
pro·nounce′ment
pro·nun′ci·a′tion
proof′read′
·read′ ·read′ing
prop′a·gan′da
prop′a·gan·dize
·dized ·diz·ing
prop′a·gate′
·gat′ed ·gat′ing
prop′a·ga′tion
prop′a·ga′tor
pro′pane
pro·pel′
·pelled′ ·pel′ling
pro·pel′lant or
·lent
pro·pel′ler
pro·pen′si·ty
·ties
prop′er·ly
prop′er·tied
prop′er·ty
·ties
proph′e·cy n.
·cies
proph′e·sy′ v.
·sied′ ·sy′ing
proph′et
(*predictor;* SEE
profit)
pro·phet′ic
pro·phet′i·cal·ly
pro′phy·lac′tic

pro′phy·lax′is
·lax′es
pro·pin′qui·ty
pro·pi′ti·ate′
·at′ed ·at′ing
pro·pi′ti·a′tion
pro·pi′ti·a′tor
pro·pi′ti·a·to′ry
pro·pi′tious
pro·po′nent
pro·por′tion
pro·por′tion·al
pro·por′tion·al·ly
pro·por′tion·ate
pro·por′tion·ate·
ly
pro·pos′al
pro·pose′
·posed′ ·pos′ing
prop′o·si′tion
pro·pound′
pro·pri′e·tar′y
·ies
pro·pri′e·tor
pro·pri′e·tress
pro·pri′e·ty
·ties
pro·pul′sion
pro·pul′sive
pro ra′ta
pro·rat′a·ble
pro·rate′
·rat′ed ·rat′ing
pro′ro·ga′tion

pro·sa′ic
pro·sa′i·cal·ly
pro·sce′ni·um
·ni·ums or ·ni·a
pro·sciut′to
pro·scribe′
·scribed′
·scrib′ing
(*forbid;* SEE
prescribe)
pro·scrip′tion
prose
pros′e·cut′a·ble
pros′e·cute′
·cut′ed ·cut′ing
(*legal term;*
SEE persecute)
pros′e·cu′tion
pros′e·cu′tor
pros′e·lyte′
·lyt′ed ·lyt′ing
pros′e·lyt·ism
pros′e·lyt·ize′
·ized′ ·iz′ing
pros′o·dy
·dies
pros′pect
pro·spec′tive
(*expected;* SEE
perspective)
pros′pec·tor
pro·spec′tus
pros′per
pros·per′i·ty

233

pros'per·ous
pros'tate
  (*gland;* SEE
  prostrate)
pros'the·sis
  ·the·ses'
pros·thet'ic
pros'ti·tute'
  ·tut·ed ·tut'ing
pros'ti·tu'tion
pros'trate
  ·trat·ed ·trat·ing
  (*prone;* SEE
  prostate)
pros·tra'tion
pros'y
  ·i·er ·i·est
pro·tag'o·nist
pro·tect'
pro·tec'tion
pro·tec'tive
pro·tec'tor
pro·tec'tor·ate
pro'té·gé'
  (*one helped by
  another;* SEE
  prodigy)
pro'tein
pro tem'po·re'
pro·test'
Prot'es·tant
prot'es·ta'tion
pro·test'er *or*
  ·tes'tor

pro·thon'o·tar'y
  ·ies
pro'to·col'
pro'ton
pro'to·plasm
pro'to·typ'al
pro'to·type'
pro'to·zo'an
pro·tract'
pro·tract'ed·ly
pro·tract'i·ble
pro·trac'tile
pro·trac'tion
pro·trac'tor
pro·trude'
  ·trud'ed
  ·trud'ing
pro·tru'sile
pro·tru'sion
pro·tru'sive
pro·tu'ber·ance
pro·tu'ber·ant
proud'ly
prov'a·bil'i·ty
prov'a·ble
prov'a·bly
prove
  proved, proved
  or prov'en,
  prov'ing
prov'en·der
prov'erb
pro·ver'bi·al
pro·ver'bi·al·ly

pro·vide'
  ·vid'ed ·vid'ing
prov'i·dence
prov'i·dent
prov'i·den'tial
pro·vid'er
prov'ince
pro·vin'cial
pro·vin'cial·ism
pro·vin'cial·ly
pro·vi'sion
pro·vi'sion·al
pro·vi'sion·al·ly
pro·vi'so
  ·sos *or* ·soes
pro·vi'so·ry
prov'o·ca'tion
pro·voc'a·tive
pro·voc'a·tive·ly
pro·voke'
  ·voked' ·vok'ing
pro'vo·lo'ne
pro'vost
prow'ess
prowl'er
prox'i·mal
prox'i·mate
prox·im'i·ty
prox'i·mo'
prox'y
  ·ies
pru'dence
pru'dent
pru·den'tial

pru'dent·ly
prud'er·y
prud'ish
prune
  pruned prun'ing
pru'ri·ence
pru'ri·ent
pry
  pries,pried pry'ing
psalm'book'
psal'mo·dy
psal'ter·y
 ·ies
pse·phol'o·gy
pseu'do
pseu'do·nym'
pseu'do·nym'i·ty
pseu·don'y·mous
psit'ta·co'sis
pso·ri'a·sis
psy'che
psy·che·de'li·a
psy·che·del'ic
psy·che·del'i·cal·ly
psy·chi·at'ric
psy·chi·at'ri·cal·ly
psy·chi'a·trist
psy·chi'a·try
psy'chic
psy'chi·cal·ly
psy·cho·a·nal'y·sis

psy'cho·an'a·lyst
psy'cho·an'a·lyt'ic
psy'cho·an'a·lyt'i·cal·ly
psy'cho·an'a·lyze'
 ·lyzed' ·lyz'ing
psy'cho·dra'ma
psy'cho·dy·nam'ics
psy'cho·gen'ic
psy·cho·log'i·cal
psy·chol'o·gist
psy·chol'o·gize'
 ·gized' ·giz'ing
psy·chol'o·gy
psy·chom'e·try
psy'cho·neu·ro'sis
 ·ses
psy'cho·neu·rot'ic
psy'cho·path'ic
psy'cho·path·ol'o·gy
psy'cho·sex'u·al
psy·cho'sis
 ·ses
psy'cho·so·mat'ic
psy'cho·ther'a·py
psy·chot'ic
pter'o·dac'tyl
pto'maine
pu'ber·ty
pu·bes'cence
pu'bic

pub'lic
pub'li·ca'tion
pub'li·cist
pub·lic'i·ty
pub'li·cize'
 ·cized' ·ciz'ing
pub'lic·ly
pub'lish
puck'er
pud'ding
pud'dle
 ·dled ·dling
pudg'i·ness
pudg'y
 ·i·er ·i·est
pueb'lo
 ·los
pu'er·ile
Puer'to Ri'co
puff'i·ness
puff'y
 ·i·er ·i·est
pu'gil·ism
pug·na'cious
pug·nac'i·ty
pul'chri·tude'
pul'chri·tu'di·nous
pull
pul'let
pul'ley
 ·leys
pull'out'
pull'o'ver

235

pul′mo·nar′y
pul′mo·tor
pul′pit
pulp′wood′
pulp′y
·i·er ·i·est
pul′sate
·sat·ed ·sat·ing
pul·sa′tion
pulse
pulsed puls′ing
pul′ver·iz′a·ble
pul′ver·i·za′tion
pul′ver·ize′
·ized′ ·iz′ing
pum′ice
(rock; SEE pomace)
pum′mel
·meled or
·melled
·mel·ing or
·mel·ling
pump′er·nick′el
pump′kin
pun
punned
pun′ning
punch card
pun′cheon
punc·til′i·o′
·os′
punc·til′i·ous
punc′tu·al
punc′tu·al′i·ty

punc′tu·al·ly
punc′tu·ate′
·at′ed ·at′ing
punc′tu·a′tion
punc′tu·a′tor
punc′tur·a·ble
punc′ture
·tured ·tur·ing
pun′dit
pun′gen·cy
pun′gent
pu′ni·ness
pun′ish
pun′ish·a·ble
pun′ish·ment
pu′ni·tive
pun′ster
pu′ny
·ni·er ·ni·est
pu′pil
pup′pet
pup′pet·eer′
pup′py
·pies
pur′chas·a·ble
pur′chase
·chased
·chas·ing
pure′bred′
pu·rée′
·réed′ ·ré′ing
pure′ly
pur·ga′tion
pur′ga·tive

pur′ga·to′ry
purge
purged purg′ing
pu′ri·fi·ca′tion
pu′ri·fi′er
pu′ri·fy′
·fied′ ·fy′ing
pur′ism
pu′ri·tan
pu′ri·tan′i·cal
pu′ri·ty
purl
(stitch; SEE pearl)
pur·loin′
pu·ro·my′cin
pur′ple
pur′plish
pur·port′
pur′pose
·posed ·pos·ing
pur′pose·ful
pur′pose·ful·ly
pur′pose·less
pur′pose·ly
purr
purs′er
pur·su′ance
pur·sue′
·sued′ ·su′ing
pur·suit′
pu′ru·lence
pu′ru·lent
pur·vey′
pur·vey′ance

pur·vey′or
pur′view
push′cart′
push′o′ver
push′-up′
pu·sil·lan′i·mous
pus′sy
·si·er ·si·est
(*with pus*)
puss′y
·ies
(*cat*)
pus·tu·lant
pus·tule
put
put put′ting
(*place;* SEE putt)
pu′ta·tive
pu′tre·fac′tion
pu′tre·fy′
·fied′ ·fy′ing
pu·tres′cence
pu·tres′cent
pu′trid
putt
(*golf term;* SEE put)
put·tee′
putt′er
(*golf club*)
put′ter
(*busy oneself*)
put′ty
·tied ·ty·ing

puz′zle
·zled ·zling
puz′zler
pyg′my
·mies
py′lon
py·or·rhe′a
pyr′a·mid
py·ram′i·dal
pyre
py·ret′ic
Py′rex
py·rog′ra·phy
py·ro·ma′ni·a
py·ro·ma′ni·ac′
py′ro·tech′nics
py·rox′y·lin
Py·thag′o·ras
py′thon

Q

quack′er·y
·ies
quad′ran′gle
quad·ran′gu·lar
quad′rant
quad′rate
·rat·ed ·rat·ing
quad·rat′ic
quad·ren′ni·al
quad′ri·lat′er·al

qua·drille′
quad·ril′lion
quad′ri·ple′gi·a
quad′ru·ped′
quad·ru′ple
·pled ·pling
quad·ru′plet
quad·ru′pli·cate′
·cat′ed ·cat′ing
quaff
quag′mire′
quail
quaint′ly
quake
quaked
quak′ing
qual′i·fi·ca′tion
qual′i·fi′er
qual′i·fy′
·fied′ ·fy′ing
qual′i·ta′tive
qual′i·ty
·ties
qualm
quan′da·ry
·ries
quan′ti·ta′tive
quan′ti·ty
·ties
quan′tum
·ta
quar′an·tin′a·ble
quar′an·tine′
·tined′ ·tin′ing

quar'rel
·reled *or* ·relled
·rel·ing *or*
·rel·ling
quar'rel·some
quar'ry
·ries
·ried ·ry·ing
quart
quar'ter
quar'ter·back'
quar'ter-deck'
quar'ter·ly
·lies
quar'ter·mas'ter
quar'ter·saw'
·sawed', ·sawed'
or ·sawn',
·saw'ing
quar·tet' *or* ·tette'
quar'tile
quar'to
·tos
quartz
qua'sar
quash
qua'si
qua'ter·na'ry
·ries
quat'rain
qua'ver
quay
(*wharf;* SEE key)
quea'si·ness

quea'sy
·si·er ·si·est
queen'li·ness
queen'ly
·li·er ·li·est
queen'-size'
queer
quell
quench'a·ble
quer'u·lous
que'ry
·ries
·ried ·ry·ing
quest
ques'tion
ques'tion·a·ble
ques'tion·naire'
queue
queued
queu'ing
(*line;* SEE cue)
quib'ble
·bled ·bling
quick'en
quick'-freeze'
-froze' -fro'zen
-freez'ing
quick'sand'
quick'sil'ver
quick'-tem'pered
quick'-wit'ted
quid'nunc'
qui·es'cence
qui·es'cent

qui'et
(*still;* SEE quite)
qui'e·tude'
qui·e'tus
quill
quilt'ing
quince
qui·nel'la
quin·quen'ni·al
quin·tes'sence
quin·tet'
or ·tette'
quin·til'lion
quin·tu'ple
·pled ·pling
quin·tu'plet
quin·tu'pli·cate'
·cat'ed ·cat'ing
quip
quipped
quip'ping
quire
(*of paper;* SEE
choir)
quirk
quis'ling
quit
quit *or* quit'ted
quit'ting
quit'claim'
quite
(*fully;* SEE quiet)
quit'tance
quit'ter

238

quiv′er
quix·ot′ic
quiz
 quiz′zes
 quizzed
 quiz′zing
 quiz′zi·cal
quoin
 (*wedge; corner;*
 SEE coign, coin)
quoit
quon′dam
Quon′set hut
quo′rum
quo′ta
quot′a·ble
quo·ta′tion
quote
 quot′ed quot′ing
quo′tient

R

rab′bet
 (*cut;* SEE rabbit)
rab′bi
 ·bis *or* ·bies
rab·bin′i·cal
rab′bit
 (*hare;* SEE rabbet)
rab′ble
 ·bled ·bling

rab′id
ra′bies
rac·coon′
race
 raced rac′ing
race′horse′
rac′er
race track
race′way′
ra′cial
ra′cial·ly
rac′i·ly
rac′i·ness
rac′ism
rack′et
rack′et·eer′
rack′-rent′
rac′on·teur′
rac′y
 ·i·er ·i·est
ra′dar
ra′di·al
ra′di·ance
ra′di·ant
ra′di·ate′
 ·at·ed ·at·ing
ra′di·a′tion
ra′di·a′tor
rad′i·cal
rad′i·cal·ism
rad′i·cal·ly
ra′di·o′
 ·os′, ·oed′ ·o′ing
ra′di·o·ac′tive

ra′di·o·gram′
ra′di·o·graph′
ra′di·og′ra·phy
ra′di·o·i′so·tope′
ra′di·ol′o·gist
ra′di·ol′o·gy
ra′di·o·phone′
ra′di·o·pho′no·
 graph′
ra′di·o·pho′to
 ·tos
ra′di·os′co·py
ra′di·o·sonde′
ra′di·o·tel′e·
 phone′
ra′di·o·ther′a·py
ra′di·o·ther′my
rad′ish
ra′di·um
ra′di·us
 ·di·i′ *or* ·di·us·es
ra′dix
 ra′di·ces′ *or*
 ra′dix·es
ra′don
raf′fi·a
raf′fle
 ·fled ·fling
raft′er
rag′a·muf′fin
rage
 raged rag′ing
rag′ged
rag′lan

239

ra·gout'
rag'pick'er
rag'time'
rag'weed'
raid'er
rail'ing
rail'ler·y
·ies
rail'road'
rail'-split·ter
rail'way'
rai'ment
rain
(*water;* SEE
reign, rein)
rain'bow'
rain check
rain'coat'
rain'drop'
rain'fall'
rain'i·ness
rain'proof'
rain'storm'
rain'y
·i·er ·i·est
raise
raised rais'ing
(*lift;* SEE raze)
rai'sin
rai'son d'etre'
ra'jah *or* ·ja
rake
raked rak'ing
rak'ish

ral'li·er
ral'ly
·lies
·lied ·ly·ing
ram
rammed
ram'ming
ram'ble
·bled ·bling
ram'bler
ram·bunc'tious
ram'e·kin *or* ·quin
ram'i·fi·ca'tion
ram'i·fy'
·fied' ·fy'ing
ram'jet'
ramp
ram·page'
·paged' ·pag'ing
ram·pa'geous
ramp'ant
ram'part
ram'rod'
ram'shack·le
ranch'er
ran'cid
ran'cor
ran'cor·ous
ran'dom
ran'dom·ize'
·ized' ·iz'ing
range
ranged
rang'ing

rang'i·ness
rang'y
·i·er ·i·est
ran'kle
·kled ·kling
ran'sack
ran'som
rap
rapped rap'ping
(*strike;* SEE wrap)
ra·pa'cious
ra·pac'i·ty
rape
raped rap'ing
rap'id-fire'
ra·pid'i·ty
rap'id·ly
ra'pi·er
rap'ine
rap'ist
rap'port'
rap·proche'ment
rap·scal'lion
rap·to'ri·al
rap'ture
rap'tur·ous
rare
rar'er rar'est
rare'bit
rar'e·fy'
·fied' ·fy'ing
rare'ly
rar'i·ty
·ties

ras'cal
ras·cal'i·ty
ras'cal·ly
rash'er
rash'ness
rasp'ber'ry
·ries
rasp'i·ness
rasp'ing
rasp'y
·i·er ·i·est
rat
rat'ted rat'ting
rat'a·ble or rate'·
ratch'et
rate
rat'ed rat'ing
rath'er
raths'kel·ler
rat'i·fi·ca'tion
rat'i·fi'er
rat'i·fy'
·fied' ·fy'ing
ra'tio
·tios
ra'ti·o'ci·nate'
·nat'ed ·nat'ing
ra'tion·al
ra'tion·ale'
ra'tion·al·ism
ra'tion·al'i·ty
ra'tion·al·i·za'tion
ra'tion·al·ize'
·ized' ·iz'ing

ra'tion·al·ly
rat'line or ·lin
rat'tail'
rat·tan' or ra·tan'
rat'tle
·tled ·tling
rat'tle·brained'
rat'tler
rat'tle·snake'
rat'tle·trap'
rat'tly
rau'cous
rav'age
·aged ·ag·ing
rave
raved rav'ing
rav'el
·eled or ·elled
·el·ing or ·el·ling
ra'ven
rav'e·nous
ra·vine'
ra·vi·o'li
rav'ish
raw'boned'
raw'hide'
ray'on
raze
razed raz'ing
(demolish; SEE
raise)
ra'zor
ra'zor·back'
reach

re·act'
(respond)
re'-act'
(act again)
re·ac'tion
re·ac'tion·ar'y
·ies
re·ac'ti·vate'
·vat'ed ·vat'ing
re·ac'tive·ly
re·ac'tor
read
read read'ing
read'a·bil'i·ty
read'a·ble
read'i·ly
read'i·ness
re'ad·just'
read'out'
read'y
·i·er ·i·est
·ied ·y·ing
read'y-made'
re·a'gent
re·al'
(actual; SEE reel)
re'al·ism
re'al·ist
re'al·is'tic
re'al·is'ti·cal·ly
re·al'i·ty
·ties
(real thing; SEE
realty)

re·al·iz'a·ble
re·al·i·za'tion
re·al·ize'
 ·ized' ·iz'ing
re'al-life'
re'al·ly
realm
Re'al·tor
re'al·ty
 (*real estate;* SEE reality)
ream'er
re·an'i·mate'
 ·mat'ed ·mat'ing
reap'er
re'ap·por'tion
rear guard
re·ar'ma·ment
re'ar·range'
re'ar·range'ment
rear'ward
rea'son·a·ble
rea'son·a·bly
re'as·sur'ance
re'as·sure'
 ·sured' ·sur'ing
re'bate
 ·bat·ed ·bat·ing
reb'el *n.*
re·bel' *v.*
 ·belled' ·bel'ling
re·bel'lion
re·bel'lious
re·birth'

re·bound'
re·buff'
 (*blunt refusal*)
re'-buff'
 (*buff again*)
re·buke'
 ·buked'
 ·buk'ing
re'bus
re·but'
 ·but'ted
 ·but'ting
re·but'tal
re·cal'ci·trant
re·call'
re·cant'
re·cap'
 ·capped'
 ·cap'ping
re'ca·pit'u·late'
 ·lat'ed ·lat'ing
re'ca·pit'u·la'tion
re·cap'pa·ble
re·cap'ture
re·cede'
 ·ced'ed ·ced'ing
re·ceipt'
re·ceiv'a·ble
re·ceive'
 ·ceived'
 ·ceiv'ing
re·ceiv'er·ship'
re·cen'sion
re'cent

re·cep'ta·cle
re·cep'tion
re·cep'tive
re·cep'tor
re'cess
re·ces'sion
re·ces'sive
re·charge'a·ble
re·cher'ché
re·cid'i·vism
rec'i·pe
re·cip'i·ent
re·cip'ro·cal
re·cip'ro·cal·ly
re·cip'ro·cate'
 ·cat'ed ·cat'ing
re·cip'ro·ca'tion
re·cip'ro·ca'tor
rec'i·proc'i·ty
re·ci'sion
re·cit'al
rec'i·ta'tion
rec'i·ta·tive'
re·cite'
 ·cit'ed ·cit'ing
reck'less
reck'on·ing
re·claim'
 (*restore for use*)
re'-claim'
 (*claim back*)
rec'la·ma'tion
re·cline'
 ·clined' ·clin'ing

rec′luse
re·clu′sion
rec′og·ni′tion
rec′og·niz′a·ble
re·cog′ni·zance
rec′og·nize′
 ·nized′ ·niz′ing
re·coil′
 (*draw back*)
re′-coil′
 (*coil again*)
re·coil′less
rec′ol·lect′
 (*remember*)
re′-col·lect′
 (*collect again*)
rec′ol·lec′tion
rec′om·mend′
rec′om·men·
 da′tion
re′com·mit′
rec′om·pense′
 ·pensed′
 ·pens′ing
rec′on·cil′a·ble
rec′on·cile′
 ·ciled′ ·cil′ing
rec′on·cil′i·a′tion
rec′on·dite′
re′con·di′tion
re·con′nais·sance
re′con·struct′
re′con·noi′ter
re′con·sid′er

re′con·ver′sion
re′con·vert′
re·cord′ *v.*
rec′ord *n.*
re·cord′er
re·count′
 (*narrate*)
re′-count′
 (*count again*)
re·coup′
re′course
re·cov′er
 (*get back*)
re′-cov′er
 (*cover again*)
re·cov′er·y
 ·ies
rec′re·ant
rec′re·ate′
 ·at′ed ·at′ing
 (*refresh*)
re′-cre·ate′
 ·at′ed ·at′ing
 (*create anew*)
rec′re·a′tion
re′-cre·a′tion
re·crim′i·nate′
 ·nat′ed ·nat′ing
re·crim′i·na′tion
re·cruit′
rec′tal
rec·tan′gle
rec·tan′gu·lar
rec′ti·fi′a·ble

rec′ti·fi·ca′tion
rec′ti·fi′er
rec′ti·fy′
 ·fied′ ·fy′ing
rec′ti·lin′e·ar
rec′ti·tude′
rec′tor
rec′to·ry
 ·ries
rec′tum
 ·tums *or* ·ta
re·cum′ben·cy
re·cum′bent
re·cu′per·ate′
 ·at′ed ·at′ing
re·cu′per·a′tion
re·cur′
 ·curred′
 ·cur′ring
re·cur′rence
re·cur′rent
rec′u·sant
re·cy′cle
re·dact′
re·dac′tion
re·dac′tor
red′bait′
red′-blood′ed
red′den
re·deem′a·ble
re·demp′tion
re′de·ploy′
re′de·vel′op·ment
red′-hand′ed

243

red′head′
red′-hot′
re′di·rect′
re·dis′trict
red′-let′ter
re·do′
  ·did′ ·done′
  ·do′ing
red′o·lence
red′o·lent
re·dou′ble
re·doubt′
re·doubt′a·ble
re·dound′
red′out′
re·dress′
  (*remedy*)
re′-dress′
  (*dress again*)
re·duce′
  ·duced′ ·duc′ing
re·duc′i·ble
re·duc′tion
re·dun′dan·cy
  ·cies
re·dun′dant
re·du′pli·cate′
re·du′pli·ca′tion
re·ech′o
reed′i·ness
re·ed′it
re·ed′u·cate′
reed′y
  ·i·er ·i·est

reek
  (*emit a smell;* SEE
  wreak)
reel
  (*whirl; dance;*
  spool; SEE real)
re′e·lect′
re′e·lec′tion
re′em·bark′
re′em·bod′y
re′em·brace′
re′e·merge′
re·em′pha·sis
re·em′pha·size′
re′em·ploy′
re′en·act′
re′en·dow′
re′en·gage′
re′en·list′
re·en′ter
re·en′try
re′e·quip′
re′es·tab′lish
re′e·val′u·ate′
re′ex·am′ine
re′ex·change′
re′ex·hib′it
re′ex·pe′ri·ence
re′ex·plain′
re′ex·port′
re·fec′tion
re·fer′
  ·ferred′
  ·fer′ring

ref′er·a·ble *or*
  ·eed′ ·ee′ing
ref′er·ee′
  ·eed′ ·ee′ing
ref′er·ence
ref′er·en′dum
  ·dums *or* ·da
ref′er·ent
re·fer′ral
re·fill′a·ble
re·fine′
  ·fined′ ·fin′ing
re·fine′ment
re·fin′er·y
  ·ies
re·fit′
re·fla′tion
re·flect′
re·flec′tion
re·flec′tive
re·flec′tor
re′flex
re·flex′ive
re′for·est·a′tion
re·form′
  (*make better*)
re′-form′
  (*form again*)
ref′or·ma′tion
re·form′a·to·ry
  ·ries
re·fract′
re·frac′tion
re·frac′to·ry

re·frain'
re·fran'gi·ble
re·fresh'
re·fresh'ment
re·frig'er·ant
re·frig'er·ate'
 ·at'ed ·at'ing
re·frig'er·a'tion
re·frig'er·a'tor
ref'uge
ref·u·gee'
re·ful'gent
re·fund'
re·fur'bish
re·fus'al
re·fuse' v.
 ·fused' ·fus'ing
ref'use n.
re·fut'a·ble
ref·u·ta'tion
re·fute'
 ·fut'ed ·fut'ing
re·gain'
re'gal adj.
re·gale' v.
 ·galed' ·gal'ing
re·ga'li·a
re·gal'i·ty
 ·ties
re·gard'ing
re·gard'less
re·gat'ta
re'gen·cy
 ·cies

re·gen'er·ate'
 ·at'ed ·at'ing
re·gen'er·a'tion
re·gen'er·a'tive
re·gen'er·a'tor
re'gent
reg'i·cide'
re·gime' or ré·
reg'i·men
reg'i·ment
reg'i·men'tal
reg'i·men·ta'tion
re'gion·al
reg'is·ter
reg'is·trant
reg'is·trar'
reg'is·tra'tion
reg'is·try
 ·tries
re'gress
re·gres'sion
re·gres'sive
re·gret'
 ·gret'ted
 ·gret'ting
re·gret'ful
re·gret'ful·ly
re·gret'ta·ble
re·gret'ta·bly
reg'u·lar
reg'u·lar'i·ty
 ·ties
reg'u·late'
 ·lat'ed ·lat'ing

reg'u·la'tion
reg'u·la'tor
re'ha·bil'i·tate'
 ·tat'ed ·tat'ing
re·gur'gi·ta'tion
re'ha·bil'i·tate'
 ·tat'ed ·tat'ing
re'ha·bil'i·ta'tion
re·hears'al
re·hearse'
 ·hearsed'
 ·hears'ing
reign
 (rule; SEE rain,
 rein)
re'im·burs'a·ble
re'im·burse'
 ·bursed'
 ·burs'ing
rein
 (control; SEE
 rain, reign)
re'in·car'nate
 ·nat·ed ·nat·ing
re'in·car·na'tion
re'in·cur'
rein'deer
re'in·force'
 ·forced'
 ·forc'ing
re'in·force'ment
re'in·state'
 ·stat'ed
 ·stat'ing

re·it′er·ate′
  ·at′ed ·at′ing
re·ject′
re·jec′tion
re·joice′
  ·joiced′ ·joic′ing
re·join′der
re·ju′ve·nate′
  ·nat′ed ·nat′ing
re·lapse′
  ·lapsed′
  ·laps′ing
re·lat′a·ble
re·late′
  ·lat′ed ·lat′ing
re·la′tion·ship′
rel′a·tive
rel′a·tive·ly
rel′a·tiv′i·ty
re·lax′
re·lax′ant
re′lax·a′tion
re′lay
  ·layed ·lay·ing
  (send by relay)
re′-lay′
  -laid′ -lay′ing
  (lay again)
re·lease′
  ·leased′
  ·leas′ing
  (set free)
re′-lease′
  (lease again)

rel′e·gate′
  ·gat′ed ·gat′ing
rel′e·ga′tion
re·lent′less
rel′e·vance
rel′e·vant
re·li′a·bil′i·ty
re·li′a·ble
re·li′a·bly
re·li′ance
re·li′ant
rel′ic
re·lief′
re·liev′a·ble
re·lieve′
  ·lieved′ ·liev′ing
re·liev′er
re·li′gion
re·li′gious
re·lin′quish
rel′i·quar′y
  ·ies
rel′ish
re·luc′tance
re·luc′tant
re·ly′
  ·lied′ ·ly′ing
re·main′der
re·make′
  ·made′ ·mak′ing
re·mand′
re·mark′a·ble
re·mark′a·bly
re·me′di·a·ble

re·me′di·al
rem′e·dy
  ·dies
  ·died ·dy·ing
re·mem′ber
re·mem′brance
re·mind′er
rem′i·nisce′
  ·nisced′
  ·nisc′ing
rem′i·nis′cence
rem′i·nis′cent
rem′i·nis′cer
re·miss′
re·mis′si·ble
re·mis′sion
re·mit′
  ·mit′ted
  ·mit′ting
re·mit′ta·ble
re·mit′tance
re·mit′tent
rem′nant
re·mod′el
re·mon′strance
re·mon′strate
  ·strat·ed
  ·strat·ing
re′mon·stra′tion
re·mon′stra·tor
re·morse′ful
re·morse′less
re·mote′
re·mote′ly

246

re·mov'a·ble
re·mov'al
re·move'
 ·moved'
 ·mov'ing
re·mu'ner·ate'
 ·at'ed ·at'ing
re·mu'ner·a'tion
re·mu'ner·a'tive
re·mu'ner·a'tor
ren'ais·sance'
re·nas'cent
rend
 rent rend'ing
ren'der
ren'dez·vous'
 ·vous'
 ·voused'
 ·vous'ing
ren·di'tion
ren'e·gade'
re·nege'
 ·neged' ·neg'ing
re·new'al
ren'net
re·nounce'
 ·nounced'
 ·nounc'ing
ren'o·vate'
 ·vat'ed ·vat'ing
ren'o·va'tion
re·nown'
re·nowned'
rent'al

rent'-free'
re·nun'ci·a'tion
re·or'der
re'or·gan·i·za'tion
re·or'gan·ize'
 ·ized' ·iz'ing
re·pair'man
rep'a·ra·ble
rep'a·ra'tion
rep'ar·tee'
re·past'
re·pa'tri·ate'
 ·at'ed ·at'ing
re·pa'tri·a'tion
re·pay'
 ·paid' ·pay'ing
 (*pay back*)
re'·pay'
 ·paid' ·pay'ing
 (*pay again*)
re·peal'
re·peat'
re·pel'
 ·pelled' ·pel'ling
re·pel'lent
re·pent'
re·pent'ance
re·pent'ant
re'per·cus'sion
rep'er·toire'
rep'er·to'ry
 ·ries
rep'e·ti'tion
 (*a repeating*)

re'·pe·ti'tion
 (*petition again*)
rep'e·ti'tious
re·pet'i·tive
re·phrase'
re·place'
re·place'a·ble
re·place'ment
re·plen'ish
re·plete'
re·ple'tion
re·plev'in
rep'li·ca
re·ply'
 ·plies'
 ·plied' ·ply'ing
re·port'ed·ly
re·port'er
re·pose'
 ·posed' ·pos'ing
 (*rest*)
re'·pose'
 (*pose again*)
re·pos'i·to·ry
 ·ries
re'pos·sess'
re'pos·ses'sion
rep're·hend'
rep're·hen'si·ble
rep're·hen'sion
rep're·sent'
 (*stand for*)
re'·pre·sent'
 (*present again*)

rep're·sen·ta'tion
rep're·sent'a·tive
re·press'
  (*restrain*)
re'-press'
  (*press again*)
re·pressed'
re·press'i·ble
re·pres'sion
re·prieve'
  ·prieved'
  ·priev'ing
rep'ri·mand'
re·print'
re·pris'al
re·proach'
re·proach'ful
rep'ro·bate'
  ·bat'ed ·bat'ing
re·proc'essed
re'pro·duce'
re'pro·duc'i·ble
re'pro·duc'tion
re'pro·duc'tive
re·proof'
re·prove'
  ·proved'
  ·prov'ing
  (*rebuke*)
re'-prove'
  (*prove again*)
rep'tile
rep·til'i·an
re·pub'lic

re·pub'li·can
re·pu'di·ate'
  ·at'ed ·at'ing
re·pu'di·a'tion
re·pug'nance
re·pug'nant
re·pulse'
  ·pulsed'
  ·puls'ing
re·pul'sion
re·pul'sive
rep'u·ta·bil'i·ty
rep'u·ta·ble
rep'u·ta·bly
rep'u·ta'tion
re·pute'
  ·put'ed ·put'ing
re·quest'
Re'qui·em
re·quire'
  ·quired'
  ·quir'ing
re·quire'ment
req'ui·site
req'ui·si'tion
re·quit'al
re·quite'
  ·quit'ed
  ·quit'ing
rere'dos
re·route'
re·run'
  ·ran' ·run'
  ·run'ning

re·sal'a·ble
re'sale'
re·scind'
re·scind'a·ble
re·scis'sion
res'cu·a·ble
res'cue
  ·cued ·cu·ing
res'cu·er
re·search'
re·sem'blance
re·sem'ble
  ·bled ·bling
re·sent'
  (*feel a hurt*)
re'-sent'
  (*sent again*)
re·sent'ful
re·sent'ment
res'er·va'tion
re·serve'
  ·served'
  ·serv'ing
  (*set aside*)
re'-serve'
  (*serve again*)
re·serv'ed·ly
re·serv'ist
res'er·voir'
re·set'
  ·set' ·set'ting
re·ship'ment
re·side'
  ·sid'ed ·sid'ing

res·i·dence
res·i·den·cy
 ·cies
res·i·dent
res·i·den'tial
re·sid'u·al
re·sid'u·ar·y
res'i·due'
re·sign'
 (*give up*)
re'-sign'
 (*sign again*)
res'ig·na'tion
re·sil'i·ence
re·sil'i·ent
res'in
res'in·ous
re·sist'
re·sist'ance
re·sist'ant
re·sist'er
 (*one who resists*)
re·sist'i·ble
re·sis'tor
 (*electrical device*)
re'sole'
 ·soled' ·sol'ing
res'o·lute'
res'o·lu'tion
re·solv'a·ble
re·solve'
 ·solved'
 ·solv'ing
 (*break into parts*)

re'-solve'
 (*solve again*)
re·sol'vent
res'o·nance
res'o·nant
res'o·na'tor
re·sort'
 (*go for help*)
re'-sort'
 (*sort again*)
re·sound'
 (*echo*)
re'-sound'
 (*sound again*)
re'source
re·source'ful
re·spect'a·bil'i·ty
re·spect'a·ble
re·spect'ful
re·spect'ful·ly
re·spec'tive
re·spec'tive·ly
res'pi·ra'tion
res'pi·ra'tor
res'pi·ra·to'ry
re·spire'
 ·spired'
 ·spir'ing
res'pite
 ·pit·ed ·pit·ing
re·splend'ence
re·splend'ent
re·spond'
re·spond'ent

re·sponse'
re·spon'si·bil'i·ty
 ·ties
re·spon'si·ble
re·spon'si·bly
re·spon'sive
re·state'
 ·stat'ed ·stat'ing
res'tau·rant
res'tau·ra·teur'
rest'ful
res'ti·tu'tion
res'tive
rest'less
res'to·ra'tion
re·stor'a·tive
re·store'
 ·stored' ·stor'ing
re·strain'
 (*hold back*)
re'-strain'
 (*strain again*)
re·straint'
re·strict'
re·stric'tion
re·stric'tive
rest'room'
re·struc'ture
re·sult'
re·sult'ant
re·sum'a·ble
re·sume' *v.*
 ·sumed'
 ·sum'ing

ré·su·mé' *n.*
re·sump'tion
re·sur'face
re·sur'gence
re·sur'gent
res'ur·rect'
res'ur·rec'tion
re·sus'ci·tate'
·tat'ed ·tat'ing
re·sus'ci·ta'tion
re·sus'ci·ta'tor
re'tail
re·tain'
re·tain'er
re·take'
·took' ·tak'en
·tak'ing
re·tal'i·ate'
·at'ed ·at'ing
re·tal'i·a'tion
re·tal'i·a·to'ry
re·tard'
re·tard'ant
re·tard'ate
re'tar·da'tion
retch
(*strain to vomit;*
SEE wretch)
re·ten'tion
re·ten'tive
re'ten·tiv'i·ty
re·think'
ret'i·cence
ret'i·cent

re·tic'u·lar
re·tic'u·late'
·lat'ed ·lat'ing
ret'i·cule'
ret'i·na
·nas *or* ·nae'
ret'i·nue'
re·tire'
·tired' ·tir'ing
re·tir'ee'
re·tire'ment
re·tool'
re·tort'
re·touch'
re·trace'
(*go back over*)
re'-trace'
(*trace again*)
re·trace'a·ble
re·tract'
re·tract'a·ble
re·trac'tile
re·trac'tion
re·trac'tor
re'tread' *v.*
·tread'ed
·tread'ing
re'tread' *n.*
re·treat'
(*go back*)
re'-treat'
(*treat again*)
re·trench'
ret'ri·bu'tion

re·triev'a·ble
re·triev'al
re·trieve'
·trieved'
·triev'ing
re·triev'er
ret'ro·ac'tive
ret'ro·ces'sion
ret'ro·fire'
ret'ro·fit'
ret'ro·grade'
·grad'ed
·grad'ing
ret'ro·gress'
ret'ro·gres'sion
ret'ro·rock'et *or*
ret'ro-rock'et
ret'ro·spect'
ret'ro·spec'tion
re·turn'
re·turn'ee'
re·un'ion
re·u'nite'
re·us'a·ble
re·use'
rev
revved rev'ving
re·vamp'
re·veal'
re·veil·le
rev'el
·eled *or* ·elled
·el·ing *or* ·el·ling
rev'e·la'tion

rev'el·ry
re·venge'
·venged'
·veng'ing
re·venge'ful
re·veng'er
rev'e·nue'
re·ver'ber·ant
re·ver'ber·ate'
·at'ed ·at'ing
re·ver'ber·a'tion
re·ver'ber·a'tor
re·ver'ber·a·to'ry
re·vere'
·vered' ·ver'ing
rev'er·ence
rev'er·end
rev'er·ent
rev'er·en'tial
rev'er·ie
re·vers'
·vers'
(*part of garment*)
re·ver'sal
re·verse'
·versed'
·vers'ing
(*turned backward*)
re·vers'i·ble
re·vers'i·bly
re·ver'sion
re·ver'sion·ar'y
re·vert'
re·view'

re·view'al
re·view'er
re·vile'
·viled' ·vil'ing
re·vise'
·vised' ·vis'ing
re·vi'sion
re·vi'so·ry
re·vi'tal·ize'
re·viv'a·ble
re·viv'al
re·vive'
·vived' ·viv'ing
re·viv'i·fy'
rev'o·ca·ble
rev'o·ca·bly
rev'o·ca'tion
re·voke'
·voked' ·vok'ing
re·volt'
re·volt'ing
rev'o·lu'tion
rev'o·lu'tion·ar'y
·ies
rev'o·lu'tion·ize'
·ized' ·iz'ing
re·volv'a·ble
re·volve'
·volved'
·volv'ing
re·volv'er
re·vue' *or* ·view'
re·vul'sion
re·ward'

re·wind'
·wound'
·wind'ing
re·write'
·wrote' ·writ'ten
·writ'ing
rhap·sod'ic
rhap·sod'i·cal·ly
rhap'so·dize'
·dized' ·diz'ing
rhap'so·dy
·dies
rhe'o·stat'
rhe'sus
rhet'o·ric
rhe·tor'i·cal
rhe·tor'i·cal·ly
rhet'o·ri'cian
rheu·mat'ic
rheu'ma·tism
rheu'ma·toid'
rheum'y
·i·er ·i·est
Rh factor
rhine'stone'
rhi·ni'tis
rhi·noc'er·os
rhi'zome
Rhode Island
rho'do·den'dron
rhom'boid
rhom'bus
·bus·es *or* ·bi
rhu'barb

251

rhyme
 rhymed
 rhym'ing
 (*verse;* SEE rime)

rhythm
rhyth'mic
rhyth'mi·cal·ly

rib
 ribbed
 rib'bing

rib'ald
rib'ald·ry
rib'bon
ri'bo·fla'vin
rice
 riced ric'ing
rich'ness
rick·et·i·ness
rick'ets
rick·ett'si·a
 ·si·ae' *or* ·si·as
rick'et·y
rick'ey
rick'rack'
rick'shaw *or* ·sha
ric'o·chet'
 ·cheted' *or*
 ·chet'ted
 ·chet'ing *or*
 ·chet'ting
ri·cot'ta
rid
 rid *or* rid'ded
 rid'ding

rid'a·ble *or* ride'·
rid'dance
rid'dle
 ·dled ·dling
ride
 rode rid'den
 rid'ing
rid'er·less
ridge
 ridged ridg'ing
ridge'pole'
rid'i·cule'
 ·culed' ·cul'ing
ri·dic'u·lous
rife
rif'fle
 ·fled ·fling
 (*shoal; shuffle*)
riff'raff'
ri'fle
 ·fled ·fling
 (*gun; plunder*)
ri'fle·man
rig
 rigged rig'ging
ri'ga·to'ni
rig'ger
 (*one who rigs;*
 SEE rigor)
right
 (*correct;* SEE rite)
right'-an'gled
right'eous
right'ful·ly

right'-hand'ed
right'ist
rig'id
ri·gid'i·ty
rig'ma·role'
rig'or
 (*stiffness;* SEE
 rigger)
rig'or mor'tis
rig'or·ous
rile
 riled ril'ing
rim
 rimmed
 rim'ming
rime
 rimed rim'ing
 (*hoarfrost; rhyme;*
 SEE rhyme)
ring
 rang rung
 ring'ing
 (*sound;* SEE
 wring)
ring
 ringed ring'ing
 (*circle;* SEE
 wring)
ring'er
ring'lead'er
ring'let
ring'mas'ter
ring'side'
rink

rinse
  rinsed rins'ing
ri'ot·ous
rip
  ripped rip'ping
ri·par'i·an
rip'en
ripe'ness
ri·poste' or
  ·post'
rip'per
rip'ple
  ·pled ·pling
rip'saw'
rip'tide'
rise
  rose ris'en
  ris'ing
ris'er
ris'i·bil'i·ty
  ·ties
ris'i·ble
risk'i·ly
risk'i·ness
risk'y
  ·i·er ·i·est
ris·qué'
ris'sole
rite
  (ceremonial act;
  SEE right, write)
rit'u·al
rit'u·al·is'tic
rit'u·al·ly

ri'val
  ·valed or ·valled
  ·val·ing or
  ·val·ling
ri'val·ry
  ·ries
rive
  rived, rived or
  riv'en, riv'ing
riv'er·side'
riv'et
riv'et·er
riv'u·let
roach
road'a·bil'i·ty
road'bed'
road'block'
road'show'
road'side'
road'ster
road'way'
road'work'
roam'er
roan
roar'ing
roast'er
rob
  robbed rob'bing
rob'ber
rob'ber·y
  ·ies
robe
  robed rob'ing
rob'in

ro'bot
ro·bust'
rock'-and-roll'
rock'-bound'
rock'er
rock'et
rock'e·teer'
rock'et·ry
rock'i·ness
rock·oon'
rock'y
  ·i·er ·i·est
ro·co'co
ro'dent
ro'de·o'
  ·os'
roe
  (fish eggs; SEE
  row)
roent'gen
rogue
  rogued rogu'ing
ro'guer·y
  ·ies
ro'guish
roil
  (stir up; SEE royal)
roist'er·er
roist'er·ous
role or rôle
  (actor's part)
roll
  (revolve)
roll'a·way'

253

roll'back'
roll call
roll'er
rol'lick·ing
roll'-top'
ro·maine'
ro·mance'
·manced'
·manc'ing
ro·man'tic
ro·man'ti·cal·ly
ro·man'ti·cism
ro·man'ti·cize'
·cized' ·ciz'ing
ron'deau
·deaux
(*poem*)
ron'do
·dos
(*music*)
rood
(*cross;* SEE rude)
roof'er
rook
rook'er·y
·ies
rook'ie
room'er
(*lodger;* SEE
rumor)
room·ette'
room'ful'
·fuls'
room'i·ness

room'mate'
room'y
·i·er ·i·est
roos'ter
root beer
root'er
root'less
root'let
rope
roped rop'ing
rope'walk'
Roque'fort
ro'sa·ry
·ries
ro·sé'
ro'se·ate
rose'bud'
rose'bush'
rose'-col'ored
ro·se'o·la
ro·sette'
rose'wood'
Rosh' Ha·sha'na
ros'i·ly
ros'in
ros'i·ness
ros'ter
ros'trum
·trums *or* ·tra
ros'y
·i·er ·i·est
rot
rot'ted
rot'ting

ro'ta·ry
·ries
ro'tat·a·ble
ro'tate
·tat·ed ·tat·ing
ro·ta'tion
ro'ta·tor
rote
(*routine;* SEE
wrote)
ro·tis'ser·ie
ro'to·gra·vure'
ro'tor
rot'ten
ro·tund'
ro·tun'da
ro·tun'di·ty
rou·é'
rouge
rouged roug'ing
rough
(*not smooth;*
SEE ruff)
rough'age
rough'cast'
·cast' ·cast'ing
rough'-dry'
-dried' -dry'ing
rough'en
rough'-hew'
-hewed', -hewed'
or -hewn',
-hew'ing
rough'ly

rough'shod'
rou·lade'
rou·leau'
 ·leaux' or ·leaus'
rou·lette'
round'a·bout'
roun'de·lay'
round'house'
round'up'
round'worm'
rouse
 roused rous'ing
roust'a·bout'
rout
 (*noisy mob; dig up; defeat*)
route
 rout'ed rout'ing
 (*course*)
rou·tine'
rove
 roved rov'ing
row *n., v.*
 (*line; use oars; brawl;* SEE roe)
row'boat'
row'di·ness
row'dy
 ·dies
 ·di·er ·di·est
row'dy·ism
row'el
 ·eled *or* ·elled
 ·el·ing *or* ·el·ling

roy'al
 (*regal;* SEE roil)
roy'al·ist
roy'al·ly
roy'al·ty
 ·ties
rub
 rubbed
 rub'bing
rub'ber·ize'
 ·ized' ·iz'ing
rub'ber·y
rub'bish
rub'ble
 (*stone;* SEE ruble)
rub'down'
ru·bel'la
ru'bi·cund'
ru'ble
 (*money;* SEE rubble)
ru'bric
ru'by
 ·bies
ruche
ruch'ing
ruck'sack'
rud'der
rud'di·ness
rud'dy
 ·di·er ·di·est
rude
 (*crude;* SEE rood)
rude'ly

ru'di·ment
ru'di·men'ta·ry
rue
 rued ru'ing
rue'ful
ruff
 (*collar;* SEE rough)
ruf'fi·an
ruf'fle
 ·fled ·fling
rug'ged
ru'in·a'tion
ru'in·ous
rule
 ruled rul'ing
rul'er
rum'ble
 ·bled ·bling
ru'mi·nant
ru'mi·nate'
 ·nat'ed ·nat'ing
ru'mi·na'tor
rum'mage
 ·maged
 ·mag·ing
ru'mor
 (*hearsay;* SEE roomer)
rum'ple
 ·pled ·pling
run
 ran run
 run'ning
run'a·bout'

run'a·way'
run'-down'
rung
(*crossbar; pp. of ring;* SEE wrung)
run'-in'
run'ner-up'
run'ners-up'
run'ni·ness
run'ny
·ni·er ·ni·est
run'off'
run'-on'
run'way'
rup'ture
·tured ·tur·ing
ru'ral
ru'ral·ly
ruse
rush
rus'set
rus'tic
rus'ti·cal·ly
rus'ti·cate'
·cat'ed ·cat'ing
rust'i·ness
rus'tle
·tled ·tling
rus'tler
rust'proof'
rust'y
·i·er ·i·est
rut
rut'ted rut'ting

ru'ta·ba'ga
ruth'less
rye
(*grain;* SEE wry)

S

Sab'bath
sab·bat'i·cal
sa'ber *or* ·bre
sa'ble
sa'bot
sab'o·tage'
·taged' ·tag'ing
sab'o·teur'
sac
(*pouch;* SEE sack)
sac'cha·rin *n.*
sac'cha·rine *adj.*
sac'er·do'tal
sa·chet'
sack
(*bag;* SEE sac)
sack'cloth'
sack'ful'
·fuls'
sack'ing
sac'ra·ment
sac'ra·men'tal
sa'cred
sac'ri·fice'
·ficed' ·fic'ing

sac'ri·fi'cial
sac'ri·lege
sac'ri·le'gious
sac'ris·tan
sac'ris·ty
·ties
sac'ro·il'i·ac'
sac'ro·sanct'
sa'crum
·cra *or* ·crums
sad
sad'der sad'dest
sad'den
sad'dle
·dled ·dling
sad'dle·bag'
sad'dle·cloth'
sad'dler
sad'i'ron
sad'ism
sad'ist
sa·dis'tic
sa·dis'ti·cal·ly
sa·fa'ri
·ris
safe
saf'er saf'est
safe'-con'duct
safe'-de·pos'it
safe'guard'
safe'keep'ing
safe'ty
·ties
saf'fron

sag
  sagged sag'ging
sa'ga
sa·ga'cious
sa·gac'i·ty
sage
  sag'er sag'est
sage'brush'
sag'gy
  ·gi·er ·gi·est
sa'go
  ·gos
sail'boat'
sail'cloth'
sail'er
  (*boat*)
sail'fish'
sail'or
  (*person; hat*)
saint'li·ness
saint'ly
  ·li·er ·li·est
sa'ke
  (*rice wine*)
sake
  (*purpose*)
sa·laam'
sal'a·ble *or*
  sale'·
sa·la'cious
sal'ad
sal'a·man'der
sa·la'mi
sal'a·ried

sal'a·ry
  ·ries
sal'e·ra'tus
sales'clerk'
sales'man
sales'man·ship'
sales'peo'ple
sales'per'son
sales'wom'an
sa'lient
sa'line
sa·lin'i·ty
sa·li'va
sal'i·var'y
sal'i·vate'
  ·vat'ed ·vat'ing
sal'low
sal'ly
  ·lies, ·lied ·ly·ing
sal'ma·gun'di
salm'on
sal'mo·nel'la
  ·lae *or* ·la *or* ·las
sa·lon'
sa·loon'
sa·loon'keep'er
sal'si·fy'
salt'box'
salt'cel'lar
salt'i·ly
salt·ine'
salt'i·ness
salt'pe'ter
salt'shak'er

salt'wa'ter
salt'works'
  ·works'
salt'y
  ·i·er ·i·est
sa·lu'bri·ous
sal'u·tar'y
sal'u·ta'tion
sa·lu'ta·to'ri·an
sa·lu'ta·to'ry
  ·ries
sa·lute'
  ·lut'ed ·lut'ing
sal'vage
  ·vaged ·vag·ing
sal'vage·a·ble
sal·va'tion
salve
  salved salv'ing
sal'ver
sal'vo
  ·vos *or* ·voes
Sa·mar'i·tan
same'ness
sam'i·sen'
sam'o·var'
sam'pan
sam'ple
  ·pled ·pling
sam'pler
sam'u·rai'
  ·rai'
san'a·tive
sanc'ti·fi·ca'tion

sanc′ti·fy′
 ·fied′ ·fy′ing
sanc′ti·mo′ni·ous
sanc′ti·mo′ny
sanc′tion
sanc′ti·ty
sanc′tu·ar′y
 ·ies
sanc′tum
 ·tums or ·ta
san′dal
san′daled or
 ·dalled
san′dal·wood′
sand′bag′
sand bar
sand′blast′
sand′box′
san′dhi
sand′hog′
sand′i·ness
sand′lot′
sand′man′
sand′pa′per
sand′stone′
sand′storm′
sand′wich
sand′y
 ·i·er ·i·est
sane′ly
San′for·ize′
 ·ized′ ·iz′ing
sang′-froid′
san′gui·nar′y

san′guine
san′i·tar′i·um
 ·i·ums or ·i·a
san′i·tar′y
san′i·ta′tion
san′i·tize′
 ·tized′ ·tiz′ing
san′i·ty
San′skrit
sap
 sapped sap′ping
sa′pi·ent
sap′ling
sa·pon′i·fy′
 ·fied′ ·fy′ing
sap′phire
sap′py
 ·pi·er ·pi·est
sap′suck′er
sa·ran′
sar′casm
sar·cas′tic
sar·cas′ti·cal·ly
sar·co′ma
 ·mas or ·ma·ta
sar·coph′a·gus
 ·a·gi
sar·dine′
sar·don′ic
sar·don′i·cal·ly
sar′do·nyx
sa′ri
 ·ris
sa·rong′

sar′sa·pa·ril′la
sar·to′ri·al
sas′sa·fras′
sa·tan′ic
sa·tan′i·cal·ly
satch′el
sate
 sat′ed sat′ing
sa·teen′
sat′el·lite′
sa′tia·ble
sa′ti·ate′
 ·at′ed ·at′ing
sa′ti·a′tion
sa·ti′e·ty
sat′in
sat′in·wood′
sat′in·y
sat′ire
sa·tir′i·cal
sat′i·rist
sat′i·rize′
 ·rized′ ·riz′ing
sat′is·fac′tion
sat′is·fac′to·ri·ly
sat′is·fac′to·ry
sat′is·fy′
 ·fied′ ·fy′ing
sa·to′ri
sa′trap
sat′su·ma
sat′u·ra·ble
sat′u·rate′
 ·rat′ed ·rat′ing

258

sat′u·ra′tion
Sat′ur·day
sat′ur·nine′
sat′yr
sat′y·ri′a·sis
sauce′pan′
sau′cer
sau′ci·ness
sau′cy
·ci·er ·ci·est
sau′er·bra′ten
sau′er·kraut′
sau′na
saun′ter
sau′sage
sau·té′
·téed′ ·té′ing
sau·terne′
sav′a·ble or
save′·
sav′age
sav′age·ly
sav′age·ry
sa·van′na
sa·vant′
save
saved sav′ing
sav′ior
sa′voir-faire′
sa′vor
sa′vor·i·ness
sa′vor·y
·i·er ·i·est
sa·voy′

saw
sawed saw′ing
saw′dust′
saw′horse′
saw′mill′
saw′-toothed′
saw′yer
sax′o·phone′
sax′o·phon′ist
say
said say′ing
says
say′-so′
scab
scabbed scab′bing
scab′bard
scab′bi·ness
scab′by
·bi·er ·bi·est
scab′rous
scaf′fold
scagl·io′la
scal′a·ble
scal′a·wag′
scald
scale
scaled scal′ing
scale′less
sca·lene′
scal′i·ness
scal′lion
scal′lop
scal′op·pi·ne
scal′pel

scalp′er
scal′y
·i·er ·i·est
scam′per
scan
scanned
scan′ning
scan′dal
scan′dal·ize′
·ized ·iz′ing
scan′dal·mon·ger
scan′dal·ous
scan′na·ble
scan′ner
scan′sion
scant′i·ly
scant′i·ness
scant′ling
scant′ness
scant′y
·i·er ·i·est
scape′goat′
scape′grace′
scap′u·la
·lae′ or ·las
scap′u·lar
scar
scarred
scar′ring
scar′ab
scar′a·mouch′
scarce′ly
scar′ci·ty
·ties

scare
scared scar'ing
scare'crow'
scarf
scarfs or scarves
(long cloth)
scarf
scarfs
(joint; cut)
scar'i·fi·ca'tion
scar'i·fy'
·fied' ·fy'ing
scar'i·ness
scar'let
scarp
scar'y
·i·er ·i·est
scat
scat'ted
scat'ting
scathe
scathed
scath'ing
scat'ter
scat'ter·brain'
scav'enge
·enged ·eng·ing
scav'eng·er
sce·nar'i·o'
·os'
sce·nar'ist
scene
sce'ner·y
·ies

sce'nic
scent
(odor; SEE sent)
scep'ter
sched'ule
·uled ·ul·ing
sche'ma
·ma·ta
sche·mat'ic
sche·mat'i·cal·ly
scheme
schemed
schem'ing
scher'zo
·zos or ·zi
schism
schis·mat'ic
schiz'oid
schiz'o·phre'ni·a
schiz'o·phren'ic
schnau'zer
schol'ar·ly
schol'ar·ship'
scho·las'tic
scho·las'ti·cal·ly
scho·las'ti·cism
school'boy'
school'girl'
school'house'
school'mate'
school'room'
school'teach'er
school'work'
schoon'er

schwa
sci·at'i·ca
sci'ence
sci'en·tif'ic
sci'en·tif'i·cal·ly
sci'en·tist
scim'i·tar
scin·til'la
scin·til·late'
·lat'ed ·lat'ing
scin·til·la'tor
sci'on
scis'sors
scle·ro'sis
scoff
scold'ing
sconce
scone
scoop'ful'
·fuls'
scoot'er
scope
scorch'ing
score
scored scor'ing
score'less
scorn'ful
scor'pi·on
scot'-free'
scoun'drel
scour
scourge
scourged
scourg'ing

scout′mas′ter
scowl
scrab′ble
·bled ·bling
scrag′gly
·gli·er ·gli·est
scrag′gy
·gi·er ·gi·est
scram′ble
·bled ·bling
scrap
scrapped
scrap′ping
scrap′book′
scrape
scraped
scrap′ing
scrap′er
scrap′heap′
scrap′ple
scrap′py
·pi·er ·pi·est
scratch′i·ness
scratch′y
·i·er ·i·est
scrawl
scraw′ny
·ni·er ·ni·est
scream′ing
screech′y
screen′play′
screw′driv′er
scrib′ble
·bled ·bling

scrib′bler
scribe
scribed scrib′ing
scrim′mage
·maged ·mag·ing
scrimp′i·ness
scrimp′y
·i·er ·i·est
scrip
(certificate)
script
(manuscript)
scrip′tur·al
scrof′u·la
scroll′work′
scro′tum
·ta or ·tums
scrounge
scrounged
scroung′ing
scrub
scrubbed
scrub′bing
scrub′by
·bi·er ·bi·est
scruff
scrunch
scru′ple
·pled ·pling
scru′pu·lous
scru′ta·ble
scru′ti·nize′
·nized′ ·niz′ing
scru′ti·ny

scu′ba
scuff
scuf′fle
·fled ·fling
scull
(oar; boat; SEE
skull)
scul′ler·y
·ies
sculpt
sculp′tor
sculp′tur·al
sculp′ture
·tured ·tur·ing
scum′my
·mi·er ·mi·est
scup′per·nong′
scur·ril′i·ty
·ties
scur′ril·ous
scur′ry
·ried ·ry·ing
scur′vy
·vi·er ·vi·est
scut′tle
·tled ·tling
scythe
scythed
scyth′ing
sea′board′
sea′borne′
sea′coast′
sea′far′er
sea′far′ing

sea'food'
sea'go'ing
seal'ant
sea level
seal'skin'
seam
sea'man
seam'less
seam'stress
seam'y
·i·er ·i·est
sé'ance
sea'plane'
sea'port'
sear
(*burn;* SEE seer)
search'light'
sea'scape'
sea'shell'
sea'shore'
sea'sick'ness
sea'side'
sea'son
sea'son·a·ble
sea'son·al
seat belt
sea'ward
sea'way'
sea'weed'
sea'wor'thy
se·ba'ceous
se'cant
se·cede'
·ced'ed ·ced'ing

se·ces'sion
se·clude'
·clud'ed
·clud'ing
se·clu'sion
se·clu'sive
sec'ond
sec'ond·ar'i·ly
sec'ond·ar'y
sec'ond-class'
sec'ond-guess'
sec'ond·hand'
sec'ond-rate'
se'cre·cy
se'cret
sec're·tar'i·al
sec're·tar'i·at
sec're·tar'y
·ies
se·crete'
·cret'ed ·cret'ing
se·cre'tion
se'cre·tive
se'cre·to·ry
sect
sec·tar'i·an
sec'tion·al
sec'tion·al·ize'
·ized' ·iz'ing
sec'tor
sec'u·lar
sec'u·lar·ize'
·ized' ·iz'ing
se·cur'a·ble

se·cure'
·cured' ·cur'ing
se·cure'ly
se·cu'ri·ty
·ties
se·dan'
se·date'
·dat'ed ·dat'ing
se·date'ly
se·da'tion
sed'a·tive
se·den'tar'y
sed'i·ment
sed'i·men'ta·ry
sed'i·men·ta'tion
se·di'tion
se·di'tious
se·duce'
·duced' ·duc'ing
se·duc'i·ble
se·duc'tion
se·duc'tive
se·du'li·ty
sed'u·lous
see
saw seen see'ing
seed'bed'
seed'i·ness
seed'ling
seed'y
·i·er ·i·est
seek
sought seek'ing
seem'ing·ly

seem'li·ness
seem'ly
· li·er · li·est
seep'age
seer
(*prophet;* SEE
sear)
seer'suck'er
see'saw'
seethe
seethed
seeth'ing
seg'ment
seg·men'tal
seg'men·ta'tion
seg're·gate'
· gat'ed · gat'ing
seg're·ga'tion
seg're·ga'tion·ist
sei'del
seis'mic
seis'mi·cal·ly
seis'mo·graph'
seis·mog'ra·pher
seis·mol'o·gist
seis·mol'o·gy
seize
seized seiz'ing
sei'zure
sel'dom
se·lect'
se·lect'ee'
se·lec'tion
se·lec'tive

se·lec'tiv'i·ty
se·lec'tor
self
selves
self'-act'ing
self'-ad·dressed'
self'-ap·point'ed
self'-as·sur'ance
self'-as·sured'
self'-cen'tered
self'-con'fi·dence
self'-con'scious
self'-con·tained'
self'-con·trol'
self'-de·fense'
self'-dis'ci·pline
self'-driv'en
self'-ed'u·cat'ed
self'-em·ployed'
self'-es·teem'
self'-ev'i·dent
self'-ex·plan'a·
to'ry
self'-ex·pres'sion
self'-gov'ern·ing
self'-im'age
self'-im·por'tant
self'-im·posed'
self'-im·prove'·
ment
self'-in·duced'
self'-in·dul'gence
self'-in·flict'ed
self'-in'ter·est

self'ish
self'less
self'-load'ing
self'-love'
self'-made'
self'-pit'y
self'-por'trait
self'-pos·sessed'
self'-pres'er·va'·
tion
self'-reg'u·lat'ing
self'-re·li'ance
self'-re·proach'
self'-re·spect'
self'-re·straint'
self'-right'eous
self'-ris'ing
self'-sac'ri·fice'
self'same'
self'-sat'is·fied'
self'-seal'ing
self'-serv'ice
self'-start'er
self'-styled'
self'-suf·fi'cient
self'-sup·port'
self'-taught'
self'-tor'ture
self'-willed'
self'-wind'ing
sell
sold sell'ing
sell'-off'
sell'out'

263

sel'vage *or*
  ·vedge
se·man'tic
sem'a·phore'
  ·phored'
  ·phor'ing
sem'blance
se'men
  sem'i·na
se·mes'ter
sem'i·an'nu·al
sem'i·au'to·
  mat'ic
sem'i·cir'cle
sem'i·co'lon
sem'i·con·duc'tor
sem'i·con'scious
sem'i·de·tached'
sem'i·fi'nal
sem'i·for'mal
sem'i·month'ly
sem'i·nal
sem'i·nar'
sem'i·nar'y
  ·ies
sem'i·of·fi'cial
sem'i·pre'cious
sem'i·pri'vate
sem'i·pro·fes'·
  sion·al
sem'i·rig'id
sem'i·skilled'
sem'i·sol'id
Sem'ite

Se·mit'ic
sem'i·trail'er
sem'i·trop'i·cal
sem'i·week'ly
sem'i·year'ly
sem·o·li'na
sen'ate
sen'a·tor
sen'a·to'ri·al
send
  sent send'ing
send'-off'
se·nes'cent
se'nile
se·nil'i·ty
sen'ior
sen·ior'i·ty
sen·sa'tion
sen·sa'tion·al·ly
sense
  sensed sens'ing
sense'less
sen'si·bil'i·ty
  ·ties
sen'si·ble
sen'si·bly
sen'si·tive
sen'si·tiv'i·ty
sen'si·ti·za'tion
sen'si·tize'
  ·tized' ·tiz'ing
sen'so·ry
sen'su·al
sen'su·al'i·ty

sen'su·ous
sent
  (*transmitted;*
  SEE scent)
sen'tence
  ·tenced ·tenc·ing
sen·ten'tious
sen'tient
sen'ti·ment
sen'ti·men'tal
sen'ti·men·
  tal'i·ty
sen'ti·men'tal·
  ize'
  ·ized' ·iz'ing
sen'ti·nel
  ·neled *or* ·nelled
  ·nel·ing *or*
  ·nel·ling
sen'try
  ·tries
sep'a·ra·ble
sep'a·rate'
  ·rat'ed ·rat'ing
sep'a·ra'tion
sep'a·ra·tism
sep'a·ra'tor
se'pi·a
Sep·tem'ber
sep·tet' *or*
  ·tette'
sep'tic
sep·tu·a·ge·
  nar'i·an

sep·tu'ple
 ·pled ·pling
sep'ul·cher
se·pul'chral
se'quel
se'quence
se·quen'tial
se·ques'ter
se'quin
se·quoi'a
se·ra'pe
ser'e·nade'
 ·nad'ed ·nad'ing
ser'en·dip'i·ty
se·rene'
se·ren'i·ty
serf
 (*slave;* SEE surf)
serge
 (*fabric;* SEE surge)
ser'geant
se'ri·al
 (*in a series;*
 SEE cereal)
se'ri·al·ize'
 ·ized' ·iz'ing
se'ries
 ·ries
ser'if
se'ri·o·com'ic
se'ri·ous
se'ri·ous-mind'ed
ser'mon
se'rous

ser'pent
ser'pen·tine'
ser·rate'
 ·rat'ed ·rat'ing
se'rum
 ·rums *or* ·ra
ser'vant
serve
 served serv'ing
serv'ice
 ·iced ·ic·ing
serv'ice·a·bil'i·ty
serv'ice·a·ble
serv'ice·a·bly
serv'ice·man'
ser'vi·ette'
ser'vile
ser·vil'i·ty
ser'vi·tor
ser'vi·tude'
ses'a·me'
ses'qui·cen·ten'·
 ni·al
ses'sion
 (*meeting;* SEE
 cession)
set
 set set'ting
set'back'
set'-in'
set'-off'
set'screw'
set·tee'
set'ter

set'tle
 ·tled ·tling
set'tle·ment
set'tler
set'-to'
 -tos'
sev'en·teen'
sev'enth
sev'en·ti·eth
sev'en·ty
 ·ties
sev'er
sev'er·al
sev'er·al·ly
sev'er·ance
se·vere'
se·vere'ly
se·ver'i·ty
 ·ties
sew
 sewed, sewn *or*
 sewed, sew'ing
 (*stitch;* SEE sow)
sew'age
sew'er
sew'er·age
sex'a·ge·nar'i·an
sex'i·ly
sex'i·ness
sex'less
sex'tant
sex·tet' *or*
 ·tette'
sex'ton

265

sex·tu′ple
　·pled　·pling
sex·tu′plet
sex′u·al
sex′u·al′i·ty
sex′u·al·ly
sex′y
　·i·er　·i·est
shab′bi·ly
shab′bi·ness
shab′by
　·bi·er　·bi·est
shack′le
　·led　·ling
shade
　shad′ed
　shad′ing
　shad′i·ness
　shad′ow
　shad′ow·y
shad′y
　·i·er　·i·est
shaft
shag
　shagged
　shag′ging
shag′gi·ness
shag′gy
　·gi·er　·gi·est
shak′a·ble or
　shake′a·ble
shake
　shook　shak′en
　shak′ing

Shake′speare′
Shake·spear′e·an
　or ·i·an
shake′-up′
shak′i·ly
shak′i·ness
shak′y
　·i·er　·i·est
shal′low
sha·lom′
sham
　shammed
　sham′ming
sham′ble
　·bled　·bling
shame
　shamed
　sham′ing
shame′faced′
shame′ful
shame′ful·ly
shame′less
sham·poo′
　·pooed′　·poo′ing
shang′hai
　·haied　·hai·ing
shank
shan′tung′
shan′ty
　·ties
shape
　shaped　shap′ing
shape′less
shape′li·ness

shape′ly
　·li·er　·li·est
share
　shared　shar′ing
share′crop′per
share′hold′er
shark′skin′
sharp′en·er
sharp′-eyed′
sharp′shoot′er
sharp′-sight′ed
sharp′-tongued′
sharp′-wit′ted
shat′ter
shat′ter·proof′
shave
　shaved, shaved
　or shav′en,
　shav′ing
shawl
sheaf
　sheaves
shear
　sheared, sheared
　or shorn,
　shear′ing
　(*cut;* SEE sheer)
shears
sheath
　(*a case; dress*)
sheathe
　sheathed
　sheath′ing
　(*put into a sheath*)

266

sheave
  sheaved
  sheav′ing
shed
  shed shed′ding
sheen
sheep′ish·ly
sheep′skin′
sheep′walk′
sheer
  (*thin; steep;*
  SEE shear)
sheet′ing
sheik *or* sheikh
shelf
  shelves
shell
shel·lac′ *or* ·lack′
  ·lacked′
  ·lack′ing
shell′fish′
shell′-like′
shell′proof′
shel′ter
shelve
  shelved
  shelv′ing
she·nan′i·gan
shep′herd
sher′bet
sher′iff
sher′ry
  ·ries
shib′bo·leth

shield
shift′i·ly
shift′i·ness
shift′less
shift′y
  ·i·er ·i·est
shil·le′lagh *or*
  shil·la′lah
shil′ly-shal′ly
  ·lied ·ly·ing
shim
  shimmed
  shim′ming
shim′mer·y
shim′my
  ·mies
  ·mied ·my·ing
shin
  shinned
  shin′ning
shine
  shone *or* shined
  shin′ing
shin′gle
  ·gled ·gling
shin′i·ness
shin′y
  ·i·er ·i·est
ship
  shipped
  ship′ping
ship′board′
ship′mate′
ship′ment

ship′own′er
ship′pa·ble
ship′per
ship′shape′
ship′wreck′
ship′wright′
ship′yard′
shirk′er
shirr′ing
shirt′waist′
shiv′a·ree′
  ·reed′ ·ree′ing
shiv′er
shoal
shock′ing
shock′proof′
shod′di·ly
shod′di·ness
shod′dy
  ·di·er ·di·est
shoe
  shod *or* shoed,
  shod *or* shoed
  or shod′den,
  shoe′ing
shoe′horn′
shoe′lace′
shoe′mak′er
sho′er
shoe′shine′
shoe′string′
shoe tree
shoo
  shooed shoo′ing

shoot
  shot shoot'ing
shop
  shopped
  shop'ping
shop'keep'er
shop'lift'er
shop'per
shop'talk'
shop'worn'
Shor'an or
  shor'·
shore'line'
shore'ward
shor'ing
short'age
short'bread'
short'cake'
short'change'
short'-cir'cuit
short'com'ing
short'cut'
short'en
short'en·ing
short'hand'
short'-hand'ed
short'horn'
short'-lived'
short'-range'
short'sight'ed
short'stop'
short'-tem'pered
short'-term'
short'-waist'ed

short'wave'
short'-wind'ed
shot'gun'
should
shoul'der
should'n't
shov'el
  ·eled or ·elled
  ·el·ing or ·el·ling
shov'el·ful'
  ·fuls'
show
  showed, shown
  or showed,
  show'ing
show'boat'
show'case'
show'down'
show'er
show'i·ly
show'i·ness
show'man
show'off'
show'piece'
show'place'
show'room'
show'y
  ·i·er ·i·est
shrap'nel
shred
  shred'ded or
  shred
  shred'ding
shrewd

shriek
shrill'ness
shril'ly
shrine
shrink
  shrank or shrunk,
  shrunk or
  shrunk'en,
  shrink'ing
shrink'age
shriv'el
  ·eled or ·elled
  ·el·ing or ·el·ling
shroud
shrub'ber·y
shrug
  shrugged
  shrug'ging
shuck
shud'der
shuf'fle
  ·fled ·fling
shuf'fle·board'
shun
  shunned
  shun'ning
shunt
shut
  shut shut'ting
shut'down'
shut'-in'
shut'-off'
shut'out'
shut'ter

shut′tle
·tled ·tling
shut′tle·cock′
shy
  shy′er or shi′er
  shy′est or shi′est
  shies
  shied shy′ing
Si′a·mese′
sib′i·lance
sib′i·lant
sib′ling
sick′bed′
sick′en
sick′le
sick′li·ness
sick′ly
  ·li·er ·li·est
sick′room′
side
  sid′ed sid′ing
side′arm′
side arms
side′board′
side′burns′
side′car′
side′light′
side′line′
side′long′
si·de′re·al
side′sad′dle
side′show′
side′slip′
side′split′ting

side′step′ v.
side′stroke′
side′swipe′
side′track′
side′walk′
side′ways′
side′wise′
sid′ing
si′dle
  ·dled ·dling
siege
si·en′na
si·er′ra
si·es′ta
sieve
  sieved siev′ing
sift′er
sigh
sight
  (*view;* SEE
  cite, site)
sight′less
sight′ly
  ·li·er ·li·est
sight′see′ing
sight′se′er
sign
  (*signal;* SEE sine)
sig′nal
  ·naled or ·nalled
  ·nal·ing or
  ·nal·ling
sig′nal·ize′
  ·ized′ ·iz′ing

sig′nal·ly
sig′na·to′ry
  ·ries
sig′na·ture
sign′board′
sig′net
sig·nif′i·cance
sig·nif′i·cant
sig′ni·fi·ca′tion
sig′ni·fy′
  ·fied′ ·fy′ing
sign′post′
si′lage
si′lence
  ·lenced ·lenc·ing
si′lenc·er
si′lent
si′lex
sil′hou·ette′
  ·et′ted ·et′ting
sil′i·ca
sil′i·cate
si·li′ceous
sil′i·cone′
sil′i·co′sis
silk′en
silk′i·ness
silk′-screen′
silk′worm′
silk′y
  ·i·er ·i·est
sil′li·ness
sil′ly
  ·lies, ·li·er ·li·est

si'lo
·los, ·loed ·lo·ing
sil'ver
sil'ver·fish'
silver plate
sil'ver·smith'
sil'ver-tongued'
sil'ver·ware'
sil'ver·y
sim'i·an
sim'i·lar
sim'i·lar'i·ty
·ties
sim'i·le'
si·mil'i·tude'
sim'mer
si'mon-pure'
sim'per
sim'ple
·pler ·plest
sim'ple-mind'ed
sim'ple·ton
sim·plic'i·ty
·ties
sim'pli·fi·ca'tion
sim'pli·fi'er
sim'pli·fy'
·fied' ·fy'ing
sim'ply
sim'u·lant
sim'u·late'
·lat'ed ·lat'ing
sim'u·la'tion
sim'u·la'tor

si'mul·cast'
·cast' or ·cast'ed
·cast'ing
si'mul·ta'ne·ous
sin
sinned sin'ning
sin·cere'
·cer'er ·cer'est
sin·cere'ly
sin·cer'i·ty
sine
(ratio; SEE sign)
si'ne·cure'
sin'ew·y
sin'ful
sing
sang sung
sing'ing
singe
singed
singe'ing
sin'gle
·gled ·gling
sin'gle-breast'ed
sin'gle-hand'ed
sin'gle-space'
sin'gle·ton
sin'gly
sing'song'
sin'gu·lar
sin'gu·lar'i·ty
sin'gu·lar·ize'
·ized' ·iz'ing
sin'is·ter

sink
sank or sunk,
sunk sink'ing
sin'ner
sin'u·ous
si'nus
si'nus·i'tis
sip
sipped sip'ping
si'phon
sire
sired sir'ing
si'ren
sir'loin
si·roc'co
·cos
si'sal
sis'ter-hood'
sis'ter-in-law'
sis'ters-in-law'
sis'ter·li·ness
sis'ter·ly
sit
sat sit'ting
si·tar'
sit'-down'
site
(place; SEE sight)
sit'-in'
sit'ter
sit'u·ate'
·at'ed ·at'ing
sit'u·a'tion
sit'-up' or sit'up'

sitz bath
six'fold'
six'pen'ny
six'teenth'
sixth
six'ti·eth
six'ty
·ties
siz'a·ble *or*
size'·
size
sized siz'ing
siz'zle
·zled ·zling
skate
skat'ed skat'ing
skein
skel'e·ton
skep'tic
skep'ti·cal
skep'ti·cal·ly
skep'ti·cism
sketch'book'
sketch'i·ly
sketch'i·ness
sketch'y
·i·er ·i·est
skew'er
ski
skis *or* ski
skied ski'ing
skid
skid'ded
skid'ding

ski'er
skil'let
skill'ful
skim
skimmed
skim'ming
skimp'i·ly
skimp'i·ness
skimp'y
·i·er ·i·est
skin
skinned
skin'ning
skin'-deep'
skin'flint'
skin'ni·ness
skin'ny
·ni·er ·ni·est
skip
skipped
skip'ping
ski'plane'
skip'per
skir'mish
skit'tish
skul·dug'ger·y
or skull·
skulk
skull
(*head;* SEE scull)
skull'cap'
sky
skies
sky'cap'

sky'-dive'
-dived' -div'ing
sky'-high'
sky'lark'
sky'light'
sky'line'
sky'rock'et
sky'scrap'er
sky'ward
sky'ways'
sky'writ'ing
slack'en
slack'er
slake
slaked slak'ing
sla'lom
slam
slammed
slam'ming
slan'der
slan'der·ous
slang'y
·i·er ·i·est
slant'wise'
slap
slapped
slap'ping
slap'dash'
slap'stick'
slash
slate
slat'ed slat'ing
slat'tern
slaugh'ter

slave
  slaved slav′ing
slav′er
slav′er·y
slav′ish·ly
slay
  slew slain
  slay′ing
  (*kill;* SEE sleigh)
slea′zi·ness
slea′zy
  ·zi·er ·zi·est
sled
  sled′ded
  sled′ding
sledge
  sledged
  sledg′ing
sleek′ly
sleep
  slept sleep′ing
sleep′i·ly
sleep′i·ness
sleep′less
sleep′walk′ing
sleep′y
  ·i·er ·i·est
sleet
sleeve′less
sleigh
  (*snow vehicle;*
  SEE slay)
sleight
  (*skill;* SEE slight)

slen′der
slen′der·ize′
  ·ized′ ·iz′ing
sleuth
slew *or* slue
  (*a lot;* SEE slue)
slice
  sliced slic′ing
slick′er
slide
  slid slid′ing
slide rule
slight
  (*frail;* SEE
  sleight)
slim
  slim′mer
  slim′mest
  slimmed
  slim′ming
slim′i·ness
slim′ness
slim′y
  ·i·er ·i·est
sling
  slung sling′ing
sling′shot′
slink
  slunk slink′ing
slip
  slipped slip′ping
slip′cov′er
slip′knot′
slip′-on′

slip′page
slip′per·i·ness
slip′per·y
  ·i·er ·i·est
slip′shod′
slip′stream′
slip′-up′
slit
  slit slit′ting
slith′er
sliv′er
sli′vo·vitz′
slob′ber
sloe
  (*fruit;* SEE slow)
sloe′-eyed′
slog
  slogged
  slog′ging
slo′gan
sloop
slop
  slopped
  slop′ping
slope
  sloped slop′ing
slop′pi·ly
slop′pi·ness
slop′py
  ·pi·er ·pi·est
slosh
slot
  slot′ted slot′ting
sloth′ful

slouch'y
·i·er ·i·est
slough
slov'en·li·ness
slov'en·ly
·li·er ·li·est
slow
(*not fast;* SEE
sloe)
slow'-wit'ted
sludge
sludg'y
·i·er ·i·est
slue *or* slew
slued *or* slewed
slu'ing *or*
slew'ing
(*turn;* SEE slew)
slug
slugged
slug'ging
slug'gard
slug'gish
sluice
sluiced sluic'ing
slum
slummed
slum'ming
slum'ber
slum'ber·ous
slump
slur
slurred
slur'ring

slush'y
·i·er ·i·est
slut'tish
sly
sli'er *or* sly'er
sli'est *or* sly'est
sly'ly *or* sli'ly
smack
small'-mind'ed
small'pox'
small'-scale'
smart
smash'up'
smat'ter·ing
smear'i·ness
smear'y
·i·er ·i·est
smell
smelled *or* smelt
smell'ing
smell'i·ness
smell'y
·i·er ·i·est
smidg'en
smile
smiled smil'ing
smirch
smirk
smite
smote, smit'ten
or smote,
smit'ing
smock'ing
smog

smog'gy
·gi·er ·gi·est
smok'a·ble *or*
smoke'a·ble
smoke
smoked
smok'ing
smok'er
smoke screen
smoke'stack'
smok'i·ness
smok'y
·i·er ·i·est
smol'der
smooth
smooth'bore'
smooth'-faced'
smooth'-shav'en
smooth'-spo'ken
smor'gas·bord'
smoth'er
smudge
smudged
smudg'ing
smudg'i·ness
smudg'y
·i·er ·i·est
smug
smug'ger
smug'gest
smug'gle
·gled ·gling
smut'ty
·ti·er ·ti·est

273

snack bar
snaf'fle
  ·fled ·fling
sna·fu'
snag
  snagged
  snag'ging
snail'-paced'
snake
  snaked snak'ing
snak'y
  ·i·er ·i·est
snap
  snapped
  snap'ping
snap'drag'on
snap'pish
snap'shot'
snare
  snared snar'ing
snarl'y
  ·i·er ·i·est
snatch
sneak'i·ly
sneak'i·ness
sneak'y
  ·i·er ·i·est
sneer'ing·ly
sneeze
  sneezed
  sneez'ing
snick'er
snif'fle
  ·fled ·fling

snif'ter
snip
  snipped
  snip'ping
snipe
  sniped snip'ing
sniv'el
  ·eled *or* ·elled
  ·el·ing *or*
  ·el·ling
snob'ber·y
snob'bish
snoop'er·scope'
snore
  snored snor'ing
snor'kel
snout
snow'ball'
snow'-blind'
snow'bound'
snow'drift'
snow'fall'
snow'flake'
snow line
snow'mo·bile'
  ·biled' ·bil'ing
snow'plow'
snow'shoe'
  ·shoed'
  ·shoe'ing
snow'storm'
snow'-white'
snow'y
  ·i·er ·i·est

snub
  snubbed
  snub'bing
snub'-nosed'
snuff'ers
snuf'fle
  ·fled ·fling
snug
  snug'ger
  snug'gest
snug'gle
  ·gled ·gling
soak'ers
soap'box'
soap'suds'
soap'y
  ·i·er ·i·est
soar
  (*fly;* SEE sore)
sob
  sobbed
  sob'bing
so'ber-mind'ed
so·bri'e·ty
so'bri·quet'
so'-called'
soc'cer
so'cia·bil'i·ty
so'cia·ble
so'cia·bly
so'cial
so'cial·ism
so'cial·ite'
so'cial·i·za'tion

274

so'cial·ize'
  ·ized' ·iz'ing
so·ci'e·tal
so·ci'e·tal·ly
so·ci'e·ty
  ·ties
so'ci·o·cul'tu·ral
so'ci·o·e'co·
  nom'ic
so'ci·o·gram'
so'ci·o·log'i·cal
so'ci·ol'o·gist
so'ci·ol'o·gy
so'ci·o·path'
so'ci·o·po·lit'i·cal
sock'et
sock'eye'
sod
  sod'ded sod'ding
so·dal'i·ty
  ·ties
sod'den·ness
sod'om·y
soft'ball'
soft'-boiled'
soft'-cov'er
sof'ten·er
soft'heart'ed
soft'-shell'
soft'-spo'ken
soft'ware'
sog'gi·ness
sog'gy
  ·gi·er ·gi·est

soil
soi·ree' *or* ·rée'
so'journ
sol'ace
  ·aced ·ac·ing
so'lar
so·lar'i·um
  ·lar'i·a
sol'der
  (*metal alloy*)
sol'dier
  (*man in an army*)
sole
  soled sol'ing
  (*bottom surface;*
  only; SEE soul)
sol'e·cism
sole'ly
sol'emn
so·lem'ni·fy'
  ·fied' ·fy'ing
so·lem'ni·ty
  ·ties
sol'em·nize'
  ·nized' ·niz'ing
so'le·noid'
sole'plate'
so·lic'it
so·lic'i·ta'tion
so·lic'i·tor
so·lic'i·tous
so·lic'i·tude'
sol'id
sol'i·dar'i·ty

so·lid'i·fi·ca'tion
so·lid'i·fy'
  ·fied' ·fy'ing
sol'id-state'
so·lil'o·quize'
  ·quized'
  ·quiz'ing
so·lil'o·quy
  ·quies
sol'i·taire'
sol'i·tar'y
sol'i·tude'
so'lo
  ·los
so'lo·ist
sol'stice
sol'u·bil'i·ty
sol'u·ble
sol'ute
so·lu'tion
solv'a·bil'i·ty
solv'a·ble
solve
  solved
  solv'ing
sol'ven·cy
sol'vent
som'ber
som·bre'ro
  ·ros
some'bod'y
some'day'
some'how'
some'one'

275

som'er·sault'
some'thing
some'time'
some'times'
some'what'
some'where'
som·nam'bu·late'
·lat'ed ·lat'ing
som'no·lent
so'nar
so·na'ta
sonde
song'ster
son'ic
son'-in-law'
sons'-in-law'
son'net
son'net·eer'
so·nor'i·ty
so·no'rous
soon'er
soothe
soothed
sooth'ing
sooth'say'er
soot'i·ness
soot'y
·i·er ·i·est
sop
sopped
sop'ping
soph'ism
soph'ist
so·phis'ti·cal

so·phis'ti·cate'
·cat'ed ·cat'ing
so·phis'ti·ca'tion
soph'is·try
·tries
soph'o·more'
soph'o·mor'ic
sop'o·rif'ic
so·pra'no
·nos or ·ni
sor'cer·er
sor'cer·y
·ies
sor'did
sore
(painful; SEE soar)
sore'ly
sor'ghum
so·ror'i·ty
·ties
sor'rel
sor'ri·ly
sor'ri·ness
sor'row
sor'row·ful
sor'ry
·ri·er ·ri·est
sor'tie
so'-so'
sou·brette'
souf·flé'
soul
(spirit; SEE sole)

soul'ful
soul'-search'ing
sound'proof'
soup'çon'
source'book'
sour'dough'
sour'ness
sou'sa·phone'
souse
soused sous'ing
South Car'o·li'na
South Da·ko'ta
south'east'
south'east'er·ly
south'east'ern
south'east'ward
south'er·ly
south'ern
south'ern·er
south'ern·most'
south'ward
south'west'
south'west'er·ly
south'west'ern
south'west'ward
sou've·nir'
sov'er·eign
sov'er·eign·ty
·ties
so'vi·et
sow
sowed, sown or
sowed, sow'ing
(plant; SEE sew)

soy'bean'
space
  spaced spac'ing
space'craft'
  ·craft'
space'flight'
space'man
space'port'
space'ship'
space'suit'
space'walk'
spa'cious
spack'le
  ·led ·ling
spade
  spad'ed
  spad'ing
spade'work'
spa·ghet'ti
span
  spanned
  span'ning
span'dex
span'drel
span'gle
  ·gled ·gling
span'iel
span'sule
spar
  sparred
  spar'ring
spare
  spared spar'ing
spare'ribs'

spar'kle
  ·kled ·kling
spar'kler
spar'row
sparse'ly
spasm
spas·mod'ic
spas·mod'i·cal·ly
spas'tic
spa'tial
spat'ter
spat'u·la
spawn
spay
speak
  spoke spo'ken
  speak'ing
speak'er
spear'head'
spear'mint'
spe'cial
spe'cial·ist
spe'cial·ize'
  ·ized' ·iz'ing
spe'cial·ly
spe'cial·ty
  ·ties
spe'cie
  (coin money)
spe'cies
  ·cies
  (kind)
spec'i·fi'a·ble
spe·cif'ic

spe·cif'i·cal·ly
spec'i·fi·ca'tion
spec'i·fy'
  ·fied' ·fy'ing
spec'i·men
spe'cious
speck'le
  ·led ·ling
spec'ta·cle
spec'ta·cled
spec·tac'u·lar
spec'ta·tor
spec'ter
spec'tral
spec'tro·scope'
spec·tros'co·py
spec'trum
  ·tra or ·trums
spec'u·late'
  ·lat'ed ·lat'ing
spec'u·la'tion
spec'u·la'tive
spec'u·la'tor
speech'less
speed
  sped or speed'ed
  speed'ing
speed'boat'
speed'i·ly
speed'i·ness
speed·om'e·ter
speed'up'
speed'y
  ·i·er ·i·est

spe'le·ol'o·gy

spell
  spelled or spelt
  spell'ing
  (*name the letters*)

spell
  spelled spell'ing
  (*work in place of*)

spell'bind'
  ·bound' ·bind'ing

spell'down'

spe·lunk'er

spend
  spent spend'ing

spend'thrift'

sper'ma·ce'ti

spew

sphere

spher'i·cal

sphe'roid

sphinx
  sphinx'es or
  sphin'ges

spice
  spiced spic'ing

spic'i·ness

spick'-and-span'

spic'y
  ·i·er ·i·est

spi'der

spi'er

spig'ot

spike
  spiked spik'ing

spill
  spilled or spilt
  spill'ing

spin
  spun spin'ning

spin'ach

spi'nal

spin'dle
  ·dled ·dling

spin'dly
  ·dli·er ·dli·est

spin'drift'

spine'less

spin'et

spin'ner

spin'off'

spin'ster

spin'y
  ·i·er ·i·est

spi'ral
  ·raled or ·ralled
  ·ral·ing or
  ·ral·ling

spir'it·less

spir'it·u·al

spir'it·u·ous

spit
  spit'ted
  spit'ting
  (*impale*)

spit
  spit or spat
  spit'ting
  (*eject saliva*)

spite
  spit'ed
  spit'ing

spite'ful

spit'fire'

spit'tle

spit·toon'

spitz

splash'down'

splat'ter

splay'foot'
  ·feet'

spleen'ful

splen'did

splen'dor

sple·net'ic

splice
  spliced
  splic'ing

splin'ter

split
  split split'ting

split'-lev'el

split'-up'

splotch

splurge
  splurged
  splurg'ing

splut'ter

spoil
  spoiled or spoilt
  spoil'ing

spoil'age

spoil'sport'

spoke
 spoked spok′ing
spoke′shave′
spokes′man
spo·li·a′tion
sponge
 sponged
 spong′ing
sponge′cake′
spon′gi·ness
spon′gy
 ·gi·er ·gi·est
spon′sor
spon·ta·ne′i·ty
 ·ties
spon·ta′ne·ous
spoon′er·ism
spoon′-feed′
 -fed′ -feed′ing
spoon′ful′
 ·fuls′
spo·rad′ic
sport′ing
spor′tive
sports′man
sports′wear′
spot
 spot′ted
 spot′ting
spot′-check′
spot′light′
spot′ti·ness
spot′ty
 ·ti·er ·ti·est

spout′less
sprain
sprawl
spray
spread
 spread
 spread′ing
sprig
 sprigged
 sprig′ging
spright′li·ness
spright′ly
 ·li·er ·li·est
spring
 sprang or
 sprung, sprung,
 spring′ing
spring′board′
spring′i·ness
spring′time′
spring′y
 ·i·er ·i·est
sprin′kle
 ·kled ·kling
sprin′kler
sprint′er
spritz
sprock′et
sprout
spruce
 spruc′er
 spruc′est
 spruced
 spruc′ing

spry
 spri′er or spry′er
 spri′est or
 spry′est
spry′ly
spry′ness
spume
 spumed
 spum′ing
spu·mo′ni or ·ne
spur
 spurred
 spur′ring
spu′ri·ous
spurn
spurt
sput′nik
sput′ter
spu′tum
spy
 spies
 spied spy′ing
spy′glass′
squab′ble
 ·bled ·bling
squab′bler
squad′ron
squal′id
squall
squal′or
squan′der
square
 squared
 squar′ing

square'-rigged'
squar'ish
squash'i·ness
squash'y
·i·er ·i·est
squat
squat'ted
squat'ting
squawk
squeak'i·ly
squeak'y
·i·er ·i·est
squeal'er
squeam'ish
squee'gee
·geed ·gee·ing
squeez'a·ble
squeeze
squeezed
squeez'ing
squelch
squig'gle
·gled ·gling
squint'-eyed'
squire
squired
squir'ing
squirm'y
·i·er ·i·est
squir'rel
squirt
stab
stabbed
stab'bing

sta·bil'i·ty
sta'bi·li·za'tion
sta'bi·lize'
·lized' ·liz'ing
sta'bi·liz'er
sta'ble
·bled ·bling
sta'bly
stac·ca'to
·tos
stack'up'
sta'di·um
·di·a or ·di·ums
staff
staffs or staves
(stick; music)
staffs
(people)
stage
staged
stag'ing
stage'craft'
stage'hand'
stage'-struck'
stag'ger
stag'nan·cy
stag'nant
stag'nate
·nat·ed ·nat·ing
stag·na'tion
stag'y
·i·er ·i·est
staid
(sober; SEE stay)

stain'less
stair'case'
stake
staked
stak'ing
(post; share;
SEE steak)
stake'hold'er
stake'out'
sta·lac'tite
sta·lag'mite
stale
stal'er stal'est
staled stal'ing
stale'mate'
·mat'ed ·mat'ing
stalk'ing-horse'
stall
stal'lion
stal'wart
stam'i·na
stam'mer
stam·pede'
·ped'ed ·ped'ing
stance
stan'chion
stand
stood stand'ing
stand'ard
stand'ard-bear'er
stand'ard·i·
za'tion
stand'ard·ize'
·ized' ·iz'ing

stand'by'
 ·bys'
stand·ee'
stand'-in'
stand'off'
stand'pat'
stand'point'
stand'still'
stand'-up'
stan'za
staph'y·lo·coc'cus
 ·coc'ci
sta'ple
 ·pled ·pling
sta'pler
star
 starred
 star'ring
star'board
starch'i·ness
starch'y
 ·i·er ·i·est
star'dom
stare
 stared
 star'ing
star'gaze'
 ·gazed' ·gaz'ing
stark'-nak'ed
star'let
star'light'
star'lit'
star'ry
 ·ri·er ·ri·est

star'-span'gled
start'er
star'tle
 ·tled ·tling
star·va'tion
starve
 starved
 starv'ing
starve'ling
stat'a·ble
state
 stat'ed stat'ing
State'hood'
state'li·ness
state'ly
 ·li·er ·li·est
state'ment
state'room'
states'man
state'-wide'
stat'ic
stat'i·cal·ly
sta'tion
sta'tion·ar'y
 (*not moving*)
sta'tion·er
sta'tion·er'y
 (*writing paper*)
sta·tis'tic
sta·tis'ti·cal
sta·tis'ti·cal·ly
stat'is·ti'cian
stat'u·ar'y
 ·ies

stat'ue
stat'u·esque'
stat'u·ette'
stat'ure
sta'tus
sta'tus quo'
stat'ute
stat'u·to'ry
staunch
stave
 staved *or* stove
 stav'ing
stay
 stayed stay'ing
 (*stop;* SEE staid)
stead'fast'
stead'i·ly
stead'i·ness
stead'y
 ·i·er ·i·est
 ·ied ·y·ing
steak
 (*meat;* SEE stake)
steal
 stole stol'en
 steal'ing
stealth'i·ly
stealth'y
 ·i·er ·i·est
steam'boat'
steam'er
steam'roll'er
steam'ship'
steam shovel

steam'y
·i·er ·i·est
steel mill
steel wool
steel'work'er
steel'yard'
stee'ple
stee'ple·chase'
stee'ple·jack'
steer'age·way'
steers'man
stein
stel'lar
stem
 stemmed
 stem'ming
stem'-wind'ing
sten'cil
 ·ciled *or* ·cilled
 ·cil·ing *or*
 ·cil·ling
ste·nog'ra·pher
sten'o·graph'ic
ste·nog'ra·phy
sten'o·type'
sten'o·typ'ist
sten'o·typ'y
sten·to'ri·an
step
 stepped
 step'ping
step'broth'er
step'child'
 ·chil'dren

step'daugh'ter
step'-down'
step'fa'ther
step'lad'der
step'moth'er
step'par'ent
steppe
 (*treeless plain*)
stepped'-up'
step'ping·stone'
step'sis'ter
step'son'
step'-up'
ster'e·o'
ster'e·o·phon'ic
ster'e·op'ti·con
ster'e·o·scope'
ster'e·o·scop'ic
ster'e·o·type'
 ·typed' ·typ'ing
ster'e·o·typ'ic
ster'ile
ste·ril'i·ty
ster'i·li·za'tion
ster'i·lize'
 ·lized' ·liz'ing
ster'ling
stern'ness
stern'-wheel'er
stet
 stet'ted
 stet'ting
steth'o·scope'
ste've·dore'

stew'ard
stew'ard·ess
stick
 stuck stick'ing
stick'i·ness
stick'le
 ·led ·ling
stick'ler
stick'pin'
stick-to'-it·ive·
 ness
stick'y
 ·i·er ·i·est
stiff'en
stiff'-necked'
sti'fle
 ·fled ·fling
stig'ma
 ·mas *or* ·ma·ta
stig'ma·tize'
 ·tized' ·tiz'ing
stile
 (*steps;* SEE style)
sti·let'to
 ·tos *or* ·toes
still'born'
still life
still'y
stilt'ed
stim'u·lant
stim'u·late'
 ·lat'ed ·lat'ing
stim'u·la'tion
stim'u·la'tive

stim'u·lus
·li'
sting
  stung sting'ing
stin'gi·ly
stin'gi·ness
stin'gy
  ·gi·er ·gi·est
stink
  stank *or* stunk,
  stunk stink'ing
stint'ing·ly
sti'pend
sti·pen'di·ar'y
  ·ar'ies
stip'ple
  ·pled ·pling
stip'u·late'
  ·lat'ed ·lat'ing
stip'u·la'tion
stip'u·la'tor
stir
  stirred stir'ring
stir'rup
stitch
stock·ade'
  ·ad'ed ·ad'ing
stock'bro'ker
stock'hold'er
stock'i·ness
stock'i·nette' *or*
  ·net'
stock'ing
stock'pile'

stock'room'
stock'-still'
stock'y
  ·i·er ·i·est
stock'yard'
stodg'i·ness
stodg'y
  ·i·er ·i·est
sto'gie *or* ·gy
  ·gies
sto'ic
sto'i·cal
sto'i·cism
stoke
  stoked stok'ing
stoke'hole'
stok'er
stole
stol'en
  (*pp. of steal*)
stol'id
stol'len
  (*sweet bread*)
stom'ach
stom'ach·ache'
stone
  stoned ston'ing
stone'-blind'
stone'cut'ter
stone'-deaf'
stone'ma'son
stone'ware'
stone'work'
ston'i·ly

ston'y
  ·i·er ·i·est
stoop
  (*porch; bend;*
  SEE stoup)
stop
  stopped
  stop'ping
stop'cock'
stop'gap'
stop'light'
stop'o'ver
stop'page
stop'per
stop'ple
  ·pled ·pling
stop'watch'
stor'a·ble
stor'age
store
  stored stor'ing
store'house'
store'keep'er
store'room'
storm'bound'
storm door
storm'i·ly
storm'i·ness
storm'y
  ·i·er ·i·est
sto'ry
  ·ries
  ·ried ·ry·ing
sto'ry·tell'er

stoup
(*basin;* SEE
stoop)
stout'heart'ed
stove'pipe'
stow'a·way'
stra·bis'mus
strad'dle
·dled ·dling
Strad'i·var'i·us
strafe
strafed straf'ing
strag'gle
·gled ·gling
strag'gler
straight
(*not bent;*
SEE strait)
straight'a·way'
straight'edge'
straight'ened
(*made straight;*
SEE straitened)
straight'-faced'
straight'for'ward
strain'er
strait
(*waterway;* SEE
straight)
strait'ened
(*limited;* SEE
straightened)
strait'jack'et
strait'-laced'

strange
strang'er
strang'est
strange'ly
stran'ger
stran'gle
·gled ·gling
stran'gle·hold'
stran'gu·late'
·lat'ed ·lat'ing
stran'gu·la'tion
strap
strapped
strap'ping
strat'a·gem
stra·te'gic
stra·te'gi·cal·ly
strat'e·gist
strat'e·gy
·gies
strat'i·fi·ca'tion
strat'i·fy'
·fied' ·fy'ing
strat'o·sphere'
stra'tum
·ta *or* ·tums
stra'tus
·ti
straw'ber'ry
·ries
stray
streak'i·ness
streak'y
·i·er ·i·est

stream'line'
·lined' ·lin'ing
street'car'
strength'en
stren'u·ous
strep'to·coc'cal
strep'to·coc'cus
·coc'ci
strep'to·my'cin
stretch'er
stretch'i·ness
stretch'y
·i·er ·i·est
streu'sel
strew
strewed, strewed
or strewn,
strew'ing
stri'ate
·at·ed ·at·ing
stri·a'tion
strict'ly
stric'ture
stride
strode strid'den
strid'ing
stri'dent
strid'u·late'
·lat'ed ·lat'ing
strife
strike
struck, struck *or*
strick'en,
strik'ing

284

strike'break'er
string
　strung
　string'ing
strin'gen·cy
　·cies
strin'gent
string'halt'
string'i·ness
string'y
　·i·er ·i·est
strip
　stripped
　strip'ping
stripe
　striped
　strip'ing
strip'ling
strip'tease'
strive
　strove or strived,
　striv'en or
　strived, striv'ing
strobe
stroke
　stroked
　strok'ing
stroll'er
strong'-arm'
strong'box'
strong'hold'
strong'-mind'ed
strong'-willed'
stron'ti·um

strop
　stropped
　strop'ping
struc'tur·al
struc'ture
　·tured ·tur·ing
stru'del
strug'gle
　·gled ·gling
strum
　strummed
　strum'ming
strut
　strut'ted
　strut'ting
strych'nine
stub
　stubbed
　stub'bing
stub'ble
stub'bly
　·bli·er ·bli·est
stub'born
stub'by
　·bi·er ·bi·est
stuc'co
　·coes or ·cos
　·coed ·co·ing
stud
　stud'ded
　stud'ding
stud'book'
stu'dent
stud'horse'

stu'di·o'
　·os'
stu'di·ous
stud'y
　·ies, ·ied ·y·ing
stuff'i·ness
stuff'y
　·i·er ·i·est
stul'ti·fy'
　·fied' ·fy'ing
stum'ble
　·bled ·bling
stun
　stunned
　stun'ning
stu'pe·fac'tion
stu'pe·fy'
　·fied' ·fy'ing
stu·pen'dous
stu'pid
stu·pid'i·ty
　·ties
stu'por
stur'di·ly
stur'di·ness
stur'dy
　·di·er ·di·est
stur'geon
stut'ter
stut'ter·er
sty
　sties
　stied sty'ing
　(pig pen)

285

sty *or* stye
  sties
  (*eyelid swelling*)
style
  styled styl′ing
  (*mode;* SEE stile)
style′book′
styl′ish
styl′ist
sty·lis′tic
styl′i·za′tion
styl′ize
  ·ized ·iz·ing
sty′lus
  ·lus·es *or* ·li
sty′mie
  ·mied ·mie·ing
styp′tic
sty′rene
Sty′ro·foam′
su′a·ble
sua′sion
suave
suave′ly
suav′i·ty
sub′as·sem′bly
sub′base′ment
sub′com·mit′tee
sub·con′scious
sub·con′tract
sub′cul′ture
sub·cu·ta′ne·ous
sub′di·vide′
sub′di·vi′sion

sub·due′
  ·dued′ ·du′ing
sub′gum′
sub′ject
sub·jec′tive
sub′jec·tiv′i·ty
sub·join′der
sub′ju·gate′
  ·gat′ed ·gat′ing
sub′ju·ga′tion
sub′ju·ga′tor
sub·junc′tive
sub′lease′
sub·let′
  ·let′ ·let′ting
sub′li·mate′
  ·mat′ed ·mat·ing
sub′li·ma′tion
sub·lime′
  ·limed′ ·lim′ing
sub·lim′i·nal
sub·lim′i·ty
sub·mar′gin·al
sub′ma·rine′
sub·merge′
sub·mer′gence
sub·mer′gi·ble
sub·merse′
  ·mersed′
  ·mers′ing
sub·mers′i·ble
sub·mer′sion
sub·mis′sion
sub·mis′sive

sub·mit′
  ·mit′ted
  ·mit′ting
sub·nor′mal
sub′nor·mal′i·ty
sub·or′di·nate′
  ·nat′ed ·nat′ing
sub·or′di·na′tion
sub′or·na′tion
sub′plot′
sub·poe′na
  ·naed ·na·ing
sub ro′sa
sub·scribe′
  ·scribed′
  ·scrib′ing
sub′script
sub·scrip′tion
sub′se·quent
sub·ser′vi·ent
sub·side′
  ·sid′ed ·sid′ing
sub·sid′i·ar′y
  ·ies
sub′si·di·za′tion
sub′si·dize′
  ·dized′ ·diz′ing
sub′si·dy
  ·dies
sub·sist′ence
sub′soil′
sub′stance
sub·stand′ard
sub·stan′tial

sub·stan'tial·ly
sub·stan'ti·ate'
·at'ed ·at'ing
sub·stan'ti·a'tion
sub'stan·ti'val
sub'stan·tive
sub'sta'tion
sub'sti·tut'a·ble
sub'sti·tute'
·tut'ed ·tut'ing
sub'sti·tu'tion
sub·stra'tum
·ta or ·tums
sub·struc'tur·al
sub'struc'ture
sub'ter·fuge'
sub'ter·ra'ne·an
sub'ti'tle
sub'tle
·tler ·tlest
sub'tle·ty
·ties
sub'tly
sub·tract'
sub·trac'tion
sub'tra·hend'
sub·trop'i·cal
sub'urb
sub·ur'ban
sub·ur'ban·ite'
sub·ur'bi·a
sub·ver'sion
sub·ver'sive
sub·vert'

sub'way'
suc·ceed'
suc·cess'
suc·cess'ful
suc·cess'ful·ly
suc·ces'sion
suc·ces'sive
suc·ces'sor
suc·cinct'
suc'cor
(*help;* SEE sucker)
suc'co·tash'
suc'cu·lence
suc'cu·lent
suc·cumb'
suck'er
(*one that sucks;*
SEE succor)
suck'le
·led ·ling
su'crose
suc'tion
sud'den·ly
sud'den·ness
su'dor·if'ic
suds'y
·i·er ·i·est
sue
sued su'ing
suede *or* suède
su'et
suf'fer
suf'fer·ance
suf'fer·ing

suf·fice'
·ficed' ·fic'ing
suf·fi'cien·cy
suf·fi'cient
suf'fix
suf'fo·cate'
·cat'ed ·cat'ing
suf'fo·ca'tion
suf'frage
suf'fra·gette'
suf'fra·gist
suf·fuse'
·fused' ·fus'ing
suf·fu'sion
sug'ar
sug'ar·coat'
sug'ar-cured'
sug'ar·plum'
sug'ar·y
sug·gest'
sug·gest'i·ble
sug·ges'tion
sug·ges'tive
su'i·ci'dal
su'i·cide'
suit
(*set;* SEE suite)
suit'a·bil'i·ty
suit'a·ble
suit'a·bly
suit'case'
suite
(*rooms; furniture;*
SEE suit, sweet)

suit′or
su′ki·ya′ki
sul′fa
sul′fur
sulk′y
·i·er ·i·est
sul′len
sul′ly
·lied ·ly·ing
sul′tan
sul·tan′a
sul′tri·ness
sul′try
·tri·er ·tri·est
sum
summed
sum′ming
su′mac
sum·mar′i·ly
sum′ma·rize′
·rized′ ·riz′ing
sum′ma·ry
·ries
(brief account)
sum·ma′tion
sum′mer·time′
sum′mer·y
(like summer)
sum′mit
sum′mon
sum′mons
·mons·es
sump′tu·ar′y
sump′tu·ous

sun
sunned sun′ning
sun bath
sun′bathe′
·bathed′ ·bath′ing
sun′bath′er
sun′beam′
sun′burn′
sun′burst′
sun′-cured′
sun′dae
Sun′day
sun′di·al
sun′down′
sun′-dried′
sun′dries
sun′dry
sun′glass′es
sunk′en
sun′lamp′
sun′light′
sun′lit′
sun′ni·ness
sun′ny
·ni·er ·ni·est
sun′proof′
sun′rise′
sun′set′
sun′shade′
sun′shine′
sun′spot′
sun′stroke′
sun′tan′
sun′-tanned′

sup
supped sup′ping
su·perb′
su′per·car′go
·goes or ·gos
su′per·charge′
su′per·cil′i·ous
su′per·e′go
su′per·fi′cial
su′per·fi′ci·al′i·ty
·ties
su′per·fi′cial·ly
su′per·fine′
su′per·flu′i·ty
·ties
su·per′flu·ous
su′per·het′er·
o·dyne′
su′per·hu′man
su′per·im·pose′
su′per·in·duce′
su′per·in·tend′ent
su·pe′ri·or
su·pe′ri·or′i·ty
su·per′la·tive
su′per·man′
su′per·mar′ket
su′per·nat′u·ral
su′per·nu′mer·
ar′y
·ar′ies
su′per·scribe′
su′per·script′
su′per·scrip′tion

su·per·sede'
·sed'ed ·sed'ing
su·per·se'dure
su·per·sen'si·tive
su·per·ses'sion
su·per·son'ic
su·per·sti'tion
su·per·sti'tious
su·per·struc'ture
su·per·vene'
·vened'
·ven'ing
su·per·ven'tion
su·per·vise'
·vised' ·vis'ing
su·per·vi'sion
su·per·vi'sor
su·per·vi'so·ry
su·pine'
sup'per
sup·plant'
sup'ple
sup'ple·ly
sup'ple·ment
sup'ple·men'tal
sup'ple·men'ta·ry
sup'ple·men·
ta'tion
sup'pli·ant
sup'pli·cant
sup'pli·cate'
·cat'ed ·cat'ing
sup'pli·ca'tion
sup·pli'er

sup·ply'
·plied' ·ply'ing
·plies'
sup·port'
sup·port'ive
sup·pose'
·posed' ·pos'ing
sup·pos'ed·ly
sup·po·si'tion
sup·pos'i·to'ry
·ries
sup·press'
sup·press'i·ble
sup·pres'sion
sup·pres'sor
sup'pu·rate'
·rat'ed ·rat'ing
sup'pu·ra'tion
su·prem'a·cist
su·prem'a·cy
su·preme'ly
sur'charge
sur'cin'gle
sure
sur'er sur'est
sure'-foot'ed
sure'ly
sur'e·ty
·ties
surf
(*waves;* SEE serf)
sur'face
·faced ·fac'ing
surf'board'

surf'boat'
surf'-cast'
sur'feit
surf'er
surge
surged surg'ing
(*sudden rush;*
SEE serge)
sur'geon
sur'ger·y
·ies
sur'gi·cal
sur'gi·cal·ly
sur'li·ness
sur'ly
·li·er ·li·est
sur·mise'
·mised' ·mis'ing
sur·mount'
sur'name'
·named'
·nam'ing
sur·pass'
sur'plice
(*cloak*)
sur'plus
(*excess*)
sur·prise'
·prised' ·pris'ing
sur·pris'ing·ly
sur·re'al
sur·re'al·ism
sur·ren'der
sur'rep·ti'tious

sur'rey
 ·reys
sur'ro·gate'
 ·gat'ed ·gat'ing
sur·round'
sur'tax'
sur·veil'lance
sur'vey
 ·veys
sur·vey'or
sur·viv'a·ble
sur·viv'al
sur·vive'
 ·vived' ·viv'ing
sur·vi'vor
sus·cep'ti·bil'i·ty
sus·cep'ti·ble
sus·pect'
sus·pend'
sus·pense'
sus·pen'sion
sus·pen'so·ry
sus·pi'cion
sus·pi'cious
sus·tain'
sus·tain'a·ble
sus'te·nance
sut·tee'
su'ture
 ·tured ·tur·ing
svelte
swab
 swabbed
 swab'bing

swad'dle
 ·dled ·dling
swag'ger
swal'low
swal'low-tailed'
swa'mi
 ·mis
swamp'y
 ·i·er ·i·est
swan's'-down'
swap
 swapped
 swap'ping
sward
 (turf; SEE sword)
swarm
swarth'y
 ·i·er ·i·est
swash'buck'ler
swas'ti·ka
swat
 swat'ted
 swat'ting
swath n.
 (strip)
swathe v., n.
 swathed
 swath'ing
 (bandage)
sway'backed'
swear
 swore
 sworn
 swear'ing

swear'word'
sweat
 sweat or
 sweat'ed,
 sweat'ing
sweat'band'
sweat'er
sweat shirt
sweat'shop'
sweat'y
 ·i·er ·i·est
sweep
 swept sweep'ing
sweep'stakes'
 ·stakes'
sweet
 (like sugar;
 SEE suite)
sweet'bread'
sweet corn
sweet'en·er
sweet'heart'
sweet'meat'
swell
 swelled, swelled
 or swol'len,
 swell'ing
swel'ter
swept'back'
swerve
 swerved
 swerv'ing
swift'ness
swill

swim
  swam swum
  swim'ming
  swim'ming·ly
  swim'suit'
swin'dle
  ·dled ·dling
swing
  swung
  swing'ing
swing'by'
swin'ish
swipe
  swiped
  swip'ing
swirl
switch'board'
switch'man
swiv'el
  ·eled or ·elled
  ·el·ing or ·el·ling
swol'len
sword
  (*weapon;* SEE
  sward)
sword'fish'
sword'play'
swords'man
syb'a·rite'
syc'a·more'
syc'o·phant
syc'o·phan'tic
syl·lab'ic
syl·lab'i·fi·ca'tion

syl·lab'i·fy'
  ·fied' ·fy'ing
syl'la·ble
syl'la·bus
  ·bus·es or ·bi'
syl'lo·gism
sylph
syl'van
sym'bi·ot'ic
sym'bol
  (*mark;* SEE
  cymbal)
sym·bol'ic
sym'bol·ism
sym'bol·is'tic
sym'bol·ize'
  ·ized' ·iz'ing
sym·met'ri·cal
sym'me·try
  ·tries
sym'pa·thet'ic
sym'pa·thet'i·
  cal·ly
sym'pa·thize'
  ·thized' ·thiz'ing
sym'pa·thy
  ·thies
sym·phon'ic
sym'pho·ny
  ·nies
sym·po'si·um
  ·ums or ·a
symp'tom
symp'to·mat'ic

syn'a·gogue'
syn'chro·mesh'
syn'chro·nism
syn'chro·ni·
  za'tion
syn'chro·nize'
  ·nized' ·niz'ing
syn'chro·nous
syn'chro·tron'
syn'co·pate'
  ·pat'ed ·pat'ing
syn'co·pa'tion
syn'co·pe
syn'cre·tize'
  ·tized' ·tiz'ing
syn'di·cal·ism
syn'di·cate'
  ·cat'ed ·cat'ing
syn'drome
syn·ec'do·che
syn'e·col'o·gy
syn'er·gism
syn'od
syn·od'i·cal
syn'o·nym
syn·on'y·mous
syn·on'y·my
  ·mies
syn·op'sis
  ·ses
syn·op'size
  ·sized ·siz·ing
syn·op'tic
syn·tac'tic

syn·tac'ti·cal·ly
syn'tax
syn'the·sis
·ses'
syn'the·size'
·sized' ·siz'ing
syn·thet'ic
syn·thet'i·cal·ly
syph'i·lis
syph'i·lit'ic
sy·ringe'
·ringed' ·ring'ing
syr'up
sys'tem
sys'tem·at'ic
sys'tem·at'i·
cal·ly
sys'tem·a·tize'
·tized' ·tiz'ing
sys·tem'ic

T

tab'ard
tab'by
·bies
tab'er·nac'le
ta'ble
·bled ·bling
tab'leau
·leaux or ·leaus
ta'ble·cloth'

292

ta'ble d'hôte'
ta'ble-hop'
ta'ble·land'
ta'ble·spoon'ful
·fuls
tab'let
ta'ble·ware'
tab'loid
ta·boo' or ·bu'
·boos' or ·bus'
·booed' or ·bued'
·boo'ing or
·bu'ing
ta'bor or ·bour
tab'o·ret
tab'u·lar
tab'u·late'
·lat'ed ·lat'ing
tab'u·la'tion
tab'u·la'tor
ta·chis'to·scope'
ta·chom'e·ter
tac'it
tac'i·turn'
tac'i·tur'ni·ty
tack'i·ness
tack'le
·led ·ling
tack'y
·i·er ·i·est
tact'ful
tact'ful·ly
tac'ti·cal
tac·ti'cian

tac'tics
tac'tile
tact'less
tac'tu·al
tad'pole'
taf'fe·ta
taf'fy
tag
tagged tag'ging
tail'gate'
·gat'ed ·gat'ing
tail'less
tail'light'
tai'lor
tai'lor-made'
tail'piece'
tail'race'
tail'spin'
tail wind
taint'ed
tak'a·ble or take'·
take
took tak'en
tak'ing
take'off'
take'out'
take'o'ver
talc
tal'cum
tale'bear'er
tal'ent·ed
ta'les·man
(juryman)
tale'tell'er

tal'is·man
  ·mans
  (*good luck charm*)
talk'a·tive
talk'y
tal'low
tal'ly
  ·lies, ·lied ·ly·ing
Tal'mud
tal'on
tam'a·ble *or*
  tame'·
ta·ma'le
tam'bour
tam'bou·rine'
tame
  tamed tam'ing
tam'-o'-shan'ter
tamp'er *n.*
tam'per *v.*
tam'per·er
tam'pi·on
tam'pon
tan
  tan'ner tan'nest
  tanned tan'ning
tan'dem
tan'ge·lo'
  ·los'
tan'gent
tan·gen'tial
tan'ge·rine'
tan'gi·ble
tan'gi·bly

tan'gle
  ·gled ·gling
tan'go
  ·gos
tang'y
  ·i·er ·i·est
tank'age
tank'ard
tank'er
tank'ful
  ·fuls
tan'ner·y
  ·ies
tan'nic
tan'nin
tan'ta·lize'
  ·lized' ·liz'ing
tan'ta·mount'
tan'trum
tap
  tapped
  tap'ping
tape
  taped tap'ing
tape deck
ta'per
  (*candle; decrease;*
  SEE tapir)
tape'-re·cord'
tape recorder
tap'es·try
  ·tries
tape'worm'
tap'i·o'ca

ta'pir
  (*animal;* SEE
  taper)
tap'pet
tap'room'
tap'root'
tar
  tarred tar'ring
tar'an·tel'la
ta·ran'tu·la
tar·boosh'
tar'di·ness
tar'dy
  ·di·er ·di·est
tare
  tared tar'ing
  (*weight deduction;*
  SEE tear)
tar'get
tar'iff
tar'nish
ta'ro
  ·ros
  (*plant*)
tar'ot
  (*playing cards*)
tar·pau'lin
tar'pon
tar'ra·gon'
tar'ry
  ·ried ·ry·ing
tar'tan
tar'tar
tar'tar sauce

tart′ly
task force
task′mas′ter
tas′sel
· seled *or* · selled
· sel·ing *or*
· sel·ling
taste
tast′ed tast′ing
taste′ful
taste′ful·ly
taste′less
tast′er
tast′i·ness
tast′y
· i·er · i·est
tat′ter·de·mal′ion
tat′tered
tat′ter·sall′
tat′tle
· tled · tling
tat′tle·tale′
tat·too′
· toos′
· tooed′ · too′ing
taught
(*trained;* SEE taut)
taunt
taupe
taut
(*tight;* SEE taught)
tau·tol′o·gy
· gies
tav′ern

taw′dry
· dri·er · dri·est
taw′ny
· ni·er · ni·est
tax′a·bil′i·ty
tax′a·ble
tax·a′tion
tax′-de·duct′i·ble
tax′-ex·empt′
tax′i
· is, · ied
· i·ing *or* · y·ing
tax′i·cab′
tax′i·der′mist
tax′i·der′my
tax′i·me′ter
tax′i·way′
tax·on′o·my
tax′pay′er
tea bag
teach
taught teach′ing
teach′a·ble
teach′er
teach′-in′
tea′cup′
tea′cup·ful′
· fuls′
teak
tea′ket′tle
team
(*group;* SEE teem)
team′mate′
team′ster

team′work′
tea′pot′
tear
tore torn
tear′ing
(*rip;* SEE tare)
tear
teared tear′ing
(*eye fluid;*
SEE tier)
tear′drop′
tear′ful
tear gas
tear′i·ness
tea′room′
tear′y
· i·er · i·est
tease
teased teas′ing
tea′sel
· seled *or* · selled
· sel·ing *or*
· sel·ling
tea′spoon·ful′
· fuls′
teat
tea′-ta′ble
tea′tast′er
tea′time′
tech′nic
tech′ni·cal
tech′ni·cal′i·ty
· ties
tech′ni·cal·ly

tech·ni'cian
tech'ni·col'or
tech·nique'
tech·noc'ra·cy
tech·nog'ra·phy
tech'no·log'i·cal
tech·nol'o·gy
te'di·ous
te'di·um
tee
  teed tee'ing
teem
  (*abound;* SEE
  team)
teen'-age'
teen'-ag'er
tee'ter-tot'ter
teethe
  teethed teeth'ing
tee·to'tal·er
tee·to'tal·ism
Tef'lon
teg'u·ment
tel·au'to·graph'
tel'e·cast'
  ·cast' *or* ·cast'ed
  ·cast'ing
tel'e·com·mu'·
  ni·ca'tion
tel'e·course'
tel'e·gen'ic
tel'e·gram'
tel'e·graph'
te·leg'ra·pher

tel'e·graph'ic
te·leg'ra·phy
tel'e·ki·ne'sis
tel'e·me'ter
te'le·o·log'i·cal
te'le·ol'o·gy
tel'e·path'ic
te·lep'a·thy
tel'e·phone'
  ·phoned'
  ·phon'ing
tel'e·phon'ic
te·leph'o·ny
tel'e·pho'to
tel'e·pho'to·graph'
tel'e·pho·tog'ra·
  phy
tel'e·play'
tel'e·prompt'er
tel'e·ran'
tel'e·scope'
  ·scoped' ·scop'ing
tel'e·scop'ic
tel'e·thon'
Tel'e·type'
  ·typed' ·typ'ing
tel'e·type'writ'er
tel'e·view'er
tel'e·vise'
  ·vised' ·vis'ing
tel'e·vi'sion
tell
  told tell'ing
tell'a·ble

tell'er
tell'tale'
tel'pher *or* ·fer
Tel'star'
te·mer'i·ty
tem'per
tem'per·a
tem'per·a·ment
tem'per·a·
  men'tal
tem'per·ance
tem'per·ate
tem'per·a·ture
tem'pered
tem'pest
tem·pes'tu·ous
tem'plate *or* ·plet
tem'ple
tem'po
  ·pos *or* ·pi
tem'po·ral
tem'po·rar'i·ly
tem'po·rar'i·ness
tem'po·rar'y
tem'po·rize'
  ·rized' ·riz'ing
temp·ta'tion
tempt'er
tempt'ing
tempt'ress
tem'pus fu'git
ten'a·ble
te·na'cious
te·nac'i·ty

ten'an·cy
·cies
ten'ant
ten'ant·a·ble
ten'ant·ry
·ries
tend'en·cy
·cies
ten'der
(soft; offer)
tend'er
(one who tends)
ten'der·foot'
·foots' or ·feet'
ten'der·heart'ed
ten'der·ize'
·ized' ·iz'ing
ten'der·iz'er
ten'der·loin'
ten'don
ten'dril
ten'e·ment
ten'et
ten'fold'
Ten'nes·see'
ten'nis
ten'on
ten'or
(tendency; singer)
SEE tenure)
ten'pins'
tense
tens'er tens'est
tensed tens'ing

tense'ly
tense'ness
ten'sile
ten·sil'i·ty
ten'sion
ten'ta·cle
ten'ta·tive
ten'ta·tive·ly
ten'ter
ten'ter·hook'
tenth
ten·u'i·ty
ten'u·ous
ten'ure
(time held;
SEE tenor)
ten·u'ri·al
te'pee or tee'·
tep'id
te·pid'i·ty
te·qui'la
ter'cen·te'nar·y
·ies
ter'gi·ver·sate'
·sat'ed ·sat'ing
ter'gi·ver·sa'tor
ter'ma·gant
ter'mi·na·ble
ter'mi·na·bly
ter'mi·nal
ter'mi·nate'
·nat'ed ·nat'ing
ter'mi·na'tion
ter'mi·nol'o·gy

ter'mi·nus
·ni' or ·nus·es
ter'mite
ter'na·ry
terp'si·cho·re'an
ter'race
·raced ·rac·ing
ter'ra cot'ta
ter'ra fir'ma
ter·rain'
Ter'ra·my'cin
ter'ra·pin
ter·rar'i·um
·i·ums or ·i·a
ter·raz'zo
ter·res'tri·al
ter'ri·ble
ter'ri·bly
ter'ri·er
ter·rif'ic
ter·rif'i·cal·ly
ter'ri·fy'
·fied' ·fy'ing
ter'ri·to'ri·al
ter'ri·to'ri·al'i·ty
ter'ri·to'ry
·ries
ter'ror
ter'ror·ism
ter'ror·ist
ter'ror·is'tic
ter'ror·i·za'tion
ter'ror·ize'
·ized' ·iz'ing

ter′ry
terse
  ters′er ters′est
terse′ness
ter′ti·ar′y
tes′sel·late′
  ·lat′ed ·lat′ing
tes′sel·la′tion
test′a·ble
tes′ta·ment
tes′ta·men′ta·ry
tes′tate
tes′ta·tor
tes′ti·cle
tes′ti·fi′er
tes′ti·fy′
  ·fied′ ·fy′ing
tes′ti·ly
tes′ti·mo′ni·al
tes′ti·mo′ny
  ·nies
tes′ti·ness
tes′ty
  ·ti·er ·ti·est
tet′a·nus
tête′-à-tête′
teth′er
tet′ra·cy′cline
tet′ra·he′dron
  ·drons or ·dra
te·tral′o·gy
  ·gies
Tex′as
text′book′

tex′tile
tex′tu·al
tex′tur·al
tex′ture
than *conj., prep.*
thank′ful
thank′less
thanks′giv′ing
that
  those
thatch
thaw
the′a·ter *or* ·tre
the·at′ri·cal
theft
their
  (*poss. form of*
  they; SEE there,
  they're)
theirs
  (*belonging to*
  them; SEE there's)
the′ism
the·is′tic
the·mat′ic
theme
them·selves′
then
  (*at that time*)
thence′forth′
the·oc′ra·cy
  ·cies
the·od′o·lite′
the′o·lo′gian

the′o·log′i·cal
the·ol′o·gy
  ·gies
the′o·rem
the′o·ret′i·cal
the′o·ret′i·cal·ly
the′o·re·ti′cian
the′o·rize′
  ·rized′ ·riz′ing
the′o·ry
  ·ries
the·os′o·phy
  ·phies
ther′a·peu′tic
ther′a·pist
ther′a·py
  ·pies
there
  (*at that place;*
  SEE their, they're)
there′a·bouts′
there·af′ter
there·at′
there·by′
there·for′
  (*for it*)
there′fore′
  (*for that reason*)
there·in′
there·in·aft′er
there·in′to
there's
  (*there is;* SEE
  theirs)

there'to·fore'
there'up·on'
there·with'
ther'mal
therm'i·on'ics
ther'mo·dy·
  nam'ics
ther'mo·e·lec'·
  tric'i·ty
ther·mom'e·ter
ther'mo·nu'cle·ar
ther'mo·pile'
ther'mo·plas'tic
ther'mos
ther'mo·stat'
ther'mo·stat'i·
  cal·ly
the·sau'rus
  ·ri or ·rus·es
the'sis
  ·ses
they'd
they'll
they're
  (they are; SEE
  their, there)
they've
thi'a·mine'
thick'en·ing
thick'et
thick'ness
thick'set'
thick'-skinned'
thick'-wit'ted

thief n.
  thieves
thieve v.
  thieved thiev'ing
thiev'er·y
  ·ies
thiev'ish·ly
thigh'bone'
thim'ble·ful'
  ·fuls'
thin
  thin'ner
  thin'nest
  thinned
  thin'ning
thing
think
  thought
  think'ing
thin'-skinned'
third'-class'
third'-rate'
thirst'i·ly
thirst'i·ness
thirst'y
  ·i·er ·i·est
thir'teenth'
thir'ti·eth
thir'ty
  ·ties
this
  these
this'tle·down'
thith'er·to'

thole
thong
tho·rac'ic
tho'rax
  ·rax·es or ·ra·ces
tho'ri·um
thorn'y
  ·i·er ·i·est
thor'ough
thor'ough·bred'
thor'ough·fare'
thor'ough·go'ing
though
thought
thought'ful·ly
thought'ful·ness
thought'less
thou'sand·fold'
thrall'dom
thrash
thread'bare'
thread'i·ness
thread'y
  ·i·er ·i·est
threat'en
3'-D'
three'-deck'er
three'-di·men'·
  sion·al
three'fold'
three'-ply'
three'-quar'ter
three'score'
three'some

three'-way'
three'-wheel'er
thren'o·dy
·dies
thresh'er
thresh'old
threw
(*pt. of throw;*
SEE through)
thrice
thrift'i·ly
thrift'i·ness
thrift'y
·i·er ·i·est
thrill'er
thrive
thrived *or* throve,
thrived *or*
thriv'en,
thriv'ing
throat'y
·i·er ·i·est
throb
throbbed
throb'bing
throe
(*pang;* SEE throw)
throm·bo'sis
throne
throned
thron'ing
throng
throt'tle
·tled ·tling

through
(*from end to end
of;* SEE threw)
through·out'
throw
threw thrown
throw'ing
(*hurl;* SEE throe)
throw'a·way'
throw'back'
thrum
thrummed
thrum'ming
thrust
thrust thrust'ing
thud
thud'ded
thud'ding
thumb'nail'
thumb'screw'
thumb'stall'
thumb'tack'
thump
thun'der·bolt'
thun'der·cloud'
thun'der·head'
thun'der·ous
thun'der·show'er
thun'der·squall'
thun'der·storm'
thun'der·struck'
Thurs'day
thus
thwack

thwart
thyme
(*herb;* SEE time)
thy'mus
thy'roid
ti·ar'a
tib'i·a
tic
(*muscle spasm*)
tick
(*click; insect*)
tick'er tape
tick'et
tick'ing
tick'le
·led ·ling
tick'ler
tick'lish
tick'-tack-toe'
tick'y tack'y
tid'al
tid'bit'
tide'land'
tide'mark'
tide'wa'ter
ti'di·ly
ti'di·ness
ti'dings
ti'dy
·di·er ·di·est
·died ·dy·ing
tie
tied ty'ing
tie'back'

299

tie'-dye'
  -dyed' -dye'ing
tie'-in'
tie'pin'
tier
  (*row;* SEE tear)
ti'er
  (*one that ties;*
  SEE tire)
tie tack
tie'-up'
ti'ger
ti'ger's eye
tight'en
tight'fist'ed
tight'fit'ting
tight'knit'
tight'-lipped'
tight'rope'
ti'gress
tile
  tiled til'ing
till'a·ble
tilt'-top'
tim'bale
tim'ber
  (*wood*)
tim'ber·line'
tim'bre
  (*quality of sound*)
time
  timed tim'ing
  (*duration;*
  SEE thyme)

time'card'
time clock
time'-con·sum'ing
time'-hon'ored
time'keep'er
time'less
time'li·ness
time'ly
  ·li·er ·li·est
time'out'
time'piece'
tim'er
time'sav'ing
time'ta'ble
time'-test'ed
time'worn'
time zone
ti·mid'i·ty
tim'id·ly
tim'or·ous
tim'o·thy
tim'pa·ni
tim'pa·nist
tin
  tinned tin'ning
tinc'ture
  ·tured ·tur·ing
tin'der·box'
tin'foil'
tinge
  tinged, tinge'ing
  or ting'ing
tin'gle
  ·gled ·gling

tin'gly
  ·gli·er ·gli·est
ti'ni·ness
tin'ker
tin'ker·er
tin'kle
  ·kled ·kling
tin'ni·ness
tin·ni'tus
tin'ny
  ·ni·er ·ni·est
tin'-plate'
  -plat'ed -plat'ing
tin'sel
  ·seled *or* ·selled
  ·sel·ing *or*
  ·sel·ling
tin'smith'
tin'tin·nab'u·
  la'tion
tin'type'
tin'ware'
ti'ny
  ·ni·er ·ni·est
tip
  tipped tip'ping
tip'-off'
tip'pet
tip'ple
  ·pled ·pling
tip'sy
  ·si·er ·si·est
tip'toe'
  ·toed' ·toe'ing

tip'top'
ti'rade
tire
  tired tir'ing
  (*weary; rubber
  hoop;* SEE tier)
tired'ly
tire'less
tire'some
tis'sue
ti'tan
tithe
  tithed tith'ing
ti'tian
tit'il·late'
  ·lat'ed ·lat'ing
tit'il·la'tion
ti'tle
  ·tled ·tling
ti'tle·hold'er
tit'mouse'
  ·mice'
tit'ter
tit'u·lar
toad'stool'
toad'y
  ·ies, ·ied ·y·ing
toad'y·ism
to'-and-fro'
toast'mas'ter
to·bac'co
  ·cos
to·bac'co·nist
to·bog'gan

toc·ca'ta
toc'sin
  (*alarm;* SEE toxin)
to·day'
tod'dle
  ·dled ·dling
tod'dler
tod'dy
  ·dies
to-do'
toe
  toed toe'ing
toe'-dance'
  -danced'
  -danc'ing
toe'hold'
toe'-in'
toe'less
toe'nail'
tof'fee *or* ·fy
to'ga
  ·gas *or* ·gae
to·geth'er
tog'gle
  ·gled ·gling
toi'let
toi'let·ry
  ·ries
toil'some
toil'worn'
to'ken
tole
tol'er·a·ble
tol'er·a·bly

tol'er·ance
tol'er·ant
tol'er·ate'
  ·at'ed ·at'ing
tol'er·a'tion
tol'er·a'tor
toll'booth'
toll bridge
toll call
toll'gate'
toll'keep'er
toll road
tom'a·hawk'
to·ma'to
  ·toes
tom'boy'
tomb'stone'
tom'cat'
tom'fool'er·y
to·mor'row
tom'-tom'
ton
  (*weight;* SEE tun)
ton'al
to·nal'i·ty
  ·ties
tone
  toned ton'ing
tone'-deaf'
tongs
tongue
  tongued
  tongu'ing
tongue'-lash'ing

tongue'-tie'
-tied' -ty'ing
ton'ic
to·night'
ton'nage
ton·neau'
·neaus' or
·neaux'
ton'sil
ton'sil·lec'to·my
·mies
ton'sil·li'tis
ton·so'ri·al
ton'sure
·sured ·sur·ing
ton'tine
tool'mak'er
tooth
teeth
tooth'ache'
tooth'brush'
tooth'paste'
tooth'pick'
tooth'some
top
topped top'ping
to'paz
top'coat'
top'-drawer'
top'-dress'ing
top'-flight'
top'-heav'y
to'pi·ar'y
top'ic

top'i·cal
top'knot'
top'less
top'-lev'el
top'most'
top'-notch'
to·pog'ra·pher
top'o·graph'i·cal
to·pog'ra·phy
(*surface features;*
SEE typography)
top'ple
·pled ·pling
top'sail
top'-se'cret
top'soil'
top'sy-tur'vy
toque
to'rah or ·ra
torch'bear'er
torch·ier' or
·iere'
torch'light'
tor'e·a·dor'
tor'ment
tor·men'tor
tor·na'do
·does or ·dos
tor·pe'do
·does
tor'pid
tor·pid'i·ty
tor'por
torque

tor'rent
tor·ren'tial
tor'rid
tor·rid'i·ty
tor'sion
tor'so
·sos or ·si
tort
(*wrongful act*)
torte
(*cake*)
tor·til'la
tor'toise
tor·to'ni
tor'tu·ous
(*winding*)
tor'ture
·tured ·tur·ing
tor'tur·ous
(*agonizing*)
toss'up'
to'tal
·taled or ·talled
·tal·ing or
·tal·ling
to·tal'i·tar'i·an
to·tal'i·ty
to'tal·i·za'tor
to'tal·ly
tote
tot'ed tot'ing
to'tem
tot'ter
touch'back'

touch'down'
tou·ché'
touch'hole'
touch'i·ly
touch'i·ness
touch'stone'
touch'-type'
touch'-typ'ist
touch'y
·i·er ·i·est
tough'en
tough'-mind'ed
tou·pee'
tour' de force'
tours' de force'
tour'ism
tour'ist
tour'ma·line
tour'na·ment
tour'ney
·neys
tour'ni·quet
tou'sle
·sled ·sling
tow'age
to·ward'
tow'boat'
tow'el
·eled or ·elled
·el·ing or ·el·ling
tow'er·ing
tow'head'
tow'line'
town'ship

towns'peo'ple
tow'path'
tow'rope'
tox·e'mi·a
tox'ic
tox'i·cant
tox'i·col'o·gy
tox'in
(*poison*; SEE
tocsin)
trace
traced trac'ing
trace'a·ble
trac'er
trac'er·y
·ies
tra·che·a
·ae' *or* ·as
tra·cho'ma
track
(*trace*)
tract
(*land; leaflet*)
trac'ta·ble
trac'tile
trac'tion
trac'tor
trad'a·ble *or*
trade'a·ble
trade
trad'ed trad'ing
trade'-in'
trade'-last'
trade'mark'

trade name
trades'man
trades'peo'ple
trade wind
tra·di'tion
tra·di'tion·al
tra·duce'
·duced' ·duc'ing
traf'fic
·ficked ·fick·ing
traf'fick·er
tra·ge'di·an
tra·ge'di·enne'
trag'e·dy
·dies
trag'ic
trag'i·cal·ly
trag'i·com'e·dy
·dies
trag'i·com'ic
trail'blaz'er
trail'er
train·ee'
train'man
trait
trai'tor
trai'tor·ous
trai'tress
tra·jec'to·ry
·ries
tram'mel
·meled *or* ·melled
·mel·ing *or*
·mel·ling

tram′ple
·pled ·pling
tram′po·line′
trance
tranced
tranc′ing
tran′quil
·quil·er or ·quil·ler
·quil·est or
·quil·lest
tran′quil·ize′
or ·quil·lize′
·ized′ or ·lized′
·iz′ing or ·liz′ing
tran′quil·iz′er or
·quil·liz′er
tran·quil′li·ty or
·quil′i·ty
tran′quil·ly
trans·act′
trans·ac′tion
trans·ac′tor
trans·at·lan′tic
trans·ceiv′er
tran·scend′
tran·scend′ent
tran′scen·den′tal
trans·con·ti·
nen′tal
tran·scribe′
·scribed′ ·scrib′ing
tran′script′
tran·scrip′tion
tran′sept

trans·fer′
·ferred′
·fer′ring
trans·fer′a·ble
or ·fer′ra·ble
trans·fer′al
or ·fer′ral
trans·fer·ee′
trans·fer′ence
trans·fer′rer
trans·fig′u·ra′tion
trans·fig′ure
trans·fix′
trans·form′
trans·for·ma′tion
trans·form′er
trans·fuse′
trans·fus′i·ble
trans·fu′sion
trans·gress′
trans·gres′sion
trans·gres′sor
tran′sient
tran·sis′tor
tran·sis′tor·ize′
·ized′ ·iz′ing
trans′it
tran·si′tion
tran·si′tion·al·ly
tran′si·tive
tran′si·to′ry
trans·lat′a·ble
trans·late′
·lat′ed ·lat′ing

trans·la′tion
trans·la′tor
trans·lit′er·ate′
·at′ed ·at′ing
trans·lit′er·a′tion
trans·lu′cence
trans·lu′cent
trans·mi′grate
·grat·ed ·grat·ing
trans′mi·gra′tion
trans·mis′si·ble
trans·mis′sion
trans·mit′
·mit′ted
·mit′ting
trans·mit′tal
trans·mit′tance
trans·mit′ter
trans·mut′a·ble
trans′mu·ta′tion
trans·mute′
·mut′ed
·mut′ing
trans′o·ce·an′ic
tran′som
tran·son′ic
trans·pa·cif′ic
trans·par′en·cy
·cies
trans·par′ent
tran·spire′
·spired′ ·spir′ing
trans·plant′
tran·spon′der

trans·port′
trans·por·ta′tion
trans′pos′a·ble
trans·pose′
·posed′ ·pos′ing
trans′po·si′tion
trans·sex′u·al
trans·ship′
·shipped′
·ship′ping
tran′stage′
tran′sub·stan′ti·
ate′
trans·val′ue
trans·ver′sal
trans·verse′
trans·verse′ly
trans·ves′tite
trap
trapped trap′ping
trap′door′
tra·peze′
tra·pe′zi·um
trap′e·zoid′
trap′per
trap′pings
trap′shoot′ing
trash′i·ness
trash′y
·i·er ·i·est
trau′ma
·mas or ·ma·ta
trau·mat′ic
trau·mat′i·cal·ly

trav′ail
 (hard work)
trav′el
 ·eled or ·elled
 ·el·ing or ·el·ling
 (journey)
trav′el·er or
 ·el·ler
trav′e·logue′ or
 ·log′
trav·ers′a·ble
trav·ers′al
trav·erse′
 ·ersed′ ·ers′ing
trav′er·tine′
trav′es·ty
 ·ties
 ·tied ·ty·ing
trawl′er
tray
 (holder; SEE
 trey)
treach′er·ous
treach′er·y
 ·ies
trea′cle
tread
 trod, trod′den or
 trod, tread′ing
trea′dle
 ·dled ·dling
tread′mill′
trea′son
trea′son·ous

treas′ure
 ·ured ·ur·ing
treas′ur·er
treas′ure-trove′
treas′ur·y
 ·ies
treat′a·ble
trea′tise
treat′ment
trea′ty
 ·ties
tre′ble
 ·bled ·bling
tree
treed
tree′ing
tree′nail′
tree′top′
tre′foil
treil′lage
trek
trekked
trek′king
trel′lis
trem′ble
 ·bled ·bling
tre·men′dous
trem′o·lo′
 ·los′
trem′or
trem′u·lous
trench′ant
trench mouth
trend

trep'i·da'tion
tres'pass
tress'es
tres'tle
tres'tle·work'
trey
  (*a three;* SEE
  tray)
tri'a·ble
tri'ad
tri'al
tri'an'gle
tri·an'gu·lar
tri·an'gu·late'
  ·lat'ed ·lat'ing
tri·an'gu·la'tion
trib'al
trib'al·ism
tribes'man
trib'u·la'tion
tri·bu'nal
trib'une
trib'u·tar'y
  ·ies
trib'ute
tri'cen·ten'ni·al
tri'ceps
  ·cep·ses *or* ·ceps
tri·chi'na
  ·nae
trich'i·no'sis
tri·chot'o·my
tri'chro·mat'ic
trick'er·y

trick'i·ly
trick'i·ness
trick'le
  ·led ·ling
trick'ster
trick'y
  ·i·er ·i·est
tri'col'or
tri'cot
tri'cy·cle
tri'di·men'sion·al
tri·en'ni·al
tri·en'ni·um
  ·ums *or* ·a
tri'er
tri'fle
  ·fled ·fling
tri·fo'cal
trig'ger
trig'o·no·met'ric
trig'o·nom'e·try
tri·lat'er·al
tri·lin'gual
tril'lion
tril'li·um
tril'o·gy
  ·gies
trim
trimmed
trim'ming
trim'mer
trim'mest
tri·mes'ter
tri·month'ly

trin'i·ty
  ·ties
trin'ket
tri·no'mi·al
tri'o
  ·os
trip
  tripped trip'ping
tri·par'tite
trip'ham'mer
tri'ple
  ·pled ·pling
tri'ple-space'
tri'plet
trip'li·cate'
  ·cat'ed ·cat'ing
tri'ply
tri'pod
trip'per
trip'tych
tri·sect'
triste
tris·tesse'
trite
  trit'er trit'est
trite'ly
trit'u·rate'
  ·rat'ed ·rat'ing
tri'umph
tri·um'phal
tri·um'phant
tri·um'vi·rate
triv'et
triv'i·a

triv'i·al
triv'i·al'i·ty
·ties
triv'i·al·ly
tri·week'ly
·lies
tro'che
(*lozenge*)
tro'chee
(*poetic meter*)
trod'den
trof'fer
trog'lo·dyte'
troll
trol'ley
·leys
·leyed ·ley·ing
trol'lop
trom·bone'
trom·bon'ist
troop
(*of soldiers;*
SEE troupe)
troop'ship'
tro'phy
·phies
trop'ic
trop'i·cal
tro'pism
trop'o·sphere'
trot
trot'ted trot'ting
trot'ter
trou'ba·dour'

trou'ble
·bled ·bling
trou'ble·mak'er
trou'ble-shoot'er
trou'ble·some
trough
trounce
trounced
trounc'ing
troupe
trouped
troup'ing
(*of actors;*
SEE troop)
troup'er
trou'sers
trous'seau
·seaux *or* ·seaus
trout
trow'el
·eled *or* ·elled
·el·ing *or* ·el·ling
tru'an·cy
·cies
tru'ant
truce
truck farm
truck'le
·led ·ling
truc'u·lence
truc'u·lent
trudge
trudged
trudg'ing

true
tru'er tru'est
trued tru'ing
or true'ing
true'-blue'
true'-life'
true'love'
truf'fle
tru'ism
tru'ly
trump
trumped'-up'
trump'er·y
·ies
trum'pet
trum'pet·er
trun'cate
·cat·ed ·cat·ing
trun·ca'tion
trun'cheon
trun'dle
·dled ·dling
trunk line
trun'nion
truss
trus·tee'
·teed' ·tee'ing
(*manager;* SEE
trusty)
trus·tee'ship'
trust'ful
trust'ful·ly
trust'i·ness
trust'wor'thy

307

trust'y
·ies, ·i·er ·i·est
(*relied upon;*
SEE trustee)
truth'ful
truth'ful·ly
truth'ful·ness
try
tries
tried try'ing
try'out'
tryst
tset'se fly
T'-shirt'
tsim'mes
tsor'is
T square
tsu·na'mi
tub
tubbed tub'bing
tu'ba
·bas *or* ·bae
tub'ba·ble
tub'bi·ness
tub'by
·bi·er ·bi·est
tube
tubed tub'ing
tu'ber
tu'ber·cle
tu·ber'cu·lar
tu·ber'cu·lin
tu·ber'cu·lo'sis
tu·ber'cu·lous

tube'rose'
(*plant*)
tu'ber·ous
(*having tubers*)
tu'bu·lar
tuck'er
Tu'dor
Tues'day
tuft'ed
tug
tugged tug'ging
tug'boat'
tu·i'tion
tu'la·re'mi·a
tu'lip
tulle
tum'ble
·bled ·bling
tum'ble·down'
tum'bler
tum'ble·weed'
tum'brel
tu'me·fy'
·fied' ·fy'ing
tu·mes'cence
tu·mes'cent
tu'mid
tu'mor
tu'mor·ous
tu'mult
tu·mul'tu·ous
tun
tunned tun'ning
(*cask;* SEE ton)

tun'a·ble
or tune'·
tun'dra
tune
tuned tun'ing
tune'ful
tune'less
tun'er
tune'up' *or*
tune'-up'
tung'sten
tu'nic
tun'nel
·neled *or* ·nelled
·nel·ing *or*
·nel·ling
tu'pe·lo'
·los'
tur'ban
(*headdress*)
tur'bid
tur'bine
(*engine*)
tur'bo·jet'
tur'bo·prop'
tur'bu·lence
tur'bu·lent
tu·reen'
turf
tur'gid
tur'key
tur'mer·ic
tur'moil
turn'a·bout'

308

turn'a·round'
turn'buck'le
turn'coat'
turn'down'
tur'nip
turn'key'
·keys'
turn'off'
turn'out'
turn'o'ver
turn'pike'
turn'stile'
turn'ta'ble
tur'pen·tine'
tur'pi·tude'
tur'quoise
tur'ret
tur'tle
tur'tle·dove'
tur'tle·neck'
tus'sle
·sled ·sling
tu'te·lage
tu'te·lar'y
tu'tor
tu·to'ri·al
tut'ti-frut'ti
tu'tu
tux·e'do
·dos
TV
TVs or TV's
twang
tweak

tweed
tweed'y
·i·er ·i·est
tweeze
tweezed
tweez'ing
tweez'ers
twelfth
twelve'fold'
twen'ti·eth
twen'ty
·ties
twen'ty·fold'
twice'-told'
twid'dle
·dled ·dling
twi'light'
twi'lit
twill
twine
twined twin'ing
twin'-en'gined
twinge
twinged
twing'ing
twi'-night'
twin'kle
·kled ·kling
twirl'er
twist'er
twitch
twit'ter
two'-by-four'
two'-edged'

two'-faced'
two'-fist'ed
two'fold'
two'-hand'ed
two'-leg'ged
two'-piece'
two'-ply'
two'-sid'ed
two'some
two'-way'
ty·coon'
tym·pan'ic
typ'a·ble or type'·
typ'al
type
typed typ'ing
type'bar'
type'cast'
·cast' ·cast'ing
(in acting)
type'-cast'
-cast' -cast'ing
(in printing)
type'script'
type'set'
·set' ·set'ting
type'set'ter
type'write'
·wrote' ·writ'ten
·writ'ing
type'writ'er
ty'phoid
ty·phoon'
ty'phus

typ′i·cal
typ′i·cal·ly
typ′i·fy′
 ·fied′ ·fy′ing
typ′ist
ty·pog′ra·pher
ty′po·graph′i·cal
ty·pog′ra·phy
 (*setting of type;*
 SEE topography)
ty·pol′o·gy
ty·ran′ni·cal
tyr′an·nize′
 ·nized′ ·niz′ing
tyr′an·nous
tyr′an·ny
 ·nies
ty′rant
ty′ro
 ·ros
ty′ro·thri′cin

U

u·biq′ui·tous
u·biq′ui·ty
ud′der
 (*milk gland;*
 SEE utter)
u·fol′o·gist
ug′li
 (*fruit*)

ug′li·ness
ug′ly
 ·li·er ·li·est
u′kase
u·ku·le′le
ul′cer
ul′cer·ate′
 ·at′ed ·at′ing
ul′cer·ous
ul′ster
ul·te′ri·or
ul′ti·mate
ul′ti·mate·ly
ul′ti·ma′tum
 ·tums *or* ·ta
ul′tra
ul′tra·con·serv′·
 a·tive
ul′tra·ism
ul′tra·ma·rine′
ul′tra·mi′cro·
 scope′
ul′tra·mod′ern
ul′tra·na′tion·al·
 ism
ul′tra·son′ic
ul′tra·sound′
ul′tra·vi′o·let
ul′u·late′
 ·lat′ed ·lat′ing
um′ber
um·bil′i·cal
um·bil′i·cus
 ·ci′

um′bra
 ·brae *or* ·bras
um′brage
um·bra′geous
um·brel′la
u′mi·ak′ *or* ·ack′
um′laut
um′pire
 ·pired ·pir′ing
un·a′ble
un′a·bridged′
un′ac·count′a·ble
un′ac·count′ed-
 for′
un′ac·cus′tomed
un′af·fect′ed
un′-A·mer′i·can
u′na·nim′i·ty
u·nan′i·mous
un·apt′
un·armed′
un′as·sum′ing
un′at·tached′
un′a·void′a·ble
un′a·ware′
un′a·wares′
un·bal′anced
un·bear′a·ble
un·beat′a·ble
un′be·com′ing
un′be·known′
un′be·lief′
un′be·liev′a·ble
un′be·liev′er

un·bend'
·bent' *or* ·bend'ed,
·bend'ing
un·bi'ased *or*
·assed
un·bid'den
un·bolt'ed
un·bos'om
un·bound'ed
un·bri'dled
un·bro'ken
un·buck'le
un·but'ton
un·called'-for'
un·can'ni·ly
un·can'ni·ness
un·can'ny
un·cared'-for'
un·cer·e·mo'ni·ous
un·cer'tain
un·cer'tain·ty
·ties
un·char'i·ta·ble
un·chris'tian
un'ci·al
un·civ'il
un·civ'i·lized'
un·clad'
un·class'i·fied
un'cle
un·clothe'
·clothed' *or*
·clad', ·cloth'ing

un·com'fort·a·ble
un·com'pro·
mis'ing
un'con·cerned'
un'con·di'tion·al
un·con'scion·a·
ble
un·con'scious
un'con·sti·
tu'tion·al
un·cou'ple
un·couth'
unc'tion
unc'tu·ous
un·daunt'ed
un·de·cid'ed
un·de·ni'a·ble
un'der·age'
un'der·age
un'der·brush'
un'der·buy'
·bought' ·buy'ing
un'der·car'riage
un'der·class'man
un'der·clothes'
un'der·coat'
un'der·cov'er
un'der·cur'rent
un'der·cut'
un'der·de·vel'·
oped
un'der·do'
·did' ·done'
·do'ing

un'der·dog'
un'der·em·ployed'
un'der·es'ti·mate'
un'der·fired'
un'der·foot'
un'der·gar'ment
un'der·glaze'
un'der·go'
·went' ·gone'
·go'ing
un'der·grad'u·ate
un'der·ground'
un'der·growth'
un'der·hand'
un'der·hand'ed
un'der·hung'
un'der·lay'
·laid' ·lay'ing
un'der·lie'
·lay' ·lain'
·ly'ing
un'der·line'
un'der·ling'
un'der·lin'ing
un'der·mine'
un'der·neath'
un'der·nour'ish
un'der·pants'
un'der·part'
un'der·pass'
un'der·pay'
·paid' ·pay'ing
un'der·pin'ning
un'der·play'

un'der·priv'i·
  leged
un'der·proof'
un'der·rate'
un'der·score'
un'der·sea'
un'der·sec're·
  tar'y
  ·ies
un'der·sell'
  ·sold' ·sell'ing
un'der·sexed'
un'der·shirt'
un'der·shot'
un'der·side'
un'der·signed'
un'der·sized'
un'der·staffed'
un'der·stand'
  ·stood' ·stand'ing
un'der·stand'a·
  ble
un'der·stand'a·bly
un'der·state'ment
un'der·stud'y
  ·ies, ·ied ·y·ing
un'der·take'
  ·took' ·tak'en
  ·tak'ing
un'der·tak'ing
un'der·tone'
un'der·tow'
un'der·val'ue
un'der·wa'ter

un'der·wear'
un'der·weight'
un'der·world'
un'der·write'
  ·wrote' ·writ'ten
  ·writ'ing
un·do'
  ·did' ·done'
  ·do'ing
un·doubt'ed·ly
un·dress'
un·due'
un·du'lant
un·du·late'
  ·lat'ed ·lat'ing
un·du'ly
un·dy'ing
un·earned'
un·earth'
un·eas'y
un·em·ploy'a·ble
un·e'qualed
  or ·qualled
un·e·quiv'o·cal·ly
un·err'ing
un·es·sen'tial
un·e'ven·ness
un·e·vent'ful·ly
un·ex·cep'tion·
  a·ble
un·ex·cep'tion·al
un·ex·pect'ed
un·faith'ful
un·fa·mil'iar

un·feel'ing
un·feigned'
un·for·get'ta·ble
un·for'tu·nate
un·found'ed
un·freeze'
  ·froze' ·froz'en
  ·freez'ing
un·frock'
un·furl'
un·gain'ly
un·god'ly
un'guent
un'gu·late
un·hand'
un·heard'-of'
un·hoped'-for'
un·horse'
  ·horsed'
  ·hors'ing
u'ni·cam'er·al
u'ni·cel'lu·lar
u'ni·corn'
u'ni·cy'cle
u'ni·fi'a·ble
u'ni·fi·ca'tion
u'ni·fi'er
u'ni·form'
u'ni·form'i·ty
u'ni·fy'
  ·fied' ·fy'ing
u'ni·lat'er·al
un·im·peach'a·ble
un·in·hib'it·ed

un·in·tel'li·gi·ble
un'ion
un'ion·ize'
·ized' ·iz'ing
u·nique'
u'ni·son
u'nit
U'ni·tar'i·an
u·nite'
·nit'ed ·nit'ing
u'nit·ize'
·ized' ·iz'ing
u'ni·ty
·ties
u'ni·ver'sal
u'ni·ver·sal'i·ty
u'ni·ver'sal·ly
u'ni·verse'
u'ni·ver'si·ty
·ties
un·kempt'
un·known'
un·lade'
·lad'ed, ·lad'ed
or ·lad'en,
·lad'ing
un·law'ful
un·less'
un·let'tered
un·like'li·hood'
un·like'ly
un·lim'it·ed
un·list'ed
un·looked'-for'

un·loose'
·loosed' ·loos'ing
un·loos'en
un·luck'y
un·make'
·made' ·mak'ing
un·man'
·manned'
·man'ning
un·men'tion·a·ble
un·mer'ci·ful
un·mis·tak'a·ble
un·mit'i·gat'ed
un·nat'u·ral
un·nec'es·sar'y
un·nerve'
·nerved'
·nerv'ing
un·num'bered
un·oc'cu·pied'
un·or'gan·ized'
un·paid'-for'
un·par'al·leled'
un·pleas'ant
un·prec'e·dent'ed
un·prej'u·diced
un·prin'ci·pled
un·qual'i·fied
un·ques'tion·a·
bly
un'quote'
un·rav'el
·eled or ·elled
·el·ing or ·el·ling

un·re·al·is'tic
un·rea'son·a·ble
un·re·gen'er·ate
un·rest'
un·rul'i·ness
un·rul'y
·i·er ·i·est
un·said'
un·sa'vor·i·ness
un·sa'vor·y
un·scathed'
un·scru'pu·lous
un·seat'
un·seem'ly
un·shod'
un·sight'li·ness
un·sight'ly
un·speak'a·ble
un·stead'y
un·strung'
un·sung'
un·tan'gle
·gled ·gling
un·ten'a·ble
un·think'a·ble
un·thought'-of'
un·ti'dy
un·tie'
·tied' ·ty'ing or
·tie'ing
un·til'
un·time'ly
un·told'
un·touch'a·ble

un·to'ward
un·truth'ful
un·tu'tored
un·u'su·al
un·veil'ing
un·want'ed
 (*not wanted;*
 SEE unwonted)
un·war'y
un·whole'some
un·wield'i·ness
un·wield'y
un·wit'ting·ly
un·wont'ed
 (*not usual;*
 SEE unwanted)
un·wor'thy
un·writ'ten
un·zip'
up'-and-com'ing
up'-and-down'
up'beat'
up·braid'
up'bring'ing
up'coun'try
up·date'
up·end'
up'grade'
up·heav'al
up'hill'
up·hold'
 ·held' ·hold'ing
up·hol'ster
up·hol'ster·er

up·hol'ster·y
 ·ies
up'keep'
up'land
up·lift'
up·on'
up'per-case'
 -cased' -cas'ing
up'per·class'man
up'per·most'
up'right'
up'ris'ing
up'roar'
up·roar'i·ous
up·root'
up·set'
 ·set' ·set'ting
up'shot'
up'stage'
 ·staged'
 ·stag'ing
up'stairs'
up·stand'ing
up'start'
up'state'
up'stream'
up'swept'
up'swing'
up'take'
up'thrust'
up'-tight' *or*
 up'tight'
up'-to-date'
up'town'

up·turn'
up'ward
u·ra'ni·um
ur'ban
 (*of the city*)
ur·bane'
 (*socially poised*)
ur'ban·ism
ur·ban'i·ty
 ·ties
ur'ban·i·za'tion
ur'ban·ize'
 ·ized' ·iz'ing
ur'chin
u·re'mi·a
u·re'ter
u·re'thra
 ·thrae *or* ·thras
urge
 urged urg'ing
ur'gen·cy
 ·cies
ur'gent
u'ri·nal
u'ri·nal'y·sis
 ·ses'
u'ri·nar'y
u'ri·nate'
 ·nat'ed ·nat'ing
u'rine
urn
u'ro·log'i·cal
u·rol'o·gy
u·ros'co·py

us'a·ble *or* use'·
us'age
use
  used us'ing
use'ful
use'less
us'er
ush'er
ush'er·ette'
u'su·al
u'su·al·ly
u'su·fruct'
u'su·rer
u·su'ri·ous
u·surp'
u'sur·pa'tion
u'su·ry
  ·ries
U'tah
u·ten'sil
u'ter·ine
u'ter·us
  ·ter·i'
u·til'i·tar'i·an
u·til'i·ty
  ·ties
u'ti·liz'a·ble
u'ti·li·za'tion
u'ti·lize'
  ·lized' ·liz'ing
ut'most'
u·to'pi·a
ut'ter
  (*speak;* SEE udder)

ut'ter·ance
U'-turn'
ux·o'ri·ous

V

va'can·cy
  ·cies
va'cant
va'cate
  ·cat·ed ·cat·ing
va·ca'tion
vac'ci·nate'
  ·nat'ed ·nat'ing
vac'ci·na'tion
vac·cine'
vac'il·late'
  ·lat'ed ·lat'ing
vac'il·la'tion
vac'il·la'tor
va·cu'i·ty
  ·ties
vac'u·ous
vac'u·um
  ·ums *or* ·a
vag'a·bond'
va·gar'y
  ·ies
va·gi'na
  ·nas *or* ·nae
va'gran·cy
  ·cies

va'grant
vague
vague'ly
vain
  (*futile; conceited;*
  SEE vane, vein)
vain'glo'ri·ous
vain'glo'ry
val'ance
  (*drapery;* SEE
  valence)
vale
  (*valley;* SEE veil)
val'e·dic'tion
val'e·dic·to'ri·an
val'e·dic'to·ry
  ·ries
va'lence
  (*term in chemis-*
  try; SEE valance)
val'en·tine'
val'et
val'iant
val'id
val'i·date'
  ·dat'ed ·dat'ing
val'i·da'tion
va·lid'i·ty
va·lise'
val'ley
  ·leys
val'or
val'or·i·za'tion
val'u·a·ble

315

val'u·a'tion
val'ue
 ·ued ·u·ing
val'ue·less
valve
val'vu·lar
vam'pire
van'dal
van'dal·ism
van'dal·ize'
 ·ized' ·iz'ing
Van·dyke'
vane
 (*blade;* SEE
 vain, vein)
van'guard'
va·nil'la
van'ish
van'i·ty
 ·ties
van'quish
van'tage
vap'id
va'por
va'por·i·za'tion
va'por·ize'
 ·ized' ·iz'ing
va'por·iz'er
va'por·ous
va·que'ro
 ·ros
var'i·a·ble
var'i·a·bly
var'i·ance

var'i·ant
var'i·a'tion
var'i·col'ored
var'i·cose'
var'ied
var'i·e·gate'
 ·gat'ed ·gat'ing
var'i·e·ga'tion
va·ri'e·tal
va·ri'e·ty
 ·ties
var'i·o'rum
var'i·ous
var'nish
var'si·ty
 ·ties
var'y
 ·ied ·y·ing
 (*change;* SEE very)
vas'cu·lar
vas de·fe·rens'
vas'e·line'
vas'sal
 (*a subordinate;*
 SEE vessel)
vast'ness
vat
 vat'ted vat'ting
vat'-dyed'
vaude'ville
vault'ing
vaunt
vec'tor
vec·to'ri·al

V'-E' Day
veer
veg'e·ta·ble
veg'e·tar'i·an
veg'e·tate'
 ·tat'ed ·tat'ing
veg'e·ta'tion
veg'e·ta'tive
ve'he·mence
ve'he·ment
ve'hi·cle
ve·hic'u·lar
veil
 (*screen;* SEE vale)
vein
 (*blood vessel;*
 streak; SEE
 vain, vane)
Vel'cro
vel'lum
ve·loc'i·pede'
ve·loc'i·ty
 ·ties
ve·lour' *or* ·lours'
 ·lours'
ve·lure'
vel'vet
vel'vet·een'
vel'vet·y
ve'nal
 (*corrupt;* SEE
 venial)
ve·nal'i·ty
 ·ties

vend'ee'
ven·det'ta
ven'dor *or*
  vend'er
ve·neer'
ven'er·a·ble
ven'er·ate'
  ·at'ed ·at'ing
ven'er·a'tion
ve·ne're·al
Ve·ne'tian
venge'ance
venge'ful
ve'ni·al
  (*pardonable;* SEE
  venal)
ven'i·son
ven'om·ous
ve'nous
ven'ti·late'
  ·lat'ed ·lat'ing
ven'ti·la'tion
ven'ti·la'tor
ven'tri·cle
ven·tril'o·quist
ven'ture
  ·tured ·tur·ing
ven'ture·some
ven'tur·ous
ven'ue
ve·ra'cious
  (*truthful;* SEE
  voracious)
ve·rac'i·ty

ve·ran'da *or* ·dah
ver'bal
ver'bal·i·za'tion
ver'bal·ize'
  ·ized' ·iz'ing
ver'bal·ly
ver·ba'tim
ver·be'na
ver'bi·age
ver·bose'
ver·bos'i·ty
ver'dant
ver'dict
ver'di·gris'
ver'dure
verge
  verged verg'ing
ver'i·fi'a·ble
ver'i·fi·ca'tion
ver'i·fy'
  ·fied' ·fy'ing
ver'i·ly
ver'i·si·mil'i·tude'
ver'i·ta·ble
ver'i·ta·bly
ver'i·ty
  ·ties
ver'mi·cel'li
ver'mi·cide'
ver·mic'u·lar
ver·mic'u·lite'
ver'mi·form'
ver'mi·fuge'
ver·mil'ion

ver'min
Ver·mont'
ver·mouth'
ver·nac'u·lar
ver'nal
ver'ni·er
ver'sa·tile
ver'sa·tile·ly
ver'sa·til'i·ty
versed
ver'si·fi·ca'tion
ver'si·fy'
  ·fied' ·fy'ing
ver'sion
ver'sus
ver'te·bra
  ·brae' *or* ·bras
ver'te·bral
ver'te·brate
ver'tex
  ·tex·es *or* ·ti·ces'
ver'ti·cal
ver·tig'i·nous
ver'ti·go'
verve
ver'y
  ·i·er ·i·est
  (*complete; exceed-*
  ingly; SEE vary)
ves'i·cant
ves'i·cate'
  ·cat'ed ·cat'ing
ves'i·cle
ves'per

ves'sel
(*container; ship;* SEE vassal)
ves'tal
ves'ti·bule
ves'tige
ves·tig'i·al
vest'ment
vest'-pock'et
ves'try
·tries
vet'er·an
vet'er·i·nar'i·an
vet'er·i·nar'y
·ies
ve'to
·toes
·toed ·to·ing
vex·a'tion
vex·a'tious
vi'a·bil'i·ty
vi'a·ble
vi'a·duct'
vi'al
(*bottle;* SEE vile, viol)
vi'and
vi'brant
vi'bra·phone'
vi'brate
·brat·ed ·brat·ing
vi·bra'tion
vi·bra'to
·tos

vi'bra'tor
vi'bra·to'ry
vic'ar
vic'ar·age
vi·car'i·al
vi·car'i·ous
vice
(*evil conduct;*
flaw; SEE vise)
vice'-chair'man
vice'-chan'cel·lor
vice'-con'sul
vice'-pres'i·dent
vice'roy
vi'ce ver'sa
vi'chy·ssoise'
vi·cin'i·ty
·ties
vi'cious
vi·cis'si·tude'
vic'tim
vic'tim·ize'
·ized' ·iz'ing
vic'tor
vic·to'ri·a
vic·to'ri·ous
vic'to·ry
·ries
vi·cu'ña
vid'e·o'
vid'i·con
vie
vied vy'ing
view'point'

vig'il
vig'i·lance
vig'i·lant
vig'i·lan'te
vi·gnette'
vig'or
vig'or·ous
vile
(*evil; offensive;*
SEE vial, viol)
vile'ly
vil'i·fi·ca'tion
vil'i·fy'
·fied' ·fy'ing
vil'la
vil'lage
vil'lag·er
vil'lain
(*scoundrel;*
SEE villein)
vil'lain·ous
vil'lain·y
·ies
vil'lein
(*serf;* SEE
villain)
vin'ai·grette'
vin'ci·ble
vin'di·cate'
·cat·ed ·cat·ing
vin'di·ca'tion
vin'di·ca'tive
vin'di·ca'tor
vin·dic'tive

318

vin'e·gar
vin'er·y
·ies
vine'yard
vin'i·cul'ture
vi'nous
vin'tage
vint'ner
vi'nyl
vi'ol
(*instrument*;
SEE vial, vile)
vi'o·la
vi'o·la·ble
vi'o·late'
·lat'ed ·lat'ing
vi'o·la'tion
vi'o·la'tor
vi'o·lence
vi'o·lent
vi'o·let
vi'o·lin'
vi'o·lin'ist
vi'o·lon·cel'lo
·los
VIP *or* V.I.P.
vi'per
vi·ra'go
·goes *or* ·gos
vi'ral
vir'gin
vir'gin·al
Vir·gin'ia
vir·gin'i·ty

vir'gule
vir'ile
vi·ril'i·ty
vi·rol'o·gy
vir·tu'
vir'tu·al
vir'tu·al·ly
vir'tue
vir'tu·os'i·ty
vir'tu·o'so
·sos *or* ·si
vir'tu·ous
vir'u·lence
vir'u·lent
vi'rus
vi'sa
vis'age
vis'-à-vis'
vis'cer·a
vis'cid
vis·cos'i·ty
vis'count
vis'count·ess
vis'cous
vise
vised vis'ing
(*clamp*; SEE vice)
vis'i·bil'i·ty
vis'i·ble
vis'i·bly
vi'sion
vi'sion·ar'y
·ies
vis'it

vis'it·ant
vis'it·a'tion
vis'i·tor
vi'sor
vis'ta
vis'u·al
vis'u·al·ize'
·ized' ·iz'ing
vi'ta
·tae
vi'tal
vi·tal'i·ty
·ties
vi'tal·ize'
·ized' ·iz'ing
vi'ta·min
vi'ti·a·ble
vi'ti·ate'
·at'ed ·at'ing
vi'ti·a'tion
vi'ti·a'tor
vit're·ous
vit'ri·fy'
·fied' ·fy'ing
vit'ri·ol
vit'ri·ol'ic
vi·tu'per·ate'
·at'ed ·at'ing
vi·tu'per·a'tion
vi·va'cious
vi·vac'i·ty
viv'id
viv'i·fy'
·fied' ·fy'ing

319

vi·vip'a·rous
viv'i·sect'
viv'i·sec'tion
vix'en
V'-J' Day
V'-neck'
vo·cab'u·lar'y
·ies
vo'cal cord
vo'cal·ist
vo'cal·ize'
·ized' ·iz'ing
vo·ca'tion
vo·cif'er·ate'
·at'ed ·at'ing
vo·cif'er·ous
vo'cod'er
vod'ka
vogue
voice'less
voice'print'
void'a·ble
voi·là'
voile
vol'a·tile
vol'a·til'i·ty
vol·can'ic
vol·ca'no
·noes or ·nos
vol'i·tant
vo·li'tion
vol'ley
·leys
·leyed ·ley·ing

320

vol'ley·ball'
volt'age
vol·ta'ic
vol·tam'e·ter
volt'me·ter
vol'u·bil'i·ty
vol'u·ble
vol'u·bly
vol'ume
vo·lu'mi·nous
vol'un·tar'i·ly
vol'un·tar'y
vol'un·teer'
vo·lup'tu·ar'y
·ies
vo·lup'tu·ous
vo·lute'
vo·lu'tion
vom'it
voo'doo
·doos
vo·ra'cious
(greedy; SEE
veracious)
vo·rac'i·ty
vor'tex
·tex·es or ·ti·ces'
vot'a·ble or vote'·
vo'ta·ry
·ries
vote
vot'ed vot'ing
vo'tive
vouch'er

vouch·safe'
·safed' ·saf'ing
vow
vow'el
voy'age
·aged ·ag·ing
voy'ag·er
vo·yeur'
vroom
vul'can·i·za'tion
vul'can·ize'
·ized' ·iz'ing
vul'gar
vul·gar'i·an
vul'gar·ism
vul·gar'i·ty
·ties
vul'gar·ize'
·ized' ·iz'ing
vul'ner·a·bil'i·ty
vul'ner·a·ble
vul'ner·a·bly
vul'ture
vul'tur·ous
vul'va
vy'ing

W

wad
wad'ded
wad'ding

wad'dle
·dled ·dling
wade
wad'ed
wad'ing
wa'fer
waf'fle
waft
wag
wagged
wag'ging
wage
waged wag'ing
wa'ger
wag'ger·y
·ies
wag'gish
wag'gle
·gled ·gling
Wag·ne'ri·an
wag'on·load'
wa·hi'ne
waif
wail
(*cry;* SEE wale,
whale)
wain'scot
·scot·ed *or*
·scot·ted
·scot·ing *or*
·scot·ting
wain'wright'
waist'band'
waist'coat

waist'-high'
waist'line'
wait'er
wait'ress
waive
waived waiv'ing
(*give up;* SEE
wave)
waiv'er
(*a relinquishing;*
SEE waver)
wake
woke *or* waked,
waked *or* wok'·
en, wak'ing
wake'ful
wak'en
wale
waled wal'ing
(*ridge;* SEE
wail, whale)
walk
walk'a·way'
walk'ie-talk'ie
walk'-in'
walk'-on'
walk'out'
walk'-through'
walk'-up'
walk'way'
wall'board'
wal'let
wall'eyed'
wall'flow'er

wal'lop·ing
wal'low
wall'pa'per
wall'-to-wall'
wal'nut
wal'rus
waltz
wam'pum
wan
wan'ner
wan'nest
wan'der
(*stray;* SEE
wonder)
wan'der·lust'
wane
waned wan'ing
wan'gle
·gled ·gling
want'ing
wan'ton
(*unjustifiable;*
SEE won ton)
war
warred war'ring
war'ble
·bled ·bling
ward
war'den
ward'robe'
ward'room'
ware'house'
·housed'
·hous'ing

war'fare'
war'head'
war'i·ly
war'i·ness
war'like'
war'lock'
warm'blood'ed
warmed'-o'ver
warm'heart'ed
war'mon'ger
warmth
warm'-up'
warn'ing
warp
war'path'
warped
war'plane'
war'rant
war'ran·ty
 ·ties
war'ren
war'ri·or
war'ship'
wart
war'time'
war'y
 ·i·er ·i·est
wash'a·ble
wash'-and-wear'
wash'board'
wash'bowl'
wash'cloth'
washed'-out'
washed'-up'

wash'er
wash'er·wom'an
Wash'ing·ton
wash'out'
wash'room'
wash'stand'
wash'tub'
was'n't
wasp'ish
was'sail
wast'age
waste
 wast'ed
 wast'ing
waste'bas'ket
waste'ful
waste'land'
waste'pa'per
waste pipe
wast'rel
watch'band'
watch'case'
watch'dog'
watch fire
watch'ful
watch'mak'er
watch'man
watch'tow'er
watch'word'
wa'ter·borne'
wa'ter·col'or
wa'ter-cooled'
water cooler

wa'ter·craft'
wa'ter·cress'
wa'ter·cy'cle
wa'tered
wa'ter·fall'
wa'ter·front'
water glass
water hole
wa'ter·i·ness
wa'ter·less
wa'ter·line'
wa'ter·logged'
wa'ter·mark'
wa'ter·mel'on
water pipe
water power
wa'ter·proof'
wa'ter-re·pel'lent
wa'ter-re·sist'ant
wa'ter·scape'
wa'ter·shed'
wa'ter·side'
wa'ter-ski'
 -skied' -ski'ing
wa'ter-ski'er
water skis
wa'ter-soak'
wa'ter-sol'u·ble
wa'ter·spout'
wa'ter·tight'
water tower
wa'ter·way'
water wheel
water wings

322

wa·ter·works'
wa·ter·worn'
wa·ter·y
watt'age
watt'-hour'
wat'tle
·tled ·tling
watt'me·ter
wave
waved wav'ing
(*curving motion;*
SEE waive)
wave'length'
wav'er
(*one that waves;*
SEE waiver)
wa'ver
(*falter;* SEE
waiver)
wav'i·ness
wav'y
·i·er ·i·est
wax
wax'en
wax'i·ness
wax'work'
wax'y
·i·er ·i·est
way
(*route; manner;*
SEE weigh, whey)
way'bill'
way'far'er
way'far'ing

way'lay'
·laid' ·lay'ing
way'side'
way'ward
weak'en
weak'-kneed'
weak'ling
weak'ly
·li·er ·li·est
weak'-mind'ed
weak'ness
weal
(*ridge; welfare;*
SEE wheal, wheel)
wealth'i·ness
wealth'y
·i·er ·i·est
wean
weap'on
wear
wore worn
wear'ing
wear'a·ble
wea'ri·ly
wea'ri·ness
wea'ri·some
wea'ry
·ri·er ·ri·est
·ried ·ry·ing
wea'sel
weath'er
(*atmospheric con-*
ditions; SEE
whether)

weath'er·beat'en
weath'er·bound'
weath'er·cock'
weath'er·man'
weath'er·proof'
weath'er·strip'
·stripped'
·strip'ping
weather vane
weave
wove, wov'en *or*
wove, weav'ing
(*interlace*)
weave
weaved
weav'ing
(*move in and out*
as in traffic)
weav'er
web
webbed
web'bing
web'foot'
·feet'
web'-foot'ed
wed
wed'ded,
wed'ded *or*
wed, wed'ding
we'd
wedge
wedged
wedg'ing
Wedg'wood'

323

wed'lock
Wednes'day
wee
  we'er we'est
weed'i·ness
week'day'
week'end' or
  week'-end'
week'ly
  ·lies
weep
  wept weep'ing
weep'i·ness
weep'y
  ·i·er ·i·est
wee'vil
weigh
  weighed
  weigh'ing
  (*measure weight
  of;* SEE way, whey)
weight'i·ness
weight'less
weight'y
  ·i·er ·i·est
weir
  (*dam;* SEE we're)
weird
wel'come
  ·comed ·com·ing
weld'er
wel'fare'
well'-ad·vised'
well'-ap·point'ed

well'-bal'anced
well'-be·haved'
well'-be'ing
well'-be·loved'
well'born'
well'-bred'
well'-chos'en
well'-con·tent'
well'-dis·posed'
well'do'ing
well'-done'
well'-fa'vored
well'-fed'
well'-found'ed
well'-groomed'
well'-ground'ed
well'-han'dled
well'head'
well'-in·formed'
well'-in·ten'·
  tioned
well'-knit'
well'-known'
well'-made'
well'-man'nered
well'-mean'ing
well'-meant'
well'-nigh'
well'-off'
well'-or'dered
well'-pre·served'
well'-read'
well'-round'ed
well'-spo'ken

well'spring'
well'-thought'-of'
well'-timed'
well'-to-do'
well'-turned'
well'-wish'er
well'-worn'
we'll
Welsh rabbit
  or rarebit
welt'er
welt'er·weight'
we're
  (*we are;* SEE
  weir)
weren't
were'wolf'
  ·wolves'
wes'kit
west'er·ly
  ·lies
west'ern·er
west'ern·ize'
  ·ized' ·iz'ing
west'-north'west'
west'-south'west'
West Vir·gin'ia
west'ward
wet
  wet'ter wet'test
  wet or wet'ted
  wet'ting
  (*moistened;*
  SEE whet)

wet′back′
wet′ta·ble
whale
  whaled whal′ing
  (*fishlike mammal;*
  SEE wail, wale)
whale′boat′
whale′bone′
whal′er
wharf
  wharves *or*
  wharfs
wharf′age
wharf′in·ger
what·ev′er
what′not′
what′so·ev′er
wheal
  (*pimple;* SEE
  weal, wheel)
wheat
whee′dle
  ·dled ·dling
wheel
  (*disk for turning;*
  SEE weal, wheal)
wheel′bar′row
wheel′base′
wheel′chair′
wheel′house′
wheel′wright′
wheeze
  wheezed
  wheez′ing

wheez′y
  ·i·er ·i·est
whelp
when
whence
when·ev′er
where
where′a·bouts′
where·as′
where·by′
where′fore′
where·in′
where·of′
where′up·on′
wher·ev′er
where·with′
where′with·al′
wher′ry
  ·ries, ·ried ·ry·ing
whet
  whet′ted
  whet′ting
  (*sharpen;* SEE wet)
wheth′er
  (*if;* SEE weather)
whet′stone′
whey
  (*thin part of milk;*
  SEE way, weigh)
which·ev′er
whiff
while
  whiled whil′ing
  (*time;* SEE wile)

whim
whim′per
whim′si·cal
whim′sy
  ·sies
whine
  whined whin′ing
  (*cry;* SEE wine)
whin′i·ness
whin′ny
  ·nies
  ·nied ·ny·ing
  (*neigh*)
whin′y
  ·i·er ·i·est
  (*complaining*)
whip
  whipped
  whip′ping
whip′cord′
whip′lash′
whip′pet
whip′poor·will′
whip′saw′
whip′stitch′
whip′stock′
whir *or* whirr
  whirred
  whir′ring
whirl
whirl′pool′
whirl′wind′
whisk broom
whisk′er

whis'key
·keys *or* ·kies
whis'per
whis'tle
·tled ·tling
whis'tler
whit
(*bit;* SEE wit)
white
whit'ed whit'ing
white'cap'
white'-col'lar
white'-haired'
white'-hot'
white'-liv'ered
whit'en·er
white'ness
whit'en·ing
white room
white'wall'
white'wash'
whith'er
(*where;* SEE
wither)
whit'ing
whit'tle
·tled ·tling
whiz *or* whizz
whizzed
whiz'zing
who·ev'er
whole'heart'ed
whole'sale'
·saled' ·sal'ing

whole'sal'er
whole'some
whole'-wheat'
whol'ly
(*completely;* SEE
holey, holy)
whom·ev'er
whom·so·ev'er
whoop'ee
whop'per
whore
whorl
who's
(*who is; who has*)
whose
(*poss. of* who)
who'so·ev'er
why
wick'ed
wick'er·work'
wick'et
wide'-an'gle
wide'-a·wake'
wide'-eyed'
wid'en
wide'-o'pen
wide'spread'
widg'et
wid'ow
wid'ow·er
width
wield
wield'y
·i·er ·i·est

wie'ner
wife
wives
wife'ly
wig'gle
·gled ·gling
wig'gly
wig'let
wig'wam
wild'cat'
·cat'ted ·cat'ting
wil'de·beest'
wil'der·ness
wild'-eyed'
wild'fire'
wild'life'
wile
wiled wil'ing
(*trick;* SEE while)
wil'i·ness
will'ful *or* wil'·
will'ing·ness
will'-o'-the-wisp'
wil'low·y
will'pow'er
wil'ly-nil'ly
wil'y
·i·er ·i·est
wim'ple
·pled ·pling
win
won win'ning
wince
winced winc'ing

wind
  wound wind'ing
wind'blown'
wind'-borne'
wind'break'er
wind'burn'
wind'fall'
wind'i·ness
wind'lass
  (*winch*)
wind'less
  (*without wind*)
wind'mill'
win'dow
win'dow·pane'
win'dow-shop'
wind'row'
wind'shield'
wind'storm'
wind'-swept'
wind'up'
wind'ward
wind'y
  ·i·er ·i·est
wine
  wined win'ing
  (*drink;* SEE whine)
wine cellar
wine'-col'ored
wine'glass'
wine'grow'er
wine press
win'er·y
  ·ies

Wine'sap'
wine'skin'
wing chair
wing'span'
wing'spread'
win'ner
win'now
win'some
win'ter
win'ter·green'
win'ter·ize'
  ·ized' ·iz'ing
win'ter·time'
win'try
  ·tri·er ·tri·est
wipe
  wiped wip'ing
wire
  wired wir'ing
wire'draw'
  ·drew' ·drawn'
  ·draw'ing
wire'hair'
wire'-haired'
wire'less
Wire'pho'to
wire'pull'er
wire'tap'
wire'work'
wir'i·ness
wir'y
  ·i·er ·i·est
Wis·con'sin
wis'dom

wise
  wis'er wis'est
wise'ly
wish'bone'
wish'ful
wisp
wist'ful
wit
  (*sense;* SEE whit)
witch'craft'
witch'er·y
  ·ies
with·draw'
  ·drew' ·drawn'
  ·draw'ing
with·draw'al
with'er
  (*wilt;* SEE whither)
with·hold'
  ·held' ·hold'ing
with·in'
with·out'
with·stand'
  ·stood'
  ·stand'ing
wit'less
wit'ness
wit'ti·cism
wit'ti·ness
wit'ty
  ·ti·er ·ti·est
wiz'ard
wiz'ard·ry
wiz'ened

wob'ble
·bled ·bling
woe'be·gone'
woe'ful
wolf
wolves
wolf'hound'
wom'an
wom'en
wom'an·hood'
wom'an·kind'
wom'an·li·ness
wom'an·ly
womb
wom'en·folk'
won'der
(*marvel;* SEE
wander)
won'der·ful
won'der·land'
won'der·work'
won'der·work'er
won'drous
wont
(*accustomed*)
won't
(*will not*)
won' ton'
(*food;* SEE wanton)
wood'carv'ing
wood'chuck'
wood'craft'
wood'cut'
wood'ed

wood'land'
wood'peck'er
wood'pile'
wood pulp
wood'shed'
woods'man
wood'sy
·si·er ·si·est
wood'wind'
wood'work'
wood'y
·i·er ·i·est
woof'er
wool'en
wool'gath'er·ing
wool'grow'er
wool'lies *or*
wool'ies
wool'li·ness *or*
wool'i·ness
wool'ly *or*
wool'y
·li·er *or* ·i·er
·li·est *or* ·i·est
Worces'ter·shire'
word'age
word'book'
word'i·ly
word'i·ness
word'less
word'-of-mouth'
word'play'
word'y
·i·er ·i·est

work
worked *or*
wrought
work'ing
work'a·ble
work'a·day'
work'bench'
work'book'
work'day'
work'house'
work'ing·man'
work'load'
work'man·like'
work'man·ship'
work'out'
work'room'
work'shop'
work'ta'ble
work'week'
world'li·ness
world'ly
·li·er ·li·est
world'ly-wise'
world'-shak'ing
world'-wea'ry
world'wide'
worm'-eat'en
worm gear
worm'hole'
worm'i·ness
worm wheel
worm'wood'
worm'y
·i·er ·i·est

worn'-out'
wor'ri·er
wor'ri·ment
wor'ri·some
wor'ry
 ·ries
 ·ried ·ry·ing
wor'ry·wart'
worse
wors'en
wor'ship
 ·shiped *or*
 ·shipped
 ·ship·ing *or*
 ·ship·ping
wor'ship'er *or*
 wor'ship'per
wor'ship·ful
worst
wor'sted
wor'thi·ly
wor'thi·ness
worth'less
worth'while'
wor'thy
 ·thi·er ·thi·est
would
would'-be'
wound
wrack
wraith
wran'gle
 ·gled ·gling
wran'gler

wrap
 wrapped *or*
 wrapt
 wrap'ping
 (*cover;* SEE rap)
wrap'a·round'
wrap'per
wrath'ful
wreak
 (*inflict;* SEE reek)
wreath *n.*
wreathe *v.*
 wreathed
 wreath'ing
wreck'age
wreck'er
wrench
wres'tle
 ·tled ·tling
wres'tler
wretch
 (*miserable
 person;* SEE
 retch)
wretch'ed
wrig'gle
 ·gled ·gling
wring
 wrung wring'ing
 (*twist;* SEE ring)
wrin'kle
 ·kled ·kling
wrin'kly
 ·kli·er ·kli·est

wrist'band'
wrist'let
wrist pin
wrist'watch'
writ
write
 wrote writ'ten
 writ'ing
 (*inscribe;* SEE
 right, rite)
write'-in'
write'-off'
writ'er
write'-up'
writhe
 writhed
 writh'ing
wrong'do'er
wrong'do'ing
wrong'ful
wrote
 (*pt. of* write;
 SEE rote)
wrought
wrought'-up'
wrung
 (*pt. and pp. of*
 wring; SEE rung)
wry
 wried wry'ing
 wri'er wri'est
 (*twisted;* SEE rye)
wry'ly
Wy·o'ming

329

X

x
  x-ed *or* x'd
  x-ing *or* x'ing
xan'thous
xe'bec
xen'o·pho'bi·a
xe·rog'ra·phy
xe·roph'i·lous
Xe'rox
Xmas
X'-ray' *or*
  X ray
xy'lo·phone'
xy'lo·phon'ist

Y

yacht
yachts'man
Yan'kee
yard'age
yard'arm'
yard'mas'ter
yard'stick'
yarn'-dyed'
yawl
yawn

yea
year'book'
year'ling
year'long'
year'ly
yearn
year'-round'
yeast
yel'low
yelp
yen
  yenned yen'ning
yeo'man
yes
  yessed yes'sing
ye·shi'va
yes'ter·day
yes'ter·year'
yet
yew
  (*tree;* SEE ewe)
Yid'dish
yield
yip'pie
yo'del
  ·deled *or* ·delled
  ·del·ing *or*
  ·del·ling
yo'del·er *or*
  yo'del·ler
yo'ga
yo'gi
  ·gis
yo'gurt

yoke
  yoked yok'ing
  (*harness*)
yolk
  (*of an egg*)
Yom Kip'pur
yon'der
you'd
you'll
young'ster
your
  (*poss. of* you)
you're
  (*you are*)
yours
your·self'
  ·selves'
youth'ful
you've
yowl
yo'-yo'
yule log
yule'tide'

Z

zai'ba·tsu'
  ·tsu'
za'ni·ness
za'ny
  ·nies, ·ni·er
  ·ni·est

zeal
zeal'ot
zeal'ous
ze'bra
ze'brass'
ze'bu
Zeit'geist'
Zen
ze'nith
ze'o·lite'
ze'o·lit'ic
zeph'yr
zep'pe·lin
ze'ro
 ·ros or ·roes
 ·roed ·ro·ing
zest'ful·ly
zest'ful·ness

zig'zag'
 ·zagged'
 ·zag'ging
zinc
 zincked or zinced
 zinck'ing or
 zinc'ing
zin'ni·a
Zi'on·ism
zip
 zipped zip'ping
ZIP code
zip'per
zir'con
zith'er
zo'di·ac'
zo·di'a·cal
zom'bie

zon'al
zone
 zoned zon'ing
zoo
zo'o·ge·og'ra·phy
zo'o·log'i·cal
zo·ol'o·gist
zo·ol'o·gy
zoom lens
zoy'si·a
zuc·chet'to
 ·tos
zuc·chi'ni
 ·ni or ·nis
zwie'back
zy'gote
zy·mol'o·gy
zy'mur·gy

PUNCTUATION

The following covers the most important usages. Practice in punctuation often differs in particulars among writers, publishing houses, etc., but the modern trend is toward simplification.

PERIOD
The period (.) is used:
1) to mark the end of a sentence;
2) as one of a series (usually three) to indicate missing material or a break in continuity. When the missing material ends with a period, that period is added;
   Ex.: "I pledge allegiance . . . and to the Republic . . . ."

COMMA
The comma (,) is used:
1) between independent clauses of equal value that are short and have no commas within them;
   Ex.: He worked hard, he saved his money, and he bought a house.
2) between two independent clauses joined by coordinating or correlative conjunctions;
   Ex.: We went to the party, but Ralph wasn't there.
3) after a dependent clause, usually a fairly long one, that precedes an independent clause;
   Ex.: When it became apparent that they would not cooperate, we stopped all negotiations.

4) before and after a dependent clause that comes in the middle of a sentence;

   Ex.: The apples, although they had been freshly picked, became spoiled in shipment.

5) to set off a nonrestrictive, as distinguished from a restrictive, clause, phrase, or word;

   Ex.: Tim, who is my brother, is not here. (But *not* in: The boy who is my brother is sitting there.)

6) to avoid initial confusion in interpretation;

   Ex.: Run, for your life is in danger.

7) to set off conjunctive adverbs, such as *however, moreover,* etc., or short transitional phrases;

   Ex.: We are, however, pleased with your suggestion.

8) to separate clauses, phrases, or words in a series;

   Ex.: Find out who he is, what he wants, and where he comes from. Ann, Lois, or Jane will be here.

9) after terms (e.g., i.e., namely) that introduce a series or example;

   Ex.: Some of our presidents, e.g., Jefferson, J. Q. Adams, and Buchanan, had previously been secretaries of state.

10) to set off a parenthetical clause, phrase, or word;

    Ex.: By the end of the month, when the bill is due, I will have the money. The family, along with the servants, has left for the summer.

11) between two adjectives which modify the same substantive and can be interchanged in position;

    Ex.: a large, modern building

12) to indicate omitted material;

    Ex.: The infant becomes a child; the child, an adolescent; and the adolescent, an adult.

13) to set off the one spoken to in direct address;

    Ex.: "Go, Dick, and shut the window."

14) to set off direct quotation;

    Ex.: He said, "Welcome." "Thank you," we replied.

15) to set off titles, addresses, names of places, etc.;
  Ex.: R. T. Fisher, Ph.D., Secretary, 110 Elm Street, Akron, Ohio, handles all correspondence.

16) before, and sometimes after, the year in dates;
  Ex.: On February 12, 1809, Lincoln was born.

17) after the salutation of a personal letter;
  Ex.: Dear Max and Alice,

18) after the complimentary close of a letter;
  Ex.: Very truly yours,

19) to separate thousands in numbers;
  Ex.: The area of the earth is about 197,260,000 sq. mi.

20) to separate inverted names, phrases, etc., as in a bibliography, index, or catalog;
  Ex.: Jones, Harold T.

SEMICOLON

The semicolon (;) is used:

1) in compound sentences between independent clauses not joined by connectives, especially if they are long or have commas within them;
  Ex.: Detroit, on one side of the river, is in the U.S.; Windsor, on the other side, is in Canada.

2) in compound sentences between independent clauses joined by conjunctive adverbs;
  Ex.: We are pleased with your suggestion; moreover, we intend to put it into effect.

3) in a series where commas have already been used;
  Ex.: The contestants came from Albany, New York; Seattle, Washington; and London, England.

COLON

The colon (:) is used:

1) to introduce a series;
  Ex.: The following materials will be needed: pencil, pen, eraser, ruler, and notebook.

2) to introduce a part of a sentence that exemplifies, restates, or explains the preceding part;
   Ex.: Some of the greatest creative artists never became wealthy: Mozart died a very poor man.
3) before an extended quotation;
   Ex.: Lincoln arose and spoke as follows: "Fourscore and seven years ago . . . ."
4) between chapter and verse in Biblical references;
   Ex.: The story of Noah begins in Gen. 5:28.
5) between the volume and page numbers in references;
   Ex.: The article is in *U.S. Encyclopedia* 34:1747.
6) after the salutation of a business letter;
   Ex.: Dear Sir:
7) to separate the hours from the minutes in time;
   Ex.: The train will depart at 10:47 P.M.
8) to separate the parts of a ratio;
   Ex.: Wins and losses were in the ratio 3:1.

CAPITALIZATION

A capital letter is used as the initial letter of:
1) the first word in a sentence;
2) the first word in a direct question within a sentence;
   Ex.: This story answers the question, Where does true happiness really lie?
3) every word in all proper nouns or names;
4) every word, except conjunctions, articles, and short prepositions that are not the first word, in the titles of works of literature, music, art, etc.
   Ex.: The Decline and Fall of the Roman Empire
5) every word, except conjunctions, articles, and short prepositions, in the names (or derived words) of organizations, institutions, businesses, agencies, religions, holidays, etc. Sometimes the initial article is capitalized as part of the official name;
   Ex.: the Boy Scouts of America, Fourth of July

6) salutations and complimentary closes of letters;
   Ex.: Gentlemen, Dear Sir, Very truly yours

DASH
The dash (—) is used:
1) to show a break in continuity or thought in a sentence;
   Ex.: Give it to John—I mean, to George.
2) before and after parenthetical material that is a result of a break in thought or continuity;
   Ex.: I wrote a letter—and what a chore it was—to my lawyer concerning the problem.
3) between numbers, dates, times, places, etc. that mark limits;
   Ex.: You will find it on pages 89–104. Franklin lived 1706–1790. The hotel is open June–September. The office hours are 8:00–5:00 daily. He will arrive on the New York–Chicago flight.
4) to indicate the omission of letters, numbers, etc.;
   Ex.: Don't tell Mr. B—.
5) before the citation of the author or source of a quotation;
   Ex.: "Every dog has his day."—Cervantes.

QUOTATION MARKS
Double quotation marks (" ") are used:
1) to enclose a direct quotation;
   Ex.: I replied, "I will try to help them."
2) to enclose the titles of divisions, parts, chapters, etc. of books, periodicals, etc. Titles of plays, operas, and other works of art are either set off by quotation marks or italicized.
   Ex.: I have just read "The Gold Bug." "The Knight's Tale" is one of *The Canterbury Tales*.
3) to enclose words out of grammatical context;
   Ex.: The word *silly* originally meant "happy."

4) to enclose terms that are technical, ironical, coined, etc.;

   Ex.: How "considerate" of him to make us wait.

Single quotation marks (' ') are used to enclose a direct quotation within other quoted material;

   Ex.: The teacher said, "William Hazlitt's dying words were 'It was a happy life.'"

Note: Commas and periods are usually placed inside quotation marks;

   Ex.: "I am seven," he said. The answer was "No."

Colons and semicolons are placed outside quotation marks;

   Ex.: Answer these questions on the "Gettysburg Address": In what year was it given? What was the occasion? I had not read Francis Bacon's essay "Of Truth"; in fact, I had never heard of it.

An interrogation mark or exclamation mark is placed outside or inside depending on the part of the sentence to which it applies;

   Ex.: "What did you say?" he repeated. Did I hear you say, "It's snowing"? She exclaimed, "Never!" You had better not call me "yellow"!

APOSTROPHE

The apostrophe (') is used:

   1) to indicate an omitted letter or letters;

      Ex.: The sec'y. will attend if he's in town.

   2) to form the possessive of nouns and some pronouns;

      Ex.: Sam's, lass's, Horace's, wolves', everyone's

   3) in forming the plural of letters, numbers, etc.;

      Ex.: He pronounced his *th*'s like *s*'s.

PARENTHESES

Parentheses, ( ), are used:

   1) to enclose nonessential, explanatory material;

      Ex.: He ran 1500 meters (a little less than a mile).

2) to enclose letters or numbers of reference;
> *Ex.:* The candidate spoke on three subjects: (1) housing; (2) roads; (3) recreation.

Note: A period, an interrogation mark, or an exclamation mark is placed inside or outside parentheses depending on the part of the sentence to which it applies;
> *Ex.: Veni, vidi, vici.* (I came, I saw, I conquered.)
> I have many faults (as does everybody else).

BRACKETS

Brackets, [ ], are used:

1) to enclose parenthetical material that falls within other parenthetical material;
> *Ex.:* Dr. Lee (a person I feared [no, dreaded] as a child) was a kindly man.
2) to enclose comments, corrections, insertions, etc. made by a person other than the author of the quoted material;
> *Ex.:* "He was a friend of the nineteenth-century British statesman [Randolph] Churchill."

ITALICS

Italicized type is used:

1) to indicate foreign words;
> *Ex.:* His motto was *omnia vincit amor.*
2) to set off the titles of books, periodicals, newspapers, etc. Titles of plays, operas, and other works of art are either italicized or set off by quotation marks.
> *Ex.: David Copperfield* is a great novel.
3) to indicate words whose meaning is stressed;
> *Ex.:* Please do *not* use this door.
4) to indicate terms, letters, numbers, etc. used as words instead of for their meanings;
> *Ex.: Charry* means "like charcoal." The expression *to wit* is being used less frequently nowadays.

338